UNDERCOVER AGENT

Mark Seaman is an historian with the Cabinet Office in London, and before that with the Imperial War Museum, who has studied SOE and the French Resistance for nearly forty years. Given his close association with many SOE veterans over the years, and his extensive knowledge of secret archives in Britain and abroad, he holds an unrivalled expertise in his subject. His other published works include *Bravest of the Brave*, the biography of the wartime SOE agent 'Tommy' Yeo-Thomas, GC, codenamed 'the White Rabbit'.

Mark has written for newspapers, been a frequent broadcaster on special operations and resistance, and has acted as historical adviser to several feature films and television programmes, including Steven Spielberg's *Band of Brothers*. In 2014 he was appointed MBE for 'services to the study of the history of intelligence'.

Tony Brooks asked Mark Seaman to write his story and together they worked on the book for many years, visiting the scenes of the agent's adventures, recording hundreds of hours of interviews and sifting through private and public papers. Brooks's extraordinary endeavours as a wartime secret agent for SOE were recognised by another branch of British Intelligence. After the war he became a career officer of the Secret Intelligence Service – sometimes known as MI6. But that, as they say, is another story...

UNDERCOVER AGENT

How one of SOE's youngest agents helped defeat the Nazis

MARK SEAMAN

JOHN BLAKE

Published by John Blake Publishing,
80–1 Wimpole Street,
Marylebone
London W1G 9RE

www.facebook.com/johnblakebooks
twitter.com/jblakebooks

First published, under the title *Saboteur*, in hardback in 2018
This retitled paperback edition first published in 2020

Paperback ISBN: 978-1-78946-143-5
Ebook ISBN: 978-1-78946-021-6
Audiobook ISBN: 978-1-78946-346-0

British Library Cataloguing-in-Publication Data:

A catalogue record for this book is available from the British Library.

Designed and set by seagulls.net

Printed and bound in Great Britain by Clays Ltd, Elcograf S.p.A

1 3 5 7 9 10 8 6 4 2

Text copyright © Mark Seaman 2018

John Blake Publishing is an imprint of Bonnier Books UK

www.bonnierbooks.co.uk

This book is dedicated to Tony's wife, Lena. Her devotion to him was manifest to the very end. She was a wonderful person in her own right and enriched the life of anyone who had the good fortune to come into contact with her.

The men and women of the National Health Service also deserve mention. The marvellous care and attention they paid to Tony and Lena towards the end of their lives owed nothing to their patients' celebrity. They were unaware that they had a war hero and his wife in their care and simply showed an exemplary dedication to caring for two citizens in need.

Contents

Glossary

Abwehr	German military intelligence
ALPHONSE	Field name for Tony Brooks
Armée Secrète	French Resistance 'Secret Army'
Baker Street	Primary location in London of SOE headquarters
BCRA	Bureau Central de Renseignement et d'Action – Free French secret service
Beaulieu	SOE training centre in Hampshire
BISHOP	Codename for Marcus Bloom's wireless link
CGT	Confédération Générale du Travail – principal French Trades Union Federation
CHARLES	SIS codename for Bertholet
Circuit	F Section name for an operational network
CNR	Conseil National de la Résistance – French National Resistance Council
CO	Commanding officer
Dead-letter drop	Site for the clandestine delivery and reception of messages; also known as a 'postbox'
DF	SOE section organising agent escape routes
D/F	Direction-finding (wireless)
DSO	Distinguished Service Order
DZ	Dropping zone
EUGENE	Field name for Maurice Pertschuk
F	French or Independent Section, Symbol of Head of F Section
FANY	First Aid Nursing Yeomanry
Feldgendarmerie	German military police
FFI	Forces Françaises de l'Intérieur

Franc	French monetary unit
Funkspiel	'Radio Game' – exploitation of captured British wireless links
Gardes Mobiles	Vichy security force
Gestapo	Nazi security service
GMR	Groupes Mobiles de Réserve – Vichy paramilitary force
ITF	International Transport Workers' Federation
ISK	Internationaler Sozialisticher Kampfbund
Jedburgh	Three-man Allied Special Forces team
JUDEX	Codename for F Section missions to visit post-liberation networks
Laissez-passer	Pass/permit
Lysander	RAF light aircraft employed on clandestine operations delivering and picking up personnel from Occupied France
Maquis	Rural resistance fighters
MBE	Member of the Order of the British Empire
MC	Military Cross
Message personnel	Simple phrase broadcast by the BBC that conveyed a coded message
MEW	Ministry of Economic Warfare
MI(R)	Military Intelligence (Research)
MI5	Military Intelligence Section 5 – British Security Service
MI6	Military Intelligence Section 6 – British Secret Intelligence Service
MI9	Military Intelligence Section 9 – British escape and evasion organisation
Milice	Vichy paramilitary police force
OKW	*Oberkommando der Wehrmacht* – German Armed Forces High Command
OSS	Office of Strategic Services – US intelligence and special operations organisation
PE	Plastic explosive
PIERRE	Codename for René Bertholet
PIMENTO	Tony Brooks's circuit

PWE	Political Warfare Executive
RAF	Royal Air Force
RDX	Research Department Explosive (British)
RENE	Codename for René Bertholet
RF	Section of SOE liaising with the Free French
ROBERT	Codename for René Bertholet
SD	See *Sicherheitsdienst*
SFHQ	Special Force Headquarters
SFIO	Section Française de l'Internationale Ouvrière – French Socialist Party
SHAEF	Supreme Headquarters Allied Expeditionary Force
Sicherheitsdienst	Nazi Party intelligence service
SIS	Secret Intelligence Service, also known as MI6
SNCF	Société Nationale des Chemins de Fer Français
SO2	Early title for SOE
SOE	Special Operations Executive
SRFD	Service de Répression des Fraudes Douanières – French Customs Investigation Branch
SS	*Schutzstaffel* – elite organisation within the Nazi Party
STO	Service du Travail Obligatoire – Vichy forced-labour programme
STS	Special Training School (SOE)
THEODORE	Field name for Tony Brooks
TONTON	Codename for René Bertholet
URBAIN	Field name for Marcus Bloom
WAAF	Women's Auxiliary Air Force
Waffen-SS	Military wing of the SS
Wehrmacht	German Armed Forces
WO	War Office
WPM	Words per minute (Morse transmissions)
W/T	Wireless telegraphy
W/T/O	Wireless telegraphy operator

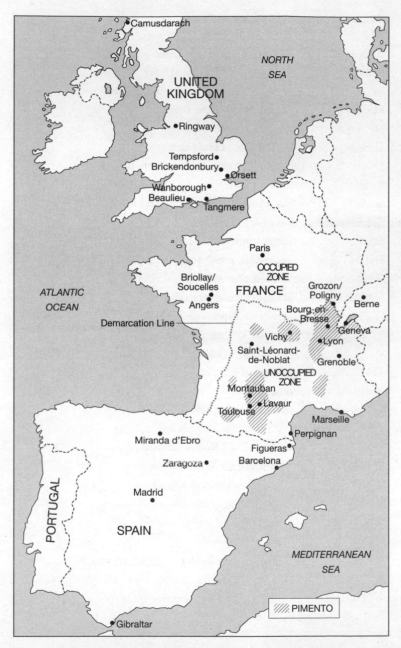

The primary locations where Tony Brooks carried out his wartime activities.

Introduction

I first met Tony Brooks in 1983. At the time I was an historian at the Imperial War Museum and engaged on mounting an exhibition about European Resistance in the Second World War. Given that it was less than forty years since the end of the conflict, our team was able to draw on the support of many Resistance veterans, of whom Tony proved to be one of the most engaged, lending his time, his advice and an impressive collection of personal documents and artefacts for display. I held responsibility for the overall historical content of the exhibition, so in the light of this task initially knew Tony as but one of a constellation of heroes and heroines whose stories were featured in the displays.

The exhibition served as the catalyst that transformed an interest in the Resistance into a preoccupation. Following the conclusion of the project, I studied and wrote about the subject and enjoyed close contact with wartime veterans and, in particular, members of the British secret service that worked intimately with the Resistance – the Special Operations Executive (SOE). On both a professional and social level I absorbed insights offered by the SOE alumni: the latter permitted my getting to know these remarkable men and women as people; the former translated into a major project to make the IWM a centre for the study and commemoration of their history. Tony Brooks was one of this group who befriended me and, after several years of weighing me up, one day he asked me to write his story.

Even when assessed against the myriad, remarkable personal contributions in the field of special operations during the Second World War, Tony Brooks's exploits were extraordinary. However, in the decades following the conflict, only a few fragments of his story emerged, here and there in books about SOE and it was not until the publication of the official history of SOE in France in 1966 that a partial (and partially inaccurate) intimation of his wartime efforts emerged. Ironically, it was as a result of his continuing government service that Tony was one of the few SOE veterans that the author, M. R. D. Foot, had been permitted to interview. Presumably it was felt that Tony would be a safe conveyor of his secret memories given his continuing post-war career in British Intelligence, but this inevitably restricted opportunities for him to amplify the book's account of his wartime activities.

It was not until Tony's retirement that he gradually emerged into public view. He began to engage with academics, lectured to students and schoolchildren on both sides of the Channel, and was interviewed by newspaper journalists and in television documentaries (usually with some reluctance and unease). His memory was prodigious and he could keep any audience – a dinner party to a packed auditorium – spellbound. His honesty and gallant mien were so evident (supplemented by his innate modesty) that, allied to his apparently perfect recall, the task of any prospective biographer seemed, on the face of it, simply to transcribe his oral testimony. But Tony wanted more. He acknowledged that even his remarkable memory was imperfect and he was highly critical of the published memoirs of his contemporaries that contained abundant and inaccurate embellishments crafted by ghost writers and in which uncomfortable and unpalatable incidents were 'airbrushed' out of the historical narrative.

After some two decades of preparation (albeit part-time), this biography of Tony Brooks must seem a pretty feeble return for an endeavour of such a long gestation. Sometimes a friendship between subject and author can improve a biography, but it can also disrupt it. Tony Brooks's descent into ill health resulted in a change of priorities; more time was needed on personal-care duties than the research and writing of the book; he and his wife Lena became the real priorities. But the book crept along to completion and Tony and Lena were able to read early drafts, and expressed their approval of them. Theirs are the most important critical appraisals that this biographer can receive.

Over many years of close collaboration and friendship with Tony, in addition to making hundreds of hours of taped interviews, he gave me complete access to his extensive personal archive (described as 'AMB Papers' in the notes) – or so I thought. During our work together he showed me some files and even lent them for extended periods of time. Requests for renewed access to his papers were met with the response 'help yourself' but this largesse remained largely unexploited. Latterly, there was neither the time nor the opportunity to ferret into the cupboards and filing cabinets in his study/ workshop when the two most important people were sitting upstairs needing their lunch or another cork to be drawn. It was only after Tony died in 2007 and Lena followed him two years later that friends foregathered at their house in Notting Hill Gate prior to her funeral. A mourner mentioned in passing that during his frequent social visits he had never ventured into the basement, so a brief foray was undertaken. The study/workshop had not been visited by Tony or Lena for many years due to their infirmity and the vertiginous configuration of the stairs. Their friend asked whether fresh research material might possibly be found. I answered that I really did not know and, to emphasise the point, pulled open a cupboard door commenting, 'I've no idea what's in here.' I turned to glance at the shelves and there, before me, were more than a dozen files of Tony's papers and correspondence spanning the period from 1941 to 1947. Until that moment this treasure trove was completely unknown to me for Tony and Lena had never mentioned it.

I am absolutely certain that there was never any intention to keep the papers from me. Rather, if they had remembered that the files were there, they must have assumed that I had followed up the open invitation to 'help myself'. This windfall of documents resulted not merely in a substantial re-analysis of the narrative but obliged a major re-working of the draft text. The most significant discovery was the 'Narrative', a forty-six-page typescript account by Tony of his first thirteen months as a secret agent in France. He must have written this shortly after the war and, in his typically sparse style, it provides a remarkable, near-contemporary account of his deeds and, importantly, his movements. The dates are very specific. So specific in fact that they suggest that he had kept a daily record (in spite of the security implications) of his travels in France between July 1942 and August 1943. He never mentioned having written a journal nor, sadly, has a diary survived. Comparisons with other official and semi-official documents reveal his personal account to be almost invariably correct. The 'Narrative' has facilitated a reliable chronology that even the release of the official SOE records and Tony's prodigious memory, were unable to deliver in the initial years of research for the book. The finds were not over. A little later, another important document was discovered in a pile of old magazines. This time it was a typewritten report entitled 'My trip from Proby to Goldsmiths – May the 28th to October the 12th', which chronicled Tony's 1941 flight from France, his crossing of the Pyrenees and incarceration in Spain. Written a month after his return to England, it, too, corroborated his verbal testimony while also providing some fascinating, extra details.

These new documents have been adopted as vital elements in compiling the true chronology of Tony's activities in France. Consequently, *Saboteur* contradicts a few of its subject's statements made in interviews and written accounts. Thankfully, any disparities are largely concerned with detail rather than raising more fundamental questions of whether an event did or did not happen. Tony was always most insistent that the book should be as accurate as humanly possible and our agreement (that was maintained during his life and has continued after his death) was that every effort would be made to locate reliable sources to anchor his verbal recollections. At first, this imperative had the result in early drafts that Tony had almost become marginalised in his own biography. Hopefully, this error has been corrected and Tony's 'voice' in contemporary writings and later interviews has been properly integrated in this account of his extraordinary wartime experiences.

For all the importance and prominence of his work as the leader of his network, PIMENTO, Tony's service left relatively few traces in the official SOE record. Among the explanations for this state of affairs are that he possessed a relatively uncontroversial wartime career and harboured a marked disinclination to engage in paperwork. The research for this book began long before the SOE records were transferred to the National Archives and 'SOE Advisers' attached to the Foreign Office kindly provided information from the closed records. I owe a great deal to the last two Advisers, Gervase Cowell and Duncan Stuart, for this source made available some vital records that do not seem to have been included in the SOE papers subsequently released to the public.

Understandably, given the 'fog of war' and the length of time Tony was operating in the field, there are some inconsistencies over times and dates in both the official and unofficial accounts. After the war Tony aided and abetted the confusion by sometimes shaping accounts of his PIMENTO colleagues' activities in order to secure a pension or decoration for them. It has been a constant challenge to lock his story into provable fact; even basic, empirical data such as the details of the second flight which took Tony to France have proved complex.

I have been blessed by the privilege of learning from the veterans – almost all of whom have now departed the scene. These have included Sir Robin Brook, SOE's regional controller for Western Europe, Maurice Buckmaster, the head of F Section, and Vera Atkins, Buckmaster's *eminence grise*. I was tutored in air supply by Group Captain Ron Hockey, commanding officer of No. 138 Squadron, Wing Commander Len Ratcliff, commanding officer of No. 161 Squadron, and Air Chief Marshal Sir Lewis Hodges, who collected Tony from Occupied France in August 1943. Other SOE veterans who shared their memories of Tony included Ernest van Maurik, Brian Stonehouse, Brooks Richards, Henri Despaigne and Yvonne Cormeau. In France I was granted the reminiscences of Tony's PIMENTO comrades such as Jean Monier, Maurice Rouch and Robert Marty.

The support of fellow historians is a vital feature and I am indebted in particular to Chris Baxter and Sébastien Albertelli who read the text in draft. Tony and Lena's friend (and mine) Jim Owers also gave the book a health check. Others who have lent their support and advice include the late Keith Jeffery, Duncan Stuart, Eunan O'Halpin, David Harrison, Bob Body, Nigel Perrin, Rod Bailey and Andrzej Suchcitz. Of course, my family and friends have encouraged and sustained me during the long journey in bringing the book to completion.

I owe a special note of thanks to my friends and colleagues Toby and Dominique Buchan, and Andrew Lownie for their skill and expertise in bringing Tony's story to publication.

All these men and women would, however, fully understand that their contributions were but a supplement to the most important person of all – Tony Brooks. It was a rare privilege to be able to spend so much time with such a remarkable individual and, for once using the word in its real sense, a true hero.

MARK SEAMAN

Prologue

He had never experienced a descent quite like this one. The three parachute drops at the training school near Manchester had not left him with any great confidence in the wisdom of jumping out of an aircraft but at least they had all been reassuringly similar. But this, his first operational drop, was alarmingly different. Almost as soon as he pushed himself through the hole in the floor of the Royal Air Force Halifax bomber and his parachute deployed, he began to swing in a disconcertingly random manner. At the height of the pendulum he saw the aircraft flying off into the moonlit distance, then he was swooping downwards, the fields, trees, hedgerows and houses of the French countryside flashing by beneath him. But there was nothing wrong with his training; his parachute was the problem and until this critical moment he had been blissfully unaware of its imperfections. His 'A' type parachute was notorious for 'candling' – twisting and failing to open correctly – but the parachutist was discovering another deadly defect. Its peculiar design dictated that his suitcase was suspended by webbing straps above his head and it was this ill-advised configuration that imparted a broken pendulum effect to his descent. The subsequent, uncontrolled movement prevented him from either steering the parachute or correcting the disturbing, swaying motion. To make matters worse, house lights began to come on below him and voices were shouting excitedly. But his growing assumption that his clandestine arrival had been compromised was not the most pressing problem for he now realised that it was potluck which point of his arc of descent would see him hit the ground. He could only hope that the uncontrolled landing would not inflict too bad an injury but this hasty appraisal was scarcely completed before he smashed into a tree, crashing through the smaller branches until his back struck the trunk with, as he later said, 'a hell of a thump'. He then slipped downwards through the foliage, hitting the ground awkwardly and wrenching his right knee. He released the harness and struggled out of the webbing straps, leaving his parachute and its shrouds enmeshed in the tree, then crawled painfully across the field to a ditch with the intention of hiding from search parties, gaining a moment of respite and rapidly considering his next move.

It was the early hours of 2 July 1942 at Saint-Léonard-de-Noblat in the Unoccupied Zone of France. The parachutist's name was Tony Brooks. He was twenty years old and the youngest agent sent to France by the British secret service, the Special Operations Executive (SOE). He was badly injured with damaged vertebrae and a dislocated knee. To make matters worse, he knew his less than inconspicuous arrival would soon bring the French police onto the scene. As Tony contemplated his plight, he reluctantly came to the conclusion that his secret career was about to end before it had even begun.

Chapter One
An Unusual Childhood

But just who was this parachutist and what had converted an English youth, barely out of his teens, into a secret agent and delivered him into enemy territory in the summer of 1942?

Tony Brooks's upbringing was unconventional. His father, Douglas, was the son of wealthy Quakers who held a prominent position in the British cement industry. He had become the black sheep of the family during the First World War resulting from his decision to quit the passivity of his service with the Friends' Ambulance Unit and enlist in the Royal Flying Corps. However, Douglas's distinguished service as a fighter pilot with No. 11 Squadron on the Western Front, confirmed by the award of a Military Cross, seems to have facilitated reconciliation with his parents.*

In August 1918 he married Beryl Anderson, the daughter of Herbert Anderson, an industrialist with close professional links to the Brooks dynasty.

---

* There was a family story that Douglas preceded his youngest son into the world of clandestine warfare by exfiltrating a secret agent from behind German lines near Metz. The legend stated that after landing, Douglas switched off his engine and waited until, in due course, the man appeared. He unfortunately proved of insufficient stature to swing the propeller blade to make the engine catch, so Douglas instructed him to board the aircraft while he climbed out to turn over the engine himself. His success was soon tempered by seeing the machine taxiing across the field with the luckless spy an unwitting passenger in a pilotless aeroplane. Douglas chased after it, and managed to clamber aboard, and returned to base. Regrettably, Douglas's logbook for the period July 1917 to May 1918 offers no corroboration of the episode but AIR1/20/2011 does record his 'splendid' and 'excellent' work with the squadron.

The couple's first child, Peter, was born in 1920, and soon afterwards Douglas left England to take up a post as a civil engineer in Egypt. Beryl and Peter joined him in the Middle East but they did not stay long for she became pregnant and returned to England for her confinement. A second son, Anthony Morris Brooks, was born at Orsett, Essex, on 4 April 1922.

It was a time when the demands of imperial and commercial employment obliged countless husbands to live apart from their families for years on end. While some couples coped with separation, the Brookses did not and cracks began to appear in their marriage. Moreover, medical problems exacerbated matrimonial troubles. Shortly after Tony's birth, Beryl contracted tuberculosis while her baby was diagnosed with the incurable skin condition psoriasis. Medication merely limited the discomfort of the small, red, scaly patches, intolerably itchy and painful, that appeared on his body. In addition to these health issues, Beryl's finances were in disarray. Douglas seems to have made inadequate provision for his young family and Tony recalled that the affluent patriarchs of the Brooks and Anderson families did little to help maintain them.

Beryl Brooks was not the sort of woman simply to wait around for fate to deal her a better hand and decided to move her young family to the South of France. In the 1920s the Côte d'Azur was not solely the playground of the rich and famous. It offered a low cost of living, a healthy climate to aid the delicate constitutions of Beryl and her younger son and, perhaps more tenuously, was a closer staging post to Egypt. The first two attributes were exploited to good effect with the renting of an inexpensive villa at Juan-les-Pins where the limitless sunshine resulted in improvements to Beryl's and Tony's health. It was here that, even as he began to speak his mother tongue, Tony also began to learn French from daily contact with maids, nurses, gardeners and shopkeepers.

Any hope that residence in Southern France would forge a closer link to Douglas proved illusory. Whether the family separations constituted a symptom or a cause of marital problems, the ties between Douglas and Beryl Brooks became increasingly strained. The former remained intent on pursuing his work in the Middle East while his wife's health kept her from joining him in the unforgiving Egyptian climate. As time passed, the marriage showed no signs of improvement and Tony's parents formally separated; thereafter, for more than a decade, Douglas, to all intents, vanished from his sons' lives.

Such was Beryl's financial predicament that even the relatively frugal existence on the Côte d'Azur could not be sustained and in 1927 she moved to Switzerland where the exchange rate was favourable and the mountain air promised to have a commensurately therapeutic effect on the family's health. Beryl and her sons slipped easily into the large British expatriate community around Lake Geneva, though their membership of this colony of exiles did little to inhibit Tony's growing fluency in the French language.

At first Beryl and her sons lived on the lakeside, then moved to a small residence, the Villa du Château, in the hills above Clarens near the village of Planchamp. Although the family remained well-nigh impecunious, the alpine life helped the two boys to grow up fit and strong. Tony later recalled that childhood illnesses only befell him when he went to England to complete his schooling. The family's daily routine reflected a far from pampered upbringing and the boys' household duties bred an acceptance of hard work and self-reliance. For Beryl the hardships of bringing up two young children in a foreign country on limited resources were somewhat alleviated by her friendship with Bill Barton, an employee at Montreux of the travel company, Thomas Cook & Sons. They had met when Barton was assigned responsibility for handling Beryl's finances and, gradually, a romance blossomed. In January 1930, after years of separation, Beryl divorced Douglas and, in November, married Barton. It was hardly surprising, given the tight, insular relationship that prevailed between the mother and her sons, that there were problems. While he easily accepted the situation and called his stepfather 'Daddy B', Tony recalled that his brother loathed Barton, comparing him unfavourably to the idealised image he had created of the long-absent Douglas.* But, tragically, the new family was denied the chance of building a life together. Beryl's doctors advised that her age and weakened constitution made having another child a serious threat to her health, but, even so, she fell pregnant. Recognising the risks, she sought to prepare her children for the worst and made special efforts to teach them to be even more self-sufficient. On 14 October 1932 Beryl gave birth to a daughter, Ann, but complications soon set in. She had steadfastly

---

* In fact, Barton possessed heroic qualities of his own. In 1934 he apprehended an armed robber in Montreux, for which act he was awarded the Carnegie Medal. During the Second World War he worked with British officials to assist servicemen seeking sanctuary in Switzerland.

refused to be admitted to hospital to have the baby, and died three weeks later. In retrospect, Tony considered that he was less affected than his brother by their mother's death but, nevertheless, felt 'a great void' at the loss. Perhaps with a presentiment, on her deathbed Beryl gave wristwatches to the two boys; Tony's became a talisman for him in the difficult, dangerous and frequently lonely years to come. Meanwhile Barton's grief was compounded by the realisation that he was a widower, and responsible not just for his baby daughter but also two stepsons. He assumed these challenges with a commendable sense of duty, and a maid, Cécile, was engaged to look after the house and the baby. In 1937 the lease on the Villa du Château expired and the family moved from the mountain slopes back to the lakeside.

Peter and Tony now became beneficiaries of a Brooks family trust fund that provided the wherewithal for their education at Chillon College, a school on the shores of Lake Geneva. This Swiss-English 'public school' did not inhibit the boys understanding the growing European political crises. The ramifications of Nazi racial persecution were all too evident even in the artificial, British ambience of the college; both Brooks boys had Jewish classmates who were refugees from oppression in Germany. While Tony later categorised most of his fellow pupils as 'acquaintances' (rather than friends), he was close to Gottlob, who had been assisted by an American welfare agency to reach the safety of Switzerland. Gottlob willingly described to his classmate the Nazi racism that had culminated in his parents' incarceration in a concentration camp. This chilling insight into Nazi depredations had a powerful effect upon Tony and, even as a schoolboy, he began to develop a keen interest in the turbulent politics of the Europe around him.*

In Douglas's absence, members of the Brooks family kept a spasmodic watching brief over his sons and their education. Peter left Switzerland in July 1937 to attend a crammer in England while Tony remained at Chillon, now as a weekday boarder, until he completed his School Certificate examination. Then Douglas's older brother, Norman, who had assumed the role of Tony's legal guardian decided that the boy should be sent to England and enrolled at Felsted School, situated near to the Brooks family home at Orsett in Essex.

---

* In a post-war letter of 11 November 1945, John 'Jubilee' Stuart, a Chillon classmate, wrote to Tony, 'Often I thought of our plans during the Abysinnian [sic] war when we wanted to buy an old fighter aircraft and fight Fascisme!' AMB Papers.

Joining a British public school can be an intimidating experience to even the best prepared of youths and Tony, in spite of Chillon's emulation of British scholastic standards, felt an acute strangeness about Felsted's practices. The uniforms, tuck boxes, prefects and three church services every Sunday (the school was High Church) seemed peculiar while a further, unexpected, difficulty soon confronted him; for a boy hardened by the healthy, Swiss, outdoor life, Tony succumbed to a succession of illnesses. His previous, relatively isolated upbringing failed to provide adequate resistance against common childhood maladies. That first year, his sick record at Felsted was dismal: first term – chicken pox; second term – virulent influenza; third term – scarlet fever. He recalled that during his first terms at the school he was rarely out of the Sanatorium; nevertheless, he derived some benefit from this as he was able to pursue his studies without the usual classroom distractions, and came to know his school textbooks almost by heart. He also became an ardent admirer of the school nurse, developing what he admitted was a full-fledged 'crush'. It is not surprising that Tony should have vested his affections on a stranger, for he did not receive much support from the Brookses at this time. His Uncle Basil regularly visited the school in his Bugatti motor car to take his son, Edward, a Felsted student, to lunch, but Tony was only invited to join them on one occasion. In spite of the school's proximity to 'Goldsmiths', the Brooks residence at Orsett, Tony spent the half-term holidays at Felsted. When he did pay a visit to his family, his relatives provided neither affection nor the schoolboy's essential requirement of pocket money; the few treats coming his way being offered by the servants, rather than his grandparents, uncles and aunts. The austere ambience of Goldsmiths, a large detached villa outside Basildon, owed as much to the previous century as the 1930s. Every Sunday morning the entire household of four gardeners, the chauffeur, the cook, the kitchen maid, the housemaid, and Maude the housekeeper, paraded for prayers led by Grandfather Brooks.

Amidst this Dickensian saga, there were occasionally more convivial distractions. One of Tony's friends at Felsted was Martin 'The Goat' Wilkinson, the son of the Rector of Thetford in Norfolk, and during an Easter vacation Tony was invited to spend the holiday with the family. The Reverend Wilkinson's previous incumbency had been at Leverington, near Wisbech, and he had maintained contact with the Mundays, fruit farmers and prominent members of the local community. During the holiday, Martin and Tony went to stay at Leverington, a decision perhaps not unconnected with the presence there of the two Munday daughters, Hope and Penelope. Tony became close friends with Hope and he remained in touch with her (largely by letter) over the following years. Later, Peter Brooks was brought into the circle and took something of a shine to Penelope.

Back at Felsted, Tony met with mixed fortunes in his examinations. A 98 per cent pass in French and distinguished marks in Science, Maths and Geography were not matched in other subjects and the score he received for his Latin and Divinity papers suggested that he managed to write his name and the title of the paper correctly but little more. Meanwhile, after his initial ill-health, Tony's natural fitness had returned. Felsted was very sports-minded and every day the boys engaged in some form of compulsory games. The school was a bastion of rugby, causing Tony some disquiet because he disliked the game and favoured soccer. (Inevitably, Tony was put into the scrum where, to compound his fundamental dislike for the sport, the physical chafing disturbed his psoriasis and made his ears bleed.)[1] He did well at other sports, notably athletics, where his natural stamina was put to good effect in long-distance running.* Something of a loner, he nevertheless made a sufficiently favourable impression on his schoolmates and teachers to be elected head of his house Middle Room. While he participated in most aspects of Felsted life, one was denied him: engagement in the Officer Training Corps required an extra payment by the pupil's family, and Tony's (as Quakers and pacifists) declined the subvention. He was not particularly upset by this restriction and joined the Scouts whose freer discipline proved in tune with his own personality.

It was while coming to the end of his schooling at Felsted that Tony briefly renewed acquaintanceship with his father when Douglas visited Goldsmiths, accompanied by his wife Ruth Hoffmann. Neither of the Brooks boys had received letters from their father during their childhood and, given the absence of paternal contact, the overriding impression that the reunion left in Tony's memory was primarily of his stepmother's décolletage rather than the encounter with the stranger who was his father. (He later recollected

---

* In 1936 he had won the Junior Cross Country race at Chillon (the engraver misspelt his name 'Brookes' on the egg cup-sized trophy).

that while Barton signed himself 'Daddy' in post-war correspondence with him, Douglas tended to conclude his letters with the formal 'D. Brooks'.)

Tony's interests were characterised by a focus on technology and engineering. Lorries, cars, trains, aviation and mechanics fascinated him and he aspired to join the transport branches of his family's cement industry businesses. His teachers advised that in order to realise his ambitions, he should apply for a place at the City and Guilds Institute where his brother was already a student. Tony's application was successful, but his age dictated that he could not enrol until September the following year. He left Felsted in July 1939 and went to stay with his mother's father, 'Gramps', at Folkestone. As a treat, he recalled, he was taken to see an air show, where he experienced the contrasting excitement of his first air flight and the trauma of witnessing a parachute descent that ended in tragedy.*

That summer, Tony and Peter left England to visit the French home of Norman Brooks, their father's elder brother. Tony's uncle had served with the British Army during the First World War and then stayed in France as a representative of Associated Portland Cement Manufacturers. In 1922 he was appointed managing director of a plaster works, Plâtrières Modernes de Grozon, near the town of Poligny in the Jura region. Norman turned the fortunes of the failing company around and in the early 1930s the Brooks family became its majority shareholders. The plan was that Tony would remain in France after the summer vacation to gain work experience at Grozon until it was time to take up his studies in London. Tony was content with the arrangements; there was nothing to keep him in England and he looked forward to a return to France.

---

* Tony remembered it as Sir Alan Cobham's Flying Circus, but this programme ended in 1935. Perhaps it was a different event or the outing took place at another time.

Chapter Two
'This Country is at War'

In August 1939 Tony and Peter arrived at Norman Brooks's impressive home, the Château de Proby near Poligny. The young men caught up on family news with their Aunt Ruth and cousin Joan, and then settled into a leisurely existence punctuated by occasional contributions to minor chores around the estate. It was a pleasant, uncomplicated sojourn; the brothers were healthy, privileged and looking forward to their future education in England. But the serenity of the Brookses' life in the small town in the Jura was not immune from an unfolding international crisis.

There was a growing realisation that the Anglo-French diplomatic appeasement of Nazi Germany embodied in the 'settlement' of the Munich Crisis of September 1938 had merely postponed war rather than prevented it. Britain and France embarked on substantial rearmament programmes while Hitler implemented a series of political and military coups that included the dismemberment of Czechoslovakia, an alliance with Italy and, perhaps most surprising of all, a non-aggression pact with the Soviet Union.

As was its custom, the French nation 'closed down' for the August holiday, but elsewhere it was business as usual. Throughout that month Germany stepped up diplomatic pressure on Poland while, at the same time, completed its war plans. Then, on 1 September 1939, the Wehrmacht launched an overpowering invasion, forcing Britain and France rapidly to review their treaty obligations to the Poles. The tension gripped the whole of Europe, the momentous events even touching the Château de Proby, and Tony and his brother were among the millions who avidly tuned into radio broadcasts for updates on the deteriorating crisis in Poland until, on 3 September 1939, they heard that Britain and then France (six hours after its ally) had declared war on Germany. Far from sharing the dismay voiced by their uncle, the two young men greeted the news with the approbation, 'Thank God!'* Peter soon returned to London where he joined the editorial staff of *The Aeroplane* magazine, later becoming the air correspondent of the *Manchester Evening News* before joining the Fleet Air Arm with which he flew Swordfish aircraft.[1]

Meanwhile, Tony stayed on in France. He applied to the British Embassy in Paris asking to join the RAF but was rejected as his age group was not yet eligible, and he reluctantly accepted that he would have to remain at Poligny until he could return to Britain either to continue his education or to enlist. Unsurprisingly, he did not find his duties at the Grozon plaster works stimulating and, as the boss's nephew and marked as a future member of 'management', his duties were very 'white collar'. One consolation was his twice-weekly visits to Lons-le-Saunier to learn shorthand, typing and accountancy. He formed a friendship with his tutor, Marcel Mégard, while another, very different, relationship blossomed after Tony spotted Marcelle 'Lelette' Mornand, a dental nurse, as she passed by the office. He contrived a meeting with her and they began courting. While the romance failed the test of time, Lelette, like several of Tony's friends from this period, would play a supporting role in his wartime adventures.[2]

The Grozon plaster works boasted an impressive array of vehicles and industrial machinery that offered a welcome distraction from the stuffy confines of Tony's office work. He struck up a friendship with Camille Bouillet, the chief mechanic, who recognised the young man's enthusiasm and encouraged him to learn to drive both cars and trucks. Under Bouillet's tutelage, Tony acquired vehicle maintenance and driving skills but also, perhaps more important for his subsequent career, a deep insight into the mores and argot of the French working class. In spite of his privileged surroundings, he felt much more at home with the drivers and mechanics than amidst the luxury and servants of his uncle's château.

---

* The portentous nature of the day is somewhat diminished by the only surviving Brooks record of it – a rather mundane photograph of Tony showing Peter 'his' Berliet truck.

Tony was now fully immersed in the French lifestyle and by Christmas 1939 had become, in his own words, 'completely frogified'. He daily experienced contrasts between the grime of the factory workshop and the evening opulence of his uncle's château (where English was used to converse among the family but French to speak with the servants). Then a welcome temporary role arose for him chauffeuring his uncle on business trips throughout France; on one of the visits to Paris, Tony called at the British Air Attaché's office to enquire about volunteering. Once again, he was told to be patient. In February 1940 Norman travelled to Iraq on business, presumably to see Douglas, leaving Tony free to devote more time to working with the transport section of the firm.[3]

Tony's frustration at being unable to contribute to his country's war effort was somewhat assuaged by the stalemate that characterised the conflict from its very outset. This was the period of the 'Phoney War' or, as the French named it, the '*Drôle de Guerre*', during which the British gradually built up an Expeditionary Force in northern France, the French manned their Maginot Line defences and the Germans showed a comparable lack of martial ambition behind their Siegfried Line. Only an occasional raid into no-man's-land or the odd air sortie broke the all-pervading sense of inertia. Meanwhile, as a counterpoint, commercial life continued and Tony drove the firm's lorries throughout France, steadily improving his understanding of the country's geography, customs and people, and forging a familiarity with the cities of Lyon, Marseille and Toulouse.

In April 1940, the dormant conflict at last erupted with German invasions of Denmark and Norway. But, even then, the fighting in the far-away snows of Scandinavia seemed to reinforce the phoniness of the war at the heart of Europe. The despatch of an Anglo-French-Polish expeditionary force to aid the Norwegians seemed as if it might dispel the 'Phoney' epithet but, meanwhile, the Allied armies in France remained as inactive as ever. Then, suddenly, on 10 May 1940, the 'Phoney War' became very, very real. Over 140 German divisions smashed into Luxembourg, Holland, Belgium and France. Although the strengths of the invading and defending forces were almost identical, the Germans' co-ordination of their strategy and tactics was in stark contrast to the confusion and ineptitude shown by the Allies. Luxembourg was quickly overrun and the Netherlands collapsed in a couple of days. Every time the Belgian, British and French forces sought to consolidate their defences, a new German breakthrough was achieved, and a further retreat ensued. The chaos was not confined to the battlefield and an immense flood of refugees took to the roads and railways of France. During a campaign lasting less than two months, between eight and ten million French and Belgian civilians fled to regions where they hoped to escape the German onslaught. It was not just the citizens of the great cities who ran before the invader; the town of Evereux in Normandy shrank from a peacetime population of 20,000 to a mere 172 on 11 June.[4] A writer vividly described the mayhem:

> Cars ran out of petrol or broke down or got stuck in ditches when the sound of approaching Stukas made them swerve for cover. Weighed down with people and possessions, farm carts broke wheels or axles. There were traffic jams, pile-ups and arguments. Some people simply got lost. Others had to abandon their vehicles, with most of the possessions they had thought precious enough to bring, and join those already trudging along on foot with overloaded prams or bicycles. They got used to sleeping on floors of churches, in disused buildings and in the open. They began to run short of food, despite the efforts of overwhelmed local authorities. Even water could run dangerously low: in several places there were reports of canny locals standing at the roadside selling it by the bottle and the glass.[5]

Among those who joined the flight southwards were the Brooks family. Tony's diary cryptically records the deteriorating situation before their departure with aircraft being heard over the château on 9 May followed by German air raids launched against French aerodromes near Lyon and Dijon. The next day the war had evidently come a lot closer: 'Bombs shook the ceiling in Joan's [Tony's cousin] room at Proby.' The diary logs German aerial incursions into the region and Tony's growing realisation that the Allies were failing to stem the enemy tide: 'Barricades in the Jura across the road to stop cars. 7 Heinkel 111 [German bombers] came over Proby at 5.00' (25 May 1940). The appearance of six British Blenheim aircraft in the skies above the château on 10 June and Tony's observing three RAF officers in Lyon on the 13th appeared to augur better things, but the Brookses were soon to join the exodus. The next day Tony wrote, 'Bigays [colleagues and friends] came and stayed at Proby. Prepared to leave if the emergency arose.' The following day the 'emergency' had arisen, Tony noting, 'Left at 7.30 p.m. in the Cadillac, Peugeot and Citroën.' The party's ultimate destination was the town of Montauban in the *département* of the Tarn-et-Garonne some three hundred miles to the south-west. There were two reasons for the choice: Montauban seemed a reassuringly long way from the German advance, and Marcel Guerret, a Deputy at the Assemblée Nationale and deputy mayor of the town, was the father-in-law of Norman's son, Francis.*

The small convoy of vehicles made determined progress. It was impossible for the Brookses to gauge just how far in advance of the battlefront they might be, but suddenly they were overtaken on the road by German Army motorcyclists. This was Tony's first sight of the enemy, but he recalled that he felt quite unmoved and was able dispassionately to appraise the soldiers' appearance and equipment. Far more worrying to the party was the lawlessness that now prevailed in central France. The country was in turmoil, with French Army deserters joining the millions of civilians clogging the roads. Tony was concerned that a vehicle breakdown might leave the party hopelessly stranded and vulnerable to the depredations of the French flotsam and jetsam that now constituted as much of a threat to person and property as did the German armed forces.

They reached La Clette in the early hours of the 16th, then, after a brief rest, were on the road again, lunching at Billom and stopping overnight at Aurillac. Norman drove the Cadillac, Tony was behind the wheel of a Citroën and Jeunet, one of the factory workmen, conveyed the family possessions in a Gazogène-fuelled truck.[6] Jeunet decided en route to return home and Tony drove the lorry the remainder of the journey.

On the 17th the party left Aurillac and reached Montauban at four o'clock that afternoon. The town's population had trebled during the crisis and was in turmoil, leaving Tony to note in his diary, 'Lorries and refugee cars all along the roads.' But French bureaucracy still needed to be appeased and they

---

* A year earlier, Francis Brooks had married Lucette Guerret whom he had met in Paris when she was studying at the Sorbonne and he was at the École Centrale. At the time of the fall of France they were living in England.

registered on arrival with the Montauban police as refugees.[7] Guerret's house at 4 rue Léon Cladel was already full to bursting but, nevertheless, space was found and Tony acquired a billet in the attic. Among the other residents were Guerret's sister, Lelette, with her husband, Gustave Hirschfeld, former chief librarian of the Senate in Paris, and their nineteen-year-old daughter, Colette.[8]

For Tony and his family, there now seemed little alternative but to sit it out in Montauban and await the outcome of world events. News reports revealed that matters were reaching a critical stage as the French military and political collapse continued. On 14 June the Germans had entered Paris and, with the French will to continue the fight crumbling, Marshal Philippe Pétain assumed power. As France's military saviour leading the defence of Verdun during the First World War, the eighty-four-year-old Pétain seemed, on the surface, the ideal man to handle the crisis. The Marshal concurred with this widely held public opinion and considered he was the only figure capable of maintaining any semblance of national morale and of guiding the nation through its present disaster.

Meanwhile, the Brooks party in Montauban seemed to have come up with an escape plan. On 21 June Tony and his uncle travelled the fifty kilometres south to Toulouse to seek assistance from the British Consul. Tony's understated diary entry succinctly captures the moment, 'He was leaving and gave us no information. Other Brit. subjects in panic.' But the crisis peaked the following day when an armistice was signed between France and Germany and, as far as most French men and women were concerned, the war was over. In the meantime the Brookses gamely sought to find a means of getting out of the country. On the 23rd Tony wrote, 'Uncle went to Toulouse with Mr Guerret to try and get visas for Spain,' but the diary entry for the following day illustrated the rapidity with which plans changed, 'Uncle succeeded in getting visas for England by Marseilles. Spanish frontier closed on Sunday. On Monday decided not to leave yet.' It can surely be no coincidence that this volte-face took place two days after the armistice when the prospect of peace and a modicum of stability seemed about to return to France. That a calmer period had arrived is reflected in Tony's diary for the 27th, 'Refugees died down on the road from Paris. Not so many troops to be seen.'

The full terms and conditions of the armistice took a while to come into effect but the demarcation 'front line' at the conclusion of hostilities was roughly transformed into a frontier dividing France into a northern, 'Occupied' Zone under German control and a southern, 'Unoccupied' or 'Free' Zone administered by Pétain's new government. The Marshal's regime established itself at the spa town of Vichy whence Guerret was summoned to take part in the chaotic political process that would determine France's future. On 10 July the National Assembly voted itself out of existence, passed power to Pétain as head of state, and thereby terminated the French Republic. Guerret, a Socialist Party member of the Chambre des Députés since 1936, voted in favour of the motion, and thereby exemplified the scale of the malaise gripping French politics. Surprisingly he found time on the day of the great vote to send Tony at Montauban a postcard of the Vichy Casino, the temporary home of the Assembly.[9]

If the French nation was shocked and numbed by the enormity of defeat, its people nevertheless soon tried to regain a level of normality and resume their day-to-day lives. Norman Brooks was delighted to discover that Poligny fell within the Unoccupied Zone and therefore, even though a British citizen, he would be permitted to return home. Most of the Brooks entourage departed on 15 July but Tony did not accompany them, staying on at Montauban to oversee the conversion of the Citroën car to burn charcoal as fuel. It was no hardship for the young man to remain in the south-west, where a romance with Colette Hirschfeld had developed so that by 13 October he confided in his diary, 'Three months have passed since the 1st K. [kiss?] Now I am engaged unofficially.' The teenager's thoughts were, understandably, preoccupied with his new, 'unofficial' fiancée, but he still found time to discuss the war and the turbulent French political scene with Guerret. Most important, the latter introduced him to some personalities who were to become immensely influential in Tony's work as a British secret agent.

Amongst the most notable Montauban figures was Michel Comte, a garage owner and local politician – assistant mayor and member of the town council. Comte, the proprietor of the Garage des Pyrénées, a heavy-goods vehicle repair shop, had a no-nonsense attitude to life and his abundant friendliness and sociable nature made him an appealing companion for the young Englishman. A rather more shadowy figure in Guerret's Montauban circle of contacts was René Bertholet, a Swiss left-wing journalist and political activist. Tony surmised that the two men had come into contact before the war when Guerret's official duties included refugee affairs and Bertholet was working for Swiss aid charities. Bertholet's wealth of experience and his engaging personality quickly made an impact on Tony. A friendship developed and, during their conversations, Bertholet discreetly offered to arrange for the young man to cross the frontier into neutral Switzerland. Tony declined the proposal, but it provided an early manifestation of Bertholet's generosity and, just as significantly, an intimation of his influence.

At the time, Tony was unaware of the true measure of the man with whom he had become acquainted. Born in 1907, Bertholet was from a Geneva family that constituted a veritable bastion of socialism. Naturally, he became immersed in his parents' political beliefs and in 1926 took a secretarial job at Mulhouse in Alsace where he maintained his socialist connections and took his first steps as a fledgling journalist. Bertholet soon recognised that political activism was his true vocation and enrolled at the Internationaler Sozialistischer Kampfbund (ISK) School at Walkemühle in Germany. This was, effectively, a seminary for left-wing activists, and at the conclusion of his studies Bertholet became engaged in organising political groups in Germany and France. His motivation was no mere theoretical pipedream but, rather, was firmly rooted in a conviction that the rampant right-wing and fascist movements in Europe during the early 1930s needed to be challenged. Although a political idealist, he recognised that his beliefs could only be realised by action rather than the immutability of socialist theory, and he was drawn into the clandestine world, notably assisting fugitives to escape from political persecution. Initially, Bertholet's nationality offered him some protection while he was operating in Germany but in November 1933 he was betrayed to the Nazi authorities, arrested and sentenced to five years' imprisonment. He had served half of the sentence before Swiss officials managed to secure his release, but his commitment to the political struggle remained undimmed and in the mid-1930s there was no shortage of causes for a dedicated anti-fascist to pursue. He switched his activities to Spain where he wrote articles on the Civil War for the newspaper *Le Peuple*, drove an ambulance for the Republicans and maintained a variety of clandestine activities. Following the Nationalist victory in March 1939, he moved to France where he remained a prominent member of the international militant socialist scene. His articles (written under the *nom de plume* 'Pierre Robert') had a wide circulation including the British periodical *Socialist Vanguard*, while booklets such as *'Spain Calling!'* informed English-language readers of his views. Now, in the summer of 1940, he had become part of the exodus fleeing the catastrophe of the German invasion and France's defeat. One can only speculate on the effect that such a resounding Nazi victory inflicted upon the morale of one of that regime's most inveterate opponents.[10]

René Bertholet brought a strong, early whiff of the secret world to Montauban but now Tony's own clandestine career was about to commence. In the middle of August, while waiting for the work on the Citroën to be completed, he was stopped in the street outside Guerret's house by the local butcher. Excitedly the Frenchman pointed at a man walking away from them and confided that he was *'un soldat anglais'*. Thanking the butcher, Tony ran after the man and introduced himself in English. The response from the *'soldat anglais'* was decidedly guarded but, after Tony established his bona fides, the soldier accepted an invitation to visit Guerret's house and relate his story.

The *'soldat anglais'* was Albert Manser, a thirty-year-old private in the Queen's Own Royal West Kent Regiment. A pre-war member of the Territorial Army, he had served with the British Expeditionary Force during the fighting in northern France until taken prisoner. Manser was a resourceful individual and averse to being submissively marched off to a prisoner-of-war camp. As his column of captives approached the Belgian-German border, he saw the city of Aachen in the distance and realised he had to act soon. He discussed this with two fellow prisoners and they agreed to make a dash for it. Calculating that the German guards' priority would be the hundreds of other soldiers in their charge rather than giving chase to a trio of fugitives, Manser estimated that if the first fusillade of shots missed, he stood a good chance of making his escape. This is just the way it transpired. However, success meant he was at large in German-occupied Belgium, unable to speak any French other than *'oui'* or *'non'* and aware that his British Army battledress did little to help his cause. He lay up in a wood for a while and then headed south, living off vegetables he found growing in the fields. Occasionally he risked asking a farmer for help and once spent a whole day with a peasant who, as a veteran of the First World War, was willing to assist a fellow soldier in need. Manser developed a routine of walking early in the morning and then lying up during the remainder of the daylight hours. His anonymity was greatly enhanced when he stole a pair of blue overalls from a washing line and put them over his army uniform. His objective was Spain and he navigated his way using *départementale* maps that he tore out of directories found in public telephone kiosks. Unfortunately, his masterplan did not take account of the irregular configuration of the maps that owed more to the aesthetic criteria of their designer than a logical north–south axis. His route southwards therefore followed a distinctly wayward path as he zigzagged from one *département* to another. In spite of this hindrance, by mid-August he had achieved the remarkable feat of having walked from the English Channel coast via the Ardennes and the borders of Germany to the Tarn-et-Garonne.

Manser received a warm welcome at Guerret's house. He later reminded Tony, 'I so vividly remember all the good things you fixed me up with, even to needle and thread, and spare bootlaces, a lovely bath and a very fine meal, new clothes and French currency, and what to me was vastly important: confidence and kindness to see me on my way.'[11] Manser's somewhat eccentric collection of personal effects evidently intrigued his host: 'I remember you laughing at my bag I carried. It was the things in it amused you. I had a jar for my butter and another for jam, a tin for coffee, a knife and fork and a pipe and tobacco. You could not believe I had come right through Occupied France like that but assuredly I had.' Tony asked if he would like to stay the night in Montauban but Manser was determined to press on. So, with Guerret's instructions as how best to cross the frontier into Spain committed to the soldier's memory, Tony took him to the outskirts of town and the road to Toulouse. From there, the indomitable Manser planned to catch a train to Foix, in the foothills of the Pyrenees, whence he hoped to cross into Spain. This encounter with a fellow countryman marked a turning point for Tony. Albert Manser was an inspiration and with further tales of thousands of other evaders wandering around the country, the brief acquaintanceship convinced Tony that there must be something, however mundane, that he could do to assist the fugitives and aid his country's war effort. He might be a civilian, marooned in Vichy France, but if there were other Albert Mansers out there, he resolved to help get them home.[12]

With the work on the Citroën at last completed, on 30 October 1940 Tony left Montauban and headed back to Grozon. On his return, he found the old Proby routine, on the face of it, undisturbed. He took up his former duties at the factory and, if his diary is an accurate barometer, spent much of his leisure time composing letters to Colette Hirschfeld back in Montauban. However, it was soon apparent that the armistice had wrought some significant changes upon the Brooks family. His relations with Norman had never been close but they became even more distant when Tony found that his uncle seemed unconcerned by the recent British military setbacks and the dire threat now facing their homeland. In contrast, Norman's wife Ruth was in her nephew's opinion 'a saint', an estimation reinforced by Tony's discovery that she had already begun to assist British soldiers and civilians evade internment by the Vichy authorities. Amongst Ruth Brooks's 'clients' was a British fugitive, Christine Chilver, who had been studying at the Sorbonne in Paris at the time of the German invasion. She and her mother had been interned but Christine was released to escort a wounded British soldier to the French Military Hospital at Besançon. Her duty done (the soldier was eventually repatriated), Chilver seized the opportunity to escape into the Unoccupied Zone in the company of a French doctor. They made their way to Poligny where the head of the local gendarmerie, Capitaine Faure, informed them of a British family living in the vicinity that might be able to help them. Christine duly turned up at Proby where Ruth Brooks provided sanctuary before sending her to Lyon where the Red Cross arranged for her to act as companion to William Simpson, an RAF pilot suffering from extensive burns, during his repatriation to Britain via Lisbon.[13] In the months following the encounter with Chilver, Capitaine Faure continued to collect British waifs and strays and passed them to Ruth Brooks for feeding, clothing and transportation to the south and, hopefully, a return to the United Kingdom.

Tony needed no prompting to join his aunt in her endeavours and, gradually, they developed a system; the British soldiers were sheltered around Grozon until it was possible to conduct them to Lyon or convey them directly to Marseille and their ultimate destination, the Seamen's Mission at 46 rue de Forbin in the Vieux Port area of the city. This establishment, a converted garage, was run by the Reverend Donald Caskie, a Minister of the Scottish Church in Paris (where Ruth Brooks had met him before the war). The priest had fled the capital shortly before the Germans' arrival and made his way to Marseille where a former British Consul in Nice proposed that he make the Mission a sanctuary for military personnel who had evaded capture or internment.[14] Caskie then embarked upon a complex game of cat-and-mouse with the French authorities who were under pressure from the Germans to inhibit the activities of the British servicemen who had congregated in the city. To appease the sensibilities of the French officials, Caskie installed a sign outside the Mission stating 'Now open to British civilians and seamen ONLY', an affirmation that belied the continuing 'open house' nature of the establishment.[15] It was a complicated state of affairs with the British soldiers holding an ambivalent status in Marseille – neither fully fledged prisoners on the run nor welcomed visitors,

> Once they got over the demarcation line they were still liable to arrest by the local police, but they were no longer at all likely to be handed over to the enemy. The Vichy government's policy was to concentrate them successively at Marseilles, where they were lodged at Fort St Jean; from January 1941, at St Hippolyte du Fort at Nîmes; or at La Turbie, just outside Monte Carlo; not quite prisoners, not quite free. In Marseilles, officers were only required to report for a Monday morning roll call at which rations were issued; most of them promptly sold their rations on the black market and lived in lodgings on the proceeds.[16]

Caskie's work was complicated. Members of the British community on the Riviera contributed money and supplies to support him while their efforts were supplemented by funds provided (clandestinely) by the American Consul. These early, ad hoc efforts in Marseille did not escape the notice of the authorities in London, in particular MI9, a branch of the War Office responsible for assisting service personnel to escape or evade capture in enemy territory. There was clearly a need to organise helpers to assist fugitives on the Continent and, as MI9 was part of the military establishment, the Secret Intelligence Service (SIS) assumed responsibility for funding and coordinating the nascent, clandestine escape networks.

Among the first and most effective of those organising affairs in the South of France was Captain Ian Garrow of the Seaforth Highlanders. He managed to better Manser's flight from Saint-Valéry-en-Caux and reached Marseille in October 1940 with four other members of his regiment. His command of the local language has been debated ('he knew little French', 'Schoolboy with a strong Scottish accent' and 'perfect') but what is not in question is that he took to clandestine work with aplomb. He was en route to the Pyrenees and a putative escape into Spain, when he realised that he could perform a greater service for his country by remaining in France and helping others to freedom. He therefore returned to Marseille. A fellow escaper and MI9 officer offered an appreciation of Garrow's achievements,

> In the first ten months of 1941, Garrow set the pattern for future escape operations over the Spanish frontier. He organised a chain of guides from Paris and northern France over the demarcation line and a system of reception in Marseille and Toulouse. The administrative problems were great. The strict rationing of food, increasing controls, and general disillusionment, made his position precarious.[17]

It was this organisation that Tony and Ruth Brooks had – inadvertently – joined. Word would be brought to them of groups of British soldiers and refugees who had found their way to the demarcation line some thirty kilometres north of Grozon. On receiving news of the fugitives' arrival, Tony would drive a lorry across the frontier, ostensibly to fetch firewood from a supplier in the Occupied Zone. Hiding the evaders in amongst the load, he would smuggle them to Proby before eventually ferrying the group to Lyon and delivering it into the care of the Fellot sisters who maintained an office at the British Consulate (now operating under the protection of the Swiss government). On other occasions, Tony acted as a personal escort, accompanying the evaders by rail from Lyon to Marseille. He found this task infinitely more stressful than driving them by lorry; the evaders consistently failed to do what they were told, hung around in groups in public places and could not resist the temptation to speak in English. In spite of his youth, Tony proved a hard taskmaster and admonished miscreants regardless of their age or rank. He presumed this did not endear him to his charges but, with a maturity beyond his years, took his obligations very seriously. He did not relish the prospect of internment or jail just because one of his charges lacked the self-discipline to do what they were told.

Under the terms of the Franco-German armistice, the Brookses were permitted to continue to reside in Unoccupied France. Tony kept his British identity papers with him at all times but his fluency in French was now so complete that when he came in contact with Vichy officialdom he was taken for a student or apprentice. He felt under no personal threat as his confidence in the loyalty of his workmates was underpinned by a presumption that his uncle's business clout would protect him from unwelcome attention from the authorities. But he recognised there was no room for complacency and, as the months passed, his position became increasingly precarious. By the beginning of 1941, he faced the imminent prospect of internment as he had reached the age of military service and was liable to be taken into custody under the terms of the armistice agreement. A scheme was devised to register him (not entirely untruthfully) as a sufferer of acute psoriasis that rendered him unfit for military service and, consequently, no longer subject to internment. On 15 January 1941, a medical certificate supporting the diagnosis was signed by a local doctor and authorised by the Mayor of Poligny.[18] But the document failed to do the trick and two months later Tony was warned that German armistice officials had requested his papers for scrutiny. Incarceration now seemed a certainty unless he fled. Capitaine Faure, as ever, offered stalwart support and provided Tony with a set of false identity papers in the name of 'François Bertrand'. This new persona (the first of many he would possess over the succeeding years) bore an age a couple of years younger than his own in order for him to appear a schoolboy rather than a young adult. Faure warned him, however, that he should exercise caution in the use of the documents for, although they might satisfy German checks, they would be unlikely to pass scrutiny by French officials.

In March Tony visited Caskie in Marseille to discuss his increasingly pressing need to escape from France. Exfiltration by sea was rejected and the priest suggested that as an interim step Tony join him at the Seamen's Mission while a place was found on one of the overland escape parties to Spain. They agreed that this was the best option and Tony returned to Proby to await a summons from Caskie to go back to Marseille. On 4 April Tony celebrated his nineteenth birthday at Grozon in the certain and disconcerting knowledge he was living on borrowed time. So, when the note from Caskie duly arrived, he hastily obtained the necessary travel permits, gathered together his few possessions and headed for Marseille and the Seamen's Mission.

Chapter Three
A Walk in the Mountains

Tony left Proby on 27 May 1941 and made his way to Lyon where, at the Thomas Cook office in the place Bellecour, he bought a third-class train ticket to Marseille's Gare St Charles.[1] He arrived at the Mediterranean port shortly after five o'clock that evening and, such was the level of bureaucracy extending over Vichy France, was required to have his identity card stamped by the authorities and a ten-day permit issued enabling residence in the city. His next stop was the rue de Forbin and the Seamen's Mission. Caskie was unable to offer much more than an assurance that he would do what he could to get Tony out of the country – eventually. In the meantime, he could provide accommodation in the Mission and, welcoming the arrival of an additional member of staff, invited the fluent French speaker to assist in the day-to-day running of the establishment. It was a reasonable request and, as Tony knew the city fairly well from recent visits delivering fugitives, he undertook a variety of tasks; running errands, buying food on the black market and acting as an escort for British servicemen who needed to be moved around the city. Tony did not enjoy any special privileges among the Mission inmates and his relationship with Caskie was not particularly close. The cleric was a kind man who exuded a discernible air of divinity but, years later, Tony would recall that he was a little too 'precious' for any real friendship to develop. Caskie's alter ego, Ian Garrow, was not much in evidence at this time for he was lying low having come under unwelcome scrutiny by the Vichy authorities. Consequently, Tony had little contact with him save for a few meetings in Caskie's office or an occasional rendezvous on a street corner to receive instructions or money. It was clear to Tony, even from these few brief meetings, that Garrow was very well connected and obtaining funds from London via the United States Consul in Nice.

In contrast to the shadowy, unapproachable figure of Garrow, Tony found a far more congenial colleague in a French member of Caskie's network; Louis Nouveau. A wealthy businessman, Nouveau lived with his wife, Renée, in an apartment on the quai de Rive-Neuve. An inveterate anglophile, in December 1940 he had been introduced to Garrow and other British officers as they attempted to establish the escape lines. Nouveau was soon using his own money to fund them and arranging loans from other benefactors in the city and along the Côte d'Azur. He did not restrict his generosity to members of the British armed forces and Tony was a frequent recipient of his hospitality. Whenever Tony called on him, the Frenchman was a paragon of kindness and generosity; making no distinction between the young civilian and the British servicemen he was risking everything to help.[2]

By the time Tony arrived in Marseille, the clandestine organisation in the Unoccupied Zone had undergone major changes from its early days. London was taking a greater interest in the escape lines and was increasing its efforts to control them. In Unoccupied France, funds were secured from wealthy individuals and businesses against a promise from MI9 that equivalent sums would be deposited in British bank accounts. But the development of the networks achieved the commensurate effect of attracting hostile attention from the Vichy (and German) authorities, 'Caskie's ramshackle mission became dangerously exposed. The incessant searches, interrogations, and harassment by Vichy police agents soon flared up into a diplomatic imbroglio involving Great Britain, France, and the United States.'[3] The 'imbroglio' in large part centred round the local United States representative, Hugh S. Fullerton, the Consul General in Marseille. The escape lines had come to rely heavily upon the goodwill of the American diplomatic service but in Fullerton, Caskie possessed an equivocal ally. By the summer of 1941, Fullerton, rather than offering assistance, appears to have sought to curb Caskie's activities and chastised him for obtaining money from British residents in France. The American diplomat called on the Vichy authorities in Marseille to safeguard his own reputation and was informed that they knew full well what was happening at the Mission and that 'There were a great many German agents in this part of France and the German government was very accurately informed as to what was going on.'[4] The strain was beginning to tell on Caskie. In May he had been brought before a French Military Tribunal and received a suspended two-year prison sentence. Moreover, his relationship with Garrow had deteriorated, Caskie complaining to Fullerton that he was being 'victimised' by his fellow Scot. Perhaps part of the reason for this dissension was the appearance of a new character on the scene, Harold Cole. On the face of it, Cole was a much-needed reinforcement to the network. A sergeant in the Royal Engineers, he said he had been cut off from his unit in the retreat to Dunkirk and had then lain low with local Frenchmen and women who had befriended him. Bit by bit, he became involved in helping his fellow countrymen escape south to the relative safety of the Unoccupied Zone. His achievements did not go unnoticed and Garrow made him a trusted confederate in the north, where Cole organised safe houses, secured false identity documents and carried out audacious escort duties across the demarcation line. As a close associate of Garrow, Cole seems to have stayed away from the Seamen's Mission and Tony did not recall encountering him. This was just as well, for Cole was to acquire a reputation as, arguably, the worst British traitor of the Second World War.[5]

At first, Cole's faults seemed only to be a tendency to carry to excess the attributes he deployed so well in working for the organisation: cockiness, a marked propensity for chasing women, a tendency to over-indulge in the black-market 'necessities' of clandestine life, a penchant for over-embellishing a story. Eventually, these traits became too marked and too frequent to go unnoticed by his colleagues. Allegations of peculation were levelled (and proven) against him. In October 1941 a drumhead court-martial was convened in Marseille by leading members of the escape network, but they vacillated between the options of killing him or sending him back to the United Kingdom where others might more properly judge him. True to type, Cole seized the moment and fled back to the north. He soon fell into the hands of the Germans (a cuckolded husband rather than a security investigation proving to be his undoing), at which point he promptly betrayed the escape network and his former comrades-in-arms. [6] His proximity to Tony at this time adds yet one more close shave to the many that populated a long and dangerous secret career.

Against this background of tension and incipient treachery, Caskie saw Tony's appearance in Marseille not as a liability but a very useful asset. His value was made evident when, in an act of great confidence or perhaps a rather laissez-faire attitude to his responsibilities, on 2 June Caskie left the Mission for a fortnight's break, entrusting responsibility to the newcomer. It was an early example of what would become a frequent occurrence, the willingness of Tony's elders to invest their trust in him. At the same time, it highlighted Tony's confidence in his own abilities that was far in advance of his nineteen years.

Thus, within a few days of arriving in Marseille, Tony assumed the running of the mission in Caskie's absence. He supervised the forty-five inmates, drew up a work roster each day and managed the purchasing of food (much of it on the black market) at a daily rate of 1,000 francs. Meanwhile, he oversaw the secret exodus of parties (each of half a dozen fugitives) to Spain twice a week. In spite of these administrative burdens, Tony found the time to take a particular interest in the fate of four RAF aircrew who had been rescued by the French authorities after days at sea following the crash of their aeroplane. The men were being held in a military hospital under armed guard but Tony managed to visit most days and keep them supplied with food and cigarettes. He discussed their plight with Nouveau and agreed that there might be an opportunity to spirit the airmen out of Marseille before their transfer to the internment camp at Saint-Hippolyte-du-Fort. Tony undertook to check the hospital's security arrangements while the Frenchman agreed to enlist Garrow's help with the scheme. During the following days, Tony encountered difficulties in arranging a rendezvous with the Scots officer and, when the latter finally made an appearance, the meeting did not go well, Tony later admitting that the vexed teenager 'was rather curt with him'. True to form, Garrow failed to make the next appointment with Tony and, consequently, the plan to rescue the airmen collapsed.[7]

But Tony soon had other, more personal, worries. While running the mission in Caskie's absence, his Marseille residence permit expired. He took a sanguine attitude to his plight, however: 'It was obviously hopeless to try to renew it. The only thing to do was to hope for the best and stay on.'[8] For once, Garrow contributed some helpful advice and agreed that while Tony should remain in Marseille for the present, he ought to make ready to leave with one of the next groups for Spain. The need to get Tony away became even more pressing when the French police called at the Mission looking for him. Fortuitously, he was absent at the time but the hostile interest in him was manifest and no less than five subsequent visits were made by the Vichy authorities to the rue de Forbin over the next few days.

The increased threat of arrest by the French police and Caskie's return from his 'holiday' resulted in Tony being assigned the leadership of the next group of fugitives to be sent to Spain. He suspected that the suddenness of his departure was, in part, engineered by Garrow following their recent dispute, 'I was not warned the previous night that I was going. So I never even had the chance to prepare my things. This was arranged by Garrow so that I should not have an excuse for meeting him again.'[9] The six-man party left the Mission at five o'clock in the morning of 14 June 1941. Tony led the group to the Gare Saint-Charles where he met a contact who passed him their return rail tickets to Perpignan and introduced the guide who would escort them to a safe house at their destination.* The tickets were distributed to each man individually and Tony instructed them to travel separately in the train. It proved a forlorn hope, 'They were keeping contact with each other and yet not keeping together.'

Unusually the party did not contain any British servicemen and Tony's companions were a very mixed bunch, including two quarrelsome Maltese brothers named Castagna who argued incessantly, Kenneth Doggett, a rotund merchant-seaman cook who had undertaken catering duties at the Mission, and an Australian, Leslie Price.[10] During their time together in Marseille, Tony became friendly with Price who related that he had stayed on in Belgium following First World War army service. He spoke a near impenetrable French/Flemish and Australian/English that was so full of profanities that he was difficult to understand in any of these languages. Tony later recalled, 'Apart from the F-word there was no really regular feature that appeared in his English lingo.' Nevertheless, Price was a man of character and resolve who had walked the length of France to avoid internment. He

---

* The use of return tickets to camouflage the real purpose of a journey was a piece of tradecraft that was not lost on Tony and he employed it throughout his clandestine career.

was someone who Tony felt he could trust although he was evidently no Boy Scout. Although Price explained his purpose in leaving Belgium was to protect his girlfriend, when Tony got to know him better, he concluded that the decision to depart owed as much to domestic boredom as altruism.

The party changed trains at Narbonne and made its way to Perpignan without incident. The fugitives did not encounter any security checks at the station and duly reported at the Garage Maso for the rendezvous with their local guide. The proprietor assured Tony that the party would soon be collected and moved closer to the border, but his optimism was ill-founded, and the escort failed to appear. The group could not hang around the premises indefinitely so decamped to a restaurant, then moved on to a couple of cafés while Tony returned to the garage to get an update. The news was not good, 'I was calmly told that we should have to stay in the town until Monday; it was a Saturday. This was going to be a very risky thing to do as the town is [sic] absolutely filled with Gendarmes and Legionnaires, who are Pétain's Brown Shirts.* We managed to find beds in the Hôtel de la Loge. We spent both nights there. Sunday we spent at the cinema.'

The weekend sojourn was not followed by a marked improvement in the escape line's arrangements. The guide once again failed to put in an appearance and at six o'clock on the Monday morning, with the group becoming too conspicuous to allow a more protracted stay, they were ferried by truck to Argelès-sur-Mer, a few miles from the Spanish border. The vehicle halted in the foothills and the driver pointed out a hut where, he affirmed, their mountain guide awaited them. Tony paid him the money he had been given by Caskie and the lorry drove off. But the hut proved to be empty and they settled down (presumably now with fading optimism after their recent experiences) to await the arrival of their escort. As time passed and still with no sign of the *passeur*, they reluctantly concluded that they had been deceived. A debate about their next course of action followed, with Tony and Price advocating pressing on across the mountains while the others expressed doubts about handling the Pyrenees without expert help. Eventually, the faint-hearts were swayed and the group set off. In the absence of a map to guide them, Tony found that his alpine upbringing and Boy Scout training

---

* 'Brownshirts' was the nickname for the *Sturmabteilung*, a Nazi paramilitary organisation.

came in useful. He employed a system of navigation using his watch and the position of the sun to calculate the direction of their march and arranged the party in Indian file in order that they could maintain a consistent direction while traversing, at first undulating and, later, mountainous terrain. The 'few' miles to the border increased as they were obliged to zigzag up the slopes and take detours to follow the course of the valleys. The Maltese Castagna brothers soon dropped out and headed back to France, leaving Tony, Price and Doggett, to continue the trek.[11] The trio found little sustenance in the meagre rations that they carried – Tony began the expedition with only two tins of sardines and a small loaf in his knapsack. But Price proved a true stalwart, exhorting Tony and Doggett to press on regardless of their hunger, pounding alongside them in his outsize British Army boots that stood him in much better stead than his companions' ordinary shoes. They were not the only fugitives attempting a crossing and encountered a party of Poles whose guide offered to escort them into Spain but Tony and his comrades declined to pay him the 600 francs a head demanded. On the evening of the third night in the mountains they found a large, lichen-covered stone slab, and revelled in the warmth that it retained from the summer sunshine. This idyll lasted long enough for them to fall asleep before the coldness of the mountain night descended. Upon waking the next morning, they were dismayed to find that the slab marked the edge of a cliff, and uneasily concluded that any restless sleeper would have rolled to certain death on the rocks hundreds of feet below.

Even allowing for their haphazard navigation, the trio eventually determined that they must be nearing the Spanish frontier, which was reinforced when Tony spotted a marker on a distant peak that he assumed was a frontier sign. By now, their water bottles were empty and, observing a large stream running through the valley below them, they descended to slake their thirst. The cold mountain water was welcome after their long and exhausting haul but, as they drank, washed and filled their flasks, they suddenly heard the cry, *'Alerta! Alerta!'* Tony turned to observe a member of the Spanish *Guardia Civil* under a nearby bridge, trying to achieve simultaneously the acts of bringing his rifle to his shoulder, pulling up his trousers and pushing away the young woman who, until that moment, had been the object of his attentions. Desperately tired, and as yet unaccustomed to the sight of a man in uniform pointing a firearm at him, Tony did not flee but, along with his colleagues, gave himself up. With the benefit of hindsight and a lifetime's experience, he would later reproach himself for his timidity and reflect on an adage he picked up, 'Man with trousers around ankles does not run fast'. The *Guardia Civil* soldier, having recovered his breeches, if not his decorum, took their papers and led them to the local village of Espolla where they were questioned and admitted to being civilian refugees from France.[12] Price was all for saying that they were escaped prisoners-of-war, doubtless hoping that this might allow them a combatant's preferential status but the group's ages and physical appearance rendered the story highly improbable.

The three prisoners were searched and razors and knives taken from them. A sergeant at first 'impounded' Tony's French money, but, in spite of being profoundly disconcerted by the amount of Spanish cash, returned it, 'I afterwards learnt that it was about equivalent to his salary for six months.' The temporary loss of part of their funds was bad enough but the seizure of personal papers was more worrying, 'All our letters and diaries and address books went into their pockets. The sergeant took our identity papers too. I put my hand forward to reach for my passport, but he pushed it away from me and handed me my other papers only. About ten minutes later while he was trying to read through my letters he turned away from me. I seized the chance and the passport. They never saw it again until I entered the concentration camp of Miranda de Ebro.'[13] The party was then locked in a cellar that proved to be already occupied by a Spaniard and a colony of rats. Early the next morning, Tony and his companions were allowed a brief wash at the village pump and then installed in 'a very ramshackle old bus' for the journey to Figueras. 'It was already loaded to the roof with fat women and hen coops … one person got off and the rest of us were pushed in. One male passenger and one of our escort sat on the luggage rack.' At Figueras they were searched and interrogated once more at the local prison, a modern but unfinished building. Nevertheless, it was alive with bugs and the only amenity their cell boasted was a hole in the corner of the floor. The British party was now supplemented by two Spanish prisoners and, offering an intimation of the precariousness of their position, a Frenchman who was about to be sent back across the frontier. Tony and his companions demanded to see the British Consul but this merely elicited disdainful laughter from their guards.

The next day Tony and his companions were arraigned for having crossed the border illegally – and without the opportunity to say a word were found guilty. Then they were interrogated by a Spanish officer and an interpreter. Tony only admitted to speaking English, fearing that if his excellent French was revealed, it might offer the Spanish authorities a convenient option to send him back to Vichy France. He was subjected to yet another search that revealed his 10,000 pesetas. This provoked a bout of even more aggressive questioning, including accusations that he intended to bribe Spanish officials. A receipt for the impounded cash was made out in Spanish and English for his signature but, even at this early stage, Tony carefully assessed the situation. He signed his name only over the English text, trusting that this action would leave no opportunity for subsequent falsification of a 'confession' written in Spanish. For the first time since their arrest, he was separated from his companions and placed in solitary confinement. He recalled, 'It was a good education. I'm very glad of it. To hear that cell door shut and the bolts go across – the first time you hear it, it's very frightening – especially when you don't understand much of the language. But once you've heard it several times and known that it can be opened again, you take a more philosophical view.' By now, even Tony's natural resilience and self-confidence had reached low ebb. His fate seemed very uncertain as he was warned that as a civilian 'illegal frontier crosser' he could not expect the protection of the Geneva Convention.

After two nights in Barcelona, the captives were taken by lorry to the railway station and put on a train to Reus (near Tarragona) where they were locked up in a war-damaged monastery that served as temporary prison. Thus far, the ravages of the Spanish Civil War had not been too evident but here the scars of a conflict that had ended two years earlier were all too visible. Before leaving Tony, Price and Doggett in their cell, the guard indulged in a little theatre by demonstrating the significance of the white chalk mark drawn on the floor in front of the remains of the cell window that contained neither bars nor glass. He instructed them not to cross the demarcation line and showed them the deadly consequences of breaking the rule by throwing a piece of newspaper towards the aperture. From somewhere outside the building a shot rang out and a bullet whipped through the paper. It seemed too well rehearsed to have been anything other than a dangerous party trick, but it had the desired effect and the open window remained inviolate. During the night they heard more shooting and the next morning an inmate informed them that several communist prisoners had been executed.

The following day, they were on the move again with Tony handcuffed to Price for the train journey to Zaragoza. On arrival, the British prisoners were separated, and Tony found himself sharing a cell with a Spanish prisoner, 'a funny little man about 45 years old', who was a left-wing politician awaiting the result of an appeal against his death sentence. The two men communicated in a mixture of Spanish/French that included morsels of the Toulousain patois that Tony had picked up in Montauban. The other inmate offered snippets of jailhouse philosophy on the vicissitudes of Spanish political life and a few prison survival tips that included how to train fleas to combat body lice. That evening, the Spaniard unexpectedly asked Tony to pray with him to entreat his Maker that the death sentence be commuted. It was an unlikely communion of faith with the Catholic, socialist, Spanish politician and the Quaker British teenager conjoined in a heartfelt appeal to whomever or whatever was controlling their destinies. The next morning the guards came for Tony's cellmate and a few hours later he was back, elated with the news that his sentence had been commuted to twenty-five years' imprisonment. Stoically and optimistically, he presented a master plan of life's ups and downs and propounded an engaging faith in a future cycle of freedom, power, prison, freedom, power, prison ...

The next morning Tony, Price and Doggett were on their way again and now, for the first time since their arrival in Spain, there seemed to be a real opportunity for escape. Their train was only moving at about fifteen miles an hour and the guard at the far end of the compartment was far from vigilant, dozing off at increasingly regular intervals. The carriage was crowded with prisoners (including several Poles) all of whom were handcuffed together in pairs. A length of chain had been passed over one prisoner's left wrist and the two strands then inserted through a ring. The chain was next looped over the right wrist of the second prisoner and fixed with a padlock. Tony was handcuffed in this manner to Price and realised that 'By bending my hand and pulling the chain onto the flesh of Leslie's wrist, I was able to free my hand.' They were soon unshackled and, as they were only two seats from the end of the carriage, their chances of making it to the door seemed very good indeed. Moreover, theirs was the last passenger carriage of the train with a few goods trucks making up the rear. They therefore assumed that none of the other guards would be in a position to raise the alarm if the soldier in their carriage failed to notice their escape. Their knapsacks were by now an essential part of their existence so Tony slowly and unobtrusively reached up for the bags from the rack above their heads. But their luck was out. The guard proved more alert than anticipated and realised that something was very amiss when he saw a prisoner using both hands to reach for the luggage. He immediately raised the alarm and Tony and Price were soon tightly manacled once again and, for extra security, their chain was passed through the seat armrest. To compound their woes, their popularity with their fellow prisoners plummeted as the escape attempt resulted in everyone having their handcuffs painfully tightened.

In the early afternoon, the train drew into a railway siding. The prisoners disembarked 'and were handed over to the army at the station. We saw the last of the civil guards that we were beginning to hate. But we soon realised how pleasant they were in comparison to our new masters.' They were marched off (with the occasional encouragement of a rifle butt) towards a camp that displayed the sign 'Viva Franco. Arriba España. Campo de concentración de Miranda d'Ebro' above its gates. It had been opened during the civil war to accommodate seven hundred prisoners-of-war but by the time Tony arrived the number of inmates had vastly increased. Barbed-wire fences surrounded the rows of huts, each of which now accommodated almost one hundred men. Tony estimated there were several thousand prisoners, 'of whom probably about half were Spaniards. A lot were Poles. They were not necessarily Poles who had escaped from France but had been members of the International Brigades during the civil war. A lot of chaps were saying that they were French-Canadians to try and get onto the British escape system. They knew that the French who said this were often given assistance by the British Consul.' Gordon Instone, a British soldier who passed through Miranda a few months before Tony, described its cosmopolitan nature:

At the time of my arrival in the camp, there were about fifty Polish officers and two hundred and fifty Polish N.C.O.s and men; sixty Belgians; thirty-five Frenchmen, five of whom were officers; six Yugoslavs; twenty German deserters and about fifty British soldiers and airmen, some of whom I recognised as having been in Fort St. Jean. In addition, there were Dutchmen, Algerians, Armenians, Hungarians, Rumanians, Czechs and Greeks – it is doubtful indeed if there was a country in Europe that was not represented. Five hundred Spaniards brought the total number up to about a thousand.[14]

Once inside the barbed-wire perimeter, Tony and his intake were paraded before a gold-braided commandant. Then they were processed by the prison authorities; their fingerprints were taken, they were given a cursory medical examination, their heads were shaved and their bodies painted with an unknown substance that, they hoped, was some form of antiseptic. They were inoculated: 'This was a unique experience. They jabbed a needle that was rusty into one's back side and injected an un-measured quantity of liquid. They then passed on to the next man without as so much as wiping the needle.'[15] Uniforms were not issued and they were expected to wear the clothes in which they had arrived. Footwear was not supplied either, and Tony spent most of his time in bare feet in order to lengthen the life of his already dilapidated shoes. The prisoners were next given a roll call before being dismissed to their billets in the wooden huts. On entering Barrack 23, Tony observed that the sleeping area comprised wooden shelves fixed around the interior walls. He was simply instructed to take one of the available spaces. Near the door of the hut was a cubicle, sectioned off from the rest of the barrack by draped blankets. This was the private domain of the Kapo or leader of the hut, an Austrian who had fought in the civil war as a member of the International Brigades. Although the Kapo was unpopular with most of his fellow inmates, Tony took a different view, considering him a fair man who did what he could to protect the prisoners from the Spanish guards' spot searches:

He was a first-class chap – absolutely wonderful. A lot of the English prisoners there hated him. In actual fact, he was a damn good chap because if the chaps had got a candle or were smoking when lying down after curfew, he would come along and bang the uprights of the bunks with his gnout. Shouting 'Silence!' and he would swear at us. Some chaps went, 'Oh, fuck off.' And then he'd hit them on the soles of their feet, pretty hard. Because he had spotted or heard that a patrol was coming around. If a chap was caught smoking, he'd be taken outside and given a hell of a thrashing. So, in actual fact, if you listened to him and took notice of what he said you'd have never got into trouble at all.

The segregation of inmates in the camp was primarily determined by nationality and Tony was reassured to find himself mostly surrounded by his fellow countrymen. Each day, the prisoners attended a roll call and were ordered to salute the Spanish flag with cries of '*Viva Franco! Una grande Libre! Viva España! Arriba, Arriba!*' They were then divided into groups and marched out of the camp to the nearby flood plain of the River Ebro. 'We went down to the riverbed and picked up these stones about the size of a melon and put them into baskets with one handle that you carried on your back,' Tony recalled. 'Then you climbed up the riverbank and tipped them beside the road.' Any slacking by the labourers resulted in a whiplash from the guards while the only break was a midday halt when they were fed a ladleful of watery soup and half a *bocadillo* (black bread roll). 'The soup was often made out of the outside husks of broad beans. And if you know anything about broad beans you'll know they're always covered with blackfly. So the blackfly would be floating on the top of the soup. But with skill and using a piece of paper you could skim the top and get them out.' Occasionally, the food might be augmented by a little extra nutritional ingredient and once Tony found in his mess tin some gruel fortified by parts of a hoof and horseshoe. The unexplained disappearance of the camp mule was now no longer a mystery. Its carcass had been put to good use. 'I must say the soup tasted better but I found I suddenly wasn't hungry.' The only day occasion when the menu was markedly different was a national holiday, and lunch included white rice with green olives in it – 'We couldn't believe our ruddy eyes.'

Work ended at five o'clock in the afternoon and they returned to the camp where another roll call was taken, followed by compulsory 'community shouting' of Fascist slogans and renditions of *Viva España*. (In time-honoured way, the British soldiers in the camp had devised an obscene version.) The evening 'meal' consisted of acorn coffee and half a *bocadillo*. This meagre fare ostensibly could be supplemented by food purchased from a canteen that opened for business in the middle of the afternoon. Tony remembered, 'You never knew when the canteen was going to open but there was always a Pole there. As soon as the shutters opened up there were two hundred Poles in the queue in front of you.' As he settled into what passed for a routine, Tony began to learn the ways of the camp. Of the various nationalities present, the Poles impressed him with their sense of unity even if this manifested itself in their securing all the sandwiches in the camp shop before others could even get near them.

The British servicemen were kept in two huts, separate from their civilian countrymen, and their military status meant that they did not carry out any menial work. Once a fortnight, a member of the British Military Attaché's staff at the Madrid Embassy visited the camp with extra provisions for the servicemen, who generously shared these treats with the civilian inmates and some of the 'French Canadians'. The Senior British Medical Officer at this time was Captain Geoffrey Darke of the Royal Army Medical Corps who, accompanied by an RAF Flight Lieutenant, questioned Tony following his arrival in order to establish the newcomer's credentials. As Tony recalled,

> He said 'Where were you born?' and I said, 'Orsett (and spelt it for him) in Essex.' 'Oh yes,' he replied. 'And what do you know about Orsett?' I said, 'It's got a big hospital and a loony bin.' The interrogation continued with 'Oh yes, and what do you know about this loony bin?' And I said, 'Well, my grandmother is Chairman of the Governors,' To which he responded, 'Oh yes, and what is she like?' I went on to describe her and mentioned the enormous straw hat she usually wore and the immense hatpin with an artificial pearl that she used to plunge into her hair. Darke then said, 'I used to worry about that too because I was always terrified that she was going to spike herself in the head.' Then he revealed that he was Chief Registrar at that hospital and knew Gran very well indeed. So my identity was established *tout de suite*.[16]

Although the Nazi concentration camps in Germany set levels of bestiality and violence that put the treatment exacted in other prisons into the shade, Miranda was no holiday camp. Instone recorded,

> The Spanish political prisoners had as bad a time as the rest of us. A sixty-five-year-old man was kicked from one end of our hut to the other by the

guards because he had been caught selling his boots; he was screaming for mercy and bleeding profusely and although we did our best to draw off the guards, he was unconscious when we succeeded. Another Spaniard was caught one day passing a packet of cigarettes to a friend of his who was in a solitary confinement cell; the sentry on the outer enclosure who saw him, fired and as the man threw himself flat on his face, the bullet flew past his head, embedding itself in the wall and missing him by inches.[17]

Tony's experiences mirrored those of Instone. An inmate in his hut acquired a loaf of bread but refused to share it. Concerned that it would be stolen during the night while he slept, he kept it under his head, using it as a pillow. When he awoke in the morning, his head was resting on the stump of bread that was all that remained after his comrades had silently sawn away the ends. Thefts of personal goods also occurred amongst the prisoners. As Instone wrote, 'It was never safe to take your eyes off any possession, however humble, for it would be whisked away while your head was turned and sold to someone at the other end of the camp while you were still looking around for it.' One night, while asleep on his bunk, Tony awoke to feel something touching his wrist. He instinctively lashed out, believing it to be one of the camp's more adventurous rats but quickly realised that it was one of his hutmates attempting to steal his watch – the one given to him by his mother on her deathbed. The figure slipped away into the darkness but a man in the bunk opposite him pointed to another berth where the occupant was pretending to sleep. Tony knew the identity of the would-be thief – it was one of his fellow countrymen.

Unsurprisingly, the Spartan conditions in Spain and the absence of proper medication resulted in the return of Tony's psoriasis:

> During the trip I had got rather sunburnt. This and my skin trouble looked rather awful when I reached the camp. On the second day the camp doctor plaster[ed] my face, head and neck with a very strong ointment. After about four hours I could no longer move my head and my neck was very badly swollen. My eyes were hurting as well.'[18]

The 'salve' with which Tony had been 'treated' seemed corrosive rather than a balm for inflamed skin. Within an hour he was in serious pain, 'God, I was in agony. I was going round the twist. I was going to go over the wire, anything to stop the pain.' Even the Kapo realised he was in a bad way and attended him but, in spite of the torment, Tony still had to go to work. For the next twenty-four hours, although physically exhausted, he could not sleep because of the pain and discomfort from his inflamed skin. He bought a bottle of Malaga wine at the canteen and, although a virtual teetotaller, drank it, 'I slept well that night but felt like death the next morning.' In desperation, he sought out Darke who immediately took the matter in hand, issuing instructions that the British servicemen should donate any Brylcreem hair cream or shaving soap from their personal kit. The substances were then applied as a protective barrier to Tony's tormented skin once Darke had freed his scalp from the 'medication' administered by the Spanish doctor: 'I used to be well known among the other prisoners as I went about with a face covered in white zinc ointment.'[19]

The Spanish authorities offered no intimation when Tony could expect to be released. The only fragments of news from the outside world came from Darke who, Tony presumed, had passed on information about him during the visits of the Embassy staff. But Tony assumed that there was every chance of his having to wait out the war incarcerated in Spain. He had been in Miranda for six weeks but 'It seemed an eternity. It just shows how unpleasant moments in your life seem to have lasted much longer. Periods of hardship are lengthened in your mind.'* So much had happened since he left the comfort and security of his uncle's château. It was a lot for a young man to assimilate and, even if his war was to end at Miranda, he had made every effort to do his bit in serving his country's interests. But Tony's war was not to end in Spain.

A visit to the camp by a British Embassy official resulted in momentous news, 'On August the 9th I was awakened during the afternoon and told that my release had come through.' The weeks that he had spent in Miranda had made him grow up very quickly and his education in the art of survival had developed apace. From the outset, he had been self-sufficient, content to be either on his own or, as occasion allowed, in company. He enjoyed a level

---

* In later life Tony stated that he had been interned for six months. When the author's research suggested that the length of his stay should be amended to six weeks, Tony took the revision gracefully but commented, 'Well it fucking well seemed like six months.'

of adaptability that was perhaps derived from his hybrid English, Swiss and French influences, but there was no question that Miranda had taught him a great deal. He had seen humanity and bestiality at their most extreme. He had known physical pain and fatigue that had brought him to the edge of total exhaustion. Mindless brutality and unexpected kindness had featured in his experience of imprisonment but, unlike his Figueras cellmate, he was not dependent on the merry-go-round of politics to free him. Instead, he had simply to wait for the British diplomatic service to pluck him from the ghastliness of the concentration camp and take him home – wherever, in Tony's case, that might be. As agreed, the diplomat returned to Miranda with a shooting brake and together with Price, Doggett, 'a Belgian major and sergeant and a Free French sergeant-pilot', Tony was driven to Madrid and taken to the British Embassy in the Calle Fernando el Santo.[20] Here, they were given a bath and clean overalls, but were denied the slap-up meal about which they had been fantasising during their incarceration. Instead, they were offered a glass of cold tea and a small white loaf in order that empty stomachs and damaged digestions might slowly be weaned off their near-starvation diets. They were then taken to the Hotel Mora, a large, modern establishment where they savoured the sublime pleasures of their own room, a soft bed and the chance to sleep once more between clean sheets. Tired and somewhat overawed by being at liberty, Tony was disinclined to explore Madrid and stayed the next two days at the hotel, awaiting instructions from the Embassy regarding the next stage of his repatriation.

It was not a long wait. On the morning of 12 August they left Madrid by an Embassy bus and, after an overnight stay at Córdoba, reached the Spanish town of La Linea on the border with Gibraltar the following evening. The Crown colony was a pivotal feature of Britain's war effort. Gibraltar had been the strategic portal to the Mediterranean for centuries and remained a potent symbol of British naval power in the region in the opening years of the Second World War. It came to assume an even greater importance following the military reverses Britain had endured since 1940 and by the summer of 1941, its indomitable, rocky mass at the entrance to the Mediterranean made it a vital staging post for British convoys to the Middle East and Malta. Uncertainty over the depth of General Franco's allegiance to his fellow fascist states, Germany and Italy, accentuated concerns of its vulnerability to attack

The Hotel Mora in Madrid where Tony briefly stayed following his release from the Miranda de Ebro concentration camp.

from land and sea. However, in August 1941, Gibraltar was still an integral feature of British strategic interests in the Atlantic and Mediterranean and – for a nineteen-year-old – it was an encouraging embodiment of his country's continuing strength and defiance.

Tony's party was instructed during the journey south that, as soon as the vehicle stopped at the frontier, they were to make a dash across two hundred yards of no-man's-land and head for the entrance to a pillbox on the British side of the border. Although the plan seemed highly perilous, the group was reassured by a strong hint that the Spanish guards had been bribed to look the other way. It all went like clockwork. Tony and his companions took off like Olympic sprinters and arrived at a chicane of sandbags on the home side of the border where their progress was arrested by the solidly reassuring form of a Gibraltar policeman whose British 'bobby' appearance signified that they were truly safe at last. They were led straight away to a reception centre where they were stripped, shaved (in every conceivable place) and deloused. Given clean denims, they were loaded onto an army truck and taken to the Spanish Pavilion where they were billeted on the Garrison Employment Company and later attached to No. 7 Platoon, 'A' Company of the 4th Battalion of the Devonshire Regiment in the Grand Casemates. Tony 'mucked in' straight away and helped out in the unit's cookhouse both to avoid boredom and in the hope of acquiring some extra rations.[21]

Gibraltar was a point of arrival for hundreds of refugees fleeing Nazi occupation and, by the summer of 1941, the authorities had put in place a sophisticated interrogation and filtering arrangement. British Intelligence needed information about conditions in occupied Europe while, at the same time, the security services faced the challenge of identifying enemy agents posing as refugees. Thus, shortly after he had settled in, Tony was interviewed by a Field Security Police sergeant during which his bona fides were established and he attempted to pass on information about airfields and aircraft factories in France. The sergeant's report formed the basis of British Intelligence's first, but by no means last, documented interest in Tony Brooks. His account of the meeting was sent to London on 1 September 1941 with a covering memorandum stating 'Attached note of interview (51960/C) with a British Subject who has offered his services, is forwarded in case his particulars are of interest.' In addition to a list of Tony's personal details, it recorded his willingness to return to France: 'Under the circumstances [Tony's concern that his psoriasis would prevent his acceptance for military service] Mr Brooks believes he will be able to perform more useful service for the Country if he is returned to France from England ... His particular idea is collection of any information regarding engineering works, and sabotage of such works if necessary.' In order to establish his credentials and confirm his contacts in France, Tony had provided a list of 'old personal friends' of whom he was 'prepared to guarantee their genuineness and pro-British activities'. The candidates included his Uncle Norman's business associate, Mademoiselle Bigay, and Monsieur Mégard, his former tutor at Lons-le-Saunier. The interviewer concluded his report with the endorsement, 'I believe Brooks to be as he represents, and that he is safe from a security point of view.'[22]

The Secret Intelligence Service (SIS) replied a fortnight after the notification of Tony's arrival in Gibraltar and his offer to return to France. The favourable impression Tony had made at the local interview was evidently not shared by SIS Headquarters in London who were less than enthusiastic about the young volunteer. A wireless message sent to Gibraltar on 15 September 1941 starkly stated: 'Do not repeat not consider this man could return to France. Letter in bag.' The missive that subsequently arrived in the diplomatic bag did not mince its words with the author displaying all the confidence to be expected of a senior member of SIS's staff. The notes were written by Commander Kenneth Cohen, an officer of long standing who, after the French Armistice, had assumed responsibility for a great deal of SIS's cross-Channel operations. An extremely experienced intelligence practitioner, he did not hold back in expressing his scepticism at the prospect of any Englishman, let alone the nineteen-year-old Tony, being able to pass himself off as a Frenchman: 'I think it is not much good considering sending this man back again. Our experience here goes to show that unless the circumstances are very exceptional, the sending of Englishmen to France is suicidal. If they could really pass as Frenchmen, or were exceptionally debrouillard [resourceful], the case might be considered, but I do not think that in this case such conditions obtain.'[23]

While the Secret Service pondered, Tony tried to find his feet in Gibraltar. After his recent experiences, he was deeply reassured by immersion into the British enclave on the southern tip of Spain. Everyday British life was there in abundance including pubs, tearooms and branches of high street shops. In the barracks, there was a calm and stability that had been absent from Tony's life for so long.

After a stay of several weeks, it was finally time for the last stage of his journey home. The SS *Leinster*, an Irish Sea ferry, had originally arrived in Gibraltar as part of Operation 'Substance', whose objective was the delivery of reinforcements and supplies to Malta. The convoy sailed into the Mediterranean on 21 July 1941 but the *Leinster*, carrying service personnel, ran aground, and while the rest of the convoy continued on their way, the ferry limped back to Gibraltar. Having failed in its mission to transport men into the Mediterranean, it was now to be employed repatriating casualties from the Middle East and Malta. Space was found for Tony and some thirty other civilians on the ship and in the early hours of 1 October 1941 they set sail. The *Leinster* formed part of a small convoy of merchant vessels escorted by the cruiser HMS *Edinburgh* and a couple of Polish destroyers.[24] Once at sea, they were passed by a warship that, it was rumoured, was sailing north to cover an attempt by the German raiders, *Scharnhorst* and *Gneisenau*, to break out from their blockade in Brest.[25] Partly as a result of this threat, the convoy steered well out into the Atlantic before making its way northwards towards the British Isles. The weather became rough and the combination of the swaying hammocks and his proximity to the galley with its attendant, unrelenting smell of salted pork, gave Tony a bad attack of seasickness. But help was at hand in the form of another passenger, a merchant navy first mate, who had survived the disturbing experience of having no fewer than three ships torpedoed under him. During one of the rare periods when the passengers were allowed out on deck, the sailor helped Tony stow away in one of the lifeboats. He covered for Tony at roll calls and brought food to the hideaway, thereby allowing his young friend to spend the rest of the voyage blissfully free from queasiness. The *Leinster* set a course to the west of Ireland but there was a moment of concern when smoke was seen on the horizon and it was feared that it was the *Scharnhorst*. In the event, it proved to be the *Edinburgh* returning from a sweep to look for the German raider. This was by no means the last excitement and a submarine attack alert resulted in one of the accompanying destroyers unleashing a pattern of depth charges to no discernible effect. Eventually, the convoy arrived in Liverpool on 11 October 1941. Tony was among the last to disembark and reported to the dockyard Field Security office where he was given a railway warrant to Laindon in Essex – the nearest station to his grandparents' home – and sent on his way out of the port. He was at a loss as to how to continue his journey but was 'rescued' by some soldiers on an army lorry who spotted the plight of the waif, still dressed in ill-fitting fatigues, and they gave him a lift to Lime Street Station.

On arriving in London the following morning, Tony, not realising that his warrant was good for the Underground, walked the three miles from Euston to Fenchurch Street Station to catch the train to Laindon. Once at Goldsmiths, he feared that his unexpected arrival might prove a substantial shock for his aged grandparents and first went to the kitchen where he was greeted by Mrs Rouble the cook, and Maude the housemaid. After an affectionate welcome from the servants, his presence was announced and he reported to his grandparents in the drawing room. He received, as anticipated, a warm response from his grandmother but his grandfather's reaction came as something of a surprise. 'The police have been looking for you.'

Chapter Four

'We'll Be in Touch'

In the following days spent at Goldsmiths, Tony became acquainted with the innumerable layers of bureaucracy that had descended over wartime Britain. One of his first tasks was to report to the local police station where he duly explained his lengthy absence from the United Kingdom and was issued with a Ration Book and National Registration Card. Less mundane was the arrival, a few days later, of a letter from the 'War Office' requesting that he attend an interview on 18 October 1941. He had no idea what to expect but he took the train to London and duly presented himself at Room 055 of the Northumberland Hotel, now a requisitioned government office, off Trafalgar Square.

Tony was unaware that this was to be no ordinary War Office interview, for his host was a representative of the Security Service (MI5). An official history explains:

Room 055 served as a liaison section between parts of the Security Service and the War Office in certain respects. It was also used as a convenient point for contact with the public where individuals wrote to the authorities about subjects coming within the sphere of the Security Service, or for other interviews with members of the public, if and when appropriate, by officers of the Security Service who were thus able to act under cover of the War Office.[1]

The officer who interviewed Tony subsequently addressed a report of the meeting to Captain Guy Liddell, the Director of MI5's B Division, responsible for counter-espionage, and a copy was also sent to Cohen of SIS. The latter extended the document's circulation by adding a marginal note for yet another member of the shadowy Whitehall world, asking 'IVZ' to 'please speak as convenient'. The MI5 report was brief – barely a page and a half of typescript – and rehearsed details of Tony's personal history, family background and involvement with the escape lines in France. The interviewer had attempted to test Tony's command of French but soon gave up as it was perfectly clear that the interviewee's was greatly superior. The final paragraph of the report confirmed, 'Brooks appeared to me to be a pretty intelligent youth for his years. He speaks fluent French, knows many dialects and expressed willingness to be sent back to France to work for us over there.'[2]

Tony emerged from the MI5 interview with no understanding either of the meeting's purpose or the impression he had created. During the following weeks he festered at his grandparents' house, anxiously awaiting news from the nameless government officer with whom he had spoken. Increasingly, he felt that if they had no use for him, they should just inform him so that he might enlist in the RAF and serve his country. But the uncertainty was to be compounded by another British secret organisation showing an interest in him; the Special Operations Executive (SOE).

SOE had been formed in July 1940 by the amalgamation of a War Office Department, MI(R), and the Secret Intelligence Service's Section D. Both had been created in the late 1930s to examine the potential of clandestine warfare in a future conflict and, prior to the outbreak of war, they had made substantial advances in the theory of subversion, begun the recruitment and training of personnel and initiated the development of secret devices and equipment. However, the disasters of 1940 found neither MI(R) nor Section D adequately prepared for the unexpected demands of a war that saw Europe rapidly fall under German domination. Moreover, Whitehall rivalries resulted in complex machinations for control of Britain's subversive warfare efforts. The struggle concluded with the victory of Dr Hugh Dalton (the Minister of Economic Warfare), the disbandment of MI(R) and Section D, and the creation of SOE. Although many members of the founding organisations were considered surplus to requirements, a significant number of MI(R) and

Section D officers joined Dalton's team, bringing an important element of continuity to the new organisation as it sought to discern the extent of its duties. In spite of its rich inheritance, SOE had much to learn and took some time before it was in any position to send agents into Occupied Europe and meet its aims of fostering resistance to Nazi occupation. The new organisation was divided into country sections, controlled by a headquarters executive based in Baker Street in London. The primary section working into France was known as 'F' or 'Independent French'. Created in the summer of 1940 almost as SOE was formed, its head was Major Leslie Humphreys, late of Section D. In December he passed control to Henry Marriott who remained in place (to little effect) for almost a year until he handed over to Major Maurice Buckmaster in November 1941. Tony's appearance as a prospective recruit thus took place shortly before this important change of leadership.

On receipt of yet another vaguely worded official letter, Tony made another trip to London for an interview with the unnamed government organisation. The SOE representative charged with assessing Tony's suitability was Major Lewis Gielgud, F Section's recruiting officer. He was a sound choice for this important role, being intelligent, well-educated (Eton and Oxford), possessed of military experience on the Western Front during the First World War and in the inter-war years on the staff of the International Red Cross. Tony asked Gielgud about the nature of any future employment and was vaguely told it would be associated with commando operations. The meeting over, the candidate was given no indication how he had fared and was merely informed that the (still anonymous) organisation – the real name of SOE was rarely used even by its members – would get in touch in due course; this was a phrase Tony was to hear with frustrating regularity over the ensuing weeks.

SOE was not to be the last secret organisation to show an interest in the young man. On 30 October 1941, Tony lunched at the Lansdowne Club off Berkeley Square with no less a person than the mysterious 'IVZ' to whom Cohen of SIS had written regarding his case. 'IVZ' was Captain James Langley of MI9 or, more accurately, SIS's man within MI9. Jimmy Langley was a man of wide experience and the possessor of a distinguished war record; a regular officer in the Coldstream Guards, he had fought valiantly during the British Expeditionary Force's withdrawal to Dunkirk. He sustained severe wounds and, being considered too serious a casualty to be evacuated, became a prisoner-of-war. Soon, however, gangrene set in and his arm had to be amputated. Undismayed by his disability, Langley had barely begun his convalescence when he escaped from a hospital in Lille and made his way to Lyon (perhaps observing Tony innocently driving a truck past him) and eventually reached Marseille. Langley quickly found an active role in the shadowy, clandestine life of the city. He helped establish the British escape lines, working closely with Ian Garrow, until his repatriation on medical grounds in February 1941. On his return to the United Kingdom, MI9 showed interest in him, and so did another organisation, SIS. He was summoned to an interview with Colonel Claude Dansey, the Assistant Chief of SIS, and recruited: 'Theoretically you will be on loan from MI9, which is commanded by Colonel Crockatt. In practice you will be on my staff and under my orders in MI6.'³ Langley thereafter played a pivotal role in the overlapping affairs of SIS and MI9.

Langley's report on their meeting ensured that Tony would not rejoin the MI9 escape lines. His brief, seven-point memorandum stated that the candidate was 'an intelligent youth, but in my opinion quite unsuitable for a return to France'. Langley's subsequent comments superfluously recorded 'he is not yet twenty, and consequently has had no military experience at all.' The litany continued with observations that Tony had 'no "contacts" in the North' and a return to the Jura or Marseille 'would be to court disaster'. Significantly, Langley made reference to Tony's criticisms of his erstwhile colleague, Garrow: 'He had a poor opinion of Captain GARROW which was founded on gossip heard at Miranda El Ebro in Spain.' Evidently, the Coldstream Guards captain did not appreciate adverse comments on a friend and fellow officer uttered by the civilian teenager.⁴ Tony later suspected that his chances of returning to France for MI9 might also have been blighted by reports of his chastisement of evaders who ignored his instructions when he acted as their guide. His reprimands, he felt sure, had resulted in adverse comments being made in London, although there is no evidence to substantiate this conclusion. Tony had been candid with Langley regarding the other irons he had in the fire, 'He is in touch with the Air Ministry over the question of returning to France, and with Major Gielgud (S.O.E.).' Langley's assertion however is a little misleading. Tony had received an unsolicited letter on 16 October from the Air Ministry requesting an interview to obtain 'information which would be of value to Air Intelligence' and, of course, he knew nothing specific about SOE's intentions. He did visit the Air Ministry on the 20th and surviving correspondence alludes to possible 'future co-operation with Air Intelligence' but the question of Tony's returning to France under their auspices was dropped.[5] Significantly, Langley's final note in his report was to ask whether the addressee wished him to take any further action. The handwritten initials on the note, dated the same day, scrawled at the bottom of the page told it all. Kenneth Cohen effectively ended (for the moment) Tony's SIS and MI9 career with 'NA [No Action]. Thanks.'[6]

As the days passed in his Essex limbo, Tony grew ever more despondent and filled his spare time writing a report of his adventures since leaving Proby.[7] While he had received no formal rejection by the departments who had interviewed him, he concluded that this must have been the case. His frustration left him disinclined to continue trying to persuade the authorities to use him in France and he resurrected his plans to enlist in the RAF.

The secret world had not, however, washed their hands of him, and wheels were, at last, in motion; SOE initiated a security trace on 5 November 1941 and a fortnight later MI5 responded 'Nothing Recorded Against'. Things were finally moving and, on 18 November, an SOE internal note stated that Tony was scheduled to commence his training at the beginning of January 1942. Someone belatedly recognised the confusion over Tony's official status (although not his frustration and intention to join the armed forces) and commented:

> He has not registered, having been instructed not to register by the security people (presumably MI5). This is puzzling his family and he is anxious to cover himself by enlisting if possible in the RAF. Would it be possible to enlist him in the RAF and get him attached to us for three weeks from 28.12.41 if he turns out well to transfer and commission him.'[8]

Meanwhile, Tony's anxiety about his future had not lessened and, unaware of developments, he became increasingly depressed by the protracted delays. On 26 November 1941 he took matters into his own hands, travelled to London and volunteered for the RAF at the Euston Combined Recruiting Centre. After a rigorous medical an RAF doctor casually informed him that he had been allocated a low fitness grade. Aghast, Tony asked how they had arrived at the assessment. He was told that he was fit but slightly underweight and, before he could argue that it would not take long to put on a few pounds, the doctor explained that the real difficulty was Tony's flat feet as the condition would render him unfit for aircrew selection. The would-be recruit riposted that the very nature of air warfare suggested that 'foot slogging' was not a prerequisite but the doctor countered that basic training (the passport to all future RAF careers) included marching. Feeling that he had been shunned by the 'War Office' and was now being rejected by the RAF, Tony began to contemplate a visit to the nearest Royal Navy recruiting office. But the doctor was sufficiently sympathetic to ask him whether he felt capable of meeting the marching requirements. The enquiry was all Tony needed for it gave him the chance to explain that he had recently crossed the Pyrenees on foot and was therefore pretty confident about managing a bit of 'square bashing'. The doctor saw his point and promptly altered his grade to A1.[9]

The muddled process of Tony's candidacy for secret service finally took a major step forward when, at the beginning of December 1941, SOE (still without revealing its name) sent notification of their wish to recruit him.[10] He was instructed to report to 6 Orchard Court, an apartment in a modern block in Portman Square at the Oxford Street end of Baker Street, not far from SOE's headquarters. The Orchard Court flat was F Section's home from home where agents were interviewed and briefed away from the hurly burly of the main SOE offices without compromising their security.*

The major-domo was a Mr Park who, before the war, had been a messenger at the Paris branch of the Westminster Bank. He manoeuvred the apartment's visitors and staff with consummate deftness:

He knew every agent by his training pseudonym and made each one personally welcome when they arrived at the flat for briefing. His cheerful countenance was beloved by all the members of the French section and his tact was responsible for avoiding many awkward meetings between men who were not supposed to know each other's appearance. We wanted to discourage our men from meeting each other in the field and

---

* This security was pretty threadbare, it being the habit of some bus conductors to announce the stop in Baker Street as 'spy headquarters'.

the best way to do that was to see that they did not meet each other in England more than we could help. Park would spirit people from room to room in the nick of time. Of course people did meet each other and we were not silly about forbidding it – our agents were far too intelligent to need petty regulations of that kind; but there was one thing which was absolutely against orders, that was to tell anyone where one was going. There was a particular danger of this happening when two agents met in the flat and knew that they were due to be sent at the same time. Park tried his best to stop them knowing this. In general he succeeded admirably, his tact and popularity enabling him to move people from briefing room to briefing room (and into the bathroom) with the agility of the characters in a French farce.[11]

Like most of the men and women who served under him, the head of F Section was neither a regular soldier nor a professional intelligence officer. Maurice Buckmaster's extensive association with France included employment there as a tutor, a newspaper executive and assistant manager of Ford Motors. On the outbreak of war he volunteered for the British Army, was posted to the Intelligence Corps and served with the British Expeditionary Force before being evacuated at Dunkirk. Buckmaster's language skills resulted in his attachment to the ill-fated Free French expedition to Dakar in September 1940, followed by a period of service in the United Kingdom. A posting to the 50th Division in the Middle East was cancelled and, instead, he joined SOE in March 1941. Initially attached to the Belgian Section, Buckmaster was the beneficiary of a crisis within F Section that saw the resignation of his predecessor Henry Marriott, and the decision to overlook his second-in-command, Thomas Cadett, as a successor. Buckmaster possessed reasonable, if unremarkable credentials; 'He had useful and extensive contacts in France, and knew the country well. He was a colourful and in many ways a controversial figure; he was not universally popular, but no better head for the section was ever in sight.'[12]

Buckmaster's F Section inheritance in the winter of 1941 was, to say the least, meagre. The first agent to be infiltrated into France had only been parachuted on the night of 5/6 May 1941. This was Georges Bégué, who had the distinction of sending the earliest of the Section's wireless reports but also the misfortune of being arrested by the Vichy authorities in Marseille in October.* Other agents followed him into action, but the Section's work got off to a stuttering start, leading one appraisal to claim that in October 1941 'Most F agents arrested'. The same source states that by the end of the year, the Section boasted five networks with 'connected' activity but by March 1942, the figure was down to three.[13] The conditions in which the first agents had to operate were varied, frequently confused and, usually, highly dangerous. They were uncertain of the extent or even the very existence of local resistance groups and, moreover, they knew relatively little of the prevailing conditions in the Occupied and Unoccupied Zones. The German reaction to a captured British agent could be confidently anticipated, but what would be the response of the Vichy authorities? Nor was it just the agents who had to feel their way. F Section's official remit, imposed by the War Cabinet, was that overt, violent sabotage should not take place in Vichy France. Colloquially known as the 'No Bangs Rule', it specified that 'until instructions to the contrary are received His Majesty's Government view with disfavour any act of aggression by British subjects, or British troops, against persons or objects in unoccupied France.'[14] This diktat reflected the British government's ambivalent relations with Vichy and its concern that, by overtly treating Pétain's state as hostile, the French might be pushed even further into the Axis camp.

At this stage, Tony still remained pretty much in the dark about SOE and what it had in mind for him. In later life he had no recollection of the meeting with Buckmaster at Orchard Court, never mind the topics discussed. Buckmaster, on the other hand, wrote of his first impressions of Tony, 'When he joined our service in 1941, he was a leading aircraftman in the R.A.F. I felt some scruples about taking him on, at the age of eighteen, for his extremely youthful appearance smote my conscience.'[15] Tony's overriding impression, gleaned from his first briefings, was that the organisation was concerned with paramilitary work, such as mounting raids on the French coast, rather than engaging in clandestine operations in support of the Resistance. Although it was hinted that his future employment might entail the wearing of civilian clothes rather than uniform, there was no intimation at this time of his becoming

---

* He escaped in 1942, made his way back to the United Kingdom and became a pivotal member of the Section's signals team.

a secret agent. Reluctantly, he accepted that he might never join the armed forces. Then, after more than two years of his trying to achieve military status, F Section sent him to a tailor to be fitted for a uniform that bore the rank insignia of a second lieutenant on the Army General List. He was overjoyed.

In spite of some contemporary and post-war perceptions of SOE's amateurishness, the organisation's training regimen was outstandingly comprehensive and efficient. By the time Tony was put through the mill, the process had developed into a basic, three-phase programme. A 'Preliminary' or introductory course assessed the physical and mental aptitude of the candidate, with fitness training and some rudimentary instruction in weapons and explosives completing the syllabus. A successful student would emerge from this phase to the paramilitary stage, known as 'Group A', carried out in the West Highlands of Scotland. Here, candidates would develop their stamina and physical condition, be taught yet more about weapons, explosives and unarmed combat and learn fieldcraft and boat work. The third stage was known as the 'Finishing Schools' or 'Group B', where courses on secret agent 'tradecraft' were delivered in requisitioned houses on Lord Montagu's estate at Beaulieu in Hampshire. Parachute training would be inserted into a convenient point in the programme and, if all else was satisfactory, the students' long period of preparation might conclude with specialist training as a wireless operator or learning the skills of the saboteur.

The new year marked the commencement of Tony's training. After a couple of days of interviews with security personnel at Baker Street, on 2 January 1942 he became a member of Party 27L, a preliminary training course.[16] The small group of men caught the train from London to Guildford, where they were collected by a coach and driven to Wanborough Manor, Special Training School 5, F Section's induction centre, just off the Hog's Back, thirty miles south-west of London. A large, sixteenth century pile tucked in a discreet corner of a hamlet, well off the beaten track, the red-brick Manor, with its gables, leaded windows and ivy-covered walls, was the embodiment of the Hollywood stereotype of an English country house. But, far from being part of a world of make-believe, Wanborough was the first stop on a deadly journey for scores of secret agents.

The students were put into battledress and each given a training name to protect their anonymity. Tony became 'Alphonse Bright' while two of his fellow students introduced themselves as 'Theodore' and 'Roger'. Secrecy regarding personal details was closely observed and Tony concluded – from a few idle comments and his accent – that 'Theodore' was a smuggler from Marseille. In fact, he was Ted Coppin, a twenty-four-year-old private from the Royal Army Ordnance Corps. Born in Essex, he had been brought up in the South of France where his father ran a ship chandler's business, his accent and nautical bent doubtless leading to Tony's assumption about his background.[17] 'Roger' was Raymond Flower, a man who seemed extremely mature to the nineteen-year-old Tony but was a mere ten years older than him. Flower had been born in Paris and lived in France where he had worked in the hotel business. During the Phoney War he had acted as a civilian RAF interpreter until he was evacuated to England in 1940. He enlisted in the RAF and served with No. 905 Squadron until he joined SOE. He was warm and affable, and he and Tony became close friends and roommates for the rest of their training.[18] A third member of the course was 'Evans' who bore the nickname 'Josephine'. Tony later recalled that 'Evans' was rejected by Buckmaster after training because of his youthfulness but had gone on to join the elite, Lovat's Scouts, and participated on a raid in France.[19] Only a couple more of his fellow students made significant impressions on Tony. Tony remembered 'Maurice' as a Jewish tailor who deployed his professional skills to mend a tear in a fellow student's trousers. The man was Marcel Krumhorn, a British citizen who had spent most, if not all, of his thirty years in France, to the extent that he was 'handicapped by indifferent knowledge of English'. A 'costumist' in Paris in civilian life who had joined SOE from the Royal Artillery, Krumhorn's personal file reveals that he accompanied Tony throughout all the elements of his primary and sabotage training programmes.[20] In contrast, another student, 'Benjamin Stone', Brian Stonehouse, progressed to become a distinguished, if particularly unlucky, F Section agent. Born in Devon in 1918 he had spent his childhood in Boulogne and worked as an artist and illustrator in the years preceding the war. He was undergoing training for a commission into the Honourable Artillery Company when he was seconded to SOE and joined 27L.[21]

Party 27L's conducting officer was Lieutenant Edward 'Teddy' Bisset, a bilingual member of the Intelligence Corps's Field Security, and a man who Tony came to respect for his professionalism and friendship. In a letter to his fiancée, Winifred Marshall, on the first day of the course, Bisset predicted, 'My party seems to be quite good and I hope to get good results.' A conscientious officer who chose to sleep in the same dormitory as the students and join in their daily tasks, Bisset dreaded physical training but took a phlegmatic view, 'I am awfully stiff tonight, I am all rusty now and I expect that I shall suffer for about a week before I can enjoy P.T., a bit of patience will certainly improve matters.' He offered a discreet description of his 27L charges, 'I am quite happy with my new party, there [sic] are bright, you ought to hear the dirty stories going on, you would not like it too much, but still I am used to it now. I expect that I shall enjoy my time with them. We have a real cockney from Paris.' This image of harmony continued in Bisset's letters. On 14 January he wrote describing 'terrific snowball fights, the country looks lovely ... Cold and misty morning, snow all over the ground!' and 'I am still getting on very well with my party, and they are all enjoying their work. They keep smiling and cheerful which is the main thing.' The weather was 'awfully cold, a beastly wind is blowing hard' but the house was warm. In spite of the adverse conditions, Tony and his fellow students carried out a wide range of night marches, orienteering and exercises. They were given firearms training, and a nearby quarry offered them a safe location to receive tuition in handling explosives. Their performances and behaviour were monitored by Bisset and the Wanborough staff in order that, at the conclusion of the three-week course, a balanced and considered assessment was taken on whether a student should progress to the next stage of training.[22]

Tony enjoyed his time at Wanborough and participated enthusiastically in every facet of the programme. His youth and stamina allowed him to complete the route marches with some ease, while from the outset he discovered that he had a penchant for explosives. His concluding Wanborough report of 21 January 1942 reveals a near-exemplary student:

- Physical Training – Fit, active and strong: goes hard: confident at close combat and one of few who might conceivably profit from knowledge of it.
- Fieldcraft – Considers this rather a childish form of sport, and does not take it seriously enough. Could be quite good at it.
- Weapon Training – Best shot in the party: has a good idea of searching for targets making sensible use of cover.

- Explosives & Demolitions – Confident. Good sound knowledge.
- Signalling & Communications – 6/7 – with practice could reach necessary standard.
- Reports – Excellent. Intelligent and well presented.
- Map Reading etc. – Sound knowledge considering his lack of experience. Has learnt quickly.
- Riding or Driving – [No notes]

In the midst of this praise, Tony's instructors introduced a critical note, commenting that his youthful self-assurance bordered on over-confidence, but they seemed reluctant to concede that the student had more first-hand experience of clandestine work than his tutors. Nevertheless, their remarks were perceptive:

> Would do well at any subject he put his mind to. Very intelligent, and learns quickly. In fact he is a good all-round man. Unfortunately he has a very high opinion of himself, and this reacts on his work, for he is apt to side-step the intermediate problems, and arrive at the right answer without knowing why.[23]

The Commandant of Wanborough, Major Roger de Wesselow, took the instructors' caveats on board when composing his own summary and signed off Tony's report with complimentary but candid comments: 'Excellent type. Plenty of guts, extremely capable and highly intelligent. Fly. Amenable to discipline but lacks an army background; bumptious and over-confident. Exceptional for his age.'[24]

By the end of this period of training, the students were aware that they were being prepared for work with the Resistance rather than paramilitary operations. With a deviousness that belied his years, Tony therefore took a hand in shaping his destiny by deliberately masking his capability as a signaller. Although proficient in Morse code from his years as a Boy Scout, he sought to falsify his performance –but his test marks still earned the assessment he could reach the 'necessary standard'. His effort to camouflage his competence was a prescient move, for an SOE confidential note of 18 November 1941 stated, 'The intention is to use him when trained as a W/T man in France.'

On the last night of their training at Wanborough, the students went to a local pub to celebrate, Tony, with his youth and abstemiousness, rather more restrained than other members of the group. Back at the Manor, Bisset wrote to his fiancée, 'I am staying in and will enjoy a few minutes of peace. They are all very nice but get too noisy at times.'

The next day those members of the 27L party who had passed the course left Wanborough for a new location, training school 'STS 25B', in the Highlands of Scotland. The journey was not without problems and although they secured 'a very good carriage', it was unlit and the train was so delayed that they arrived at Glasgow at 6 a.m. on the 23rd instead of the previous evening. [25] With only a daily train to the West Highlands, they had to wait to continue their journey. Bisset was pretty morose, 'It is raining, the street covered with melting snow, you have never seen such a mess in all your life, luckily the hotel is very comfortable. I intend to spend the afternoon in a picture house somewhere.' Once again though, he consoled himself with the high morale of his group, 'My party is quite bright and cheerful and they enjoy their stay at the hotel. It is a good job that they don't grumble and make my life miserable, I am very lucky with that lot.'

Their destination was Camusdarach, a lodge situated a few miles to the south of the fishing port of Mallaig overlooking the Sound of Sleath. The property had been acquired by SOE a year earlier and was part of a complex of paramilitary training schools in the Protected Area of the Highlands. Party 27L caught the train from Glasgow to Fort William and then transferred to the local line to Mallaig, alighting at Morar Station where they were picked up by an army truck. Bisset commented that the weather was quite mild although it later became cold and windy. It also rained: 'Every time I go out I am wet, it is impossible to go out without being wet.' On 28 January the house's electricity failed and remained out of action for at least five days, with hurricane lamps used for lighting. In spite of the weather and the domestic hitches, the students approached their toughening-up process in an atmosphere of boisterous rough-and-tumble as recorded by Bisset. 'My party is keeping cheerful, we have plenty of fights, luckily I usually come out on top, but it happens that I get a good lesson at times!' The group were encouraged to talk in French in the mess to maintain their command of the language. Staff and trainees ate well, despite wartime rationing, with steaks and salmon served frequently. The commanding officer, Major James Young of the Argyll and Sutherland Highlanders, frowned on any poaching carried out by the students but was perfectly happy to consume the fruits of their labours when it appeared on his plate. On one occasion, Tony's party of students met up with a gillie as they finished a cross-country march. The locals had a rough idea that special training was taking place in the area and usually refrained from any contact. However, a little earlier, Tony's group had used some explosive to 'fish' for salmon and Raymond Flower was carrying the fruit of their labours in a groundsheet. The gillie asked them if they had been poaching and whether they, too, had just heard a loud bang. They replied in the negative to both enquiries. The gillie simply expressed his hope that the salmon got to the cookhouse before it fell out of the groundsheet and wished them farewell with the gentle warning that if he caught them poaching again they were for the 'high jump'.

Five-mile route marches before breakfast usually passed without incident but one exercise was transformed into a real matter of life and death. As Tony and his usual companions, Flower and 'Evans', were completing a march, 'Evans' fell into a bog. Every move he made to extricate himself resulted in his being sucked deeper into the mire. Tony and Flower lay on their groundsheets (to spread their weight) and, as Flower inched towards 'Evans', Tony held onto his ankles. Thankfully, they managed to extricate their comrade just before he sank from view. Now, with 'Evans' covered in stinking, orange slime, Tony and Flower used their recently acquired techniques to try to stay upwind as the trio made their way back to their billet.

Other exercises included orienteering across the moors and learning how to stalk deer because, explained one of their instructors, 'If you can get within a hundred yards of a stag without it noticing you, you'll be able to slit the throat of a German sentry without him ever spotting you'. Firearms training included practising with British and foreign machine guns and pistols while tuition in unarmed combat included the use of the Fairbairn/Sykes fighting knife. Tony recalled the words of an instructor, 'Never hit a chap with a knife downwards. Always cut upwards because the Almighty made us with armour plating up here [ribs and things] but he's left all this [the stomach area] empty and unprotected. So always use a knife upwards. You either get his sex, his lunch or his lungs by coming up from below.'

The seashore was used to carry out live firing exercises and instruction in working with small boats in readiness for a need to infiltrate the agents into France by sea. This training did not extend to improving Tony's deficiencies as a swimmer and he became the only student allowed to wear a lifejacket on the boat. Lessons on the shore included various types of rope work such as descending a hawser that stretched from the cliff top to the beach. Far and away the most adept exponent was Coppin who, with a wealth of experience in the entry and exit of cargo ships in French harbours, showed off by walking down the rope line in the manner of a high-wire artiste. The instructors saw this act of bravado as a challenge and, at the next session, had fixed a rat collar over the rope. Undismayed, Coppin overcame the obstacle with ease and repeated his feat of the previous day.[26]

Training with explosives was not confined to unsporting fishing expeditions and the students were tasked to lay dummy charges on the single-track railway to Morar station. The train crews were sometimes tipped off that an exercise was taking place, rendering them even more vigilant than usual. When a student failed to conceal himself sufficiently well, the railwaymen on the footplate indulged themselves by pelting the trainee saboteurs with coal from the tender. Further indignity was heaped on the battered and bruised students when, as a forfeit for being spotted, Teddy Bisset ordered them to collect the coal as supplementary fuel for the Mess fire.

Even the instructors conceded that they were being put through the mill, and Bisset affirmed, 'We shall be working all day long and late at night.' The mood of the usually upbeat leader of 27L deteriorated as the weather worsened and the temperature dropped, 'It is awfully cold outside, so sitting in the mess is rather a pleasant thing, because it is very warm. We have a dog who spent his day sitting by the fire, he thought it was too cold to go out.' Moreover, by 10 February 1942, Bisset was 'getting a bit fed up with the job'; he had another reason for feeling disgruntled, 'I am broke. I have not been paid for a long time and I am on my last pennies. I spent a lot of money on my party and I have not been refunded by H.Q. yet.'

However, there was still opportunity for a little fun and Brian Stonehouse was prevailed upon to add some exotic decor to the Mess. Bisset reported to his fiancée, 'One of my lads was an artist before the war, he was working for shops well known in London and Paris, so the CO here asked [him] to draw some nude women for the wall of our mess. Now it looks like if we were in a nightclub, mind you they are really well drawn and in the wilds of Scotland, it helps one to remember that there are beautiful things in the world. He made 3 of them, one that we call the wife, the 2nd the mistress and the 3rd is of Eastern type, they all smile at us.'* In addition to the seductive enhancement of the decor, Tony found that Stonehouse's efforts achieved an unheralded level of solicitousness from the Mess staff. Whereas it had formerly proved difficult to find a steward to refill a glass, the students and staff were now harassed by attentive soldier/waiters who made frequent appearances to ask if anything was required while stealing glances at the sketches.

Bisset's last letter from Camusdarach was written on 13 February as the group prepared to leave the following day. It was very cold, had snowed a great deal and he hoped that his next billet would not be so beset by inclement weather. One consolation was the farewell party that was planned for that evening and the prospect of '*une bonne réserve de whisky*'.

While Bisset was entitled to treat himself to his glass of whisky at the conclusion of this phase of training, so, too, was (the near teetotal) Tony, for his finishing report was, once again, most favourable. He had steadily matured and the reporting officers' comments reveal insights into the character and abilities of the young man,

1.	Physical Training	Very good. Young and agile despite bulk for age. Athletic type.
2.	Close Combat	Very good. Has the aggressive spirit.
3.	Rope Work	Very good.
4.	Fieldcraft	Good. Particularly at night, appears to have good night vision.
5.	Weapon Training	Very good. Not very fast, but most accurate of party. Very sound knowledge of all weapons.

---

* Tony had a different recollection of the CO Major Young's attitude towards the drawings. Far from asking Stonehouse to carry out the work, Young wished them to be removed. However, they were left *in situ* and were still there later in the spring to lift the spirits of subsequent courses although one source states that they were now to be found at another training establishment (King, *Jacqueline*, p. 88).

6.	Explosives & Demolitions	Exceptionally good. Test 95%. Practical, also very good. Showed great interest in all branches. Could instruct.
7.	Signalling and Communications	Good. Morse Test, Reading 8 W.P.M., Sending 7 W.P.M. Was not very interested. Could do better.
8.	Reports etc.	Fairly good.
9.	Map Reading etc.	Very good. Test 92%. Practical, very good. Sketching poor.
10.	Schemes & Tactics	Shows ability to plan and has powers of leadership which will develop.
11.	Boat work	Handles boats well.
12.	Navigation	[No entry]
13.	Special Training	[No entry]

Instructors Remarks:- A first class Student who showed great interest in practically all subjects, particularly Demolitions. Absorbed all the teaching with ease and showed originality of ideas.

Commandant's Report:- A non-smoker, and while here a tee-totaller, possesses abundant vitality, is cheerful, a great talker, but usually knows his subject. Owing to his talkativeness and his attitude of superiority to other Students, was not a favourite, except in the case of one Student of his own type. He was always most corteous [sic] to all members of the School Staff. Has plenty of guts and is much older than his years. Should prove a useful member as he is undoubtedly most capable and has a strong personality. Perhaps would require a strong hand to control him in first instance.[27]

This training report reflects Tony's emergence as a highly promising SOE student. The starved waif of the previous autumn had beefed up to be described as having 'bulk for age' but any change in his physique had not prevented praise for his physical prowess. As might have been expected, the report's least impressive comments were reserved for 'signalling and communications'. These surely were occasioned by Tony's determination to avoid wireless operator's duties; 'Was not very interested. Could do better' says it all. Undoubtedly his best subjects were 'Explosives and Demolitions' and, taken together with some promise as an organiser, he seemed set fair for selection to lead a network in France. There nevertheless remained the problem of his youthfulness, but the Commandant of Camusdarach, Major Young, exhibited commendable common sense in suggesting that Tony's other attributes should compensate for this. The few criticisms about his personality reflected the self-confidence of a teenager whose enthusiasm may have drifted towards bumptiousness and whose 'attitude of superiority' perhaps was an attempt to mask a feeling of insecurity at being so young and so unversed in the mores of the British military.

After completion of three weeks' training in Scotland (a period shorter than some other parties who stayed for a month), the group progressed to their parachute training at SOE's STS 51, close to the RAF/British Army centre for airborne forces at Ringway, Manchester. British parachuting had undergone a rapid evolution since the establishment of the Central Landing School in June 1940, and by the time Tony attended his course, considerable advances had been made in training methods. On its arrival on the afternoon of 14 February 1942, the 27L party was given an assimilation flight in a de Havilland DH89 biplane.[28] The next day, they began the first period of their training devoted to 'synthetic' groundwork with the students learning how to exit an aircraft, control their parachutes and land safely. Dummy aircraft fuselages were put to good use, as were trapeze simulators, chutes and the 'Fan' – a twenty-foot drop that saw a descent arrested by a mechanism that allowed the student to experience a similar impact to a real landing. On the 16th Tony had his first flight in a bomber, an Armstrong Whitworth Whitley Z9656, to gain experience of the drop hole in the fuselage (known in the vernacular as the 'elephant's lavatory').The following day, having mastered the basic techniques, he undertook his first genuine descent, albeit not from an aircraft but from a tethered balloon. Matters did not start well, for, soon after being issued with his parachute, he noticed feverish activity amongst a group of WAAFs. They managed to attract the attention of the instructor who immediately checked Tony's parachute and instantly gave him a replacement. Luckily, the women had noticed a white cross on his pack that denoted it was unserviceable. The seriousness of this error was not communicated to Tony until later, so, in blissful ignorance he continued onto the airfield. Here, he and three other students, together with Teddy Bisset and an instructor, were positioned in a metal and canvas basket beneath a balloon that then ascended to a height of 800 feet. In succession, the parachutists were ordered to sit with their legs over the hole in the centre of the cage and, on the instructor's orders, jump. Bisset was the first to go and Tony – apart from the instructor – the last. By the time it was Tony's turn, the cage had assumed an alarming angle and he had to clamber with some difficulty into the prescribed position over the hole. As he waited for the instructor's signal, his gaze was drawn to the disconcerting presence below him of army ambulances with large red crosses emblazoned on their roofs. On reflection he felt that the balloon jump was far worse than leaping from an aircraft when the wind, speed and noise helped distract his innate trepidation. The descent from the balloon was a silent and a stomach-churning 120-foot plummet earthwards before the parachute opened. Tony did not have to wait long for comparison with 'the real thing' and, a few hours later, he completed his first descent from a Whitley aircraft flying at 500 feet. The following day he was assigned to another balloon drop but adverse weather conditions meant that he did not jump. On the 19th, Tony made his second descent from an aircraft and the next day completed the course with a full day's work consisting of drops from a balloon (day and night) and a jump at dusk from a Whitley. While Tony had, by and large, enjoyed his time at Wanborough and Camusdarach, he found the parachute training both physically arduous and nerve-racking, leaving him to muse that it was 'a bloody stupid form of transport'. Such concerns received confirmation, if it were needed, when he observed a fatal accident caused by the parachute of a Polish student failing to open.

A note of 25 February 1942 on Coppin's file states, 'Alphonse, Theodore and Roger, it is anticipated will go to Beaulieu (date not yet decided).'[29] Brian Stonehouse's absence from the group is explained by a note of the same date on his file, 'A definite decision as to the disposal of this man (Benjamin) has not been taken but it is anticipated that he will be sent to Grendon.' It can only be assumed that the pressing need for radio operators resulted in

Stonehouse's immediate despatch to the SOE wireless instruction school at Grendon Hall in Buckinghamshire. In May Stonehouse, after two training exercises in Manchester and Leeds, was parachuted into France without having passed through the important training delivered at Beaulieu, and Tony reflected that his colleague's failure to attend the course constituted a crucial flaw in the wireless operator's preparation to meet his hazardous duties.[30]

Tony's next SOE training establishment was Station 31, the 'Finishing School' at Beaulieu near Southampton, a substantial complex consisting of several SOE-requisitioned residences on Lord Montagu's estate. The location was well chosen; it was separated from the New Forest by a heath, enhancing its isolation, while a substantial number of secluded but comfortable residences offered ideal accommodation for the discreet training of parties of students. Tony and his colleagues were billeted at 'Boarmans', a large, detached villa built in the mid-1930s. While Wanborough and Camusdarach had mostly comprised paramilitary work, Beaulieu delivered a more cerebral form of instruction and focused upon imparting the peculiar techniques required of a secret agent. By this time, Tony felt a real sense of progression through his training courses and, although there remained ample opportunities for skylarking, he approached this stage with a genuine sense of purpose. The standards of teaching and examination at Beaulieu would be the most rigorous to date and any flaws in a student's character or capabilities were subjected to the closest scrutiny.

The Beaulieu course made a great impression on Tony. Regardless of earlier criticisms by his instructors of over-confidence, there is no doubt that he took this phase of his training very, very seriously. Decades later, he reflected that throughout his time as an agent in France, he always tried to follow the precepts passed to him at Beaulieu. Moreover, he judged that a high proportion of F Section's operational disasters resulted from the failure of his contemporaries to adhere to the axioms laid down in the Hampshire classrooms.

In addition to agent tradecraft, the students were given extensive briefings on the enemy that awaited them across the Channel. Lectures outlined details of the make-up of the German occupying forces and charts of enemy uniform and insignia informed the students of the myriad security forces stationed in France. Every student had to have a basic grounding in SOE's codes, including the double transposition system for which Tony adopted his grandparents' address as his 'key' phrase; 'Goldsmiths Langdon Hills Essex'. While for many agents, codes constituted an essential feature of their work; Tony never had recourse to use his during the whole of the war.[31]

The Beaulieu tutor who made the greatest impression upon Tony was Lieutenant Peter Folliss. Some ten years Tony's senior, he spoke French fluently and had been an actor before the war, his thespian background giving him special insights into dissimulation and disguise, which he conveyed to his students. Like many of the staff, his parent unit was the Intelligence Corps and by the end of the war he had become Beaulieu's Chief Instructor.[32]

Included in the training syllabus were lessons on how to handle hostile interrogation. This was hardly unknown territory for Tony who had experienced some rough handling in Spain the previous year but Folliss provided invaluable insights. He told the students that they should never answer a question quickly. A slow, ponderous response to even the simplest of enquiries would camouflage any indication of which were easy and which difficult. He explained it was natural to provide rapid, truthful answers to innocuous questions while a slower, contemplative response was the automatic reaction when a lie was necessary. The tempo of a question and answer session could give a skilled interrogator a clear insight into a prisoner's probity. By adopting a slow, almost dull-witted, demeanour throughout, a captured agent could win vital time to consider the dangers of questions and construct effective responses. If an agent was caught, 'play for time' was the brief. Unlike most of the other students, Tony's personal experiences ensured that his tuition at Beaulieu was not a one-way process; Folliss gleaned information from his pupil about recent, first-hand details of everyday life in France and the reality of clandestine work.

The training was not confined to the classroom. A night exercise included the burying of a parachute and, as usual, Tony and Flower were working as a team although they were not doing well. Their instructions stated that on landing, an agent would dig a hole and bury his/ her jumpsuit and parachute in order to eradicate any trace of their arrival. The only problem was that the spade included in the parachutist's equipment was minuscule given the substantial bulk of the parachute and jumpsuit, suggesting that completion of the task would necessitate several hours' digging. Unable to find a solution to the dilemma, Flower went away to relieve himself but only compounded his problems by urinating on Folliss who was observing the team's performance from the undergrowth.

An all-day exercise in Bournemouth required Tony to assimilate a detailed cover story. He was taken to the seaside resort by truck where he completed the relatively simple tasks of contacting a man (whose description had been given to him), exchanging a message by hand, clearing an improvised 'letter box' in a public convenience and transferring the document to a similar cache in a pub lavatory. The students carried out their tasks individually, but the pretence of anonymity was broken when Tony bumped into Flower who was engaged in completing his own, parallel set of instructions at an identical location. At the conclusion of the exercise, Tony was debriefed at Beaulieu, ate his supper and went to bed. In the middle of the night, he was rudely awoken by a 'German soldier' whom he soon identified as Kennedy, the Mess Steward. Unceremoniously pulled out of bed, Tony was propelled downstairs (with some encouragement from his 'guard') and frog-marched across the gravel yard to the garage. It was brightly lit with a stool in the middle of the room facing a table behind which sat Folliss in German uniform accompanied by other training staff who were similarly dressed. Tony was told to sit down but, as he attempted to do so, the stool was pulled away by means of a string tied around one of the legs. This was not a practical joke: the intention was to disorientate the 'prisoner', make him fear the unexpected and recognise that there were no rules in the hostile situation in which he found himself. In Tony's words, 'It was round one to the interrogator.'

Having picked himself up off the floor, he felt humiliated and unnerved as he began to answer the questions in English about his exercise in Bournemouth. He stuck closely to the cover story given to him at his briefing and handled the interrogation as if it were for real. He responded in the way Folliss had taught him; answering everything slowly or vaguely to camouflage the need to devote time to consider difficult, important or dangerous questions. Eventually, Folliss concluded the questioning and Tony went back to bed. The next day, conversation over breakfast revealed that the other students who had taken part in the Bournemouth exercises had received similar nocturnal surprises. Some, however, stated that they had not taken the interrogation seriously and told Folliss 'not to be so bloody silly' at the interview. Perhaps it was Tony's youth that shaped his decision to play the questioning for 'real'. Maybe it was the experiences gained in France and Spain that persuaded him that preparation for the deadly work ahead demanded more than the levity of a parlour game. Whatever the reason, his mature response to the simulated interrogation at Beaulieu would later make a vital contribution to his survival.

The concluding exercise of the course required the deployment of the range of clandestine skills learnt during training. The programme began with a verbal briefing at Orchard Court during which Tony was given a set of instructions that included a questionnaire concerning the docks and power stations in and around Liverpool. He was warned that the training exercise would not be easy; the city's police force had been alerted and its Special Branch would use the hunt for him to hone its investigative skills. Tony's first priority on arrival in Liverpool was to find digs but his knowledge of the city only consisted of the few hours spent there on his arrival from Gibraltar. Nevertheless, he managed to locate a modest guest house and, following the adage of making a lie as near to the truth as possible, told his landlady that he was engaged on a military exercise. His challenge was not merely to find the 'secrets' on his list – he was also confronted by a personal survival test. He did not know the north of England at all, scarcely drank alcohol and felt distinctly uneasy about operating in pubs – the milieu where he calculated that he stood the best chance of collecting information. His experience of life in England had been very limited, largely comprising his schooling at Felsted and visits to his grandparents in Essex and Kent. He later commented that he would have had a tougher time living life as a clandestine agent in Britain than he did in France. In spite of his vulnerability in Liverpool as an all too conspicuous outsider, Tony was not apprehended – a fate that befell other SOE students during their exercises. But he did not consider himself a success: 'If I got three out of ten I would have been doing very well' and rated himself 'a complete failure'. He returned to London to be debriefed by a supercilious officer at Orchard Court whose air of superiority was perhaps inspired by Tony's mediocre performance. Sadly, the report has not been located.

The only surviving record of the 'Finishing School' period of Tony's training comprises a single page dated 6 April 1942. It was signed (and perhaps compiled) by the Beaulieu Commandant, Lieutenant-Colonel Stanley Woolrych. It contains more criticisms of Tony than his previous training reports, perhaps reflecting the different standards demanded by Beaulieu's unique and exacting programme. Woolrych's long experience of secret service work doubtless informed his perspicacious description of Tony as a 'Bright and intelligent type of man who is keen on the job and learns quickly, but his mind is not yet entirely mature. He is far too inclined to jump to conclusions without thinking out his problems logically. He has a considerable natural capacity for leadership but is, unfortunately, handicapped in this respect by his youthfulness. He would undoubtedly make a loyal and efficient subordinate under sound leadership. A charming and cheerful personality.'[33]

At the conclusion of his Beaulieu training, Tony was sent on leave. Three days later he was confirmed in the acting rank of Second Lieutenant, but he neither felt the need of a holiday nor was he distracted by the pip on his epaulette. Tony was keen to get going, to put his hard-earned training to the test and make a contribution to a war that the newspapers and newsreels daily revealed was very much in the balance. An opportunity of reviving his friendship with Hope Munday and her family lifted his spirits but even this pleasant diversion could not dispel the frustration at remaining excluded from active involvement in the war. In his impatience to enter the fray, his leave 'was soul destroying' and as the days passed, he became ever more desperate to be sent to France and get to work.

Chapter Five

'For Christ's Sake Let's Get Going'

Now Tony was a fully trained agent (apart from an imminent specialist course on sabotage techniques), he naturally pondered where and when he would be deployed to France. His recollections of this period threw little light on the process as he was not privy to the executive deliberations of F Section and SOE Headquarters. However, it has proved possible to piece together the course of events from a disparate set of SOE records.

On 10 April 1942 Colonel David Keswick, a senior SOE staff officer in London with responsibility for France and the Low Countries, sent a message to his representative in Berne in Switzerland. Its contents were intended for onward transmission to a shadowy figure, 'Robert', traces of whose activities feature in the files of F Section, X Section (Germany) and J Section (Switzerland). Keswick's signal included 'ACSS' (Assistant Chief of the Secret Intelligence Service, Claude Dansey) as a co-addressee.[1] 'Robert', an extremely well-connected, left-wing activist, served as a vital connection between SOE and socialist groups in France, Germany, Switzerland and Italy. Moreover, he also provided intelligence to SIS that explained Dansey's interest in the signal. Keswick's signal related to an earlier internal SOE minute of 18 March 1942 that recorded: 'ROBERT wishes he had one or two more people to help with his work.'[2] It seems that this influential agent was spreading himself too thinly, operating in Switzerland and the Unoccupied Zone of France for SOE and trying to serve too many masters at once. The telegram from Keswick to

Berne acknowledged that 'ISK [Internationaler Sozialistischer Kampfbund] work is first obligation and R. ['Robert'] cannot give full time to our affairs in France.' The Swiss agent evidently needed help and in the same message London proposed a solution: 'In order to hasten and simplify organisation in France we suggest we send organiser and w/t [wireless telegraph] operator soonest possible. Have two suitable candidates already trained. Organiser will work under R.'s direction to develop trade union resistance groups in France. By this method we shall have direct communication and possibility early delivery materials.'

The message concluded, 'If R. agreeable foregoing instruct how contact in France with our organiser can be made and where.' Although Tony's name was not mentioned, there is little doubt that he was one of the 'suitable candidates', not least because he had completed his training on 6 April, four days before Keswick's signal was sent to Berne.

The state of the French Resistance in the early spring of 1942 offers an explanation why the recruitment of members of the trades unions was desirable. France remained divided into the 'occupied' and 'unoccupied' zones although much else had altered since the signing of the Armistice. The Vichy government's fantasy that France could heal the scars of 1940 in splendid isolation under a benign, German leadership of Europe was now difficult to sustain; even in the eyes of the most fervent or resolutely optimistic supporter of Pétain. The Axis invasion of the Soviet Union in June 1941 had propelled the not inconsiderable resources of the French communist party into resistance. The most immediate impact of these changes upon France, was that experienced, clandestine communist cells organised themselves, responding to Moscow's instructions that every possible action should be taken to damage the Nazi war effort. Violence against German personnel stationed in France increased and, consequently, so did the reprisals against the local community. Meanwhile, the Free French movement led by General Charles de Gaulle was taking steps to coordinate the many, disparate resistance groups within the Occupied and Free zones. The Bureau Central de Renseignement et d'Action (BCRA) under Colonel André Dewavrin (codenamed 'Passy') sent representatives to investigate the state of affairs in France and seek out nascent resistance movements. Once identified, the aim was to secure the resisters' adherence to the Free French movement and to weld them into a unified whole. This was easier said than done. France was, in large part, a confused, morass of political dejection, apathy and fear. Moreover, those men and women who contemplated resistance or had stepped beyond thought to action were not necessarily willing to acknowledge de Gaulle's primacy. Léon Morandat, codenamed 'Yvon', was the earliest emissary sent to France by the Free French minister of the interior. Born in 1913 in the Bourg region (north of Lyon) to a family of farmers, Morandat became an active trade unionist. He served with the French expeditionary force to Norway and following the failure of this Allied endeavour he briefly returned to France before being evacuated to Britain where he became one of the first to rally to de Gaulle. His knowledge of trade unions resulted in his being shifted from military service to the headquarters staff. Unsurprisingly, he was chosen as the ideal candidate to be sent to France as the first Free French political emissary. On 6/7 November 1941 he was parachuted by the RAF near Toulouse on Operation 'Outclass' with a brief to assess the state of existing and potential resistance movements amongst the Christian trade unions in the Unoccupied Zone. During Morandat's mission 'Robert' became a vital communications conduit to SOE and the Free French. It seems likely that Morandat's report on his survey of resistance was conveyed by 'Robert's' links to Switzerland and thence to Britain.[3]

The arrival in London of Morandat's report and 'Robert's' need for an assistant to run his contacts in the Unoccupied Zone were presumably the triggers for the burst of activity that led to Tony's deployment into the field. No operational instructions have survived but Buckmaster's memoirs give some hints of the selection process, 'His mission was no easy one. It was a question of establishing liaison between the C.G.T. (the French equivalent of the T.U.C.) and the Allied staff, a task which a man twice Alphonse's age might well have found onerous.'[4] Any meetings with Buckmaster at this time scarcely registered with the new recruit as he later affirmed, 'I can't say that he made a great impression on me'. But F Section's head recalled, 'We told him [Tony] all we knew about the C.G.T. – which, in fact, was not a very great deal. We gave him a list of the principal personalities in both the French and British councils. We emphasised that there was no political significance in this liaison. Alphonse had no authority to give orders or to negotiate'.[4]

Buckmaster's candour in expressing the limitations of the briefings for Tony's mission was borne out by the recollections of the agent. But at least one major political task was assigned to him; Tony was instructed to contact the influential political figure Léon Jouhaux, the Secrétaire Général of the Confédération Générale du Travail (CGT). Jouhaux, a man in his early sixties, had played a leading role in the turbulent inter-war French political scene and Hugh Dalton, the Minister of Economic Warfare with responsibility for SOE, possessed a strong personal interest in his fate. The British politician strongly advocated that labour organisations should form the basis for resistance: 'Dalton's attitude towards S.O.E. was far from non-political: he expected the natural allies of the organisation to be found among the European Left. At Baker Street, he urged his staff to make use of pre-war international trade union networks; thus one leading official of the World Federation of Trade Unions was attached to SO2, to help explore ways of arousing active opposition among conscripted workers.'[5] Dalton instructed F Section to contact Jouhaux in order to achieve these objectives but the French trade unionist was arrested by the Vichy authorities in December 1941 before a link could materialise. The failure to implement the Minister's instruction was then compounded by SOE's apparent inactivity in securing Jouhaux's release. This was interpreted by Dalton as obstructionism by F Section and disloyalty to a newly appointed controller, Robin Brook.[6] The Minister wrote a memo complaining of 'underlings playing reactionary politics' and, in the subsequent fall-out, Marriott resigned as head of F Section and was replaced by Buckmaster.[7] In February 1942, Dalton also concluded his SOE connections but Jouhaux evidently remained a sufficiently high priority that Tony was tasked to contact him.

As part of the mission briefings, Tony was sent with an F Section colleague, Robert Bourne-Paterson, to meet Sir Walter Citrine, the General Secretary of the Trades Union Council and a longtime friend of Jouhaux.[8] It was a bizarre encounter with the novice secret agent having no idea what to say to the vastly experienced leader of British trade unionism. The unsatisfactory and, thankfully, brief conversation was concluded with Citrine asking Tony to convey his best wishes to Jouhaux with a casualness that suggested the two men might chance to bump into each other in a London club rather than as part of a perilous mission into the heart of Hitler's Europe.

After the trip to Citrine, Tony was taken to Orchard Court, ushered into a room by an F Section staff officer and told to read a briefing file that had been prepared for him. It revealed that he would be dropped without a reception committee into the Unoccupied Zone of France. Further examination of the file showed a focus on Lille with maps of the city, aerial photographs and details of important sabotage targets in northern France, in particular, the marshalling yards at Fives Lille. As Tony recollected, 'It was fascinating but it did intrigue me as to why you had to be dropped in the Unoccupied Zone and face the danger of crossing the demarcation line to attack targets in the Occupied Zone.' A few days later, Bourne-Paterson asked him if he had any questions on the brief. Tony queried why he had been given data on Lille when he thought he was being deployed to the Unoccupied Zone to report on resistance amongst the French trade unions. Bourne-Paterson was visibly perplexed and departed to make enquiries. On his return he confessed that the Lille file had been intended for another F Section agent destined for northern France. It is not known whether the other individual had been given Tony's file containing notes on trade union activity in the Unoccupied Zone. If he had, he was better informed than Tony who never saw the file. With his customary inexactness, Buckmaster claimed, 'Alphonse was a receptive pupil. He said more than once that he found these lessons more entertaining than university lectures.'[9]

Perhaps surprisingly, the administrative error neither led Tony to question F Section's competence nor did it diminish his determination to be sent to France. He recalled that he was so intent on pressing on with the operation and ending the interminable hanging around, that bureaucratic mistakes did not worry him. His mantra was, simply, 'For Christ's sake let's get going'.

The meeting with Citrine proved of little value to Tony but he anticipated that more relevant insights would accrue from a briefing on the French trade unions provided by the Political Warfare Executive (PWE) School at Woburn. PWE was yet another of Britain's myriad secret agencies and was primarily concerned with the use of propaganda to influence anti-Nazi opinion in Germany and Occupied Europe. Tony's appointment was with Dr Leslie Beck, 'a mysterious figure whose role in the obscurer corridors of wartime Anglo-French relations was undoubtedly more important than most of his colleagues in PWE's French Section realised.'[10] A small, bespectacled man in his mid-thirties, Beck was the Chief Intelligence Officer of PWE's French Section but Tony assessed his knowledge was academic rather than practical. Beck had studied at the Sorbonne and was an authority on the French philosopher Descartes but he failed to make a favourable impression on the fledgling secret agent: 'I took an instant dislike to him which is why I remember him so well.' The brief audience with Beck, conducted in English, provided neither insights into the French trade unions nor any worthwhile advice as to how the twenty-year-old was going to convince Léon Jouhaux to fall in with SOE's plans. Tony (a lapsed member of the trade union Syndicat du Bâtiments du Jura) possessed first-hand experience of the working class, described Beck as 'a know-all' and concluded that the meeting was 'interesting but it served no concrete purpose to my mission'. Beck had acquaintances amongst the higher echelons of the French unions but Tony later considered that the academic 'knew bugger-all about how to organise a strike in a small factory'.[11]

After the disappointment at PWE, Tony found his next course, three weeks at STS 17, SOE's sabotage school at Brickendonbury, near Hertford, far more rewarding. Having already displayed an aptitude for handling explosives, this was a phase of training that Tony relished. The programme was wide-ranging, comprising 'A Basic Course in Industrial Sabotage, including the Sabotage of Engineering Factories, Steam and Hydraulic Power Stations, Transmission Networks, Telecommunications Systems, Vegetable Oil Factories and Railways. A little revision in Demolition Work, and making up Charges was also included.'[12] The sabotage school was part of the inheritance from Section D. The premises had been acquired in June 1940, shortly before the creation of SOE, and became the new organisation's first training establishment.[13] By the time Tony became a student on 27 April 1942, Brickendonbury had been given over to the special instruction of sabotage. The commandant was Major George Rheam of the Royal Army Ordnance Corps, a man described as 'tall' and 'dour' and 'the real inventor of modern scientific methods of attack on machinery. He was an outstandingly efficient teacher, with strong imaginative capacity allied to exacting standards.'[14] As far as Tony was concerned, Rheam 'had the humour of Stalin'.

By the spring of 1942 when Tony began his course at STS 17, SOE had developed an impressive armoury of sabotage devices. Several owed their origins to Section D and remained the mainstay of F Section's sabotage operations for the rest of the war. There were many types of military and commercial explosives available but SOE considered that the types most suitable for resistance groups were Nobel's 808, gelignite and RDX – better known as plastic explosive (PE). The latter substance was still a relatively new invention and, initially, '808' was in far greater supply. Both '808' and gelignite had the chemical side-effect of bestowing an acute headache on anyone handling it. PE, on the other hand, did not possess such unpleasant properties. Tony already knew the basic principles of explosives from his time at Wanborough and Camusdarach but at STS 17 he received detailed instruction on the individual properties and capabilities of detonators, fuses, bombs, delays, initiators and incendiaries. Not only was he taught the chemical and physical characteristics of the devices but was extensively briefed on how best to attack the types of targets he would find in France such as transformers, pylons, railway equipment, machinery and buildings.

SOE saboteurs preferred not to be around when their explosive charges detonated so 'delay' or 'time' fuses were essential features of their armoury. A charge could be initiated by a slow-burning fuse but this required the saboteur to be in attendance to light it and 'slow', when used to describe the detonation of explosive, is very much a relative term. The time delay that was most frequently deployed by SOE was the time pencil. Developed by Section D, this instrument relied upon precision engineering and chemistry to achieve an accurate means of initiating an explosive charge. It had the merits of being quite cheap and, at the same time, *quite* effective. It relied upon the crushing of an ampoule of corrosive liquid that ate away at a retaining wire holding a striker under pressure. When the wire broke, the striker was released, hitting a percussion cap that was in contact with the detonator (or Bickford or instantaneous fuse) and the explosive charge was thereby initiated. But the time pencil was not perfect. It was manufactured with a variety of delay options that were determined by the strength of the acid in the ampoule or the thickness of the wire. Moreover, the speed of corrosion was also affected by temperature – the colder the conditions, the longer the delay. Similarly, too robust bending of the copper sheath to break the glass ampoule might result in the wire snapping, which would lead either to a non-initiation of the charge or one so precipitate that the saboteur did not survive. In spite of the instructors' faith in the time pencil, Tony considered it a 'snare and a delusion'. He calculated that when he issued his saboteurs with time pencils, there was a one-in-two failure rate through over-enthusiastic bending of the copper tube.

While time delays allowed saboteurs to lay explosive charges and make their escape before they were caught up in the results of their actions, other SOE fuses relied on booby trap techniques. The mechanisms of the release, pressure and pull switches were self explanatory; lifting of a weight, the exertion of pressure or a pull would release a striker that impacted upon a detonator. Time, pressure and pull switches could all be employed on blowing up railway tracks but there was also a specific fuse to detonate the charge under the train. This was the 'fog signal igniter' that converted a pre-war, benign device (employed to warn railway crews of danger on the line) to a means of initiating a charge under a train. The igniter was clipped on the top of the rail and connected via a snout to the explosive charge by instantaneous or Bickford fuse. When the train passed over the fog signal, it crushed percussion caps in the body of the device that led to the detonation of the explosive charge. It was ostensibly foolproof but, as Tony was to discover, the amateur saboteur could incorrectly orientate the snout inwards with the result that the train's flanged wheel would sever the fuse, rendering the charge inactive.

Tony and his fellow students at STS 17 were given a comprehensive grounding in all aspects of sabotage but the prevailing diplomatic relations with Vichy France inhibited British agents in the Unoccupied Zone to carrying out discreet, non-attributable forms of attack. Aggressive, overt forms of sabotage were unacceptable under the 'no bangs' ruling as long as the vestige of Vichy/British 'neutrality' was maintained. Special emphasis was therefore placed on 'accidental' types of attack. These relied heavily upon incendiary devices, it being anticipated that any compromising evidence would be destroyed by the conflagration that they initiated. Several types were produced by SOE that ranged from incendiary cigarettes and 'pocket incendiaries' to more substantial weapons such as the 2½lb Thermite bomb.

In addition to explosives and incendiaries, there was a less dramatic form of sabotage attack: abrasive grease – a carborundum (silicon carbide) material that, if introduced into an engine, gearbox or any industrial moving part would (it was hoped) cause the mechanism to seize. The carborundum was used in powder form or ready-mixed with grease. It had the advantage of not appearing to be a sabotage weapon and so was unlikely to arouse suspicion even in close proximity to its targets – locomotive yards, factories, workshops and garages. In 1942 SOE placed great reliance upon the potential of this weapon to disrupt German transportation links both in the occupied countries and in Germany itself and it would be a major feature of Tony's early sabotage activities in France.

Tony's STS 17 course was not confined to the classrooms of a country house. Visits were made to industrial sites comparable to the types of targets that the students were likely to attack in enemy territory. One day, Rheam and Captain 'Bill' Hazeldine, a Brickendonbury instructor, took Tony's group to a power station in North London. There, they were shown where to place explosives against the weakest and most important parts of machinery. They were told that all the larger components of a steam turbine were made of cast *steel*, so, for the best destructive result, explosives should be used against alternative, cast *iron* features. No potential target was ruled out and Tony's training included inspection of a paper mill and even a margarine factory in London.

Tony enjoyed himself at Brickendonbury, feeling that the atmosphere was 'a bit of a joke – fun'. The subject suited his interest in chemistry and engineering and, as a bonus for someone with a lifelong love of railways, there was even an opportunity to drive a steam engine when his course included a visit to the Royal Engineers at Longmoor in Hampshire. Along with industrial sabotage, railways were essential targets. Building on what he had learnt at Camusdarach, Tony received instruction on how to prepare and place a variety of charges on railway lines. The exercises included work in tunnels: in the darkness the trainee saboteurs were obliged to keep their positions at the level of the train's wheels as it passed by and Tony recalled it was 'First-class training because you weren't terrified when you did it for real'. There was little in the way of formal, written theory and chemical analysis on the course but the students learned basic rules such as 'Never run away from a primed explosive'. Improvisation featured in lectures, and they were encouraged to improve on the efficacy of the devices – for example, by placing inflammable material around a pocket incendiary. They were shown that, in the absence of PE, petrol would make a perfectly suitable replacement demolition explosive. An ordinary, gallon can of fuel, when detonated in a confined area by a primer placed under the handle, possessed an awesome destructive capability. The course at STS 17 was intended to instruct Tony to be a saboteur but, just as importantly, he was trained to pass on his skills to his future recruits. It was one thing to carry out a sabotage attack himself but he was to discover that it was far more difficult to teach willing but inexperienced French resistance fighters, 'Training the saboteur was the hardest thing of all.'

Once again, Tony acquitted himself well on this, the last of his SOE training courses, which finished on 16 May 1942. Rheam's report was of a similar vein to the others written about him over the preceding months; 'A little light-hearted, but worked well and was well up in most of the subject [*sic*] taught. He was attentive and exceptionally observant on all visits. His Mutual Instruction was good.'[15] The comment about light-heartedness may perhaps have reflected Rheam's response to a practical joke in which Tony was an accomplice. The School pet, a Scottish terrier, received a label on its collar that read 'For God's sake don't stick a detonator up my arse, I've swallowed some PE'.

Back at F Section, preparations continued for Tony's departure to France. Buckmaster was convinced that, although Tony was already the youngest of SOE's agents, he should have a cover story that made him several years younger. The head of F Section recalled, 'His youth was his best protection. At a time when Frenchmen between eighteen and forty were liable to be drafted forcibly into German war factories, his identity card, showing a date of birth in 1926, proved invaluable.'[16] Buckmaster's recollections are, once again, unreliable. The 1942 compulsory worker legislation was imposed after Tony's return to France while the even more stringent Service du Travail Obligatoire (STO) was not introduced until 16 February 1943.[17] The argument for making him younger than his real age could not therefore have been inspired by a threatened call-up to work in Germany. When Tony got sight of the proposed brief for his cover story, he requested an interview with Captain Gerry Morel, one of Buckmaster's senior staff officers, in order that he might propose some amendments. He argued that his papers should make him old enough to have been a soldier in 1940 and, rather than accept documents stating that he had been captured and released by the Germans, he wished to claim that he had not been taken prisoner. Tony proposed that in order to operate in the *Unoccupied* Zone, he needed to have been born in the *Occupied* Zone to facilitate opportunities for bureaucratic snags if the Vichy authorities tried to check up on his false identity. He had a place in mind; Cormeilles-en-Parisis on the outskirts of Paris. From first-hand experience he knew that it was a place inhabited by groups of Chinese immigrants and communists

RIGHT A young Tony Brooks in pensive mood.

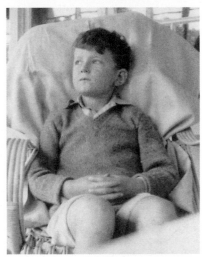

BELOW Tony (left) and his brother, Peter, on the Swiss ski slopes in 1934.

BELOW Tony (second from left) and his Chillon School rowing crew, 1937. His friend Gottlob, the German refugee, is to his left.

ABOVE The Brookses' family residence in France, the Château de Proby.

BELOW Tony (left) with family and friends at Proby, 22 May 1941,
five days before his departure for Marseille and the Seamen's Mission.
His aunt Ruth, with whom he assisted British evaders, is on the far right.

RIGHT The Reverend Donald Caskie, Marseille, May 1940 – photograph taken by Tony.

ABOVE The Seamen's Mission, Marseille, which became a centre for British personnel trying to escape to Spain.

RIGHT Tony's companions, Kenneth Doggett (right) and Leslie Price, who accompanied him in the crossing of the Pyrenees. The photograph was probably taken shortly before their departure from Marseille.

ABOVE Maurice Buckmaster, the head of SOE's F Section – Tony's commanding (if somewhat distant) officer.

ABOVE Brian Stonehouse, Tony's colleague in their F Section training party. A wireless operator, he did not share Tony's luck but miraculously survived imprisonment in several concentration camps.

ABOVE Marcus Bloom 'Urbain' – the wireless operator sent to work with Tony and PIMENTO. Sadly, his SOE career was short-lived and ended in tragedy.

ABOVE Studio portrait of a very youthful Lieutenant Anthony Brooks taken shortly before his departure for France in July 1942.

ABOVE RAF Tempsford – the base for clandestine flights in support of SOE from 1942 until the end of the war in Europe. Gibraltar Farm, the buildings in which SOE agents received their final preparations, is on the right of the photograph inside the taxiing perimeter.

BELOW L9613 V, the Halifax aircraft of No. 138 Squadron that flew Tony to France on 1/2 July 1942. This photograph was taken during a subsequent operation to Egypt.

LEFT The tree on the Citerne farm on to which Tony landed on the night of 1/2 July 1942.

BELOW The Citerne farmhouse, Saint-Léonard-de-Noblat.

BOTTOM Tony with Jean Citerne and his wife during a post-war visit.

René Bertholet – the Swiss political activist who became Tony's mentor and friend.

Tony with his friend and PIMENTO colleague Raymond Bizot after the war.

and the transitory nature of some of its population might inhibit suspicion if records 'appeared to have been lost'. To Tony's relief, his representations proved successful and F Section produced forged documents with 4 April 1917 as his date of birth, five years older than reality. His birthday (if not the real year) was, like much of his cover story, based on his real life:

My [notional] father had died from wounds shortly after the First World War on the date my brother was in fact born so I would not forget the date. My mother had been ill and moved to Switzerland in 1927 (this was fact) and had died there in 1932 (again fact). I had done my

*French demobilisation certificate provided by SOE as
part of Tony's 'Antoine Brévin' false documentation.*

schooling in Switzerland (fact and which could account for any slip in my French accent). My higher education had been at the École Central, the engineering College of Paris University (in fact my cousin had been there and I knew the place), but my call up prevented me getting a degree.[18]

He was given the alias 'Antoine Brévin' in keeping with SOE's policy that an agent's false identity should bear the initials of their real name. F Section practice dictated he was also to have a 'field name', 'Theodore', by which he would be addressed in communications with London. However, Tony decided that 'Theodore' was not for him. He wanted to have a name that, if overheard, possessed a ready explanation. There was no reason why someone might address an 'Antoine' as 'Theodore', however, 'Alphonse', his training name, was another matter entirely. He knew that there were many smutty French jokes featuring characters called 'Alphonse' and he trusted that his ability to recount one of these humorous tales might defuse unwelcome questions if he was questioned about the name. Finally, it was decided that Tony's putative network or, in F Section's more favoured term, 'circuit', was to be called PIMENTO.[19]

The next phase of the evolution of Tony's mission has not left a clear trace in SOE records but a telegram of 12 May 1942 from its representatives in Berne provides an indication of progress:

1. Robert fixed following for meeting with your organiser: Friday May 29th at office of Colis Suisse 17 Boulevard Bon Repos Toulous [sic]. Offices are ground floor. Time of meeting 11am.

2. Organiser should say in French 'I want to meet Monsieur Pierre'. When Robert presents himself organiser should say in French 'It is you Monsieur Pierre'. Robert will answer in affirmative. Organiser should say 'I come from Henri'. Robert will reply 'Henri Hauck is my friend.'[20]

The May date evidently slipped as Tony did not complete his STS 17 training until the 16th of the month. A message from London to Berne on 19 June 1942 provided revised arrangements, 'Organiser leaving probably 1st July we agree rendezvous 3rd, 4th or 6th, time and passwords'. 'Robert' was asked to arrange safe lodging for the newcomer but was not to concern himself regarding the arrival of a second agent, for, it was revealed, 'W/T operator and set not ready will follow next moon.'[21]

As the Baker Street planning gradually unfolded, Tony found a welcome distraction from the tension and frustration of endless SOE meetings and briefings. He visited Hope Munday at her family's home in Cambridgeshire and their courtship blossomed in the respites granted from Tony's demanding training regime. The prospect of his imminent departure was perhaps a factor in their decision to become engaged, but this happy event was but a brief interlude of normality in the young peoples' lives as the clandestine war began to engulf them.

While Tony awaited his despatch to France, his training colleagues were starting to embark on their missions. Tragically, their fortunes ranged from bad to catastrophic. Ted Coppin left by air for Gibraltar on 31 May 1942 en route to a clandestine insertion by sea to the South of France. His mission was to establish the BAY sabotage group and develop the clandestine delivery of SOE supplies on the Mediterranean coast. The few, surviving, fragmentary documents suggest that Coppin did well but after almost a year operating in France, he was arrested in April 1943. The precise details of his ultimate fate are uncertain and the official record starkly states he was 'killed in captivity' on 27 September 1943.[22] A month after Coppin's departure, Tony's close friend, Raymond Flower, was parachuted into France on 27/8 June 1942. His mission as 'Gaspard' was to create the MONKEYPUZZLE circuit, but his performance was unimpressive; Flower was labelled 'undistinguished for security sense or forethought' and his circuit 'never really got going properly'.[23] The agent encountered problems with members of his network to the extent that he suspected his courier and a locally recruited assistant of being German agents. So substantial were Flower's concerns, that he asked London to send him poison to liquidate the 'traitors' should the need arise. Thankfully, his fears proved unfounded and the lethal tablets remained unused. Nevertheless, enmity within the network was strong and one of Flower's associates made the unflattering description of him, 'I have met some rats in my time but never one like this with all the vices contained in one man.'[24]

Brian Stonehouse, who had left Tony's 27L training course before the Beaulieu stage, was parachuted to Chédigny in the Unoccupied Zone of

France on 30 June/1 July 1942, while Bob Sheppard, a fellow Miranda de Ebro inmate, dropped near to Villefranche-sur-Saône a month earlier. Both men were luckless. Sheppard had the appalling ill-fortune to land on the roof of a gendarmerie billet and was arrested almost before he had got out of his parachute harness. He escaped from captivity a year later but was recaptured when attempting to cross into Spain. After further trials and tribulations Sheppard was sent to Dachau concentration camp where he encountered Stonehouse.[25] The latter, bearing the field name 'Celestin', had been sent to France to serve as the wireless operator of the DETECTIVE circuit. He lost his set on landing, then, having recovered it, went to Lyon. In spite of illness and technical difficulties, Stonehouse played an important role in establishing early radio links between London and the city that was to acquire the title, 'capital of French resistance'. The sheer scale of wireless traffic he was obliged to maintain (eighty-one messages transmitted in less than two months) proved detrimental to the observance of sound security procedures. Moreover, Denise Bloch, one of Stonehouse's helpers, reported, 'he did not speak French very well' and commented that he always had a sketchbook to hand even though she 'was continually telling him it was dangerous'. Bloch also stated that the agent spoke English while walking in the street with her and these flaws led her to conclude that 'he was very homesick and was too young for his job'. Stonehouse was eventually tracked down by the Vichy security services and arrested on 24 October 1942 when transmitting from a château outside Lyon. The French authorities subsequently handed him over to the Germans and he spent the rest of the war miraculously surviving a succession of Nazi prisons and concentration camps.[26]

While his contemporaries were putting their heads into the lion's mouth, Tony languished in inactivity in London. A brief visit to see Hope in Cambridge where she was working for the Admiralty brought some temporary respite from his professional frustrations. But the notification of his promotion on 22 June 1942 to the acting rank of lieutenant failed to compensate for his increasing fretfulness that found its outlet in the constant invocation to his F Section superiors, 'For Christ's sake, let's get going'.[27]

Chapter Six
'Je Veux Voir Monsieur Pierre'

By the end of June 1942 the seemingly never-ending, stop-go planning for Tony's departure for France at last really seemed to be drawing to a conclusion. He was sent to one of SOE's specialist tailors and kitted out with a set of French clothes appropriate for his age and cover story as 'Antoine Brévin'. The simple ensemble consisted of a suit, a pair of slacks, a couple of shirts, a tie, two pairs of shoes and washing kit. All of the material was checked for its authenticity and some had been bought in British shops from stocks of French manufactured goods or acquired from refugees arriving in the United Kingdom from Occupied Europe. Next, a series of briefings provided Tony with the details of his infiltration into France. He was to be parachuted 'blind' – without a reception committee of helpers waiting for him on the ground – into the Unoccupied Zone near Limoges. On landing, he was to make for Le Bas Soleil, the house of 'Gauthier' one of F Section's most important agents, who would afford him a starting point for the next stage of his journey to Toulouse. Tony was given the precise location of the house and a password with which he might establish his bona fides but was not furnished with any other details of his contact.

In the early summer of 1942, the Royal Air Force's resources in effecting clandestine flights were very limited. A small unit, No.419 Flight, had been formed in August 1940 to infiltrate agents into enemy territory but, as the secret war burgeoned, demand soon far exceeded supply. On 25 August

1941, the Flight became No.138 (Special Duty) Squadron but expansion and elevation to full squadron status did not solve the problems of meeting the requirements of both SOE and SIS in parachuting agents and supplies into enemy territory. These difficulties were compounded by the reluctance of senior RAF officers to release aircraft for secret missions as they held firm convictions that the war was best prosecuted by dropping bombs on enemy factories rather than infiltrating saboteurs behind the lines. Nevertheless, on 15 February 1942 a second special duties squadron, No.161, was formed and given the primary task of servicing the requirements of SIS. Then, in March 1942, No.138 Squadron moved to a new and permanent home at Tempsford airfield in Bedfordshire. This became the centre of the RAF's clandestine parachute operations for the rest of the war, a place of departure for hundreds of agents and thousands of tons of stores for the Resistance. While some F Section agents were infiltrated by sea across the English Channel or landed on the southern coast of France, Tony discovered to his immense relief, that he was destined to be one of those sent in by parachute.

On the afternoon of 1 July 1942 he was collected from his London hotel and driven in the company of his conducting officer, Bourne-Paterson, to SOE's holding establishment, Station 61, Gaynes Hall, a country house situated a short drive from Tempsford airfield. Here, he was the recipient of the VIP treatment extended to agents about to undertake that momentous journey into enemy territory. SOE appreciated that the parachutists' morale might, understandably, be uncertain and that it should be strengthened by making their last few hours in England memorable with the provision of good food, comfortable surroundings and engaging company. Apart from distracting the agents from the prospect of dangers ahead, it was intended that their memories of 'home' would be warm and affectionate, and, in any future moments of loneliness and peril, these recollections would form an enduring reminder of the colleagues who were supporting them and working for their safe return. On Tony's arrival at Gaynes Hall a pre-prandial gin and orange was followed by an excellent dinner. The meal was accompanied by copious amounts of wine and completed by an enormous glass of brandy that left the normally teetotal Tony feeling decidedly 'mellow' as was the intention. Eventually, word arrived from the airfield that the weather and aircraft readiness were satisfactory, and Tony was chauffeured in a shooting brake the ten miles to the aerodrome.

Passing through the station's tight security, he was driven to the eastern side of the airfield where they alighted at Gibraltar Farm, a cottage and outhouses that had been retained from the days when the airbase was nothing but farmland. In these buildings SOE had established a dressing room and final embarkation point for agents. Already wearing his French civilian clothes, Tony was issued with his false papers and 200,000 francs – a substantial amount of money – while a close check was made for any potentially incriminating British manufacturers' labels, notes, tickets or cash on his person.*

It was then time to kit him out in the full paraphernalia of an SOE parachutist. An RAF Flight Sergeant helped him get into his 'striptease' jumpsuit, a voluminous one-piece garment. Its nickname was derived from the configuration of two zips that ran from the neck to the ankle of each leg, allowing an agent to disrobe in an instant. That was the theory, but the many and capacious pockets of Tony's 'striptease' were now filled with an array of survival equipment. A special jackknife on a cord was placed in a pocket on his arm, while first aid and 24-hour survival packs, field dressings, a spade and shaft (it being pointed out that this made a passable splint in the event of a rough landing) and a hip flask full of rum all found their designated homes in the overall. The suit contained not one but two pockets for pistols, but when the Flight Sergeant proffered a Colt .32 automatic, the first hitch of the evening occurred. Politely but firmly, Tony told him that he did not want the firearm. The RAF man was nonplussed and evidently assumed that the rejection was either an act of bravado or a loss of nerve by the agent. In fact, it was another example of Tony's self-confidence, informed by his understanding of the true state of affairs in France. A gun would be an asset in a shoot-out, but its discovery could demolish a cover story in an instant and transform an innocuous spot check for black-market contraband into the unmasking of a terrorist or gangster. Tony intended from the outset to rely on his wits and, perhaps even more importantly, to follow the Beaulieu precepts of detailed preparation and a watertight alias to avoid trouble. He gauged

---

* The checking of the agents' clothes and pockets was essential. One conducting officer was censured for failing to take appropriate action when it was noticed that the metal heels on an agent's shoes bore a British manufacturer's name. For details of SOE equipment see *The Secret Agent's Handbook of Special Devices*.

that the risks of carrying a gun far outweighed the likelihood of it solving a crisis. But the rejection of the pistol necessitated a search for official-issue ledgers in order that the list of allocated stores be duly amended. There soon followed a repeat performance when Tony declined his 'L Tablet' – a lethal poison pill. The Flight Sergeant was now becoming rather exasperated. It was not his place to question why Tony would not accept his suicide pill but, had he done so, the agent could not have given a clear-cut reason. Tony later commented that he simply could not envisage a situation when he would have felt capable of taking his own life. So, the paperwork was once again amended, and the Flight Sergeant resumed the rest of his duties, kitting out Tony with overshoes, gauntlets and a helmet that made up the remainder of the agent's regalia. Now, rather than rejecting an item of equipment, Tony turned his thoughts to acquiring something – his parachute. He was reassured to learn that he would find this on the aircraft along with his suitcase.

Tony and Bourne-Paterson were driven to the dispersal bay where the aircraft awaited them. Introductions were made to the Polish captain, the pilot and the RAF dispatcher whose duties were to look after the agent during the flight and ensure his safe exit from the aeroplane. The aircraft was a Handley Page Halifax bomber, 9613, of No. 138 (Special Duty) Squadron, captained by Flying Officer Radomir Walczak.[1] In keeping with Polish practice, the captain was the senior officer of the crew, not necessarily the pilot – Walczak was the observer/navigator. He had only undertaken two other special duty flights to France. The first, at the beginning of June, had been completed while the second, only four days before Tony's flight, had been unsuccessful.[2]

Just as Tony was about to board the aircraft, Bourne-Paterson requested a quiet word. Expecting some form of valedictory pep talk, Tony was surprised to be informed that there was still time for him to pull out of the operation. The frustrations of the preceding months, never mind his uncompromising determination to enter the fray, ensured that Tony had no intention of losing his resolve at this late stage and he immediately declined the offer. Bourne-Paterson next explained that as Tony had now affirmed his intention to proceed, he would need to sign a will. It was hardly a morale booster yet Tony managed to find some macabre humour in the request. He appended his signature, wished his conducting officer *au revoir* and clambered into the Halifax's fuselage. Once on board, the dispatcher suggested that Tony would be more comfortable and appreciably warmer if he availed himself of the sleeping bag that had been laid out for him. The Halifax took off from Tempsford at 11.45 p.m., and, in spite of the clamour of the engines and the adrenalin rush engendered by the start of his mission, Tony's sangfroid (perhaps supplemented by the after-effects of the dinner and alcohol) resulted in his falling fast asleep.[3] So deep was his slumber that the next thing he knew was the dispatcher waking him and proffering a mug of cocoa and a sandwich. Tony's experiences in the Spanish concentration camp had taught him never to turn down the offer of food and drink: 'I always applied the principle that if trouble was looming, go to it with a full stomach', and he gratefully consumed the snack. Soon the dispatcher announced the pilot had notified their approach to the dropping zone and they should ready themselves. Tony's parachute proved to be the relatively experimental, 'A' Type. Wing Commander John Corby, the Air Ministry representative on SOE's Operations Section, wrote:'The theory was that the Joe [agent] jumped, and this time released his package suspended in the fuselage over the exit-hole. The package in its turn pulled the cord and deployed the parachute.'[4] That was the theory, but as Corby continued, 'Unfortunately, in operation, this type of parachute tended to "Roman Candle" twist round and round, so that ultimately caused the parachute to collapse and allow the man to fall to the ground unsupported.' Tony was to find out that this was not the only shortcoming.

Walczak and his pilot completed their tasks with remarkable accuracy and, in the early hours of 2 July 1942, Tony was delivered to the agreed drop zone, north-east of the village of Saint-Léonard-de-Noblat, near Limoges.[5] The sound of the aircraft's engines resulted in many of the local denizens appearing in their gardens to watch the parachutist's descent. Meanwhile, Tony had other issues to occupy his thoughts for, soon after leaving the Halifax, he was acutely aware that his fourth parachute jump from an aircraft was not to be the most pleasant. Thanks to luck and a tree in the middle of his landing ground, he survived the imperfections of the parachute's design and, very battered by the experience, finally arrived on French soil. But this was hardly a time for elation; his overriding emotions as he crawled away to the edge of the field were shock, apprehension and considerable pain.

From his hiding place in the ditch, Tony thought he heard horses approaching out of the darkness. Peering into the gloom he managed to pick out a tall man dressed in a long, white nightshirt and woollen hat, accompanied by a slim youth, similarly attired. As the figures approached, Tony realised that the 'horses' hoofs' were in fact the men's wooden clogs clipping against each other as they ran. On reaching the tree, the man instructed his companion, 'We must take all this away and hide it and cover up the traces in case the police come. We will then look for him in case he is injured.'[6] These comments seemed so promising that Tony gambled on giving a whistle to attract the attention of the peasant. The man approached and enquired if he was injured. Tony replied that he had damaged his leg and, without demur, he was effortlessly picked up and carried the short distance to a small farmhouse.

Once in the kitchen, the only room on the ground floor, the man gently set his burden down in a chair by a large fireplace, opened a door at the base of an enclosed staircase and shouted '*Femme!*' In response, a middle-aged woman appeared and greeted the stranger nervously but with an attempt at a smile. The peasant instructed her to heat some '*jus*' and to add '*un bon verre de St James*' to the bowl. Having given his orders, the man disappeared into the night. In her husband's absence, the woman set about her duties, lighting an oil lamp and heating some coffee. Moving to the far side of the room, she lifted a floorboard and brought out a square, straw-covered bottle of St James rum. By now, the contents of the saucepan were boiling and, pouring a little into a bowl, she added several lumps of sugar and a substantial tot of alcohol. Tony drank the sweet and strongly fortified acorn coffee with relish and, having already taken a large swig of rum before leaving the aircraft, his morale, if not his sobriety, began rapidly to improve.

The peasant eventually returned, looking very pleased with himself and announced that the parachute, together with Tony's jump suit and suitcase, was well hidden in his hay stack. The youth, now identified as the couple's son, René, had also reappeared but was packed off to bed while his father turned his attention to Tony's injured leg. He confirmed that it was dislocated, adding that there was nothing seriously wrong and that the same thing had happened to 'Julie' only a few days previously. This matter-of-fact demeanour reassured Tony as he was told to finish his drink and stand against the side of the kitchen table. A rolled-up towel was put in his groin and his damaged leg was laid along the tabletop. The peasant now drew up Tony's trousers and, murmuring '*Ce n'est rien*', suddenly put all his weight on the damaged knee and thigh. Tony felt a nasty jarring and a shot of pain as his knee straightened and then, to his amazement, found he could flex it and that it could bear his weight. Aware of the risks the farmer was running by harbouring him, Tony asked if there was a copse nearby where he might hide. The farmer 'flew off the handle' at this suggestion and told the agent that he would be spending the night in the farmhouse.[7]

The peasant, a wiry individual, in his late forties, was clearly a man of few words but now introduced himself to Tony as Jean Citerne. Neither man was disposed to enter into a detailed discussion. Citerne asked no questions, and Tony, in turn, was disinclined to interrogate his saviour, doctor and host. However, the Englishman could not help but notice a citation for the Médaille Militaire hanging on the wall that offered further proof, if it was needed, that Citerne was a man of some calibre. Any possible thoughts of conversation were halted when Citerne told Tony that he should rest and helped the injured man up the steep stairs and into a small bedroom that contained little more than a large double bed. Predicting his guest's concerns, Citerne assured Tony that he would be quite safe in the farmhouse as nobody could have seen him enter. But he then spoilt Tony's good humour by reporting that a search was being carried out further down the valley where it was assumed that the parachutist had landed. Citerne then blew out the candle and left Tony to his thoughts. The Frenchman could be heard moving around in the room below and Tony assumed that his host was simply preparing for bed but, after ten minutes, Citerne was back. He proffered an immaculately clean French Army service revolver and with the sangfroid that Tony now began to expect, Citerne said it held six bullets, that there were five gendarmes in Saint-Léonard and that, if it came to a shoot-out: '*Tirez bien*' – 'Shoot well.'[8]

In spite of this warning that he was a hunted man and the continuing pain from his injuries, Tony fell asleep. Some time later he awoke to the sound of voices in the kitchen below. Exploiting a crack in the floorboards he made out the form of Citerne talking to two gendarmes illuminated by the glow of the kitchen's oil lamp. The peasant was doing far more than just talking and was complaining vociferously that the noise of the aircraft had frightened 'Julie'. Only now did Tony realise that 'Julie' was not a member of the family but a cow in calf with a dislocated leg. Warming to his task, the farmer was telling the gendarmes just what he intended doing to the parachutist if he showed his face, culminating in a mock decapitation with his trusty scythe. So convincing was Citerne's performance that the gendarmes even felt the need to pacify him. They instructed him neither to harm nor confront the fugitive (as he was doubtless armed and dangerous) and he must report any sightings to them. Suitably mollified, Citerne poured a round of rum for his guests and the gendarmes went on their way.

The excitement, the rum and the pains in his leg and back did not prevent Tony sleeping until Citerne woke him at mid-morning the next day. He mentioned the gendarmes' visit but the peasant dismissed it with the comment, '*Ceux sont des braves gars* [They are good chaps].' More reassuringly, Citerne reported that he had visited the village and no one had the faintest idea that 'the parachutist' was at his farm, it being assumed that the fugitive must have progressed further up the valley. He related that last night a notorious local busybody (and suspected police informant) had attempted to find where the parachutist had landed. In his haste, the would-be sleuth failed to notice a barbed-wire fence, became entangled and sustained serious cuts. The injuries curtailed the man's snooping but searches continued for three more days with gendarmes returning to the farm to enquire if the parachutist had been sighted. While the investigations continued Citerne refused to allow Tony to leave his sanctuary until his injuries had healed.[9]

Tony Brooks had enjoyed astounding good luck. His descent had been observed by a worryingly large number of Saint-Léonard-de-Noblat inhabitants, he had sustained considerable physical injuries and at first it seemed likely that he would achieve the dubious distinction of possessing one of the most short-lived careers of any secret agent parachuted into France. His salvation was Jean Citerne; a modest man who embodied the best traditions of French patriotism. Citerne unquestioningly took the young agent under his protection and, in so doing, put himself and his family at immense risk. Yet the taciturn farmer neither sought explanations nor assurances – he simply took the decision to offer sanctuary to a complete stranger. During the rest of the war Tony met many brave and resourceful Frenchmen but Citerne was the first and assuredly amongst the very best. It proved a sound start to his clandestine career – but without Jean Citerne it would have been catastrophic. The peasant's remarkable qualities provided hope that things would surely get better.

At this time, F Section was suffering the worst of both worlds in infiltrating its agents into France. There were so few circuits in operation that many new arrivals were, like Tony, dropped 'blind'. Obviously, this meant that agents were without assistance if landings resulted in physical injury – not everyone was as lucky as Tony in encountering a Citerne. Similarly, the fragile morale of new arrivals in a strange and hostile land could be seriously damaged if they were delivered alone and many miles off target from their intended dropping zone. On the other hand, there were security benefits in a solitary drop – there was always the risk that a network might have been penetrated by the enemy, and agents were sometimes parachuted straight into the hands of a German-controlled reception.[10] But the advantages of a 'blind' drop were frequently negated by F Section instructing new arrivals to make contact with existing networks. Thus, Tony had been told to make for Le Bas Soleil, the estate of one of F Section's earliest locally recruited agents, code-named 'Gauthier'. This *nom de guerre* was soon found to be redundant for, when Tony asked Jean Citerne if he knew of a house called Le Bas Soleil, he received the reply that he was acquainted with the property and 'Gauthier', Baron Philippe de Vomécourt.

On 5 July Tony told the Citernes that he was fit enough to make his way to Le Bas Soleil which, Citerne had informed him, was only a few kilometres from the farm. His decision was inspired by more than a desire to get on with his mission, for he was also concerned for the family's safety if he remained with them any longer. His worries were confirmed that afternoon when Citerne's daughters returned from school and reported that Germans from the Armistice Commission based in Limoges had arrived in the village. In spite of this news, Citerne attempted to persuade Tony to stay but the agent was adamant that he needed to press on to Le Bas Soleil. They arrived at a compromise and Tony accepted the offer that Citerne's daughters would escort him through the woods to the vicinity of de Vomécourt's house. In the late afternoon, Tony finally took his leave of Jean Citerne. Even as a novice secret agent, he recognised how remarkably fortunate he had been to find himself in the care of such a kind, resourceful and patriotic Frenchman. The debt Tony felt towards his unassuming saviour did not fade but continued to grow with the passage of the years.[11]

At dusk, Tony and the Citerne girls reached a vantage point overlooking Le Bas Soleil. Having said farewell to his guides, Tony kept the house under observation until dark and then made his way down the hill and across the fields to his objective. The château was quite modest and Tony felt it compared unfavourably to his uncle's home, Proby. De Vomécourt described it as 'a colonial style house, square, with balconies running round it, built about a hundred years ago by my wife's great-grandfather'.[12] As Tony approached the property he had little time to scrutinise it at close quarters, for a middle-aged woman was soon running towards him calling out, *'Ah, vous êtes le parachutiste!'* In spite of the woman's cavalier attitude to tradecraft, Tony would not be deprived of his first operational use of a password and duly delivered it. Disappointingly, this failed to elicit the correct response so he asked for 'Gauthier'.[13]. The woman informed him that his contact was due back at suppertime and Tony should wait for him. Introducing herself as Madame Lot, the woman ushered him into the house and led him upstairs through darkened rooms to an obscure part of the house where the footprints they left in the dust on the floor bore witness that this part of the château had been unopened for a long time. Mme Lot continued to prattle away leaving Tony to understand that she anticipated he would be a resident at Le Bas Soleil for several days.

Later that evening de Vomécourt arrived. Tony had not been told what to expect but considered that the short, bespectacled man, aged about forty, did not cut an impressive figure; but the de Vomécourt family possessed close and longstanding connections with the United Kingdom. Tony's host, Philippe, had been educated in England during the First World War, while a brother, Jean, had served as a pilot with the Royal Flying Corps. Following the armistice of 1940, Philippe and Jean remained in France while yet another sibling, Pierre, escaped to Britain where he volunteered his services to SOE and was amongst the first of F Section's agents to be sent back to his homeland. Dropped 'blind' near Châteauroux on 9/10 May 1941, Pierre de Vomécourt wasted no time in calling on his brother at Le Bas Soleil and recruited him. Thereafter Philippe had done excellent work, receiving in June 1941 the RAF's very first supply drop to France. Adopting the codename 'Gauthier', he developed a substantial network in the Limousin region although, as was typical, his undertakings suffered as a result of the shortage of wireless operators needed to maintain contact with London.

In his memoirs, Philippe de Vomécourt does not mention Tony's arrival.[14] The omission is not particularly significant as Le Bas Soleil served as a reception point for other new agents from England and Tony was merely one of several. But if de Vomécourt later forgot about this newcomer, at the time he was sufficiently well informed to comment that London had told him that Tony was bound for Toulouse. The young agent found this disturbing; it seemed a needless dissemination of information about his mission. Consequently, he felt the need to take the wind out of the sails of the omniscient de Vomécourt and, more important, create a smoke screen. He informed his host, falsely, that his real destination was Paris.[15] The two men ate a simple meal, engaged in a little laboured conversation and then retired early to their beds.

Tony did not stay long with de Vomécourt.[16] He accepted a single railway ticket to Limoges from his host, bade him a somewhat formal farewell and cycled off to the nearby station of Brignac with his injured knee and back standing up pretty well to the journey. Brignac, from which he was to catch a local train to the city, proved to be little more than a halt at a level crossing. Tony examined the ticket that de Vomécourt had given him, noted the price and then tore it up and threw it away. Now knowing the cost of a single fare to Limoges, he could estimate the price of a return and avoid attracting attention by proffering too little or too much money at the ticket counter. Thus began the utilisation of a piece of Beaulieu tradecraft that he employed throughout the war: the purchase of a return ticket meant that any enquiries made about him at the station would lead to the conclusion that pursuit was unnecessary as he would be coming back to his starting point. Similarly, if Tony was questioned by security forces about his journey, a return ticket would facilitate a greater range of cover stories than if he only possessed a single. The precaution was a wise move, for the search for him had still not died down, 'About July 1942 an agent, whose name DE VOMECOURT does not know, was parachuted blind in the neighbourhood of the chateau. The chateau was visited by the French police as a result of this and searched, but nothing unusual was found, and the incident passed off without trouble.'[17]

At last the train for Limoges arrived. This proved to be a small, electric *micheline* that looked more like a tram than a railway train but, in spite of its unimpressive appearance, it maintained a good speed. As the train passed through the countryside, Tony considered the changes he might find in the France that he had left a year earlier. In many respects, there were surprisingly few differences awaiting him. Two years after the shame of defeat and occupation, the fundamental priority was still 'to get by'. Family life and gainful employment were more important than ever and, generally speaking, the risks of adhering to dangerous political principles were best left to someone else. Although living conditions had steadily deteriorated as the war continued, they were not yet so bad that people were unable to maintain the pretence that life was still 'normal'. The French political scene basically remained the same. Even Pierre Laval, who had been dismissed as deputy prime minister in December 1941, was restored to power in April the following year. Pétain still presided over the Unoccupied Zone from Vichy although it was evident that, even in this semi-autonomous state, German influence over everyday life was increasing. The façade of an equal 'partnership' with Nazi Germany and the prospect of an important role for France in the new European Order were maintained by collaborators and the far right but for most French men and women there was only one reality: France was a satellite state of Nazi Germany. A range of anti-Semitic laws was passed with alacrity and enthusiasm by the Vichy authorities. The politicians and civil servants hardly needed any prompting by the Germans to introduce legislation that at first restricted the civil rights of French Jews. Subsequent edicts brought about arrests, the enforced wearing of yellow stars marked '*Juif*' and, ultimately, deportation to the death camps in Eastern Europe. Although these excesses at first manifested themselves most strongly in the Occupied Zone, the ghastliness soon spread south into Vichy. But the Jews were not the only scapegoats for France's woes, and other victims were readily to hand. The former leaders of the Third Republic were subjected to a show trial for their mishandling in 1940 of the nation's affairs and, between February and April 1942, the old regime's politicians and generals were held to account for their 'failings' and France's defeat.

Everyday life was tougher in the north where German occupation made it all but impossible to believe in the fantasy of a genuinely independent French state. Partly as a result of these conditions, more militant forms of resistance began to manifest themselves in the Occupied Zone as many found it increasingly difficult to stay on the sidelines of the conflict. The German invasion of the Soviet Union had provoked the French communist party into resistance, it having previously stood aloof from action. Yet, in spite of its steady growth, resistance remained an activity in which only a very small fraction of the French people were engaged. In the year that Tony had been away, small groups of resisters drawn from many political persuasions had begun to organise themselves, but these cells were, in the main, fractured and ill-coordinated. The Free French in London attempted to bond these groups together, and emissaries such as Morandat were sent to France while resistance leaders made the reverse trip for consultation with de Gaulle's staff. Meanwhile, F Section continued with its pragmatic aims and objectives. Tony and other agents might be assigned limited political tasks (such as making contact with Jouhaux) but their primary purpose was to locate or create groups of patriots who would be willing to make a military contribution to the Allied war effort.

It was early evening by the time Tony reached Limoges and with his train to Toulouse not leaving until one o'clock the following morning, he did not relish hanging around the station for several hours. He therefore found a nearby cinema and watched *La Grande Valse*: 'This considerably cheered me as the last time I had seen this film was the night I left France for England almost exactly a year previously.'[18] On his return to the station, he went to the buffet and, spotting a mother with two children, asked her to look after his suitcase for a moment. His intention was to absorb the ambience of France in 1942 and pick up the tempo of everyday life. He walked around the station concourse for about ten minutes then, concerned that the guardian of his luggage might consider his absence suspicious, he bought a third-class return ticket to Toulouse and returned to her. It was now his turn to be the Good Samaritan and he minded her older child while she went to feed the baby. He remained with the young family, exploiting them as cover, until it was time to get them onto their train for La Souterraine. Now, having discharged his duties, he boarded the Toulouse express just as it was about to pull out, 'The train was already packed with people standing everywhere and yet 200 or so on the platform intended to get on. I was one of the lucky ones.' With no seats available in the third-class carriages, there was nothing for it but to sit on his suitcase in the corridor. Sustained by his last scraps of British chocolate, he settled down to a fitful and uncomfortable night's sleep – it was to be the first but by no means the last time he would pass a journey in this way.[19]

Toulouse's Matabiau station seemed at first little different from Tony's last visit in 1940 but an identity check as he left the platform gave an early indication that things had changed. He was reassured to find that any doubts he had entertained about his forged papers were dispelled when they passed police scrutiny without comment. But there was no time for complacency and the first priority was to reconnoitre his rendezvous before the eleven o'clock appointment. Leaving the station, he walked across the bridge that spanned the canal du Midi and, looking to his right, saw the boulevard Bon Repos that ran along the side of the waterway. Situated near a large warehouse, was a dingy-looking building with the name 'Colis Suisse' written above the door. Still too early for his meeting, he went to a café-bar for breakfast. Tony's identity papers had stood up well to scrutiny but now it was the test of his ration cards. He ordered a sandwich and discovered how food shortages had affected French culinary standards. The bread was grey and the pâté filling was so devoid of meat that it did not require a ration coupon. However, he received an insight into the complexities of rationing when he proferred bread coupons and received 'change' from the waitress for his large 'denomination stamps' from some smaller examples accepted from another diner. These intricacies did not spoil his appetite: for a man who had survived Miranda de Ebro, the sandwich 'filled a hole'.

Well before the outbreak of the Second World War, Toulouse had felt the effects of European political turmoil. Substantial numbers of Italian refugees fleeing from Mussolini's repressive regime had arrived, while the city became France's 'front line' during the Spanish Civil War. The 'Phoney War' had seen the city enjoy relative tranquillity compared to the military preoccupations on France's northern and eastern frontiers. But this proved merely a brief interlude of calm and the German invasion in 1940 brought a huge influx of refugees with the city's population doubling to nearly half a million.[20] In spite of its strong socialist heritage and underlying anti-Nazi sentiment, Toulouse was as susceptible as any other community of the need to accept the reality of Vichy government. Pétain paid a formal visit in November 1940 and, by and large, the city fell in with the demands of the new regime as the old political administration departed to be replaced by politicians and civil servants willing to acquiesce to Vichy's orders.[21]

Having finished his snack, Tony presented himself at the Colis Suisse. Peering into the gloom of the warehouse, he saw that it was full of wooden crates and sacks. Men and women speaking Spanish were making up parcels of foodstuffs while behind a desk constructed of empty date boxes sat a small, bald man in his late fifties. Tony offered his password in the best Beaulieu manner, '*Je veux voir Monsieur Pierre*' but was more than a little disturbed by a response that was accurately delivered in French with a hint of a German accent. '*Vous voulez voir Pierre?*' asked the man and then, on cue, a tall, thin figure emerged from the darkness at the back of the garage, introducing himself as 'Pierre'. Tony and 'Pierre' then exchanged the further litany of passwords specified in the SOE telegrams passed between Berne and London. But the secret checks were superfluous. In an instant Tony recognised his contact; it was René Bertholet, the friend of Marcel Guerret whom he had befriended during his stay at Montauban almost two years earlier. For his part, Bertholet showed no signs of familiarity and simply suggested that they stretch their legs and take a walk along the canal. Now, without any fear of being overheard, the two men were able freely to discuss their earlier acquaintanceship.

Fate had delivered Tony to a man of exceptional quality. The novice secret agent's new colleague was a seasoned master of clandestine activity who, as Tony was aware from their earlier meeting, had an impressive track record in opposing fascism in Germany, France and Spain. But how had he become involved with SOE? It is now possible to sketch some of the complexities of Bertholet's activities with information denied to Tony at the time. First and foremost, the agent's motivation was a single-minded opposition to the Nazis wherever they manifested themselves. This stance resulted in his developing associations with a variety of like-minded people and organisations. Thus, during the Phoney War period he was in contact with the 5th Bureau of French military intelligence, its Service de Renseignement (SR) and the British SIS. [22] Bertholet always took great pains to maintain his independence and refute any assumption that he was a mercenary tool of these organisations. Rather, he worked with them in their common cause of opposing the Nazis and, specifically, as a means of sustaining the beleaguered and scattered fortunes of the International Transport Workers Federation (ITF). He continued his connection with SIS throughout the war but the links with French Intelligence were presumably severed by the defeat of 1940. Details of Bertholet's recruitment into SOE are incomplete; the surviving files simply record him as, de facto, a member of its organisation 'early in 1941'. His position is further complicated by a shared allegiance to SOE's Swiss,

German, French and Italian Sections. Unusually, for an agency that sought to ensure its agents served but one master, Bertholet achieved the remarkable distinction of working for a quartet of SOE operational departments. By the end of July 1941 he had been allotted the codename 'Robert' by SOE's Swiss Section while he also answered to 'Charles' and 'Leo' in correspondence. It was inevitable that the German Section would take a close interest in him and, as early as 1 September 1941, Major Ronald Thornley, its head, wrote a memo requesting that Bertholet 'establish lines to the transport workers in Germany', promote the General Council of the ITF's appeal to German left-wingers to carry out sabotage and develop the smuggling of 'communications, small parcels and bulk material' into the Reich. Bertholet was a very important figure in resistance circles by the time of Tony's arrival. An official history of SOE records, 'The Internationalier Sozialistiche Kampfbund [*sic*] (ISK) also offered useful contacts in Switzerland, mainly through a certain René Bertholet (Charles), who proved valuable for work into France and Italy as well as into Germany. His activities as regards Germany interlocked to some extent with those of the International Transport-Workers Federation (ITF), which was a valuable line of approach to railway workers throughout Europe.'[23]

After meeting Tony in Montauban in the summer of 1940, Bertholet had returned to Switzerland where he lived in Zurich with his wife, Hanna, a German-born fellow member of the ISK. She remained for the rest of the war in her husband's homeland but Bertholet found unpaid employment (and a marvellous cover story) as the official delegate of 'l'Entr'Aide Ouvrière Suisse' in the Unoccupied Zone of France. The organisation had been founded by Swiss trade unionists during the Depression to provide aid to the families of striking workers. It also supported Spanish Civil War refugees in France and the Colis Suisse organisation was formed to distribute packages of foodstuffs to the needy. But Bertholet was disseminating more than food parcels; he collected intelligence for the Allies from France, Switzerland, Germany and Italy, and helped lay the groundwork for resistance groups among trade unions in the Unoccupied Zone. Bertholet was, above all, an idealist. That said, he was an idealist prepared to adopt pragmatic action to achieve his ultimate objectives. This probably explains how he reconciled his left-wing political beliefs with aiding Allied secret agencies. Bertholet's connections to British, French and United States secret services (he was later on the books of the Office of Strategic Services too) are a matter of record, while a connection with Soviet Intelligence is less easy to trace.[24] Whatever the full extent of Bertholet's complex portfolio of secret associations, July 1942 witnessed the beginning of one of his most important undertakings – his work with Tony to create the PIMENTO network.[25]

The intervening years since their brief encounter in Montauban had not dimmed Tony's admiration for the Swiss activist. A unity of purpose and outlook was clear and this link between the two men stood them in good stead in the difficult years to come. Moreover, while deeply committed to political aims and objectives, Bertholet retained a lively sense of humour and a friendly personality. An aesthete, he was neither austere nor without interest in creature comforts. He smoked like a chimney and Tony discovered that although his colleague was ostensibly teetotal and a vegetarian, he would take a restorative alcoholic drink and become a carnivore when the opportunity presented itself.

Bertholet had a strong interest in the practical nature of Tony's future sabotage work. As early as 2 October 1941, William Sullivan, one of SOE's men in Switzerland (JQ100), reported:

> I discussed toys and games [sabotage material] with Robert [Bertholet]. He seems to have a pretty good knowledge of this department, having worked at one time in collaboration with the French 5th Bureau. He said that our [time] pencils in the past were not at all that they might be, the acid tending to leak out of the container. The fog signal idea was new to him and he was very much interested. I explained to him that supplies for the time being would have to be very strictly limited and that in any case there would be no question of handing them out until we were sure of the discretion and capacity of those who would handle them. Robert has some quite interesting ideas about thermos flasks and narrow cylindrical explosive charges, with minute timing apparatus to be inserted in the grease boxes of railway wagons.[26]

Such was Bertholet's interest in 'active measures' that in the autumn of 1941 SOE in London was instructing its representatives in Switzerland to restrain him from carrying out sabotage in the Unoccupied Zone of France, 'Stop supplying him toys [sabotage devices] if you are not convinced he will refrain using these in France.'[27]

During the stroll along the canal side, Bertholet informed Tony that the bald-headed man at the Colis Suisse with the suspicious accent was Auguste Bottemer, alias 'Claude Denis'. He was completely trustworthy having been a journalist in Alsace before the Germans began the expulsion of French citizens after the French region was incorporated into the Reich. His status as a Jew of left-wing political beliefs had provided further inspiration for a move to the relative safety of Toulouse. Bertholet then gave Tony a rundown on the contacts with which he proposed to furnish him, including a clandestine courier link to Switzerland. Messages could be conveyed via the Colis Suisse (and associated trade union networks) to Switzerland where they would be passed to the British Embassy in Berne then communicated by wireless to SOE in London. Bertholet outlined their respective areas of responsibility, explaining that 'he had a political job to do' while Tony would 'build up a set of my own friends to do any sabotage'.[28] With the initial parameters of their future work covered, Tony confessed that the experiences of the last few days had left him exhausted. So Bertholet escorted him to an apartment at 52, rue Saint-Rémésy, the home of Bertholet's mistress, Hélène Perret, 'Mousy'. A fellow Swiss, her association with Bertholet went back to the early 1930s and the left-wing 'Cercle International de Jeunesse'. In October 1940 she had taken employment with another charitable organisation, Le Secours Suisse aux Enfants, located in Toulouse's rue du Taur. Ever the professional, Bertholet warned Tony that Perret ought to be treated with caution and should only be used to pass messages in an emergency. He added a further note of caution concerning her fellow worker, Jo Tempi, whom he described as a dedicated communist activist. Hélène Perret was not without her own strong communist connections, being the sister-in-law of Jules Humbert-Droz, a leading light in the Swiss Communist Party. Tony's first impression of Perret was that she seemed nice enough and any political complications could be avoided or addressed in the future. His immediate domestic needs constituted the greatest priority; the flat 'was very Bohemian, full of paintings, dirty linen and bicycles' but possessed sufficient facilities to 'wash and clean up generally and make myself look like a French civilian'.[29] Bertholet returned that evening and proposed that Tony rendezvous with him in Lyon in three days' time at the Café Français, Place Antonin Poncet, where some useful contacts would be introduced.

With a few days' grace before the appointment in Lyon, Tony decided to renew contact with his family and friends at Poligny. In the absence of details of his SOE briefing, it cannot be said that he was contravening instructions in making this return to his old haunts. He later conceded that his motives were both professional and personal. On the one hand, the wisdom of visiting places where he was known to be an Englishman was at odds with the elaborate construction of his French cover story. However, Tony wished to investigate the possibility of developing another alias by resurrecting his erstwhile career as a member of the transportation department of the factory at Grozon. This made some sense as he possessed the first-hand experience to create a convincing cover story as a truck driver, but there was a huge risk in pretending to be an employee of his uncle's company. He could not reappear among his old workmates without attracting a great deal of attention and unwelcome questions. On the other hand, he felt that in an uncertain world there was much to commend the acquisition of a bolt-hole amongst family and friends. Moreover, the visit would provide the opportunity of supplementing his limited wardrobe with clothes he had left behind at his uncle's château a year previously as clothes rationing in France in the summer of 1942 was stringent.

Tony left Toulouse soon after his meeting with Bertholet and arrived at Lons-le-Saunier the following evening where he contacted a family friend, Robert Dick. An Alsatian in his mid-thirties, Dick was married to an Englishwoman and had previously helped Tony in his work aiding British servicemen on the run. As the local *Greffier du Tribunal* (Clerk of the Court) Dick was a man of substance and social standing. Although Tony only related the bare minimum about the circumstances surrounding his return to France, he was confident that he could put his trust in him. The two men wasted little time in cycling the twenty-five kilometres to Proby where Tony waited outside while Dick entered the house to prepare Ruth Brooks for the shock of her nephew's return.. When he received the all-clear, Tony crept in surreptitiously so as to avoid being spotted by the gardener whom he suspected of being pro-Vichy. It was a wonderful reunion for the aunt and her nephew as they caught up on the news of the family's English and French branches. The conversation continued as they gathered together Tony's clothes and Ruth busied herself with removing any tell-tale British manufacturer's labels. Dick then departed, leaving Tony and his aunt to await the arrival of Norman Brooks.

Knowing his uncle's attitude towards the war gave Tony little ground to expect an effusive welcome; nevertheless, when his Uncle Norman finally appeared, his reaction was far worse than anticipated. He was aghast at Tony's arrival, and surprise soon turned to anger as he railed at the risk to his family and property that his nephew's appearance constituted. Grudgingly, at Ruth's prompting, he permitted Tony to spend the night in the château but stipulated that he must leave before dawn. He concluded by issuing the stark warning that Tony was not to return under any circumstances and, if he failed to heed this injunction, Norman was prepared to hand him over to the Vichy authorities. It was an unsettling experience to receive such a hostile response from one of his closest relatives (not to say a fellow countryman), but Tony's spirits were revived by a show of loyalty from an unexpected source. Norman's cook and butler, Henriette and Antoine Chreten, were of a different mettle to their employer. Discreetly, they took Tony to one side and, pointing out the window to their room, told him that if he ever needed help he only had to knock. Their generosity touched him greatly, served to help counteract his uncle's selfishness and reassured him that there were Frenchmen and women who made his return to France worthwhile.

Norman Brooks's treatment of his secret agent nephew is worthy of note on a number of levels. It provides an insight into the rationale of some men of standing in France who, in order to protect their own position, were disinclined to support the Resistance. Moreover, it is a corrective to the comforting myth of the totality of British phlegm and patriotic devotion in the Second World War. But it was not just Norman Brooks who sought to stay aloof from the reality of war. The summer of 1942 was a time when those Frenchmen who were willing to take risks, to refrain from the safe option and sacrifice their personal interests – and perhaps their lives – were distinctly in the minority. Tony's assumption that familial obligation or patriotism would outweigh Norman Brooks's self interest taught him a useful lesson – never expect help from anyone.

The next day, Tony called on Dick. They arranged that if the contacts in Lyon failed to materialise or were compromised, Lons-le-Saunier would serve as a jumping-off point for Tony's emergency escape into Switzerland. Dick offered his home as a safe house and promised to furnish discreet medical assistance should Tony have need of it. This specialist help would be provided by Dick's contact, Dr Aubertin. Tony later reported to London that the doctor 'Has a clinic for stomach operations and has a permit to keep patients up to ten days without declaring them. He dislikes the English, so that anyone using this clinic must not have an accent and must hide the fact that he is English.' In spite of the caveats, Aubertin possessed specialist talents as 'an expert at getting bullets out being an old M.O. [Army Medical Officer] and might be very useful in case of trouble.' This was a sensible precaution on Tony's part.* Perhaps less wise was his decision to send Hope Munday a telegram, 'Many happy returns for 15th am well all my love. Brooks'. Presumably this message and a subsequent telegram in September were entrusted to Dick for transmission. But for a man whose sense of personal security came to border on the obsessive, his decision to contact his girlfriend in this manner is very surprising. Equally, it perhaps reveals that the precocious secret agent still had much to learn and that even this paragon of clandestine work was capable of behaving just like any other lonely and lovelorn youth.[30]

Tony began his peripatetic PIMENTO work at a very fast pace and would maintain it. Having concluded his affairs with Dick, he departed on the morning of 9 July for Lyon, anxious that no unforeseen delay prevent his meeting with Bertholet. His conscientiousness had an unexpected consequence when he failed to secure a hotel room and had to sleep in the waiting room of the Lyon Perrache station. Tony had visited the city many times before but nearly three years of war had taken their toll. The city, like Toulouse, was spared the ghastliness of permanent occupation, for the German military units that had arrived in June 1940 soon departed under the terms of the armistice. But by July 1942, the effects of strict rationing and austerity were manifest and the city struggled to absorb thousands of refugees from the Occupied Zone and citizens expelled from the annexed regions of Alsace and Lorraine.

---

* HS9/1045/4. Later, on a visit to Lons-le-Saunier, Tony called on Dick and asked to see the doctor as the pain from his back that he had damaged on landing was troubling him. Dick arranged the consultation, introducing the patient with the explanation that the injury had resulted from a fall from a bicycle. After the examination, the surgeon dryly enquired if Tony had been riding a bike when he suffered his parachute accident.

At eleven o'clock Tony met Bertholet at the Café Français off the Place Bellecour, the city's main square. Waiting for them was 'Lucien', a smallish man, in his early forties, wearing thick, black-rimmed spectacles. In spite of this somewhat nondescript appearance, it was soon evident to Tony that here was a dedicated resister with a clear, ordered mind, 'he was a man of the greatest value & quality, determined and a complete idealist but who had nevertheless an obvious practical sense.'[31] The introductions made, Bertholet left and the two strangers took a stroll along the Rhône quayside to begin to get to know each other. 'Lucien' was Raymond Bizot, a senior member of the Vichy government's Service de Répression des Fraudes Douanières (SRFD) – the Customs Investigation Branch. Tony had, once again, fallen on his feet, for Bizot, like Bertholet, was a remarkable individual with a broad range of experiences and contacts. He had served his country all of his adult life (including in the trenches of the First World War) and was well connected with politicians, the police and, of course, the customs service. He had an intimate knowledge of the criminal underworld and walked with confidence through the dangerous haunts of smugglers, crooks and swindlers. A man of strong political convictions, he was a civil servant of liberal beliefs and had participated in a covert, illegal conspiracy to smuggle arms to the Republicans during the Spanish Civil War. Using experience gained in frustrating smugglers, the gamekeeper had briefly turned poacher and audaciously rescued some of the materiel (still in its packing cases) that was left stranded in Spain at the time of the Nationalist victory.[32] Bizot later recounted to Tony that this activity had nearly resulted in his arrest when the Germans occupied Paris in 1940. The invaders' intelligence services were apparently aware of his role in supporting the Spanish Republicans and he was therefore on their 'wanted list'. German investigators called on M. Pochelu, Bizot's superior at the customs service, for details of his subordinate's whereabouts but were informed that their quarry was absent on duty for several days. Shortly after the Germans had left, Bizot arrived at the office and was informed of his narrow escape. He clearly needed to be put beyond the Germans' clutches and was promptly posted to the relative safety of Lyon in the Unoccupied Zone.

Once Bizot had outlined his bona fides, he revealed that he had provisionally arranged a meeting to introduce his assistant (also known to Bertholet) should Tony agree. The prospect of acquiring another PIMENTO recruit was very much to Tony's liking and a few hundred yards up the riverside they came upon Jean Dorval. Tall, fair-haired and in his late thirties, Dorval was a tough Breton and as Tony recalled, 'as stubborn as they make them'. A long-time colleague and close friend of Bizot, he, too, was a Socialist and had been intimately involved in the chicanery surrounding military aid to the Spanish Republicans. He quickly became the second recruit of the day and acquired the codenames 'Plouc' and 'Poulet'.[33] Tony and Bizot continued their discussions after Dorval eventually left them and then concluded by agreeing to meet again the next morning.

Tony spent the rest of the day re-familiarising himself with the city and finding a room in a small hotel off the rue Victor Hugo. On reflection, he felt that his first visit to Lyon as PIMENTO's leader had been intense but immensely rewarding. Bertholet had handed him on a plate two intelligent, experienced and well-connected men, who in the following months would become pivotal figures in PIMENTO. All things considered, Tony slept that night with thoughts of a job well done.

The next morning Tony met Bizot at nine o'clock and was informed that Bertholet would join them an hour later on the banks of the Saône. This time Bertholet arrived with yet another companion; no less a figure than Léon Morandat, 'Yvon', who was still engaged on his mission for de Gaulle. Tony knew nothing of Morandat's work for the Free French at this time and it was not discussed, although Tony later wrote that he was 'of no use to me as he was entirely interested in the political side'. In fact, the primary purpose of the meeting was to have Léon Morandat give his approval that Tony should meet his younger brother, Roger.[34]

If Tony was to operate effectively in Lyon he needed to find permanent, safe accommodation. Hotels were too risky; there was no guarantee of a room being available when required and residents' details were, as a matter of course, submitted to the authorities every day. So, later that afternoon, Tony met Bertholet to discuss the issue and was reassured by the news that a rented room had been found for him.[35] After a second night in his hotel, Tony went to the working-class area of Grange Blanche accompanied by Bertholet and was introduced to his prospective landlady, Mme Lometro-Blois. The residence, 8, rue Seignemartin, was a dilapidated, two-storey building, divided into apartments, in a rundown, cobbled street. The room on offer came at a rent of 250 francs a month and was at the front of the house, while Lometro-Blois and his wife lived at the back of the building. For a man who had survived Spanish prisons and slept rough as a lorry driver, the room was perfectly habitable, but its amenities were basic in the extreme. Madame and her husband, a plasterer, slept in a cupboard bed in the kitchen where Tony would be permitted to fill his basin of cold water each morning. The privies for the whole house consisted of a single, ground-floor lavatory whose very basic plumbing arrangements consisted of a wooden box situated over an open sewer. When the Rhône flooded, the sewer overflowed and the water ran down the hall and over the front-door steps.

Tony considered the room was more than adequate, 'fairly big with a large double bed in an alcove and an antiquated porcelain washing set on a marble table in one corner. Everything was very dirty and dusty and one window was broken, but I was satisfied as it was on the ground floor and therefore easy to evacuate rapidly.'[36] He told Mme Lometro-Blois that he would take it and, for the month following his arrival in France, stayed there whenever he was in Lyon, citing it as his permanent residence on a fresh set of false identity documents provided by his new contacts. Bizot gave him an identity card issued by the Préfecture that carried more official weight than the one that had been forged by SOE in England. The new document was made out for 'Antoine Brévin', bearing the real identity number of someone with a similar name to Tony's alias so that if official enquiries were ever made, the deception might be more readily maintained.

The next day (the 12th) Tony met Bizot again. This encounter provided him with an intimation of the volatile state of French politics and a comforting example of Bizot's insider knowledge. He advised Tony to leave Lyon straight away as public demonstrations were planned for the 14th. It was the first (but by no means the last) occasion when the experienced customs officer steered the young British secret agent away from potential difficulties. Tony still had much to learn about his colleague, 'When I showed surprise at his knowledge of police activities, he told me that he was Inspecteur Principal on the Service de la Répression des Fraudes Douanières, and that in this capacity he had the same authority and similar access to police affairs as an inspecteur principal of the Sûreté. I suddenly realised the tremendous possibilities of this employment and asked him whether Plouc [Dorval] was the same. He told me that he was his second in command.'[37] Tony heeded the warning and left for Montauban to commence the establishment of PIMENTO in that town and its environs. Just as Bizot had predicted, a demonstration took place in Lyon on Bastille Day, 14th July. The anniversary offered a landmark opportunity for nascent resistance movements to register their opposition to the Vichy regime. Sixty-six demonstrations took place throughout the whole of France (two-thirds of them in the Unoccupied Zone) with thousands taking to the streets in Toulouse and some 15,000 people doing the same in Lyon.[38] The wisdom of Bizot's advice in getting the British agent away from potential trouble was incontestable.

Montauban offered promising opportunities for Tony to exploit his existing contacts. He met Marcel Guerret at the Pont des Consuls near the Musée Ingres but soon realised that, although the politician was a prominent figure in Montauban, his star had significantly waned in the period since Tony's stay in 1940. That said, Guerret remained a well-known personality, and the Englishman retained too many contacts in the town for them to risk spending time together in the public gaze. Therefore, after a brief conversation, they rendezvoused later at Guerret's apartment in the rue de Rémusat in Toulouse. Now in privacy, Tony gave Guerret the Brooks family news and commenced the renewal of their acquaintanceship. However, he concluded from their conversation that, for all Guerret's abundant political experience and fervent anti-fascist beliefs, he did not possess the qualities that would allow him to play a role in PIMENTO's affairs. Guerret appears to have concurred in this assessment for he offered a substitute; the garage proprietor, Michel Comte, whom Tony had met, liked and respected during his 1940 stay. Tony had no misgivings about the proposal and asked Guerret to set up a meeting.[39]

Having assumed that the security situation in Lyon had stabilised, Tony returned there on the 15th. It was now time to meet Roger Morandat, the brother of 'Yvon'. The candidate had been taken prisoner during the battle of France but had taken advantage of the lax vigilance of his captors and escaped back to Lyon. He was an early recruit into the local resistance and, although not a railway worker, had many friends and contacts in their trades union and joined their clandestine network. Morandat was from a farming family in the Bourg area north-east of Lyon and, in addition to exploiting the links to railwaymen, Tony hoped that his connections would facilitate the establishment of PIMENTO's parachute grounds. Bizot brought Morandat to a meeting at Tony's digs in the rue Seignemartin at which the SOE agent outlined his plans and, in particular, sketched in the requirements of preparing parachute drops. Morandat needed no time to consider the proposal and instantly agreed to join the team. Just as Tony had hoped, he offered his family home in the Bourg as a base from which suitable drop grounds might be located. Tony and Bizot also began to address the possibilities of commencing railway sabotage operations. As a first and very encouraging step, Bizot produced 'the traction engineer of Lyon Perrache [station] who was very willing to do passive sabotage with abrasives on all the engines under his jurisdiction'.[40]

Constant travelling was already a feature of Tony's clandestine life and he next visited the town of La Roche-sur-Foron near the Swiss border to see Bertholet. The latter confirmed that he had notified London of Tony's safe arrival but mentioned that F Section had already heard the news from another source. On 9 July 1942 a wireless message from one of its few radio operators in France, Captain Isidore Newman, gave 'news of the manner in which THEODORE (PIMENTO) had been dropped'. Two days later London sent a message thanking Newman for the information.[41] While, of course, it was important that London knew that Tony had arrived safely, the means by which they obtained the news exemplified the insecure links between F Section agents in France. Presumably the information had been passed by de Vomécourt to Newman's colleague, Lieutenant François Basin, 'Olive', whose task was to establish contact with resistance networks in the South of France. Wireless links were so rare and so precious that Newman undertook an immense amount of work, and the report of Tony's arrival was but one of more than 200 messages he sent between May and November 1942.[42] Hardly surprisingly, given this indiscriminate reporting, Tony and Bertholet agreed that they should be independent of the overstretched (and insecure) wireless links to London maintained by other networks. Consequently, the establishment of a regular courier link to and from Switzerland was essential and, to this end, Bertholet introduced Tony to Gaby Cordier, 'a short girl of about 28, not pretty to look at but obviously very capable'.[43] It was agreed that Cordier, using the cover name 'Yvette', would convey messages to and from La

Roche-sur-Foron, either delivering them personally to Bertholet or by means of a clandestine 'letter box'. An *assistante sociale* (social worker) and, a onetime member of the ISK, Cordier was intelligent and, of course, possessed the vital cachet of Bertholet's recommendation. If this was not sufficient grounds for Tony to like and trust her, he discovered that they had something in common; she, too, suffered from a skin complaint, eczema in her case. Described by Tony as 'absolutely fearless', Cordier was a true stalwart and when enemy security action made her work ever more dangerous, she resolutely continued carrying vital documents to PIMENTO's scattered outposts.

When Tony reported these new arrangements to Bizot back in Lyon, he failed to get the reaction he expected. The customs man announced that he was displeased, criticised the plans as insecure and, as an alternative, advocated the exploitation of his own connections with French government officials at Thonon-les-Bains on the southern shore of Lake Geneva. The men he had in mind were Robert Lacoste, a tax official, and a fellow customs man, Alexandre Fourre, both of whom had untrammelled opportunities for passing material to and from Switzerland. Lacoste was a civil servant, a trade unionist, a close associate of Bertholet's and, as early as November 1940, had helped found the Resistance group Libération-Nord. In addition to these affiliations, he went on to play a major role in establishing PIMENTO's courier route to Switzerland. In order to strengthen these frontier links, Bizot offered to go to Switzerland during his August vacation to enlist the support of friends in the Swiss customs service. In the meantime, he would go to Thonon and arrange a clandestine letter box there for Cordier. It was local knowledge and experience such as this that facilitated and underpinned Tony's early success in establishing PIMENTO.

Tony returned to Toulouse on the 19th and stayed the night with Bottemer and his family at their small villa in the suburbs. It marked the beginning of an important and enduring relationship that was a feature of Tony's work in France during the next two years. Moreover, it constituted an early example of Tony's forming a personal bond with select members of his network. He did not pretend to these early associates that he was anything other than a very youthful secret agent sent from England and, from the outset, showed no airs and graces. This allowed his quick absorption into the milieu and the trust of his colleagues. Bottemer resided with his wife, her elderly parents and his sister-in-law, Marthe. Théo Bernheim, 'Claude' Bottemer's brother-in-law, was also a near-permanent resident. Although the wisdom and experience of older men such as Bertholet and Bottemer offered stability, Tony welcomed the opportunity to interact with someone of his own age such as Bernheim. When he stayed at Bottemer's they shared a room, sometimes talking through the night. Bernheim, like Bottemer, was a Jew and during one of their nocturnal conversations he reflected that if anti-Semitism in Vichy France worsened, he would be physically unable to camouflage his ancestry. His new friend reassured him that circumcision was an imperfect identification for he, an Anglo-Saxon Quaker, was at the same risk. From the outset Bernheim confessed that he could not contribute to Tony's work by transporting firearms or explosives but remained willing to serve in any other capacity. He was prepared to carry messages, book hotel rooms, purchase railway tickets, undertake reconnaissance and surveillance tasks, and he even revealed that he had something to contribute as a counterfeiter, 'After supper I learnt his value, as I caught him carving on a piece of lino a tracing of a police stamp'.[44] Bernheim's candour about his limitations impressed Tony and he became a trusted and invaluable aide.

A couple of days later it was time for Tony to renew his acquaintance with Michel Comte in Montauban. Comte, a tall, dark haired man in his forties, still ran the truck and heavy goods vehicle repair workshop, Le Garage des Pyrénées, on the Toulouse road on the outskirts of the town. He lived on the premises with his exclusively female family in a flat above the workshops. His wife and three daughters – Christiane ('Titi'), Michelle ('Michou') and Nanette ('Nanou'), aged respectively, sixteen, thirteen, and two – were supplemented by 'Tata', Comte's mother-in-law, who spoke a near impenetrable patois. Comte seemed delighted to meet Tony again and needed no time for reflection before agreeing to join the network. His first contribution was to provide Tony with a cover story that proved of incalculable importance. They agreed that the Englishman would become Comte's accredited procurer of spare parts, scavenging amongst the countless abandoned trucks that still littered the French countryside after the debacle of the summer of 1940. The 'job' gave Tony a legitimate justification for roaming throughout the Unoccupied Zone while really searching for suitable parachute grounds or travelling to meetings with members of his network.[45]

The Comtes became loyal and trusted colleagues and the relationship further deepened as they welcomed Tony into their family. His visits would be frequent, usually once a fortnight, and, if staying overnight, he dossed down on their living-room couch. At a time when food was hard to come by and good food even more difficult, the Comtes always had a place at the table for him. The whole family became initiated into at least some aspects of the network's activities and within a short while, Comte's nephew, Michel Driffaud, known as 'Petit Michel', and the garage's head mechanic, René Davas, were recruited.

On 25 July Tony returned to Lyon and met again with Roger Morandat. They agreed that the latter would adopt the codename 'Martinet' and be contacted (by a system of passwords) at his wife's *parfumerie* in the rue Masséna.[46] Tony emphasised the pressing need to secure more recruits and locate suitable parachute drop grounds so they agreed to visit the Morandat farm at Polliat, north-west of Bourg-en-Bresse, to progress matters. Having taken the train to Bourg they collected bicycles that Morandat had left at a grocer's shop in the boulevard de Brou. This journey marked the first of Tony's marathon bicycle expeditions that over the next two years saw him traversing the length and breadth of Southern France. At the Morandat farm they were welcomed by the whole household comprising Roger's parents, his brother Henri, three sisters and a brother-in-law, Ernest Fromont. Henri Morandat had been brought into the Resistance by his brother Léon ('Yvon') the previous year and now offered to help Tony and PIMENTO.[47] The Englishman explained that his primary purpose was to identify likely parachute grounds in the Bresse region that he knew possessed an eminently suitable number of large, flat fields. He was looking for sites measuring about 400 metres by 400 metres that were clear of trees and any other obstructions. All areas had to be well away from electricity pylons or high ground while road or track access for the removal of supplies, and proximity to suitable cache sites were also of high importance. Encouragingly, the Morandat brothers reported that they had already located three potential dropping zones (DZs), one of which was conveniently close to the farm. The next morning they examined the sites and Tony graded the one nearest to the Morandats' as suitable for the delivery of containers but not personnel and bestowed the codename 'Date' on it. Nearer to Mézériat, a marshy field between two streams was accepted by Tony as 'Abricot' and they set about working out the map coordinates for it. They then stopped at the Café de la Gare at Mézériat where Tony was introduced to another potential PIMENTO recruit, the patron, Alphonse Pormathios, the 'father of seven daughters, all exactly the same except for each being one size smaller than the next, who did the work in his cafe'.[48] After a good meal, Fromont went back to Polliat while Tony, the Morandat brothers and Pormathios carried on to Pont-de-Veyle. Here they met André Malamard, a friend of Pormathios and station master at Mézériat who, somewhat prematurely, had already been commissioned to locate a dropping ground. Malamard, adopting the cover name 'Dedé', was a colourful character being a former communist councillor in Lille who, harbouring fears of retribution for his political views in northern France, had decided to grow an impressive white beard to disguise himself against hostile recognition. Less impressive was Malamard's domestic situation, 'He lived in one of the worst hovels I have ever seen with his mad wife who, while we were waiting for Dedé to pump up his bicycle, proceeded to dance a jig in the kitchen to our great dismay. Dedé took it all calmly as a real fatalist should.'[49] Whatever his eccentricities, Malamard had identified a very good dropping ground that was given the codename 'Brugnon'. It was important to protect Tony's anonymity and these new contacts were only told was that he was a Frenchman with an expertise in special operations and sabotage. Henri Morandat and his brother Roger were amongst the very limited circle of people who were aware that he was really an Englishman. That night, they returned to the Morandats' farm at Polliat before going to Bourg on the 27th. Here, Roger Morandat used his excellent connections with the railway workers to provide Tony with his first introduction to this vital sector of recruits. A specially selected group of candidates confirmed that they were willing to carry out sabotage under his instructions and, in return, he briefed them on the available methods – notably the application of abrasives to damage the axle boxes of goods trucks. The message was that the 'weapon' was undetectable, would not risk the loss of innocent French lives and, if all went well, the transportation of German and Vichy war materiel would be impeded. With great regret, Tony was obliged to confess that, at present, he had no supplies to issue. He tried to retain their enthusiasm by explaining his knowledge of more advanced sabotage techniques that, he assured them, they would eventually perform.

Tony recognised that it was essential that he secure abrasives for the recruits and gave Cordier a message for Bertholet that included a request for any supplies of carborundum powder that might be available from SOE's clandestine stocks in Switzerland. He also forwarded the coordinates for the three parachute DZs on which he hoped to receive his own supplies from England.

By the summer of 1942 SOE had developed a simple but highly effective system of plotting the DZs on standard Michelin road maps. The first reference points were the Michelin sheet number followed by the *'pli'* – the fold or section – of the map. Then came the name of the nearest major town to the DZ. Finally, a grid of 5mm squares was laid over one of the 70mm by 100mm sections of the map. The east–west axis on the top of the grid bore the letters 'L' to 'Y' and the north–south was given the numbers 11 to 30. Thus the location of a DZ near to Tony's uncle's home in Grozon would possess the following coordinates

'M. 70' – Michelin map
'Pli 4' – Fold number 4
'Poligny' – The largest town in the map square
'U.20' – the cross reference of the square

If approved by London (perhaps following a photographic aerial reconnaissance), Tony would give the DZ an individual codename. When agreement was received from the RAF that a supply operation was to be mounted, final warning messages would be broadcast by the BBC French service. These could be heard at the conclusion of the evening news programme, when the announcer would recite a number of *'messages personnels'*. These idiosyncratic phrases such as 'Le poulet à la crème est excellent' seemed to the uninitiated to be either complete nonsense or surreal poetry but to those 'in the know' they were a precise signal that a supply drop was 'on'. The messages were broadcast twice on the evening of a drop at 19.15 and again at 21.15. The final confirmation of the operation would be an agreed Morse recognition signal flashed by the reception committee to the aircraft on its final approach to the DZ. Later in the war, as the number of operations increased, the BBC's messages simply advised reception committees that certain DZs should simply stand by for the next 'moon period'. Careful planning and the complexities of these arrangements, could not alter the hard fact that the success of the RAF's operations still remained dependent upon moonlit nights to facilitate navigation and identification of the drop zones.

Encouraging news now arrived from Bizot. He had been as good as his word and used his contacts to establish a primary postbox (together with a secure alternative) at Thonon under Lacoste and another at Annemasse organised by Fourre with an emergency escape route into Switzerland across the border near Gex. He had also sent Dorval to Paris to contact Charles Laurent, the secretary of the Civil Service Trade Unions to obtain information on potential recruits to the network. In addition, Bizot had written to a former colleague, Gaston Cusin, who, while decidedly not a collaborator, had managed to retain an important position in Vichy's financial administration. Tony was highly impressed by Bizot's pro-activity and competence, 'I realised that my summing up of Lucien [Bizot] as a valuable man was correct and even conservative'.[50]

Tony's optimism and sense of progress were somewhat dented at his next meeting with Bertholet in Toulouse on 3 August 1942. London had sent a message to Berne chastising Bertholet that 'they [London] had expected to receive a dropping ground and safe house for a W/T operator to join him and ALPHONSE this moon.'[51] In addition, Bertholet reported that Cordier had had a narrow escape on the latest courier run and had been obliged to destroy the papers she was carrying. It was a relief that she had avoided arrest but Tony had not kept copies of the new DZ map coordinates and now faced the prospect of having to repeat all the measurement work again.

But things were about to improve. Tony's seeking out of recruits in Toulouse continued and on 5 August he met Gilbert Zaksas, leader of a left-wing, federalist political movement, Libérer et Fédérer. Zaksas was a lawyer in his early thirties, born in Lithuania. He was amongst a group of intellectuals who had frequented a bookshop in the rue du Languedoc owned by Silvio Trentin, an Italian academic and refugee from fascist oppression. This loose collection of like-minded people transformed itself into a political resistance cell named (after the liberation) the Réseau Bertaux in honour of its leader, Professor Pierre Bertaux. The group developed and made connections with Free French contacts but in December 1941 was betrayed to the Vichy authorities. Its leaders were arrested by the Surveillance du Territoire, and eventually came to trial in July the following year – about the time of Tony's arrival. Zaksas undertook a spirited defence of the accused that resulted in the court passing surprisingly lenient sentences. Unabashed, Zaksas and the other members of the network who remained at liberty started an underground political movement, 'Libérer et Fédérer', that looked to the liberation of France but also a new post-war political structure.[52] The first edition (20,000 copies) of their underground newspaper, bearing the organisation's name, appeared on 14 July 1942 (a fortnight after Tony was parachuted into France) claiming it was the '*Organe du mouvement révolutionnaire pour la libération et la reconstruction de la France*'. Although fully committed to the cause of resistance, Zaksas's activities to date had been of an exclusively cerebral nature. Tony estimated that while the lawyer might not be a man of action, his experience of clandestine activity could be useful and, moreover, his group seemed a promising source of recruits for PIMENTO. Their first meeting took place at Zaksas's office in the rue Raymond IV and Tony immediately found himself immersed in the myriad political undercurrents of French resistance. Fortunately, he was acquainted with the complexities of 'normal' French politics and appreciated that the clandestine world of the Resistance was likely to suffer from similar issues. In the main, SOE's policy was to espouse a non-political stance and Tony adopted this line, affirming that he had no desire to interfere in 'Libérer et Fédérer's' long-term aspirations and emphasised that he was merely seeking patriotic Frenchmen and anti-Nazis to join him in the fight. This seemed to reassure Zaksas but he nevertheless 'requested that it should not be known to his men that our funds were coming from London but that they should be told that they were Trade Union subscriptions'.[53] The lawyer also stipulated that Tony could only liaise with himself or his assistant, René Figarol. Zaksas wanted Figarol to receive instruction on the techniques of organising a parachute drop and proposed that Libérer et Fédérer would then store the weapons and equipment until the day of the uprising that, it was assumed, would take place in support of the Allied invasion. Tony was unhappy with this proposal and made a non-committal reply for it was his firm intention to retain control of all materiel sent by SOE; the decision as to what, if anything, Zaksas received would be his alone. In the event, Figarol became a loyal and dedicated member of PIMENTO, supervising over twenty-five parachute operations and eventually carrying out railway sabotage and maquis operations.[54] It was agreed that Tony would maintain contact with Figarol by a dead-letter drop at the Café Conti on the Place du Capitole but the British agent was at pains not to offer any additional means by which his new recruit could contact him. He was reluctant to engage in complicated and potentially dangerous cut-out arrangements until he was better organised and acclimatised to life in France.

Regardless of London's somewhat carping complaint to Bertholet on 21 July, it had overall been a promising start for Tony and his PIMENTO network. He had been immensely fortunate in being able to draw upon Bertholet's extensive range of first-rate contacts to help him lay the foundations of the circuit. More troubling though were the intimations of poor security amongst F Section's other agents and the hectoring note of some of London's 'instructions'. Far from being dispelled in the following months, these misgivings over headquarters' conduct worsened and ultimately culminated in a disaster that had near fatal results for Tony and PIMENTO.

Chapter Seven
PIMENTO's First Steps

While Tony focused on building up his network, the task of contacting the politician Léon Jouhaux went by the board. Neither Tony's later recollections nor the official files provide an explanation for the dropping of one of his primary tasks. A logical assumption is that London realised that Tony had his hands full coping with PIMENTO's development. Moreover, other F Section agents had been charged with the same mission. A wireless report from France on 12 July 1942 stated that 'They [F Section agents] wished to send a courier by felucca to bring a plan and an autograph message from JOUHAUX to Sir Walter CITRINE and to GREEN of the American Federation of Labour expressing fraternal feelings of the French movement and asking for action and liaison with them.'[1] It is not recorded whether this operation was mounted but on 5 August the wireless operator Isidore Newman sent a message to London on behalf of another F Section agent, Major Nicholas Bodington, in which the latter offered to visit Jouhaux. Bodington had landed at Cap d'Antibes on 30 July 1942 to assess a promising new resistance network, 'Carte'. A former Paris-based journalist, Bodington had joined SOE in December 1940 as a staff officer and was unquestionably better equipped to conduct high-level talks with a senior trade unionist than the twenty-year-old Second Lieutenant Anthony Brooks. Moreover, Bodington possessed the distinct advantage of having met Jouhaux before the war, when he was working for Reuters news agency. London took him up on his offer with the proviso that he should not attempt to make contact if there was any attendant risk – Jouhaux had been under house arrest in Cahors since January 1942. Bodington replied (via yet another wireless operator, Captain Henri Despaigne, 'Ulysse') that the date of the interview had been fixed for 16 August. The visit duly took place with Jouhaux quickly penetrating Bodington's false identity. Although the conversation proved to be long and detailed, the Frenchman was very specific about the type of British assistance he was prepared to accept and left the agent in no doubt of the strict parameters required for any future association. Jouhaux refused to come to England and Bodington reported succinctly, 'He would I think be somewhat difficult to handle politically.'[2]

Meanwhile, London was engaged on what was to be a protracted and ultimately fruitless struggle to exercise close control over Tony's actions. Within three weeks of his arrival, F Section had sent a message to Berne bemoaning his failure to send details of a dropping ground and a safe house for a wireless operator to join him.[3] Ten days later, they were again badgering Bertholet for a report on preparations for the new arrival and complaining about his lack of communication. London's pressing their operatives to develop the networks was understandable, but it failed to recognise that the construction of organisations required time and care. Moreover, although Bertholet was apparently able to travel from France to Switzerland almost at will, he could not be in two places at once and responses to London's messages had to await his return to Berne. On 3 August a message from Bertholet to SOE recommended that the arrival of the wireless operator be postponed for two months (the end of September); this was reinforced a week later by Tony's endorsement of the proposed delay.

Meanwhile, doubtless as a result of information passed by Bertholet, London learnt of Norman Brooks's intransigence and the thwarting of Tony's hopes for a Grozon cover for his activities 'by the refusal of his uncle to play'.[4] Baker Street did not intend taking this rebuttal lying down and one of SOE's men in Switzerland, William Sullivan, who also served as the Assistant Commercial Counsellor at the Embassy, informed London that Norman Brooks was 'a British subject but had strong Vichy sympathies' and that this sentiment and a recent trip to Cairo 'seemed to call for investigation'.[5] But in spite of this minor Brooks family blemish, Bertholet's report offered an encouraging assessment of Tony, 'The organiser [Tony] was doing very well, making friends with the right contacts and ROBERT [Bertholet] was delighted with him.' This state of affairs presumably gladdened the hearts of Tony's superiors in London but did not curtail their preoccupation with sending him a wireless operator. The moon period largely dictated the timing of air operations and F Section pressed Bertholet and Tony to make arrangements for the agent's arrival, warning that if these were not received at Baker Street by 18 September, the operation would have to be postponed for yet another month.[6] Reluctantly, and with some difficulty occasioned by Bertholet's absences, a message was eventually sent from Switzerland advising that Tony could offer dropping grounds at Châtillon-sur-Chalaronne between Bourg and Villefranche-sur-Saône: 'Reception committees had been arranged for both the landing grounds indicated and the BBC message was expected on the usual 9.15 p.m. broadcast.' The grounds would be manned from 24 to 30 September to receive the wireless operator, 'Thibaud'. But then, after all this extended debate, on 18 September London broke the news that 'Thibaud' was unwell and SOE's medical advisers would not approve his making a parachute drop. F Section proposed that it 'would arrange for him to be dropped at the same ground under the same conditions next moon period if he was all right by then, or they would substitute another operator.'[7]

Tony could not allow the putative arrival of London's wireless operator to divert him from his primary focus; the PIMENTO recruitment drive. In Lyon on 3 September 1942 Bertholet introduced him to David Donoff, a twenty-two-year-old Parisian who, together with his family, had fled south during the battle of France.[8] After the armistice, the Donoffs, as Jews, decided it would be safer to stay where they were rather than risk returning north to live under the German occupation. Donoff was an engaging, extrovert character and proved of immense help to Tony as a 'fixer'. He had spent the whole of 1941 as a helper at the Vichy internment camp at Gurs and, while employed at the Centres d'Accueil for refugees, he had embarked on an ever-increasing range of clandestine tasks using the alias 'André Donnet'. Donoff came to Tony already possessed of a reputation as someone able to procure pretty much anything on the black market and he was particularly adept at acquiring and forging official papers. One estimate suggests that during his clandestine career he dispensed some 5,000 false identities to needy individuals. Although apparently well furnished with documentation provided by SOE and Bizot, Tony personally wanted more:

> Dodo told me that he could fix me up with a [sic] official identity card stamped and signed by the Bureau de la Circulation of the Prefecture du Rhone. I gave him a photo and asked him to do this as quickly as possible. He also agreed to supply me with an escaped prisoner's demobilisation paper which I considered would be valuable if I were ever arrested by French gendarmes or police in public, as one could show the paper and say loudly so that everyone heard 'surely a Frenchman was not going to hand over another Frenchman who had escaped from the Germans and was therefore liable to be shot'.[9]

Donoff had an ecumenical relationship with Abbé Glasberg (who had helped provide Tony's safe house) of the Catholic aid organisation, l'Amitié Chrétienne, and was a pivotal figure in obtaining false documents for both political refugees and Jews fleeing the increasingly draconian anti-semitic laws on both sides of the demarcation line. Donoff's sister, Herminette, was also recruited and went on to serve with distinction as one of PIMENTO's most indispensable couriers. Donoff's landlord, Henri Combe, became a member of the network too and provided sterling service with his 38 rue Montesquieu residence being used as a safe house and, later, an arms cache.

From Lyon Tony went to Bourg and received encouraging news from Roger Morandat of the progress in recruiting teams to carry out abrasive grease attacks on railway rolling stock at Lons-le-Saunier, Saint-Amour, Saint-Etienne and Valence. Similarly, preparations for reception committees at the grounds around Bourg were well advanced and six teams were now ready to receive drops during the coming moon period.

Several other important PIMENTO recruitments were attempted at this time. Back in Toulouse, Tony and Bertholet met at the Colis Suisse on 8 September and discussed the enlistment of a couple of leading trade unionists with significant political connections. The first, Albert Guigui, was the one-time secretary of the Syndicat des Métallos (the metal workers union), a member of the national committee of the CGT and a journalist for the newspaper *Paris-Soir*. He proved reluctant to develop a close connection with Tony (perhaps due to his existing commitments with other resistance groups) but helpfully suggested that the British agent try his luck with Julien Forgues. A trade unionist and secretary of the Toulouse Labour Exchange, Forgues was not keen to become closely involved with PIMENTO either. Tony's appraisal of their meeting did not pull any punches: 'He was very little interested in the sabotage side of resistance. He gave me the impression that he considered that the time had come for England to fight and that Frenchmen should not collaborate but should certainly not take up arms to hasten the liberation of France. I pointed out to him the weakness of that theory as I considered France's revival was very closely linked with her action in the clandestine war. He would not be persuaded then, but I am glad to say that he was before 1944.'[10]

While Tony's digs at the rue Seignemartin met his needs perfectly adequately, Bizot offered him another safe haven at the SRFD headquarters in the rue Jarente. Here, during office hours and in the evening, Tony was able to come and go virtually as he pleased, it being assumed by Bizot's colleagues that the young man was one of the investigator's informants. The links to the SRFD were reinforced by the recruitment of another customs officer who became one of the small group of resisters who were aware that Tony was really their leader. This was Louis Pédémas, a forty-seven-year-old customs officer who, like Bizot, had served his country in both World Wars, having been wounded and gassed in the First and briefly captured in the Second.[11] He became a PIMENTO stalwart for the rest of the war, performing many important tasks not the least of which was concealing much of the network's cash in the safe of the Lyon Director-General of customs. The money was hidden in sealed official envelopes with bogus labels marking them as impounded currency.

Tony came to rely heavily upon his relationship with Bizot and Dorval who had rooms at the Hôtel des Variétés in the avenue Berthelot, situated in a Lyon working-class district on the east bank of the Rhône. The hotel was small and scruffy, and, as Tony recalled, 'too sordid for words … the sheets were disgusting and … the place stank,' but the owner, M. Joigny, was also one of Bizot's informants and the customs investigator exercised strong influence over the *patron*.[12] The hostelry offered a secure meeting place where the clientele assumed that Tony was simply another of Bizot's professional contacts and, therefore, prying questions either remained unasked or soon found their way back to the SRFD. It became a 'safe house' in the months to come and the scene of occasional PIMENTO 'incidents'. One of these occurred later in the war when the increased activity of Vichy security forces on the streets of Lyon resulted in Tony deciding that it was unwise to attempt to return to his digs. He was not the only extra resident at Les Variétés, for a female PIMENTO courier was in town and also needed a bed that night. It was a time when the rules of social decorum were laid aside and people were obliged to sleep wherever they could. Tony occupied the twin bed in Bizot's room while the courier took the spare mattress in Dorval's. Inevitably, Bizot and Tony speculated on the prospect of Dorval, a notorious womaniser, trying his luck with the courier. Bizot was adamant that his colleague did not stand a chance but scarcely had they turned off their light than a succession of bangs and crashes came from their friend's room above them. Inevitably, they ascribed the noises to amorous pursuits, but Dorval later explained that his bed possessed only three legs and that the carnal activity assumed by his colleagues was really his tumbling to the floor every time he turned over in his sleep.

Tony's initial contentment with the primitive conditions at the Lometro-Bloises' faded as his digs offered scant opportunity for any relief and relaxation from the growing pressures of work. Moreover, the rooms had been used for PIMENTO meetings and his innate sense of security led him to conclude that he must find a place to live that remained unknown to even his closest intimates. Bertholet and Bizot had helped establish him at Mme Lometro-Blois's but now he determined to secure somewhere else himself. To this end, he started looking at the 'small ads' in a *bureau de tabac* at the Place des Terreaux near the Mairie until, finally, one took his eye. This offered a room in a house in the Lyon suburb of Crépieux. Tony considered that it held several attributes; it was a few kilometres outside the city limits and thereby offered a haven away from his main focus of activity, and what was more, it was on the road to Bourg and the countryside north of Lyon where he had selected landing grounds for his parachute drops.

When Tony visited the house he realised, at first sight, that 3 Chemin du Panorama exceeded his best hopes. It was an ideal bolt-hole. The three-storey, semi-detached villa was situated within a large garden, surrounded by a wall with a double sheet-steel gate. One half of the house faced south, overlooking the River Rhône while its grounds descended steeply to a door at the bottom of a flight of steps onto the main road. His interview with his prospective landlady, Mme Dupeuple, took place in her lounge with Tony assessing her as a 'wizened old crone, who had come down in the world'. He noted that the room was dominated by a portrait (and several photographs) of Madame's late husband, 'The Colonel', who had served in the First World War and died shortly before the Second. In spite of the lapse of time since the colonel's demise, his portrait remained draped in black mourning cloth.

> Madame Dupeuple's late husband was a member of the P.S.F. [Parti Social Français] or the French Fascist party, and she also shared his ideas. I soon discovered this, and played up to them saying that I thought the Marechal [Pétain] was our only hope and that communism was to be avoided at any price even if it meant collaboration with our former enemies ... I realised that I would have to play my part very carefully in this household, but that I had the added security of being known to the neighbours as Mme Dupeuple's friend and therefore assumed to have the same ideas.'[13]

During the interview with Mme Dupeuple, Tony exerted as much charm as he could muster but soon realised that the crucial factor would be his ability to pay his landlady the (as yet unspecified) rent. He was invited to view the room that was situated on the first floor above the lounge. It was on the corner of the house and possessed two windows, one facing the gate and the other looking east. Tony's immediate liking of the room increased once he had realised that its position offered an escape route out of the window, onto a nearby tree and over the garden wall. The facilities included a *cabinet de toilette* consisting of a basin and bidet while the other door in the room led out onto the landing. It was explained that the occupants of the house comprised Mme Dupeuple's thirty-five-year-old divorcée daughter (who had a job as private secretary to the assistant mayor), her teenage son and another occasional lodger, M. Blanqui. The two women shared a bedroom on the first floor while the grandson and Blanqui had rooms on the second floor.

Madame Dupeuple stated that the rent was 500 francs a month and there was no room for manoeuvre. This did not bother Tony, for, at that time, money was the least of his worries. But he needed to exert some control over Mme Dupeuple and

> ... pointed out that it was excessive in present times and that it might be unwise for her to declare that I was paying that amount. She was terrified at the thought of doing anything illegal but I thought that it was impossible for her to accept the legal rate of 125 Fr[ancs] and that I fully appreciated her position, so I advised her to consider that I was staying as a friend and that I just gave her a present of 500 Fr on the first of the month. She agreed to this and said that she would not declare me to the police to avoid any complications.

Tony had noted that there were neither sheets nor towels in the room and enquired, 'as his personal effects were in Paris', whether Mme Dupeuple might provide such items as part of the fee. If this was the case, he would agree to the 500 francs payment and, from that moment on, he could do no wrong with his avaricious landlady. She accepted the provision of bed linen, its laundry and the use of an electric *bouilloire* (heated element) to make his morning coffee. Tony's requests for keys to the garden gate and front door and the storage of his bicycle in the garage were quickly granted. He concluded the deal by handing over a 500-franc deposit and a further 500-franc advance payment of his first month's rent. Even at this early stage he let the landlady know that he would not be observing a conventional daily routine, explaining that his work frequently took him away from Lyon so he would be coming and going at irregular times and intervals. Madame Dupeuple did not seem at all bothered by this, her thoughts being preoccupied by the favourable financial arrangement she had just secured. Tony left the house feeling elated by his acquisition of the accommodation and resolved that neither his PIMENTO colleagues nor his F Section controllers in London would know of his residence at the Chemin du Panorama: 'I was determined to have somewhere I could sleep in peace, knowing that nobody could betray me under torture.'

Amongst the Resistance contacts that appeared at this time was a mysterious figure known only in the records as 'Le Docteur'. He came with Bertholet's recommendation and was probably part of a speculative initiative to expand PIMENTO's Toulouse–Lyon orbit southwards towards Marseille and the Midi. However, when Tony met 'Le Docteur' at the beginning of October 1942 he was not impressed and, more important, questioned the latter's claims to possess many contacts in the Marseille docks.[14] Nevertheless at their meeting Tony gave 'Le Docteur' two precious kilos of abrasive grease, instructed him in the use of it but declined a request to visit Marseille and instruct sabotage teams there. When Tony next spoke with Bertholet, he voiced his reservations about developing the association. It is a reflection of the mutual respect that already existed between the two men that the proposal to bring 'Le Docteur' into PIMENTO was dropped.[15] With the benefit of hindsight, it was surely a blessing that Tony did not attempt to spread his activities into yet another major city. PIMENTO would grow into an organisation that encompassed much of southern France – an area more than enough for any one man to try and control.

On 8 October 1942 Tony was introduced to another Bizot contact, Gaston Cusin. He was an important figure, for his official status aided PIMENTO in many ways over the next two years.[16] Like his friend Robert Lacoste, the thirty-nine-year-old Cusin was a civil servant, trade unionist and socialist. A colleague and friend of Bizot and Dorval from his pre-war post as Contrôleur des Douanes, he had been part of the conspiracy of French civil servants engaged in providing clandestine support to the Republicans during the Spanish Civil War. After brief army service at the beginning of the Second World War, his talents were switched to the French government's blockade preparations. Following the Armistice, he was hardly a popular figure with the Vichy authorities, was demoted to the position of Contrôleur d'Etat with the Bordeaux port authority and in April 1942, was arrested and briefly taken into 'preventative custody'. His next official assignment was another unprepossessing post as travelling inspector for the Ministre de l'Economie Nationale in the southern zone, assisting the government's advisors to the regional Prefects. If the position was professionally tiresome it proved a godsend to someone looking to camouflage a burgeoning resistance career. Cusin was intelligent, personable and astute. He moved smoothly and expertly through the labyrinthine French political scene, and miraculously, given his known political affiliations (never mind his secret activities), walked with relative impunity through the murky corridors of Vichy bureaucracy. He drew on his longstanding connections in the civil service to the benefit of the Resistance and, in particular, exercised influence over what he considered his *réseau* [network], the SRFD. Cusin would play an occasional but nevertheless very influential role within PIMENTO and, while not a man to transport explosives or participate in a parachute drop, his experience and sagacity proved of incalculable help to Tony in the years to come.

In the first months following his arrival in France, Tony worked manfully to try and meet the myriad tasks he had been set by F Section. The early aims and objectives of the PIMENTO organisation had been laid out in a message from Berne to London of 20 August 1942. It summarised 'that the plans envisaged by ROBERT were to carry out, principally in the unoccupied zone, a large-scale axle doping [sabotaging] programme: to arrange with the help of Trades Unions and resistant paramilitary organisations for depots of arms and ammunition for use at zero hour'. Sabotage of the aluminium industry in the Pyrenees was also planned along with attacks on shipping at Marseille and Sète 'as soon as personnel was conditioned [*sic*] and material was available.'[17] In the same document other tentacles of Bertholet's organisation are tantalisingly mentioned: 'Arthur' was an Alsatian interpreter working at the Kommandatur in Bordeaux and an agent 'Weidenfeld' was contacting railwaymen in Périgueux.[18] Whether these latter prospects ever came to fruition is not recorded.

Meanwhile, Tony's hopes for a programme of railway sabotage relied, in large measure, upon Roger Morandat's contacts amongst the railwaymen. In particular, this concerned the formation of 'axle doping' crews. At a time when Tony was forbidden by London to carry out overt sabotage in the Unoccupied Zone, he was permitted to launch attacks by subtle means, such as inserting abrasives into the axle boxes of goods trucks – 'axle doping'. SOE's scientists had calculated that carborundum powder when introduced into the boxes (either on its own or mixed with grease) would eventually attack the bearings and cause the axle to seize. With the connivance of local contacts, Tony and Roger Morandat carried out clandestine experiments with abrasive grease on German railway wagon bearings in the Lyon marshalling yards. An inevitable drawback of this method of sabotage was the difficulty in proving that the 'treatments' had worked. Nevertheless, their efforts, at the very least, confirmed that it was possible to gain access to the targets and that abrasive grease could be inserted into the bearings. These early attempts encouraged Tony, using Morandat's links, to form PIMENTO sabotage crews in districts adjacent to Lyon's La Part-Dieu and La Guillotière railway sidings with similar recruitment amongst railway workers in Toulouse, Tarbes and Sète. Meanwhile Libérer et Fédérer began to offer volunteers from its ranks. While more than welcome, Tony stipulated that, once selected for sabotage work, these men must cease all other forms of resistance activity. As the programme developed the young SOE agent became its pivotal figure and gave 'axle doping' sabotage instruction to teams in Toulouse, Montauban, Agen, Capdenac and Brive.[19]

By now the circuit really seemed to be taking shape. It was still, of course, in its early stages and Tony's opportunities for mounting operations were restricted by the shortage of explosives and incendiaries coupled with the British government's ban on aggressive forms of sabotage in the Unoccupied Zone. Nevertheless, by the autumn of 1942, Tony found himself in command of a growing force of resisters centred on the network's two main centres, Toulouse and Lyon. Even in these first months, the harsh reality of the circuit's geographical spread could not be underestimated. Its leader was constantly on the move by train or bicycle overseeing a constituency that stretched over an area of some 550 kilometres (a greater distance than London to Carlisle – the length of England).

The size of the PIMENTO network relied heavily upon a complex courier system operating across southern France and into Switzerland. With so many government officials working for PIMENTO, it proved relatively easy for the circuit's messages to be passed between French and Swiss customs officers (controlled by Bizot and Bertholet) during meetings in the frontier zone. Later, railwaymen also played vital roles on the courier lines. For example, a French locomotive on a journey near the border was allowed, as a matter of course, to cross into Switzerland in order that it might be turned around for the return journey into France. A customary handshake and salutation on the way into Switzerland allowed the passing of an outgoing, written PIMENTO message from a French train driver to his Swiss confederate. A similar, valedictory shaking of hands on the way back allowed Bertholet's message to Tony to be slipped to the French engineer or his stoker. The notes passed in this type of operation were tiny, consisting of a couple of cigarette papers glued together and folded to a size little larger than a postage stamp.

Other PIMENTO couriers travelling within France had either to memorise messages or, if it was necessary to write them down, hide them in their clothes or luggage. When Tony carried information he would write a cryptic note on cigarette paper and conceal it inside the lining of his leather belt. Although a non-smoker, he always carried cigarettes, a pipe and matches whenever he travelled. These accessories gave him the means of destroying any secret messages he was carrying while providing him with opportunities for camouflaging other activities; the lighting of a pipe or cigarette permitted a natural pause when keeping someone under surveillance, or to check if he himself was being followed. The smoker's paraphernalia also lent ideal cover for a moment of contemplation when being questioned, as he recalled, 'Your hands are terribly big when you've got something on your conscience.'

PIMENTO's bulkier courier material was delivered to secret 'letter boxes' – safe locales where messages or packages would only be accepted from known personnel and then handed over to a designated contact. For extra security these 'letter boxes' were used only one way. A message for Roger Morandat, for instance, would be sent to one destination while Morandat's reply to Tony went via another route to avoid both parts of an exchange of correspondence being intercepted together and providing investigators with a complete picture.

One 'letter box' of particular importance was that run by Olga Vittet, a barmaid at the Café Martel in Lyon's rue de la République. Most of Tony's recruits were introduced to him by colleagues but she constituted his own, first success at enlisting a new member of PIMENTO. One day in September 1942 Tony stopped at the Café Martel for a coffee. When he paid his bill he offered part of the payment in postage stamps, a regular practice due to the shortage of coinage. As Olga Vittet placed the money and a stamp bearing Petain's image into the cash register she made a derogatory remark about the Vichy leader. Tony later recalled, 'I thought this girl's heart's in the right place so I got chatting to her and asked if she could take messages for me because I'd got people coming along with spare [automotive] parts. She said *"Bien sûr"* and it developed from there.' After a few innocuous trial messages involving his cover business were successfully relayed to him, Tony asked Bizot to check Vittet's police record and when this proved satisfactory, the two men informed her of their real work. Thereafter the Café Martel became one of the most important centres of PIMENTO activities in Lyon. The café boasted a restaurant on the first floor while a side passage allowed a variety of discreet entry and exit options without the possibility of detection. Vittet, described by Tony as 'an ugly duckling but highly intelligent', was particularly adept at sifting out innocent customers from potentially threatening investigators. By a series of pre-arranged warning signals using the positioning of liqueur bottles behind the bar, she could secretly inform any members of the network present in the café that there was danger in their midst. Olga Vittet's 'cold' recruitment was an exception. From the outset, Tony demanded that security be paramount and other recruits into PIMENTO would only be accepted if 'guaranteed' by their sponsor. It was not enough that someone should merely wish to join; their probity had to be assured and the person introducing them into the circuit was thereafter held accountable for their reliability.

PIMENTO's wide area of operations and the security restrictions maintained by the Vichy (and, later, German) authorities combined to throw a great burden on the couriers charged with conveying messages that linked the activities of the network's disparate groups. Neither telephone nor mail was an acceptably secure means of maintaining contact and most of PIMENTO's communications were conducted by written or verbal messages. Given the prevailing social conditions, security forces regarded women travellers with less suspicion than male passengers and throughout the war Tony was extremely well-served by almost all of his female couriers. One recruit was his onetime 'unofficial fiancée', Colette Hirschfeld, who helped sustain links between groups in Montauban and Toulouse and, on occasion, in Lyon. In addition to her active work, she offered Tony safe, overnight billets as the occasion demanded.

Tony continued to pay the rent on the room at rue Seignemartin and occasionally took some laundry to Mme Lometro-Blois as an excuse to check if anyone had been making enquiries about him. Meanwhile at Crépieux, Mme Dupeuple was happy to receive her regular, inflated rent; her goodwill being topped up by gifts of a bar of black market *savon de Marseille* and scarce foodstuffs acquired during Tony's frequent 'business trips'. He built up an amicable relationship with the other woman in the house, Mme Dupeuple's daughter. Her work at the Town Hall involved contact with the Armistice Commission and, after the German occupation of the Southern Zone, she helped handle the administrative needs of their representatives in Lyon, for good measure acquiring a German major as a boyfriend. Through him she obtained privileged tickets for entertainments in the city such as concerts, the opera and the theatre but she was not an aficionado of such cultural activities and offloaded her tickets on Tony. This provided opportunities for the SOE agent to snatch a few hours of relaxation, indulging his love of classical music and opera. The outings allowed him to brush shoulders with the occupiers and their Vichy collaborators but, more importantly, the tickets also facilitated the acquisition of curfew passes to cover his journey home after the concerts. At the conclusion of each performance he was issued with a special pass that granted permission to travel home unmolested by the security forces and, as there was no requirement to return the *laissez-passer*s to the authorities, he could deliver the documents to Donoff and the counterfeiters who serviced the network.

Tony considered the men living at the Chemin du Panorama as more of a security threat than the women. Although at first innocuous, Mme Dupeuple's grandson became a cause for concern when he joined the Vichy organisation, Jeunesse de France et d'Outre Mer.[20] If this was not bad enough, later in the war, the youth announced his intention to join the Milice, Vichy's most violent and unforgiving anti-resistance group. The other tenant, M. Blanqui, was rarely seen. Tony gained the impression that he, too, was involved in some form of clandestine activity although it was unclear whether his preoccupation was a resistance or criminal career. Tony encountered Blanqui, completely by chance, in Toulouse one day but, instead of extending a greeting, the two men studiously ignored each other. It was the last time Tony saw his fellow resident for the latter never returned to Mme Dupeuple's house, leaving the agent to speculate why and where his fellow tenant had gone to ground.

The customs building in the rue Jarente became even more of a sanctuary when Bizot moved out of the Hôtel des Variétés and set up home there in Pédémas's apartment on the first floor with his common law wife, Germaine, and their young child, Charles. The Bizot family lived and slept in the dining room of the flat while Pédémas, and his partner, Simone, occupied a small room next to the kitchen. In spite of the overcrowding, there was always a spare bed (or at least a couch) for Tony if he needed to stay in the city overnight. As the months passed, Tony grew ever closer to Bizot. The wisdom and experience of the older man provided incalculable support for the young agent and, with the exception of the Chemin du Panorama safe house, there was never a secret that was not shared between the two men.

Meanwhile, London continued to press Tony over the vexed question of a wireless operator for PIMENTO. On 1 October 1942 London notified Bertholet that 'Thibaud', the nominated wireless operator, was still unfit and a substitute would be sent 'whose qualifications were at least equal but whose French was slightly deficient'. The message requested a rendezvous for the agent, preferably in Toulouse, on 5 November or the following five days.[21] If the newcomer's linguistic failings were disappointing, London's admission that 'Thibaud's' substitute, codenamed 'Urbain', was unable to make a parachute jump increased Tony's concern at the calibre of the agent being wished upon him. The wireless traffic between London and Berne revealed that Tony and Bertholet were 'disappointed about URBAIN's deficiency in French' and they recommended that 'he had better have cover as a French Canadian'.[22] The Colis Suisse in Toulouse was once again proposed as the rendezvous for the newcomer and the necessary passwords were sent to London on 17 October 1942. F Section disingenuously sought to reassure Tony and Bertholet that 'they had already worked out cover on ROBERT's [Bertholet] lines to account for a slight accent in otherwise perfect French' and that the rendezvous instructions had been forwarded to Gibraltar where the wireless operator, 'Urbain', was waiting to be conveyed by boat to France.[23]

Meanwhile, a truly momentous event in PIMENTO's history was set for the night of 26/27 October 1942; Tony's first RAF supply drop. He made the arrangements just as he had been instructed during his training,

In 1942 the DZ [Dropping Zone] light pattern was made up of four torches (type WONDER) hand held by the Reception Committee. Three lights with a red filter were set out in a 50 metre triangle with a light at each corner, one of which pointed into the wind. A white light would be at the upper wind end of the triangle, 15 metres to the left when facing into the wind and would flash the recognition signal. All torches were to be aimed at the aircraft once heard and follow it round. Depending on the strength of the wind the lights would be positioned towards the upwind side of the DZ or, in extreme conditions, beyond.[24]

In spite of the readiness and eager anticipation of Tony's reception committee, the operation was frustrated by bad weather. A Whitley aircraft of No.161 Squadron attempted to reach the dropping zone at Châtillon-sur-Chalaronne but was obliged to turn back well short of the DZ after a sortie of 4 hours and 26 minutes.[25] It was hardly an auspicious start and although Tony and his comrades were to face many such disappointments in the years to come, they felt the failure of this, their first operation, most acutely. With hindsight, it was none too surprising that the flight was problematic. It was now almost winter and Tony's dropping zones in the south-east of France were at the limit of the operational range of the Special Duties aircraft flying from their base in Bedfordshire. But surely no such dispassionate, analytical thoughts passed through the minds of the disappointed men who waited in the cold, French fields for the British aircraft that failed to appear.

Chapter Eight
There but for the Grace of God Go I

In spite of their longstanding opposition to having a wireless operator wished upon them, Tony and Bertholet could not prevent F Section in London eventually getting its way. On the night of 3/4 November 1942 a constellation of its agents arrived in the South of France. The group, consisting of George Starr, Mary Herbert, Marie-Thérèse Le Chêne, Odette Sansom and Marcus Bloom, was disembarked at Port-Miou in a clandestine operation carried out by a Polish-crewed felucca, the *Seadog*.[1] Although Tony was to cross paths with some of the party over the next few years, the man sent to handle his communications was Lieutenant Marcus Reginald Bloom. The agent was a stocky, red haired man in his mid-thirties who, before the war, had been a cinema company director opening up new theatres in Britain and on the Continent.[2] His father was British and his mother Russian and he had been educated in England. He lived for a while in the Netherlands and Belgium but had spent the years 1930 to 1937 in France. This stay provided him (according to his SOE file) with 'v. good' spoken French and 'fair' reading of the language.[3] While he was there he married a Frenchwoman, Germaine Février, who chose to remain in France with her widowed mother after the outbreak of war. Meanwhile Bloom returned to England and was serving with 124 Officer Cadet Training Unit, Royal Artillery (Anti-Aircraft) when he first came to SOE's notice. Any concerns over his mastery of French and less than athletic physique were doubtless offset by a note that he was already a second-year signaller. Bloom's performance in his SOE preliminary training was undistinguished save for a mark of 14/14 for signalling in his report and the prediction 'likely to become first rate'.[4] His subsequent paramilitary training assessments reflected a stalwart character and a determination to master the courses with the instructors' assessments paying ample tribute to these qualities. Favourable comments continued throughout the remainder of his training and a security report recorded that he came through his special 'scheme' with flying colours. The 'scheme', similar in purpose to Tony's visit to Liverpool, was an exercise carried out over two days in Loughborough during which clandestine tradecraft was tested in a number of scenarios orchestrated and observed by SOE training staff. Bloom performed well: 'This student did some remarkably good work. He is neat, painstaking and intelligent, and has complete mastery of himself in every situation.' His future seemed assured and, with F Section desperate for wireless operators, once Bloom had completed his training, his despatch to France was not long delayed.[5] The usual plethora of names was bestowed upon him including the field name 'Urbain' that became almost interchangeable with the codename given to his signal plan/wireless set, 'Bishop'. His false identity papers bore the alias, 'Michel Boileau'.

Accounts of the arrival of the F Section newcomers in the South of France are confused and contradictory. What is clear is that the party was escorted from the beach to Cannes where the men and women were split up and taken to separate safe houses. Bloom's subsequent movements are uncertain. London's instructions had included, 'You are to establish contact with ROBERT [Bertholet], the head of the circuit for whom you are to work, or with TEODORE [Tony], our chief representative with the ROBERT organisation.'[6] Bloom had been provided in Gibraltar with the address and passwords for the Colis Suisse in Toulouse and there was no apparent reason why his arrival there should not have been on schedule.[7]

There now follows one of the most significant and complex features of Tony's wartime story and it is an episode that even after decades of research retains ambiguities. It concerns Tony's relationship with Bloom, the latter's connections with another F Section agent based in Toulouse, Maurice Pertschuk, and the tragedy that befell these men. The records are incomplete and sometimes inaccurate, Tony's marvellous recall on this matter is revealed as uncertain (although his statements about the events were confidently expressed throughout the years), while many of the participants did not survive the war to offer their own testimonies. The following narrative sometimes departs from previous accounts (including the official history of SOE in France) but the re-appraisal is essential as the episode marks perhaps the most hazardous period of Tony's wartime career.[8]

Following London's notification, Tony expected Bloom in the first week of November and duly arranged to be in Toulouse to receive him. On the 7th he and Bertholet rendezvoused in the city, presumably so they would meet the wireless operator together. In Bloom's absence they filled their time discussing the schedule of supply drops and PIMENTO's financial situation. Regarding the latter, things were better than might have been expected; Tony, hardly a spendthrift, reported that he still possessed 175,000 francs out of his original two hundred thousand. They agreed that 'full time' members of PIMENTO would receive financial support, and, for example, Roger Morandat would be 'employed' at a salary of 5,000 francs a month. Their business having been concluded and with still no sign of Bloom, Bertholet departed. He was never to meet the wireless operator.[9]

Bloom's failure to appear was vexatious and worrying but other PIMENTO matters were equally pressing so Tony resolved to leave Toulouse on the 10th, heading for Montauban before returning to Lyon. That day, he called at the Colis Suisse to tie up some last-minute details and just happened to be in the back of the warehouse when he observed a man approach 'Claude' Bottemer at the desk at the front of the building. After an exchange of words that Tony could not hear, Bottemer called out, '*Alphonse, c'est pour toi.*' As he emerged from the shadows, Tony's worst fears were realised when the stranger greeted him, "'Ow are yer, mate?' Of those working at the Colis Suisse, only Bottemer knew that Tony had come from England. Fortunately, the Spanish workers in the warehouse failed to react to the English greeting but they soon had something else to grab their attention. Bloom's pipe belched out clouds of aromatic, real tobacco smoke; a smell that war shortages had long ago removed from France. By November 1942, the absence of tobacco had obliged the Spaniards to smoke a variety of very inferior substitutes, so the workers contemplated the new arrival with a mixture of envy and incredulity.

To cap it all, Bloom's failure to achieve anything approaching anonymity was completed by his attire. He was wearing a check suit with plus-four trousers, topped by a pork-pie hat (replete with feather), the whole ensemble lending him, according to Tony, the stereotypical look of a cockney bookmaker. Aghast at this vision, Tony coldly responded in French to the English greeting, saying that he did not understand him. Taking Bloom by the arm, he steered him to the relative privacy of the street outside. As they walked along the boulevard Bon Repos, matters did not improve. Tony discovered Bloom's French was as bad, if not worse, than expected. Moreover, when questioned about the wisdom of smoking a type of tobacco that had not been seen in France for years, the newcomer responded he need not worry as SOE had provided replica French packaging. Bloom's whole demeanour confirmed Tony's fears that London's decision to send an assistant had landed him with a dangerous liability.[10] But worse was to follow. When questioned why he was late, Bloom confessed that he had stayed the previous night in Toulouse at the apartment of a friend's girlfriend. The 'friend' in question was not a local Frenchman but another British agent, Lieutenant Maurice Pertschuk.

Pertschuk had arrived in France by sea near Antibes in April 1942.[11] He had affiliations with SOE's sister organisation, the Political Warfare Executive (PWE), which was concerned with investigating and supporting anti-Nazi political movements in occupied countries. However, Pertschuk's SOE file focuses exclusively on his F Section ancestry, albeit one with an emphasis on propaganda. Of a similar age to Tony, Pertschuk was born in Paris on 31 July 1921 to Russian-born but naturalised British citizens resident in France. His civilian occupation was as a clerk in a fur agency but when SOE first showed an interest in him in the summer of 1941, he was serving with the Royal Sussex Regiment. Accepted by SOE and using the alias 'Martin Perkins', he underwent training at Wanborough Manor in September 1941 and then followed the customary progression to the paramilitary phase in Scotland and a parachute course in Cheshire. He acquired a collection of operational names including 'Prunus', 'Eugène', and the false identity of 'Gérard Henri Perreau'.[12]

Following his arrival in Toulouse, Pertschuk came to the conclusion that he should foment armed resistance rather than propaganda. From the outset, he was dependent on F Section communications and it is not surprising that a 'transfer' from PWE should have taken place and he was given permission to form a circuit, PRUNUS:

> One fine day Eugene reported back to London that he was in contact with a very powerful action group in the Toulouse area with numerous possibilities for the disruption of rail and telephone communications and capable, as one particular instance, of dealing with the Toulouse telephone exchange itself. It did not take London long to decide to acquiesce in this modification of Eugene's original mission, and for F Section to begin to take a direct interest in his activities.[13]

The official historian summarised, 'to everyone's surprise, this mild-mannered and likeable young man turned out to have qualities of imaginative audacity that made him a remarkable clandestine organiser. He was brave and quick-witted as well as diplomatic; yet he lacked prudence and luck.'[14] Tony possessed similar qualities to Pertschuk in abundance but, thankfully, not the failings. In spite of F Section's frequent policy of linking its agents, he had not been informed by London of this other network operating in Toulouse. He had, nevertheless, heard on the local grapevine of a 'Eugène' who was organising a resistance group in the city.

Bloom's belated arrival and admission of his association with Pertschuk gave his relationship with Tony a far from auspicious start.[15] Tony's later recollections of the conversation also included a confession from Bloom that on arrival in Toulouse, he had offered proof of his bona fides to contacts by presenting a photograph of Pertschuk wearing British army uniform.[16] If this was the case, such an act contravened just about every security rule in the book and, if true, possession of the photograph could only have been made possible by the laxity of Bloom's conducting officers in Gibraltar that was in contrast to the rigorous searches carried out at RAF Tempsford.

This meeting with 'his' wireless operator left Tony with the clear impression that Bloom was keen to promote Pertschuk's interests, which was confirmed by the request that the three agents meet to discuss PRUNUS sharing the 'Bishop' wireless facility. Bloom freely admitted that he had revealed the address of the Colis Suisse to Pertschuk and the passwords with which London had provided him.[17]

Bloom's arrival and his association with Pertschuk posed major problems for Tony. It was not just a question of whether he would accept the proposal to share Bloom's radio; more fundamentally, Tony's first inclination was to send the radio operator straight back to England as a poor security risk. He certainly felt no obligation to accede to Pertschuk's request for an immediate meeting as he needed time to consider the situation and consult with his PIMENTO colleagues. He told Bloom he would be in touch 'in due course' and they parted company.

Returning to the Colis Suisse, Tony briefed 'Claude' Bottemer on the meeting. His colleague immediately endorsed Tony's misgivings and was adamant that the wireless operator should never again be allowed anywhere near the warehouse. On the question of Bloom's future employment with PIMENTO, Tony and Bottemer weighed up the options. The wireless operator might be sent back to England via Spain but, drawing on his own first-hand experience, Tony assessed Bloom's physical condition as unequal to the demands of crossing the Pyrenees. This left the far from ideal alternative of revising the request that Bloom's services be shared, and instead handing him over to Pertschuk, lock, stock and barrel.[18]

For the time being, Tony's connections with the PRUNUS circuit ended here.[19] He had numerous PIMENTO affairs to handle other than the problems occasioned by Bloom's arrival and could not allow himself to become preoccupied with the affairs of the wireless operator and Pertschuk. Meanwhile, truly momentous events were unfolding elsewhere. On 8 November 1942, the Allies launched Operation 'Torch', the Anglo-American invasion of French North Africa. In response, German troops entered Tunisia, the Italians occupied Corsica and, at seven o'clock on the morning of 11 November 1942, implementing a well-prepared plan, Wehrmacht forces crossed the demarcation line and invaded the Unoccupied Zone of France. The small Vichy army had, in limited measure, made preparations for this moment but was denied the opportunity of salvaging even a modicum of France's martial self-respect. General Jean Bridoux, the Vichy minister of war, ordered all units to stay in their barracks and not oppose the invasion. Any resistance from the Armistice army to the Nazis' Operation 'Anton' would have constituted a symbolic gesture rather than a genuine opportunity to repel the invader.

Tony left Toulouse on the evening of 10 November and took the overnight train to Lyon. When he arrived the following morning he discovered 'the station surrounded by French troops. After questioning and search I was allowed to procede [sic] into the town where nearly all the streets were cut by gendarmes or Gardes Mobiles.'[20] Unaware of the German invasion, he simply assumed that security forces were in place to prevent another Armistice Day demonstration – until he spotted Wehrmacht tanks moving along the roads by the Rhône, and then he deduced that momentous events had taken place and the façade of an 'unoccupied' France had ended.

> I realised that perhaps our work was going to be made more dangerous and more difficult because of the presence of German troops, but on the other hand it would make up the minds of so many Frenchmen who had not yet seen what German occupation meant and who were just living on the Black Market without the slightest cares.[21]

The takeover of the city was fairly seamless with the German military authorities quickly establishing working relationships with French politicians, civil servants and police. A month later the Occupation took on an even more sinister turn when a 50-strong SS security team took up residence at the Hotel Terminus near the Perrache railway station. Amongst their ranks was Obersturmführer Klaus Barbie who would lead the city's Gestapo unit and achieve notoriety as arguably the Occupation's most infamous Nazi.

Meanwhile, back in Toulouse, on 11 November the Vichy préfet régional, Chenaux de Leyritz, ordered posters to be displayed announcing that German units would be arriving that day and instructing the inhabitants to remain calm and warning that severe punishments would be imposed on those behaving in a disorderly manner.[22] The city became the headquarters of the Armee-Oberkommando (AOK) 1 and the administration centre, Hauptverbindungsstab (HVS) 564, took up residence at the Grand Hôtel de la Poste. In addition to the military occupation, other manifestations of the new regime appeared with the establishment of a Kommandeur der Sicherheitspolizei und des SD (KDS). The *Sicherheitsdienst*, the Nazi intelligence service, occupied the Hôtel de l'Ours blanc near the Square Wilson while the Gestapo moved into 2 rue Maignac, a requisitioned town house near the Grand-Rond. For Tony and PIMENTO, the stakes had been raised alarmingly.

The German occupation of the Southern Zone greatly increased the personal threat to Tony and the other F Section agents operating in Vichy France, but it was also an operational game changer: London's 'no bangs' injunction was now lifted. PIMENTO and the other circuits ceased 'preparing' for sabotage operations and, at last, were free to carry them out. Consequently, the need for specialist equipment was greater than ever and PIMENTO's first supply drop was even more eagerly anticipated. Equally important was the need to adapt the network's security to meet the new challenges imposed by the German occupation. As ever, Bizot was a stalwart and new procedures were thrashed out. Tony went to Bourg and liaised with the Morandats before returning to Lyon and travelling to Toulouse with Bizot. The two parts of PIMENTO gained another link with Bizot's introduction to several comrades in the south-west including Bottemer. At the conclusion of their business in Toulouse, Tony headed for Montauban while Bizot went to Perpignan to try to set up links across the border to Spain.

On 22 November 1942 Tony was back in Lyon. As ever, he tuned into the 19.15 BBC French-language news broadcast but, instead of the frustration of past months, heard the momentous coded messages revealing that PIMENTO would be receiving two drops that night.* He just managed to catch the nine o'clock train to Bourg where he met Roger Morandat who was about to leave for Polliat. Tony decided that he would handle the drop at Polliat himself and instructed Morandat to look after the operation on the 'Brugnon' ground near Ceyzériat.

Assisted by Henri Morandat, Tony organised the reception committee on the 'Abricot' DZ and, at twenty-three minutes past midnight on 23 November, Pilot Officer Bunting's Whitley bomber of No.138 Squadron delivered the network's first supply drop, PIMENTO 1. The five containers holding 68 lb of plastic explosive and a selection of weapons and abrasive grease were received without a hitch save for the pilot's minor caveat, 'Correct letters were flashed but lights were not as briefed'. Thankfully, this discrepancy did not prevent the completion of the operation and the aircraft

---

* If operations were 'on' the same message would be repeated on the next broadcast at 21.15. ('Narrative' p.23.)

returned safely to RAF Tangmere three hours later.[23] Tony and the reception committee loaded the containers onto an ox cart and conveyed them to the safety of Henri Morandat's barn. Meanwhile, preceded by the BBC *message personnel*, 'Croisade de l'air pur', an aircraft of No.161 Squadron flown by Pilot Officer Herbert Wynne, completed PIMENTO 2 to Roger Morandat's team at 'Brugnon'. This material comprised three (one source states five) containers holding 56 lb of plastic explosive.[24] In a way, the actual supplies were of almost secondary importance to the immense boost in morale that these first air operations engendered within PIMENTO. Tony's band of supporters had at last received demonstrable proof that their leader delivered on his promises, while he experienced great personal relief that the RAF/SOE support programme had finally carried out its side of the bargain.

Tony felt that as PIMENTO was now an armed, viable force, a martial gesture was required. Therefore, the night after the supply drop, he launched PIMENTO's first railway sabotage operation using explosives. Accompanied by a small team comprising the Morandat brothers, together with Fromont and 'Paul', he set two charges with fog-signal igniter fuses on the line between Bourg and Saint-Amour. When the train passed over them they duly exploded but nothing else of consequence happened 'which was rather aggravating'. However, the endeavour was not a complete failure, and, on closer inspection, it was discovered that they had 'removed approximately 4 ft. of track'.[25] Tony was keen to make up for lost time by launching attacks on the enemy and inspiring the men who had waited so long for the chance to take action. He took Roger Morandat and Fromont to Mézériat where he gave training to Pormathios and others on handling explosives. Moving quickly from the theoretical to the practical, he led the group to a nearby electricity pylon that carried 15,000 volts to the Tossiat mill and cut it down using the newly arrived explosives. But the day's work was not finished. That evening he visited Malamard's team and instructed them in sabotage techniques before providing another demonstration. Gathering up the remaining fuses and explosives he set charges on the railway line between Pont de Veyle and Mâcon with the intention of removing a substantial, twelve foot length of rail track. Their preparations complete, Tony and his men retreated to the safety of a bank about 100 yards away from the line to await the appearance of the next train. They were not disappointed and Tony drily noted, 'We satisfactorily derailed the bogies of a tank engine and the first four trucks of a mixed goods train. I returned to Lyon the following morning from Mâcon where there was a police control at the station, satisfied that I had made my reputation as a saboteur'.[26]

The delivery of the supplies obliged Tony to initiate a sophisticated system to cache and transport the sabotage material securely. It was difficult for the RAF to reach south-west France at this stage of the war and some of the explosives dropped to the network's main parachute grounds in the Bourg needed to be conveyed to the Toulouse-Montauban elements of PIMENTO. Recruits amongst the railway workers devised methods of smuggling packages to their colleagues in the Lot-et-Garonne and experienced little difficulty in secretly bringing small packets of sabotage material into stations and sidings. The contraband would then be hidden for the journey in the roof spaces above the lavatories in passenger carriages. This void, which was accessed by unscrewing a ceiling panel, was known only to rail workers and the hiding place resisted searches by French police and the German authorities throughout the war. Even if the cache had been discovered, investigators would have found it all but impossible to identify the culprit who had hidden

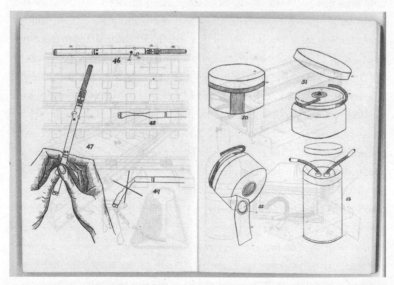

The procedure for using a time pencil (left) described in an SOE instructional booklet parachuted to the Resistance. The other devices are incendiaries.

the package. Once a train reached Toulouse, the explosives were retrieved by cleaners or railway workers; the former sometimes dropped the smaller packages down the lavatory pipe so that they could be retrieved from the railtrack underneath the carriage.

With the 'no bangs' ban lifted, the need to provide sabotage training to PIMENTO personnel grew in importance. Tony was constantly on the move instructing railwaymen in Limoges, Périgueux and Saint-Germain-des-Fossés and even organising a safe house for a wireless operator at Bellenaves should the need arise.[27] He took most of the classes himself, holding his tutorials in isolated farmhouses or railway halts where the sound of exploding detonators would not attract attention. In order to maintain his own security, he introduced himself as 'Alphonse's' representative, so that if a student was arrested they would not identify him as the leader of the circuit. The railwaymen and farmers were keen to learn the skills of a saboteur, but many struggled to understand the complexities of the equipment and, moreover, the specific drills required to construct, install and activate explosive charges. Most of the difficulties concerned the detonator, a small metal tube containing a sensitive explosive that was open at one end to receive the safety fuse. Time and again, the trainees constructed devices with the opening in the wrong place so that it failed to detonate. Even more worrying was their propensity to try to push the safety fuse into the detonator end. This was extremely dangerous because the explosive in the detonator was prone to explode if handled too robustly. But Tony consoled them (and himself) that it was still early days. He felt that the sabotage teams' morale was a vital factor and often demonstrated the effectiveness of well-placed charges on isolated sections of track. One such exercise took place near Toulouse on 14 December when he led a night-time 'training derailment' for a team of railwaymen recruited by Zaksas. The attack was made in the south-east of the city near the Montaudran aerodrome and Tony's explosive charges inflicted a six-foot cut in the rail. Although the target train's engine was not derailed, the draw bar connecting it to the first goods truck snapped, resulting in eight wagons tumbling down the embankment and breaking up. Far from being a disappointment, the locomotive's survival was a boon 'as the team were almost entirely composed of engine drivers or members of the running sheds and seeing that a sabotage could be done without hurting any railwaymen and particularly the engine driver, caused a very good impression.'[28] Another practical demonstration took place two nights later when Tony and some of his sabotage students used explosives to bring down two electricity pylons supplying the SNCF sub-station at Verlhaguet south of Montauban, 'Both pylons collapsed and the flash from the short circuit impressed the men considerably.'[29]

It was not always possible to move the sabotage material as rapidly as was desirable. On one occasion Tony delivered ten kilos of carborundum powder to Dorval for distribution to railwaymen in the Lyon marshalling yards. Although most of the consignment was successfully dispersed, Dorval still held a substantial amount hidden in a room at the Hôtel des Variétés. Normally, possession of the powder would not have posed a security problem, for his official connections should have ensured that he was not troubled by investigation for contraband. However, there was no legislating for the decision of a German patrol to carry out a snap check of the identities of hotel guests and a search of the premises. When the raid began, Dorval was in the hotel's café and duly presented his papers. His status as a government official resulted in the Germans giving him permission to go back to his room while the identity checks continued downstairs. Realising that a search of the hotel was about to ensue, Dorval extracted the carborundum powder from his cache and tipped the lot down a lavatory on the staircase's half landing. His duty done, Dorval returned to the café, confident that he had covered his tracks and destroyed the evidence. He may have covered his tracks but he had not destroyed the evidence. A short while later, a cry of alarm was heard and it was clear that Dorval's method of disposal was seriously flawed. The dense carborundum powder had blocked the hotel's lavatory drains and a cascade of water and other material had begun to flow down the staircase.[30]

Even secret agents have to take some recreation and Tony planned to spend the Christmas of 1942 in some style: 'Mme Comte bought two fat geese in the market for me, and agreed to fatten them up even more and send one to Lucien [Bizot] for Christmas.'[31] Bizot and his family had moved out of their temporary accommodation in the SRFD headquarters at the rue Jarente and were now in an apartment in a modern block, 45 avenue Maréchal Lyautey. It had been found with the help of Abbé Glasberg and was ideal for Bizot's purposes but for the fact that occupancy came with an eighty-six-year-old German lady as a lodger. The flat's owner had fled to Switzerland on the outbreak of war, leaving his mother-in-law, Mme Schnitzer, behind in the property. Tony returned to Lyon on 23 December and Bizot invited him to join his family in their new home for the festivities. With rationing becoming ever more restrictive, the cooking of a goose constituted a major culinary event. The tiny oven in Bizot's apartment could not accommodate the whole bird and major surgery had to be carried out. The impressive size of the partially dissected goose still meant that the door of the oven could not be shut properly and Bizot had to wedge it, partially closed, using a broom handle. With the gas supply intermittent and the oven having seen better days, the bird took hours to cook but, after what seemed an interminable time, it was at last ready. Now Mme Schnitzer intervened and 'tried to persuade us to boil it with onions and rice, but on being told by Lucien that I was a professional chef from a large hotel in Paris, she left us alone.'*

As the weeks passed, PIMENTO continued to draw in more Frenchmen and women whose response to the German occupation of Vichy France was to seek active roles in the Resistance. An important recruit was Rudolph Molter, known to the circuit as 'Jacquot'. Yet another member of the SRFD, he was a lively and amiable character, 'small, fat, and with a comic's face and a bawdy sense of humour. Terribly nice.' As the war progressed he played an increasingly influential part in PIMENTO's affairs.[32] Then, in January 1943, Tony was introduced to the man who was to achieve the distinction of becoming the network's 'second-in-command'.[33] The encounter took place in Toulouse on 11 January at Bottemer's. The new contact was André Moch, the twenty-five-year-old son of the prominent pre-war Socialist politician, Jules Moch. The recruit combined organisational skills acquired as an army officer with an understanding of clandestine work forged as a pre-war political activist. He had fought right-wing mobs in Paris during the political turmoil of the 1930s and served in the army during the battle of France. He was a dedicated anti-fascist, a French patriot and, not insignificantly, a Jew; his sources of motivation in the struggle against the Nazis were profound. By the time Tony met him, Moch had already developed a range of resistance

---

* 'Narrative', p. 27. The author witnessed another example of Tony's gastronomic dissimulation. When, at a restaurant in Lyon in the 1990s, his frog legs were not up to standard, Tony reinforced his complaint by affirming his own (totally fictitious) professional experience as a restaurateur.

contacts, largely in the Grenoble-Modane area, including railway workers and former army comrades-in-arms. But in spite of his credentials, Tony still provided Moch with a personal induction:

> I gave him a brief training in sabotage and in reception committees and told him that his first mission would be to organise a parachute reception in the Grenoble area to receive stores to equip teams he would have recruited to do sabotage on the lines between Lyon and Grenoble, Valence and Voiron, Grenoble and Montmelian, and Montemelian and Modane. He took this in carefully and admitted that it was a large task but said that within a month he hoped with the men he already knew, to have everything needed.[34]

Moch, given the codename 'Georges', was just the sort of individual that Tony needed as PIMENTO transcended from its modest beginnings into an organisation ready and able to wage clandestine warfare.

Meanwhile, at the turn of the new year, the affairs of the other F Section agents based in Toulouse, from whom Tony had disassociated himself, began to enter a new phase of activity. On 8 January 1943 a wireless message, ostensibly from Marcus Bloom, was sent to London: 'require another set have not lost time hidden fourty [sic] tons ammo twelve lorries ten motor cycles further ammo coming in stop require funds stop working for Teodore [Tony] and Eugene [Pertschuk] stop phone mother alls well'.[35] The impressive accumulation of war stores was not, in fact, Bloom's own work. It had been acquired by Jean d'Aligny (an erstwhile member of PRUNUS who had fallen out with Pertschuk) with the complicity of the gendarmerie of L'Isle-Jourdain, a town some thirty kilometres west of Toulouse.[36] The news of the arms seizure was doubtless a source of encouragement to F Section but the message masked the fact that after two months in France, Bloom was still incapable of plying his specialist trade: the signal had been sent over another agent's set. Moreover, the assertion that he was working for Tony was false. Bloom's decision to delude London that he was carrying out his original instructions to work for PIMENTO, while apparently innocuous, would later have deadly consequences.

The belated contact made by the 'Bishop' wireless had been carried out by an F Section operator who had come to Bloom's rescue. This was

Captain Adolphe Rabinovitch, 'Arnaud', 'a young Russo-Egyptian Jew, a wireless operator with a lurid vocabulary, as likeable as he was efficient'.[37] After studies in Egypt, France and the United States, Rabinovitch joined the French Foreign Legion and saw active service in France in 1940. Captured, he escaped and made his way to England where he joined SOE. On 28/9 August 1942 Rabinovitch was parachuted north of Grenoble with orders to head for Paris. But these original plans succumbed to local necessities and he remained in the south with the F Section organiser Peter Churchill. The dangerous linkage between F Section circuits in France is, once again, highlighted by Rabinovitch's reports to London (sent as early as 4 December 1942) regarding Bloom's difficulties and his own arrival in Toulouse to help get the 'Bishop' set in working order.[38] He stated Bloom 'did not have sufficient technical knowledge about his wireless set; he had been taught in England to use as long an aerial as possible, but he had no success with this.' Disparagingly, Rabinovitch claimed to have worked Bloom's wireless the first time he tried it, after taking the remedial step of substituting a quarter-length aerial.[39] Rabinovitch came on the air again with Bloom's second message on 23 January sent on behalf of 'Lucien'; Lazare Racheline, an agent of SOE's DF Section that handled escape lines for agents. The radio connection was short-lived and, in an attempt to improve the situation, on 11 February 1943, Rabinovitch received a message from London with instructions to inform Bloom that a new wireless set and 'red plan' had been sent on 19 January 'through Theodore [Tony] '.

Tony did receive a drop (PIMENTO 6) of four containers on 18/19 January 1943 on ground 'Iris' (Saint-Julien) but later affirmed that nothing had been delivered for PRUNUS. It is not beyond the bounds of possibility that either the set was not sent or was not retrieved. However, if London did send the material for Bloom but did not inform Tony, it constitutes yet one more flaw in the relationship between the agents and their 'controllers'. F Section still seemed to consider the networks and agents as an interlocking, cohesive whole. Baker Street might have judged such links desirable but it was a view that an impartial MI5 investigator did not share, offering the cogent, contemporary analysis, 'agents who were not supposed to be connected with each other in any way were in fact in contact.'[40] Although some F Section agents welcomed close contact with comrades, for Tony this was anathema. The security implications of these links seem to have eluded London and, throughout the first months of 1943, F section appeared content to transmit messages to pretty well any available wireless operator for forwarding to other circuits.

In the second week of February Tony sought to resolve Bloom's status and on the 12th met Pertschuk in Toulouse to discuss the matter.[41] Tony's version of their conversation – Bloom was not present – is as follows,

> When we met, we agreed that Urbain [Bloom] was a menace, but Eugene [Pertschuk] offered to house him in one of his safe houses and to look after him generally on condition that I allowed him to send his traffic via Urbain. This I agreed to most willingly and accepted in exchange to pass Eugene's bulky mail via my link with Switzerland if I were allowed to use Urbain for any urgent messages I might have. Eugene gave me his letter box at the Café Jacques, Rue d'Alsace and I gave him Olga's address in Lyon.[42]

That evening Bottemer endorsed Tony's decisions concerning Bloom and, on his return to Lyon, on the 16th he updated Bizot. Thereafter Tony was preoccupied with his customary duties arranging supply drops, recruiting personnel and, when circumstances permitted, personally carrying out acts of sabotage. Having instructed Moch's assistant and five other members of the team in Grenoble, 'I did a derailment on the Grenoble–Montmelian line in the early morning as training.'[43] Tony's return to Toulouse on 25 February presumably did not involve contact with either Bloom or Pertschuk, for his time was taken up with training new recruits to Zaksas's teams, culminating in their cutting 'six pylons, three on each of the 150,000-volt lines between the Pyrenees and Le Portet St Simon. For two days steam traction was used in the Toulouse area.'[44] As an illustration of his peripatetic and daunting workload, on 14 March, Tony was at work on the other side of the country. Accompanied by Pormathios, he attacked a train carrying petrol while it was stationary at a halt signal north of Villefranche. The 'clam' explosive charges resulted in the destruction of four wagons. Far from resting on his laurels, only a few hours later 'we derailed a supply train just a little further north than our previous operation. Eight trucks were derailed and the track was severely damaged and blocked for 24 hours. I told Martinet [Roger Morandat] to continue these operations until he had used up the spare stocks of 808 [explosive].'[45]

Meanwhile, in Toulouse Rabinovitch continued his engagement in local affairs and, on 20 February, received a wireless message from London destined for Peter Churchill that included the chilling message, 'Please warn urgent Theodore [Tony] that Robert [Bertholet] arrested by Swiss authorities stop no details yet.' As Tony had not had any contact at all with Churchill, the question has to be asked why London should think that this was an effective means of getting a message to him (other than misplaced presumptions concerning the Rabinovitch/Bloom connection). Moreover, if F Section thought that links through Pertschuk and Bloom would do the trick, this further questions London's appreciation of the real state of affairs in France. Moreover Rabinovitch was manifestly displeased with the tone of F Section's messages and on the 25th sent an irascible signal that concluded 'We are your agents and once and for all you trust us or you don't.'[46]

On 27 February a brief telegram to London by SOE's representatives in Switzerland bore the reassuring news 'Robert free. No complications. Details later.' This message was supplemented on 2 March by another from Berne requesting that Tony be informed that Bertholet was 'OK again and will let him know as soon as he can arrange to meet him'. The next day the circumstances surrounding the arrest were revealed: a smuggler carrying Bertholet's mail (and some gold) had been caught by the police. Fortunately, the documents had consisted mostly of newspaper cuttings and Bertholet managed to destroy any compromising items in his possession before the authorities arrived to search his home. SOE in Switzerland was confident, 'No one here is worried and work will go on as usual.' However, for Tony and PIMENTO, work would not carry on 'as usual'. The German occupation of Vichy France had by now made it risky for Bertholet to continue crossing the border. He was therefore largely obliged to remain in Switzerland where he continued to serve as Tony's trusted adviser (by correspondence) and facilitator of communications to and from London.[47]

Meanwhile, there was still a pressing need to resolve Bloom's role. Tony left Lyon on 19 March and the following day lunched with Pertschuk at the black-market Restaurant des Gourmets in the Place Dupuy. It 'claimed to charge 13 Francs a meal, but in the back bistro one had a most sumptuous feed on steak and chips, ham and eggs, cheese, wine and eclairs.'[48] Pertschuk was accompanied by three other members of PRUNUS; 'Jules', 'Martin' and Bloom.[49] Unfortunately, Bloom failed to improve Tony's low opinion of him, 'I realised more than ever what a menace he was, as he insisted on talking English to us. Eugene considered this a whale of a joke and replied quiet heartily.'[50]

Toulouse was not the only focus of Tony's attention and on his return to Lyon he encountered a major PIMENTO crisis. Roger Morandat had been carrying out excellent work for the network, developing the reception committees of the Bourg area with his brother Henri, and maintaining links with the railwaymen of the Lyon terminuses. But, on 15 March 1943, he and his wife were arrested by the French police and taken to the city's Saint-Paul prison.[51] One version of the circumstances surrounding his capture states that a neighbour had denounced Morandat as an escaped French prisoner-of-war living secretly in the perfume shop in the rue Masséna. Tony received word of the arrest via a warning left at Olga Vittet's dead-letter box:

> I showed this to Lucien [Bizot] who decided to use his police authority to raid Martinet's [Morandat's] shop and search it thoroughly so as to be able to remove the Michelin maps which were hidden there and any other papers he might find. In order to make this sound genuine, Lucien prepared a proces-verbal accusing Martinet of illegal traffic of saccarin [sic] and suspected traffic of cocaine. Armed with this, he and Plouc [Dorval] went to the Parfumerie du Jasmin in the Rue Massena which was under observation, very obviously. They entered but Mme Martinet did not recognise either of them, and they proceeded to search the house and remove a list of grounds and two maps very clearly marked. They did not talk to Mme Martinet as they were convinced that there was a policeman on the first floor listening to all their activities. On leaving, five policemen in plain clothes surrounded them and asked them for their papers. Lucien asked them first for theirs, and when they said 'Surete Nationale', he replied 'moi aussi' which rather startled them but when he showed his official papers they allowed him to proceed. Nevertheless they put someone to follow them, and as they had not given away the fact that they belonged to the Customs, they both went

> direct to the head office of the Police Judiciare at the Palais de Justice at
> St Jean and went in on the pretext of some other official business. When
> they came out five minutes later they were not followed.[52]

Another version states that a police search of the house revealed weapons
and plastic explosive resulting in Morandat being subjected to brutal
interrogation. Whatever the specifics of his arrest, after Morandat's initial
detention at the Saint-Paul prison, he was transferred to Montluc and Eysses
jails before being sent to German concentration camps including Dachau,
Auschwitz and Mauthausen. Tony had instituted a support programme for
the dependents of PIMENTO's casualties and Roger Morandat's wife (who
went to live with her parents) thereafter received regular financial support.[53]
While the arrest was a personal disaster, PIMENTO had now attained
sufficient maturity that the ramifications were not critical. Roger's brother,
Henri, stepped into the breach and PIMENTO's RAF supply operations in
the Bourg hardly missed a beat. Henri Morandat was a quiet, modest man
whose integrity was manifest, while the gap in the organisation occasioned
by the loss of his brother was partially compensated for by the elevation of
a colleague, Henri Gauthier, to fill the vacancy as local organiser. Given the
codename 'Jag', Gauthier was a school assistant in his mid-twenties who, as a
member of the resistance organisation Libération Sud, had excellent contacts
with other groups in the Ain. As will be seen, he was not to enjoy the most
harmonious of relations with Tony but, nevertheless, became an important
figure in this sector of the circuit.

On 2 April 1943 a PRUNUS courier, Jacques Megglé, arrived at Olga
Vittet's café. He gave her the correct passwords and handed over a large
parcel for transit to Switzerland. It was Megglé's first appearance in Lyon as
mail from Toulouse had previously been delivered by Arnault or Pertschuk
himself.[54] The messenger then requested a meeting with 'Alphonse' but failed
to pierce the rigorous PIMENTO security screen. Vittet's response was that
she had never heard of Tony but Megglé's persistence led to a meeting with
Dorval at which the courier stated that he had a message that could only be
delivered to 'Alphonse'. Dorval arranged another rendezvous that evening
on the quay of the River Rhône and reported back to Tony who 'decided to
attend it in force, Plouc [Dorval] and I going to meet Le Boiteux [Megglé]

and Lucien [Bizot], Bedat and four or five other Customs officials, all armed hanging around.'[55] The message proved to be nothing special – just a request that Tony visit Toulouse to see if he could help resolve Bloom's problems with his wireless. Tony replied that he would pay a visit but could not offer a precise date. Declining Megglé's offer to go for a drink, Tony and Dorval jumped on a passing tram but 'Lucien [Bizot] followed Le Boiteux [Megglé] "just out of curiosity" as he put it and found that he was staying in the Hotel d'Angleterre, an hotel semi-requisitioned by the Germans, which normally nobody involved in illegal matters would dare enter.'[56] Megglé's nickname 'Le Boiteux' means 'the lame one' and a PRUNUS colleague described him as 'short, broad shouldered, aged about 23–25, clean-shaven, dark haired; some chicken-pox marks on his face. He had a pronounced limp in the left leg and always carried a big walking stick.'[57] The courier later described his career in the Resistance as commencing in July 1942 with a sub-group of Philippe de Vomécourt's network. He claimed to have been very active in Paris, Port-Saint Louis, Hagetmau and Marseille until de Vomécourt's arrest forced him to go into hiding in Paris until December 1942. This account of his clandestine career included the assertion that early in 1943 he tried to penetrate the German counter-espionage services by presenting himself as a candidate for recruitment. This audacious ruse came to nothing and Megglé admitted that he pulled out of the negotiations when the Germans demanded proof of his commitment by having him denounce a colleague. Moving to Toulouse, he made several contacts in the Resistance and was eventually introduced to Pertschuk in March 1943.[58] Megglé's version of events needs to be set alongside a contradictory account offered by Marcel Petit, another member of PRUNUS, who stated that he had 'come from the Marseille group, where he had not been found satisfactory'.[59]

On 4 April 1943, PIMENTO's leader celebrated his twenty-first birthday. As with millions of his fellow countrymen serving around the world in conventional forces, it was not a time for a family party or a few drinks with pals and a girlfriend. It was business as usual and, accompanied by Dorval, Tony marked the occasion by blowing up power lines to the Berliet truck factory. 'We managed to get the 220,000 volt line to fall across the 66,000 volt line which caused a satisfactory short circuit.'[60] If he had found the time or the inclination, Tony might have reflected that he had been in France for nine months and, against the odds, had remained at liberty and created a flourishing resistance network. Bertholet was delighted with his young comrade's performance but had become concerned at the personal cost. A report to London stated he 'considers Theo's [Tony's] work to be of highest quality and pays great tribute to his courage and endurance in view of real ravages caused by his illness. Said his physical condition literally terrible.'[61] Perhaps part of the problem derived from Tony's obsessive nature. Whereas many other SOE agents adopted a leadership profile that made their true nationality a matter of common knowledge from the very first days, Tony maintained a low-key stance (apart from leading the sabotage operations). He was unassuming, parsimonious, unarmed and without bodyguards – and the strain on him was immense, but it would have taken a substantial leap of imagination for any Gestapo investigator to suspect that the youthful figure of 'Antoine Brévin' was the leader of one of SOE's most substantial networks.[62]

On 7 April Tony arrived at Bottemer's in Toulouse and went to one of the PRUNUS 'letter boxes', the apartment of Mme Odette Laroque in the rue Nègreneys. Laroque, 'small, fair, with brown eyes and a squarish face' was Pertschuk's mistress as well as being an active member of PRUNUS, and she set up a lunchtime meeting for Tony with her boyfriend at the notorious black-market restaurant, Les Truffes de Quercy.[63] Wary as ever, Tony took the precaution of having Théo Bernheim make a preliminary reconnaissance of the restaurant and check for any sign of its being under hostile surveillance.

On his arrival Tony received a surreptitious 'all clear' signal from Bernheim who, to all appearances, was busy mending a bicycle puncture on the other side of the street. On entering the restaurant, Tony was ushered to a partitioned cubicle at the back of the dining area and, as he approached, could hear the sound of animated conversation – in English. At the table introductions continued in the same language but Tony insisted that they speak in French.[64] Instead of the anticipated intimate meeting, around the table sat a group of young men and women.

Tony later affirmed that sitting next to Pertschuk was a woman, Odette Sansom, 'Lise'. An F Section courier, Sansom had landed on the same operation as Bloom and, like him, made her way to Cannes. Her original instructions were to operate in Auxerre, but circumstances resulted in her staying on the Côte d'Azur to assist one of F Section's most important agents,

Peter Churchill. A biography states she and Churchill were in Toulouse in February 1943 where they met Pertschuk. Similarly, Churchill's memoirs report a February meeting in the city attended by himself, Sansom, his wireless operator, Rabinovitch, and Pertschuk. Neither account makes reference to Tony while the PIMENTO leader never said that Churchill was at Les Truffes de Quercy. [65] The woman whom Tony later identified as Sansom is described in his near-contemporary 'Narrative' as the (unnamed) courier of George Starr, 'Hilaire'.[66] The latter was an F Section officer who had landed by the same felucca as Bloom. It had originally been intended that Starr would make his way to Lyon but the network he was to join, the DETECTIVE circuit, had suffered a succession of arrests and, instead, on meeting its leader, Henri Sevenet, in Cannes he was instructed to go to Gascony. He was to become one of F Section's most illustrious agents, developing the highly successful WHEELWRIGHT circuit through an unbroken period of service in enemy territory from November 1942 until the liberation of the south-west in September 1944.

While Mme Laroque was present at the meal, a significant absentee was Megglé. [67] This allowed Tony free reign to voice his concerns about the courier and, in particular, the odd behaviour exhibited in Lyon. Pertschuk was unconvinced by the suspicions and 'Starr's assistant' gave her own endorsement of Megglé's bona fides. But Tony was obdurate and requested that Pertschuk refrain from sending Megglé to Olga Vittet: he 'would give him in the near future a new letter box for his mail to Switzerland … on no account was he to use Olga's letter box as I suspected it was being overworked.'[68] The gathering at the restaurant unsettled Tony. Superficially, it seemed an appropriate council of war at which the leaders of F Section's endeavours in the south-west were given the opportunity to co-ordinate their efforts. On the other hand, the meeting constituted a dreadful threat to security as the agents' association risked catastrophic consequences if their networks were penetrated by enemy agents. The lunch concluded with an agreement to reconvene at the same time and place at the end of the month and the agents then went their separate ways. Their plans would not be realised.

While PIMENTO continued to develop, so too had Pertschuk's PRUNUS, its activities being centred upon Toulouse, Montréjeau, Fonsorbes, Auch, and other locations in the south west. In spite of Bloom's difficulties in making wireless contact with London, a loyal group of followers had been recruited and several RAF supply drops helped enhance Pertschuk's local standing. Moreover, PRUNUS's status was such that by April 1943 it would become involved in its most ambitious project to date: the sabotaging of the Toulouse gunpowder factory. An attack on the facility had been discussed by SOE planners in London as early as 6 August 1942 at a meeting chaired by Lieutenant-Colonel Dennis 'Bobby' Guinness, when it was described as a 'very difficult task and unlikely to be realised'.[69] Nevertheless, the question of a sabotage operation was resurrected seven months later with a telegram to F Section sent from Berne on 29 March 1943,

> Most immediate: 1) Adams has passed to us project to blow up poudrerie nationale de Toulouse. 2) Reply urgently whether you can arrange for somebody to contact on morning of April 9th following individual; 3) Monsieur Hitter, repeat Hitter, 62, Allée Jean Jaures, 3rd Floor, Toulouse. Password: De la part de Valentin. 4) Hitter is not employed in factory but will introduce our men to individuals eager to do the job.[70]

'Adams' was the codename for the SIS representative in Switzerland, so the offer had to be treated seriously but F Section was, nevertheless, cautious in a response made the same day: '1) Project smells very fishy. 2) Can Adams give indication as to reliability of his source and possibly contamination either at source or en route. 3) If Adam's [sic] reply favourable will try and arrange.' On the 31st March Berne replied:

> Hitter is absolutely reliable. He is French officer personal friend of one of Adam's [sic] most trusted agents. 2) If you do not want to contact H's friend in factory you need not. He will be content with material. But since he and his friends have been doing sabotage on their own initiative over long period consider it desirable to take them up. 3) Meantime can you guarantee completely meeting on April 9th. It has been arranged with difficulty on our behalf by Adams.

F Section replied in the affirmative on 1 April 1943 stating that Hitter would be contacted on the morning of the 9th.

In spite of F Section's concerns that the project was 'fishy', the plan possessed sound credentials having been proposed by an established network, GILBERT, run from Switzerland by Colonel Georges Groussard. An officer in the pre-war French army, after the Armistice, Groussard was appointed Inspecteur Général des Services de la Sûreté Nationale, the Vichy army's security service. Following an approach by an emissary of the Free French, in June 1941 he was secretly brought to London for consultation with the BCRA, SIS and, according to Groussard's memoirs, Winston Churchill. On his return to France, on 15 July 1941 Groussard was arrested but then escaped to Switzerland. His relations with the Free French were fraught while, in contrast, he developed strong links with SIS. From January 1943 the Toulouse sub-branch of GILBERT was led by Lieutenant François Hitter (the man to whom the London-Berne telegrams referred) who had a contact 'on the inside' of the gunpowder factory with access to blueprints of the premises. Moreover, this man, known under the cover name 'Bobby', confidently predicted that explosives could be introduced into the premises. Groussard contacted 'Adams', his SIS contact in Switzerland, regarding Hitter's proposal. But SIS was disinclined to become involved in sabotage (its priority was intelligence gathering) so it sought to engage SOE in the scheme, which culminated in Hitter's being put in touch with Pertschuk.

Having received London's approval, PRUNUS began its engagement in the proposed sabotage operation with Pertschuk's organisation offering to provide explosives for 'Bobby' to plant in the factory. Megglé became a pivotal link to Hitter's organisation. On 9 April 1943 the two men met as agreed; Hitter introduced Megglé to 'Bobby' and they concluded that the sabotage would be carried out a fortnight later.[71] But Pertschuk was unhappy with Megglé's arrangements and instructed him to have the operation brought forward. The emissary duly conveyed this news to 'Bobby'. By now Megglé felt a rapport with his new comrade-in-arms and, as a result, confided details about PRUNUS – over and above the agreed specifics of providing explosives and the handsome financial bounties for the eight saboteurs who would carry out the operation. He disclosed the 'letter box' at Mme Laroque's and there must be a suspicion that this was not all he revealed to 'Bobby'. On the 11th Megglé visited Bloom and, presumably, gave an update on developments; with this meeting surely informing the latter's wireless message to London of 12 April 1943: 'Hitter contacted stop working on op as suggested'.[72]

It was now a matter of getting the explosive devices to the saboteurs. According to Megglé, he visited 'Bobby' at nine o'clock on the Monday, discussed a range of topics including the make-up of their respective organisations, and revealed that one of PRUNUS's secret depots of explosives was maintained by Marcel Petit at the École Vétérinaire.[73] Concluding their tête-à-tête, Megglé confirmed he would return on Thursday with the explosives, and 'Bobby' escorted him to the tram. Some 500 metres into his journey, three men closed in on Megglé and seized him. The tram stopped, he was thrown into a waiting car, a blanket put over his head and his hands manacled.[74]

There was a simple explanation behind Megglé's arrest: 'Bobby' was Robert Moog, an undercover agent of the Abwehr – German military intelligence. A Frenchman, born in Paris in 1915, he apparently had connections with Alsace and, consequently, spoke German fluently. He had served in the French Army at the beginning of the war but his recruitment as a German agent may have taken place earlier and he might have acted as a member of a 'Fifth Column' organisation serving Nazi interests during the 1940 invasion. If the commencement of his traitorous behaviour is in doubt, it seems he later secured a position, thanks to his linguistic skills, as a driver for the German Armistice Commission in Toulouse. In 1942 he met, by chance, a comrade-in-arms from his army service who was working for German intelligence. Thus Moog was introduced to Hauptmann Eugen Kramer, head of Section IH of the Dijon branch of the Abwehr, and subsequently joined the German payroll as agent 'K 30' with the alias 'Steinbach'.[75] On 23 January 1943 his controllers installed him under cover with the trials team at the Toulouse gunpowder factory and in March Moog was approached by Hitter and propositioned to help sabotage the establishment. The German agent possessed an engaging personality and seemed committed to the Gaullist cause so he penetrated the GILBERT and PRUNUS networks with some ease. Having infiltrated a wide range of resistance activity in the city, all was in place for his German controllers to begin the arrests.[76]

As the first to be arrested, there has been much speculation surrounding Megglé's role in the ensuing events.[77] Moog clearly knew a great deal about PRUNUS having attended a meeting at its Toulouse headquarters, the home of the Vuillemot family at 22 rue des Pyrénées. He therefore did not necessarily require Megglé's cooperation to implement his next action, the installation of German agents in the house to await members of the PRUNUS circuit as they unwittingly walked into his trap. When the Germans first arrived on the scene, the only occupant was an eleven-year-old boy but, in the early evening, a succession of PRUNUS personnel began to call. Madame Vuillemot, the boy's mother, spotted Germans entering the house but was so concerned for her son's safety that she rushed to his side and neglected to provide warnings for her comrades. Later, further victims fell into the trap; her husband, Robert Vuillemot, their daughters, Lucien Fayman of PRUNUS and two female colleagues. Then, half an hour later, came Moog's biggest catch of all; Pertschuk. The SOE agent apparently had noticed a suspicious car parked outside the house but nevertheless entered the building.[78] Now, with the leader in the bag, the PRUNUS prisoners were taken away while a German team remained in the house, hoping to scoop up any late arrivals.

Elsewhere in the city, the arrests continued and at eleven o'clock on the 13th, Petit and a colleague were picked up at the École Vétérinaire.[79] Pertschuk's girlfriend, Odette Laroque, at first managed to avoid capture. She had not been present at the disaster at the rue des Pyrénées and briefly remained at large because the Germans had the wrong number of her home in the rue Nègreneys. But her liberty was short-lived. At 2.30 in the afternoon of 13 April she was arrested by the Gestapo at her office at the Encyclopédie Médico-chirurgicale.[80]

Two days later, another very significant arrest as far as Tony's security was concerned was made at Fonsorbes some fifteen kilometres to the south-west of Toulouse. A group of men presented themselves at the Château Esquiré where they were greeted by the proprietor, Jean d'Aligny, who, it will be recalled, had hidden firearms for PRUNUS. In spite of d'Aligny's split with Pertschuk, he continued to assist Bloom and allowed his home to be used as a safe house and site for wireless transmissions. The visitors' amiable demeanour vanished as soon as they gained entrance into the château. They arrested the inhabitants, while German *feldgendarmes* emerged from concealment and began a search of the premises. One account of the raid suggests that Bloom tried to escape but, if so, it was a forlorn gesture.[81] The operation was a triumph for Moog, crowned by the discovery of Bloom's suitcase wireless set 'hidden' under a bed. Any hope that the occupants might have held of denying their resistance activities instantly evaporated; d'Aligny, Bloom and the other residents of the château were taken to Toulouse for interrogation. PRUNUS had been destroyed in barely a week. The question now was whether the fallout would encompass Tony and PIMENTO.

Moog had not yet finished his machinations and he made short work accounting for his remaining contacts in the GILBERT network. Hitter had left for Paris on 9 April but was arrested there on the 15th.[82] Moving on to Lyon, Moog killed Captain Claude Bulard and appropriated the dead man's identity papers for his future use.[83] Meanwhile, back in Toulouse the German security forces embarked on a new operation; the 'playback' of Bloom's wireless set by sending messages to London purporting that the SOE man was still at liberty. If Bloom could not be persuaded to cooperate, they prepared to use a substitute operator.[84] An Abwehr radio expert, Karl Fischer, was already on hand but another wireless man, Joseph Goetz, of the Paris SD, was sent to Toulouse to provide assistance. Details of the 'playback' scheme are revealed in British archives but little has emerged from the German perspective apart from anecdotal comments made by a few participants. Long after the war, Goetz spoke about PRUNUS: 'Marcus Bloom should not have been sent. Marcus Bloom got the wrong gender of every word. Never he could [sic] have been taken for a Frenchman ...' After two or three days Bloom confided to him "'Dr Goetz, for the first time since I landed in France, I feel safe."'[85]

After the liberation of France, Tony wrote a very cryptic, official chronology of his clandestine career in F Section but it reveals little about the PRUNUS debacle. 'April 1943. EUGENE and URBAIN arrested. Closed letter boxes. No further breakage.'[86] The explanation for this curt assessment is not hard to find; at the time, Tony possessed a very incomplete picture of the collapse of PRUNUS. But official SOE documents then denied to him reveal that his report was hugely optimistic; the destruction of Pertschuk's circuit seriously threatened not only Tony's personal survival but the whole of PIMENTO.

Even before the PRUNUS arrests, London had failed to grasp that Bloom was not working for Tony and the two men were scarcely in contact. Consequently, Bloom's wireless traffic bearing London's messages for PIMENTO never reached Tony. On 8 April (before the arrests) SOE transmitted a message to Bloom 'For Alphonse' confirming details of one of Tony's proposed parachute DZs. Four days later, F Section asked for an explanation why PIMENTO had failed to arrange a reception committee. Tony was not the only agent to receive such unwarranted criticism. The same signal chastised George Starr and Pertschuk, concluding with the tactless and superfluous message, 'For all RAF doing utmost for us this month know your difficulties but please help pilots by perfect reception. Love and kisses.' A week later, on 19 April, the frivolity had dissipated and an ominous signal was sent by F Section to Bloom; 'One of our officers arrested by Gestapo had with him address of Mme La Rocque she therefore might be compromised stop make arrangement for her to change her residence love to all.'[87]

What remained unclear was how had London been informed of an arrest and what was the identity of the captured 'officer'? The PRUNUS disaster was not the only crisis to befall F Section that spring. On 16 April 1943 (four days after the arrest of Pertschuk) its agents Peter Churchill and Odette Sansom were arrested at the Hôtel de la Poste at Saint-Jorioz on Lake Annecy. Once again, the damage had been wrought by the Abwehr, this time in the form of a German non-commissioned officer, Hugo Bleicher, who had represented himself as a volunteer for recruitment by SOE as a double agent. London might perhaps have felt a modicum of consolation that the group's wireless operator, Rabinovitch, remained at liberty. However, the risks of linkage between the arrested agents were manifest. It seems that Churchill may well have had Mme Laroque's address on him when arrested. She is not specifically mentioned by Churchill in his post-war autobiographical accounts although he admitted to possessing a document bearing three names and telephone numbers when arrested.[88] As far as Tony's safety was concerned, his only contacts with these captured agents was the tenuous one via Rabinovitch and Bloom and the lunch in Toulouse that *might* have included Sansom. Unlike the grave danger posed by the calamitous events in Toulouse, he was not put at significant risk following the Saint-Jorioz arrests.

Had one of the other circuits learnt of the arrests in Toulouse? If so, with London believing that Tony and Starr were in regular and intimate contact with PRUNUS, why had they not been warned by other means? A second message from London was sent to Bloom on the 19th but, curiously, this had nothing to do with the reports of arrests and was yet another exhortation to

Tony, Starr and Pertschuk to achieve greater success with their reception of supply drops.

On 20 April 1943 London received information on affairs in Toulouse from another source – SOE in Berne. The message to F Section stated, '1) Most immediate: Adams [the SIS representative] informs me Hitter and others in his group arrested by Gestapo. 2) Have we had any repercussions? Instruct our men urgently to be wary.'[89] Evidently, this inspired F Section to signal agents in Toulouse on the 21st with a redundant notification of the disaster, 'For Eugene [Pertschuk] we have just been informd [sic] Hitter and others in his group arrested by Gestapo stop are there any repercussions stop take all necessary precautions.' F Section's next wireless message to Berne suggested a level of self-control that events were soon to belie, 'Sorry arrest Hitter; have advised our own people and will keep you posted.'[90]

Bloom's wireless remained silent until, on 23 April, London received 'Could not transmit recently stop can now keep contact stop notified Toulouse danger stop have left late hideout stop no news hrom [sic] Eugene stop instruct.' A second message was sent by 'Bloom' the same day, 'Still no contact with Eugene stop have found safe residence since nineteenth stop no idea what has happened region Toolouse [sic] stop uncertain what steps to take.' The messages elicited the response from London, 'You must remain at your safe house and send courier with multiple precautions to investigate condition Eugene set up stop you must remain in contact Alphonse [Tony] Hilaire [Starr] stop advise soonest.'[91]

Further messages were exchanged over the following days with 'Bishop' claiming to be safe and with friends but unable to provide news of Pertschuk or Hitter. The signals to London continued to contain errors in code security checks resulting belatedly in questions being raised in Baker Street whether 'Bloom' was just consistently slapdash or operating under duress. When decoded by SOE, the messages of the 23rd revealed that neither of the 'Bishop' signals contained their 'true check' while the 'bluff check' was present in both. These security processes were pre-arranged between F Section and its wireless operators before their departure for France. Specific spelling mistakes in a transmitted message ought to have been a reasonably reliable indicator as to whether the signal had been encoded by an agent at liberty or one who had been captured whose codes had fallen into the hands of the Germans.

The system was not flawless and Leo Marks, SOE's head of codes, had little faith in it.

> It took no account of the possibility of an agent's code being broken or tortured out of him, when the Gestapo would be in a position to work out the security checks for themselves. Nor did it make any allowances for Morse mutilation, which frequently garbled so much of the text that it was impossible to tell whether the security checks – for what little they were worth – were present.[92]

Analysis of Bloom's encoded messages revealed that he had been random in his use of the checks from the very outset. Moreover, a staff officer in London who examined the 'Bishop' transmissions felt that there would have been even greater cause for concern had 'Bloom' suddenly exhibited a suspiciously high level of diligence in encoding his messages. More disturbingly, Captain Christopher Harmer of MI5 commented, 'BISHOP transmitted very irregularly in the early stages. Moreover, in every single message from the start he omitted his security check and inserted his bluff check. This would appear, prima facie, to be evidence that he was controlled, but SOE regard it, possibly quite rightly, as of no significance.'[93]

Meanwhile Tony, in blissful ignorance of the disaster that had befallen PRUNUS, decided to visit Toulouse to carry out some PIMENTO duties but also to see Pertschuk. He took the overnight train on the 24th but it suffered a derailment and instead of arriving at 9.15 he was delayed until noon. This resulted in a change of plans; he did not call at Laroque's but instead went straight to the restaurant Les Truffes de Quercy where he anticipated finding Pertschuk. On asking the manageress if she had seen his 'friend' recently, she queried if he meant the young man who resembled the actor Jean-Louis Barrault. Recollecting Pertschuk's physical similarity to the French film star, Tony replied that he was the man in question. Without any discernible sign of emotion, the *restauratrice* informed him that she had heard that 'Jean-Louis Barrault' had been arrested, leaving Tony to admit 'I appeared amazed and said I was merely hoping to do a deal with him over a bicycle'.[94] Clearly shaken by the news, he 'apologised for disturbing her and left. For the next halfhour I travelled around on Toulouse's trams to make sure I was not followed, changing at every cross over.'[95] He could not leave the matter there and needed more than restaurant gossip. Accompanied by Theo Bernheim he went to the main post office and telephoned Laroque's number, 'A man replied and said that Croquette [Laroque] was away but would be in "incessament" [*sic: incessamment* – shortly] and that she had left him instructions for a lot of people and that if I would care to call, he would be only too willing to help me.'[96] Sensibly, Tony replied that he would call back later. On leaving the call box he spotted a man with a 'police look' who came downstairs from the telephone exchange and apparently started to follow him and Bernheim. It was a relatively simple matter for the two experienced PIMENTO men to split up and take trams going in opposite directions, their 'tail' (if that was what he was) failing to trail either of them. A few discreet enquiries around the city suggested to Tony that little more could be achieved in Toulouse and he departed for Lyon to warn London of the worrying situation.

Another set of telegrams sent by SOE in London to Bertholet in Switzerland revealed that F Section was far from being in control of the crisis. A message of 1 May 1943 read:

> Most immediate. Following for Robert [Bertholet]. Since Hitters arrest we are without news organiser Eugene [Pertschuk] instructed to contact him nor have we any news Alphonse [Tony] and we are extremely worried by a telegram just received from w/t operator Urbain [Bloom] who says he is unable contact either Alphonse or Eugene will you please ask Alphonse to give us postbox or safe house and password where Urbain can get in contact with Alphonse again as soon as possible.[97]

While London was understandably anxious to acquire information on the true course of events surrounding the PRUNUS debacle, it is surprising that, amidst the grave uncertainty, they sought to put Tony and 'Bloom' in contact. Even allowing for the longstanding misapprehension that the 'Bishop' set had been operating for PIMENTO, they should have perceived that any contact was fraught with danger. In the light of the disaster that had befallen the GILBERT and PRUNUS networks because of their association, SOE's attempt to link PIMENTO with the compromised circuit seems decidedly foolhardy. Moreover, no mention was made in the message to Bertholet of London's doubts concerning the anomalies in 'Bloom's' code checks.

No sooner had F Section sent the May Day telegram than fresh news from France necessitated a second message to Bertholet:

Have just been advised from the field that following various arrests in Toulouse British organiser though at liberty is closely watched. This may refer either to Eugene or even to Alphonse organisation in Toulouse. Germans will not take any action before Fifteenth May when they think stores delivery is to take place. Suggest you tell Alphonse with all security to warn Eugene of possible danger and advise him to leave letting Alphonse know where he is going.[98]

It is significant that messages needed to be sent from London to Bertholet in Switzerland regarding a catastrophe in Toulouse and, in part, this tortuous route justifies F Section's insistence that Tony have a wireless link. The files do not make it clear how many other F Section agents were instructed to investigate the crisis although Starr and Rabinovitch clearly did so.

Meanwhile the desultory exchange of wireless messages between London and Toulouse continued. On 2 May 1943, F Section sent to 'Bishop', 'Are trying to get in touch with Alphonse through another way and have asked for postbox where you can contact him stop are any friends mentioned in your message already connected with our work stop answer soonest cheerio.' It must be assumed that the 'other way' London proposed to contact Tony was the London–Berne–Toulouse/Lyon link. Of course, the message did not reach him. Further fragments of news concerning recent events in Toulouse appeared in a message to London from Rabinovitch of 2 May, 'EUGENE and some of his men arrested at his headquarters by Gestapo on 13th. Apparently sold out. Remainder lost contact with URBAIN, but I will try to arrange. There were also other Gestapo searches and arrests, all without using French police.'[99]

Then 'Bishop' came back on stream with two messages to London on 3 May confirming the arrest of 'Eugene' but offering reassurance that 'other safe houses' had been arranged. The second message dealt with the practicalities of parachute reception committees, stating that contact had been made with one of Pertschuk's groups but recommending that dropping grounds be cancelled until further notice. This provoked a response from F Section that they had heard 'Eugene and some of his friends arrested by Gestapo', offered the reassurance that they had 'instructed Alphonse get in contact with you' and that 'Arnaud' [Rabinovitch] might also get in touch. To facilitate the link, 'Bloom' was instructed to send details to London of a safe house or postbox (with requisite passwords). In the ensuing days, more messages were exchanged regarding parachute drop grounds and wireless schedules then, on 6 May, F Section received the contact details they had requested; from 14 May, 'Bishop's' courier would be waiting between the hours of 11.30 and noon outside the Grand Bureau de Poste in the town of Auch, 80 kilometres west of Toulouse. The courier would be carrying a green parcel as a recognition signal. The password *'Est-ce que l'autobus pour Toulouse arrête ici?'* ['Does the bus for Toulouse stop here?'] should be met by the response, *'Non, mais je vais montrer l'endroit'* ['No, but I will show you the place']. London's contact was to bring 100,000 francs with them.[100] The following day SOE confirmed receipt of the proposals, notifying 'Bishop' that they had 'instructed "Alphonse" accordingly'. By now it should not be a surprise to learn that no such instruction reached Tony.

On 8 May 1943 Rabinovitch sent a crucial message to London. It provided further details of the PRUNUS disaster but, momentously, at last reported Bloom's arrest:

> My engineer back from TOULOUSE now says URBAIN was arrested. He and his host stayed although warned to leave when EUGENE caught. Two days later house surrounded by twenty German soldiers. URBAIN and a Spaniard managed to escape to bushej [*sic*], discovered and shot at. They retreated under cover of their pistols to Gendarmerie but were handed over to Germans. Whole TOULOUSE gang obviously sold out. EUGENE knew trouble was coming and hardly moved out.[101]

This news had an immediate effect in London and, having spent so long trying to link Tony and 'Bloom', F Section now performed a complete volte-face. A wireless message to Berne instructed SOE officials 'to do their utmost to prevent ALPHONSE from keeping the rendezvous [with Bloom]'.[102]

It is plain that even now London erroneously believed that details of an appointment with 'Bloom' arranged over the 'Bishop' set would have reached the PIMENTO leader.

The next wireless message from SOE reflected the radical change in F Section's security appreciations following Rabinovitch's confirmation of Bloom's arrest. On 9 May London sent 'Bishop' a signal regarding lighting arrangements for the next supply drop and concluded, 'Message from Father quote have cancelled deal with Pinn as bank security bad and doubt his checks and called his bluff.' This apparently innocuous piece of family news appears at first to refer to an earlier message from London, sent on 8 April (before the PRUNUS disaster) that included personal details from Bloom's father, 'Everybody well Bernard fit stop have bought out Pinn'.[103] It is clear that the content of this signal formed the camouflage for the 9 May message that was critically intended to test Bloom's true status. By including wireless security jargon such as 'checks' and 'bluff', London indicated that it was questioning whether Bloom really was at liberty and operating freely. SOE hoped that references to family contacts would elude the suspicions of any German operative controlling Bloom's messages. On the other hand, the unsubtle references to 'security bad', 'doubt his checks' and 'called his bluff', suggest a degree of desperation in London's tardy probing of Bloom's predicament.

Only fragments of the wireless traffic are available to chart the course of events in the spring of 1943 and very few of the leading participants survived the war to offer their testimonies. However, sufficient data remains to enable an analysis of events, and it is clear that by the second week of May, strong apprehension about Bloom's true status had registered in Baker Street. It is unclear whether suspicions first began in SOE's Security Section, Code Section, Communications Section or F Section itself.[104] An indication of SOE HQ's disquiet is revealed in a memo of 13 May (a full month after Pertschuk and Bloom's arrests) from Major Gerry Morel to colleagues (presumably MI5) in which he volunteered to share the texts of future messages destined for 'Bloom' before their transmission. The same day, Major Richard 'Dickie' Warden of SOE's Special Section (Bayswater), the organisation's Operational Security Branch, received a letter from an MI5 officer stating that he had met Captain 'George Noble' (F Section's communications specialist) with Morel and 'later approved a message to go to BISHOP'. This is clearly not the message of the 9th while, unfortunately, the telegram in question does not seem to have survived because the next on file (16th) merely mentions hopes for supply drops, the prospect of sending money and, almost inevitably, invoked Tony as Bloom's contact, 'Alphonse instructed to make contact hope no great delay if contrary advise us stop.'[105]

These SOE and MI5 records invite the disturbing conclusion that Tony Brooks was now being used in France as an unwitting pawn in a deadly game orchestrated in Baker Street by confused staff officers against their German foe. Then, on 18 May, any residual uncertainty in London over Bloom's status was dispelled by a pronouncement made by MI5's greatest double-cross expert, Lieutenant-Colonel Thomas 'Tar' Robertson. In a typically perspicacious letter to Commander John Senter, a former MI5 officer and now SOE's Director of Security, Robertson commented, 'Our opinion is that BISHOP is now working under control.' He continued, 'At the moment I think you must regard BISHOP as blown ... We will try and give you a final opinion as soon as possible, but meanwhile I think you must ask Buckmaster to mark time on the whole Toulouse set-up.'[106]

While the security experts completed their analyses, F Section cautiously maintained the link with Bloom's wireless to try to secure further confirmation of the Germans' deadly intent. 'Bishop' messages transmitted to London continued to feature ruses intended to lure Tony (or his courier) into the enemy's net. On 23 May the Nazi operator working Bloom's set sent the signal, 'Alphonse courier not yet arrived stop let me know when I can withdraw my courier chance he may be remarked stop advise you let me know where my courier can contact that of Alphonse stop now working frrom ... (message mutilated).' The corrupted conclusion of the message received by SOE suggests that the Germans wanted to keep contact while not wishing to reveal the location of the 'Bishop' transmissions for fear of it being investigated. Then, at last, F Section went on the offensive to secure proof that the Germans were operating Bloom's wireless. They instructed him to go to the 'green pub at the usual place stop you will find your friends waiting for you with half million' – not surprisingly, the Germans were nonplussed and replied that they could make no sense of the instructions. In London it had been hoped that the real Bloom, if he was still at liberty, would recognise that the pub mentioned was the popular SOE haunt, the Manchester Arms in Adam Street, near Baker Street, and that he 'would have realised that our messages were an invitation to return at once to England.'[107] Bizarre wireless exchanges continued over the following days. London repeated the order to go to the green pub 'where you went often with Andre and Jacques' to which the Germans petulantly responded, 'What the hell are you up to your thirty five [London's previous message] useless know of no green pub or Andre or Jacques stop reply by return with full and explicit details.' But the teasing (or entrapment) continued with London calling 'Bloom' a 'silly ass' for not realising that they referred to 'the green pub in Andorra'. Yet, even at this stage, the MI5 officer entrusted with investigating the case estimated in an early draft of his report that the reaction from 'Bloom' was consistent with someone not under duress and, 'In a word, this reply is in my opinion more appropriate from an innocent but genuinely bewildered agent more than from an agent under German control, and I shall not be surprised if URBAIN turns up in Spain in the near future.'[108] This completely erroneous conclusion (that was later revised to concede that Bloom's set had been worked back immediately after the arrests) was perhaps a factor in SOE's decision to maintain the 'radio game'. Meanwhile, in order to further test their adversaries, on 27 May London flaunted tantalising prospects of secrets that they knew the Germans would be keen to possess, 'We have some new and important radio equipment it is proposed to use for D Day purposes stop we badly require to instruct a number of other operators in France on how to use it stop can you make a trip back here for a course of instruction.' This was effectively SOE's last throw of the dice and the messages that followed over the next fortnight largely concerned 'Bloom's' affirmations that he was tidying up his affairs and preparing to cross into Spain. The Germans still had not given up all hope of luring Tony or his representative into a trap, for they continued to send messages of 'Bloom's' pressing need for money. Then, on 14 June, London received the last message sent via the 'Bishop' set, 'As no help from you in any shape or form will try and cross by my own means stop will try and puss [sic] Wednesday and chance to luck.'[109]

But amidst this interchange of deceit and falsehood, what was the fate of the real Bloom and his colleague Pertschuk? Accounts by fellow prisoners who had seen the two men in the Gestapo headquarters in Toulouse record that both had been badly beaten. A report by Rabinovitch of 17 August 1943 stated: 'URBAIN was seen shortly after his arrest being escorted through TOULOUSE by Germans. His face was covered with blood.'[110] Lucien Fayman who had been arrested the same night as Pertschuk declared in a post-war report that he had seen Bloom in the Toulouse military prison with his head swathed in bandages.[111] The author of the official history affirmed, 'Bloom was caught with his set, and they managed to break his code. This they did with no help from him; beyond admitting to one of his captors, on the night of his arrest, that for the first time since his arrival in France he 'felt safe', he said nothing of interest to them.'[112] No such categorical confirmation of Bloom's stoicism has been located in SOE files nor is there a clear explanation how the Germans managed to conduct the radio game without assistance from 'Bishop'. An aside by Rabinovitch in a London debriefing revealed he 'found it hard to believe that URBAIN would submit to working his set under German control. He thinks it more likely that the Germans were working it themselves, although he is rather puzzled to know how they got hold of URBAIN's code.'[113]

Bloom was eventually sent to Fresnes prison outside Paris where he remained for almost a year until the spring of 1944. Surprisingly, he did not enter the *nacht und nabel* status imposed on other captured agents and London learnt of his presence in the jail via the Red Cross. Bloom's wife, still resident in France, was informed of her husband's whereabouts and visited him at the prison, even being allowed to furnish him with food and clothing.[114] Deported from Fresnes in the spring of 1944, his subsequent movements are obscure until he arrived at Mauthausen concentration camp near Linz in Austria on 6 September as part of a transport of forty-eight Allied personnel. A Mauthausen inmate observed the party's arrival, 'They were "registered in" in the normal way, shaved, given a shower, dressed in striped prison clothes and their number inscribed in indelible pencil on their chest.'[115] Once processed, they were marched off to Mauthausen's notorious quarry where twenty-one prisoners were shot. Bloom, along with several other F Section agents, was among the victims. The witness continued, 'Towards five o'clock, I saw personally the entry of the remainder (27), surrounded by armed SS men, being led off to the camp prison (Buncker) [*sic*] and dragging carts in which were piled the bodies of their murdered comrades.' The next day the surviving members of the party were killed.

Pertschuk was also sent to Fresnes, arriving on 28 May 1943. He remained there until January 1944 when he was sent to Compiègne in northern France before being transferred to Buchenwald concentration camp in Germany. In March he was struck down by pneumonia but had the consolation of being in the company of other F Section agents, notably, Christopher Burney and the Newton brothers, Alfred and Henry. Pertschuk was using the alias 'Martin Perkins', his SOE training name, perhaps to disguise any trace of his Russian/Jewish ancestry. By August 1944 he was a veteran inmate and greeted newly arrived, SOE prisoners with a chilling briefing, 'He warned us that we were in one of the worse concentration camps in Germany, that the life was dreadful, the death rate appalling, the treatment the worst, and that we must be very careful.'[116] Amongst the Buchenwald inmates with whom Pertschuk came in contact was François Hitter, a key figure in the plan to sabotage the gunpowder factory in Toulouse. The two men, whose fates were so closely linked, became close friends and Pertschuk entrusted Hitter with a collection of poems that he wrote while in captivity.[117] As the war drew to a close, it appeared that, after all his tribulations, Pertschuk might yet survive. But on 29 March 1945 he was hanged in the camp crematorium, barely a week before the camp's liberation.[118] Christopher Burney wrote that Pertschuk 'fought more gallantly than any of us and died more sadly'. Pertschuk's bravery did not go unrecognised; he received a posthumous MBE (Military Division), the Croix de Guerre and was made a Chevalier de la Légion d'Honneur. Bloom's only award was a British Mentioned in Despatches.

Whatever the difficulties Tony had experienced with the PRUNUS network and the disaster that befell it, there is no doubt that Pertschuk and Bloom possessed the means of dragging their fellow F Section agent down with them. The records do not offer any help in assessing the extent of the information (if any) that they gave to the Germans and Bloom's complicity in the enemy's exploitation of his wireless remains uncertain. However, it is without question that both agents knew of PIMENTO's use of the Colis Suisse and possessed the password. Similarly, they also were aware of the 'postbox' at the Café Martel in Lyon. Moreover, they had met Tony and would have been able to give a precise description of him. The 'Bishop' wireless messages reveal that the Germans were fully aware of a British agent 'Alphonse' operating in Toulouse and they made strenuous efforts to arrest him through the *Funkspiel* played out over Bloom's set. But Tony was *not* given away. Ultimately, the agents' human failings and bad luck were more than compensated for by their bravery and loyalty to a comrade they barely knew and with whom they had enjoyed a less than harmonious relationship.[119]

Moog's role as the agent provocateur was manifest but debate continued amongst the remaining members of the PRUNUS circuit and, latterly at Baker Street, of additional betrayal. Megglé came under great suspicion, although in a rare message to London about the PRUNUS debacle, Tony erroneously pointed the finger at Hitter. On 11 July 1943, he sent a message to Berne:

> 1. First to be arrested was LE BOITEUX. [Megglé] His note book contained VUILLEMOT address. EUGENE arrested when he called there on April 11th. 2. Gestapo at first did not realize importance of affair. Papers containing details of LANDES groups were not taken EUGENE's room not searched. 3. Apparently man named HITTER not repeat not arrested. He had been recommended by London to EUGENE who was reluctant to contact him. According to LE BOITEUX (in prison) it was HITTER who sold the others by selling him.[120]

After the war Hitter alleged that Meggle's behaviour after capture was reprehensible. Marcel Petit concurred and, following the liberation, reported his suspicions to SOE in London, 'He again confirmed that Jacques MEGGLE was responsible for their arrests and said that he personally wanted to liquidate MEGGLE when they met in BUCHENWALD. EUGENE forbade him to do so and said that when he got back to LONDON he would see that justice was done.'[121]

The spring of 1943 had proved to be a lamentable time for F Section but, while many of his contemporaries were succumbing to the depredations of the Nazi security services, against all the odds, Tony was still at large.[122]

Chapter Nine
The Going Gets Tough

Tony's ignorance of the scale of the PRUNUS catastrophe and the extreme threat under which it had placed him was a mixed blessing. If he had known of the Gestapo's attempts to capture him, he would have activated PIMENTO's considerable security apparatus and either initiated an investigation into the disaster or, if he deemed it necessary, made an escape to Switzerland. On the other hand, had he discovered how London had drawn him into PRUNUS's affairs and embedded him into the 'radio game' with the Germans, Tony might conceivably have decided to rupture his already strained relations with F Section. As it was, he soon found himself on the fringe of another French resistance crisis that, while it barely impinged on him, had repercussions that made the PRUNUS debacle seem like a sideshow.

Lyon, the 'Capital of the Resistance', in the early summer of 1943 was awash with clandestine movements including those sponsored by the Free French, some made up of disaffected elements of the Vichy regime, others derived from communist affiliations, and a number linked to the British. A very significant event in the city at this time was the arrival of Jean Moulin, de Gaulle's most important emissary to date. Moulin was a forty-three-year-old career civil servant who had been one of the government officials (that included Pierre Cot and Gaston Cusin) who schemed to supply Republican Spain with arms during the Civil War. The youngest Préfet in pre-war France, Moulin was dismissed in November 1940 by the Vichy authorities for refusing to implement their instructions to dismiss left-wing mayors. Freed of his professional obligations, he spent almost a year considering his next move and eventually made his way via Spain and Portugal to England, arriving in October 1941. Having received instructions from de Gaulle and some training from SOE, Moulin was parachuted back to France in January 1942. He spent the following year travelling the Unoccupied Zone, trying to weld the disparate elements of French resistance into a coherent whole. In February 1943 he was withdrawn to England for rest and consultation but returned to France a month later. On 27 May 1943 he convened the first meeting of the Conseil National de la Résistance (CNR). The ubiquitous Robert Moog, now working in concert with another double agent, Jean Multon, intercepted some of the Resistance's mail and arrested one of Moulin's Lyon-based associates, René Hardy. These successes led, in turn, to the capture on 9 June in Paris of General Charles Delestraint, the head of l'Armée Secrète. Moulin, in Lyon, was distraught when he learnt of these setbacks but resolved to press on and convened a meeting of his leading advisers on 21 June 1943 at the home of Dr Frédéric Dugoujon in the suburb of Caluire.

Tony had heard mention from his associates in Lyon of a resistance bigwig called 'Max' (one of Moulin's aliases) but had no reason to seek further information about the mystery man and his activities. The city was awash with rumours about food shortages, the black market, the occupiers' latest legislation and endless speculation about resistance activity. It was therefore a matter of no great moment when, on the morning of 21 June at the Customs Investigation Branch in the rue Jarente, Tony was told, '*Quelque chose se trame à Caluire* [Something is going on at Caluire]'. The response to his enquiry about what was 'going on' was the reply that German activity in the neighbourhood had increased and 'they' were planning 'something'. Not knowing what was in the wind, there was never a question of Tony being able to get a warning to the meeting at Dugoujon's.

The events that unfolded at Caluire on the afternoon of 21 June have become inscribed in French history. The meeting had been betrayed to the Germans, and a raid led by SS-Obersturmführer Klaus Barbie resulted in the arrest all those present. René Hardy, who had earlier escaped from German captivity, was present at the meeting. He has emerged as the strongest suspect as the Gestapo's informant not least as, against all the odds, he managed to escape from the round-up at Dr Dugoujon's; shot in the arm during his flight, he made his way to North Africa and safety. Meanwhile, Moulin's true identity at first remained concealed even though Barbie suspected he was the 'ringleader'. Appalling torture failed to elicit any information from the prisoner but the excesses of his maltreatment led to Moulin's death from his injuries a few days later.[1]

While Moulin's fate remained unknown to Tony, the reverberations of the PRUNUS affair rumbled on. A message from Bertholet to Tony of 27 June 1943 provides an insight into PIMENTO and F Section preoccupations at this time. It began with an affectionate message from Tony's girlfriend, Hope, but with the pleasantries over, it was back to basics and the lingering after-effects of the collapse of PRUNUS. The situation remained confused and Tony was instructed not to worry about 'Denis'.[2] This might have been reassuring but for the fact that the head of PIMENTO had no idea who 'Denis' was. Only after the war did he learn that this was a reference to Lieutenant Charles Duchalard, a Canadian F Section agent sent to the PRUNUS circuit on 12 April 1943 to 'act as lieutenant to PRUNUS and to advise him on demolition matters' while also helping to operate 'Rebecca' equipment.[3] Duchalard's arrival constituted yet one more headache for Tony. As nerves jangled over the fallout from the collapse of PRUNUS, in mid-May a PIMENTO postbox was approached by someone who gave the correct passwords and reported that he had been sent by 'Martin' to facilitate contact between Tony and 'Denis'. This event generated yet more queries between France, Switzerland and London about the bona fides of these unexpected and unwelcome contacts.[4] Tony decided to have nothing to do with Duchalard. This was just as well for a brief glimpse at his story reveals the doubtful quality of this F Section agent.

Duchalard could scarcely have arrived in France at a worse time. His problems might have proved even more serious had he appeared a few days earlier when he probably would have been swept up by the German arrests of the PRUNUS team. Described as a 'self-confident, even cocky' man of twenty-seven, Duchalard's sense of security proved lamentable.[5] Following the PRUNUS arrests, London ordered him to return via Spain to the United Kingdom. He reached England on 5 October 1943 but his reputation had gone before him: 'Most disappointing. A drunkard without power of self-control or sense enough to mind his p's and q's. Good-hearted but unreliable. Most keen to go on a second mission, possibly because he was stupid enough to believe that it was money for jam and didn't realise that he was being protected all the time by his comrades.' SOE returned him to the Army who consigned him to the relative obscurity of the Pioneer Corps.[6]

While one F Section agent left the scene for a somewhat discreditable but safe existence in the United Kingdom, Tony soldiered on. Bertholet's letters to him at this time convey a blend of the professional and personal. The clothes shortage in France was particularly acute and Tony was feeling the effects as much as anyone. An RAF supply drop on 18 April 1943 contained clothes for him but Henri Morandat confused the identification markings on the packages. As a result, the container holding Tony's new suit and a consignment of money was temporarily concealed under the murky waters of a drainage ditch while those bearing supplies of abrasive grease were treated with an equally disproportionate level of consideration. Two days later when preparing the contents of the drop for distribution to PIMENTO colleagues Morandat realised his mistake. Fortunately, the *maire* of Polliat had been a member of the reception committee and agreed to use his van to help retrieve the submerged container holding the clothes. He did more than simply extricate the items. His wife washed the suit and the other clothing sent from England and the council chamber of the *mairie* was pressed into service as a drying room; the mayor even ironed Tony's suit trousers himself. His sense of loyalty was greater than his knowledge of sartorial custom and he produced an immaculate crease down the side seams of the legs. When the clothing eventually reached Tony in Lyon it took quite some time to render the trousers back to their usual condition.[7] Such vicissitudes over items sent from England meant that a parcel from Switzerland for Tony containing a pair of shoes, socks and a tie was especially welcome. Bertholet apologised that a request for mechanic's overalls had not been met but assured Tony that they had been purchased and would follow. But clothes were not the priority; Tony's psoriasis still afflicted him and Vaseline and special ointment were included in the Swiss consignment. News of an additional illness had reached Bertholet but he was unable to send medicine for Tony's latest malaise – whooping-cough – that had been contracted from Michel Comte's youngest daughter, Nanou.

Bertholet's letter did not solely concern itself with domestic issues and he forwarded London's latest instructions for PIMENTO. At last Tony sensed he was receiving a real glimpse of Allied strategy, 'Reports indicate movement of German troops from France to Italy. If observations your area confirms interference possible you should successively attack to maximum extent appropriate railway target.' Bertholet had warned London that there was no guarantee that anything could be done, but Tony hoped that sabotage teams under the command of André Moch might be able to act against the Modane line and PIMENTO groups from Toulouse would try to attack anything moving on the '*grade transversale*'.[8] PIMENTO's efforts were clearly part of a broader F Section scheme to restrict the passage of German units to Italy to confront the impending Allied invasion of Sicily. Unfortunately, no statistics of the sabotage exists amongst Tony's private papers and the official record is lacking too. 'No exact indications survive in SOE's papers of the derangement caused by these line blockings to the German reinforcement plan.'[9]

By now, Tony had spent more than a year in France, building up PIMENTO, battling to meet the ever-increasing workload while trying to cope with the relentless stress of clandestine life. The strain on the young man had not escaped Bertholet's attention. He was concerned by Tony's comments that he felt disappointed by what he considered meagre results after twelve months' work. In response, the sage, older colleague attempted to reassure Tony that London appreciated his efforts and that he should not be hard on himself. But Tony had need of more than a pat on the back, for a message sent from Switzerland to London included worrying revelations about his health:

1. Theo [Tony] reports he is suffering from bad cough, nose bleeding, frequent temperature and headaches. Doctor states his skin disease will affect his heart if he does not rest.

2. Charles [Bertholet] is bitter over long neglect of request for pommade [for Tony] and again wonders whether Theo should be sent to 33 or to 53 to recover strength.[10]

Although Tony was by now a very experienced secret agent, he still exhibited a certain naivety in observing a rigorous level of rectitude over PIMENTO's finances. Bertholet suggested that he need not bother to file accounts and Tony stopped his meticulous record keeping. However, a financial statement for the first six months of 1943 (the only one to have survived) offers insights into the frugality of one of F Section's largest circuits.[11] It reveals that PIMENTO's half-year expenditure to 30 June 1943 was 253,020 francs. The sums paid to members of the circuit and Tony's living and operating expenses accounted for:

Jules [Jean Monier?]	50 000 francs
Georges [André Moch] (six months @ 3000)	18 000 francs
Costs of Martinet's [Roger Morandat] area	16 500 francs
Martinet (one month @ 3000, two months @ 4500)	12 000 francs
Jag [Henri Gauthier] (two months @ 3000)	6 000 francs
Jag's costs	3 000 francs
Dédé [Pormathios]	500 francs
Marcel [Biou] (two months @ 1000)	2 000 francs
Marcel's costs	3 000 francs
Colette [Hirschfeld] (six months of 500)	3 000 francs
Theo [Bernheim] (two payments)	20 000 francs
David [Donoff] (two payments)	20 000 francs
Diane [Robert Dick] (two months @ 1000)	2 000 francs
Georges's costs	9 500 francs
Olga [Vittet] (six months @ 500)	3 000 francs
Lucien's [Bizot's] rent (two trimesters of 3750)	7 500 francs
Georges's [Moch's] rent	4 000 francs
Alphonse's [Tony] rent	3 000 francs
Sebastien's [CFTC ex-locomotive driver?] rent	1 000 francs
Loan to Lucien [Bizot] for [his partner's] sickness	20 000 francs
Soap (33 Kgs @ 20)	660 francs
Alcohol (90°)	230 francs
Cloth (2nd piece of 10 metres)	1 000 francs
Electric batteries (60 @ 26)	1 560 francs
Repair for domestic wireless set	450 francs
Season ticket O.T.L. [Lyon tram]	212 francs
S.N.C.F. [rail reduction] card	2 383 francs

Costs of trips	6 844 francs
(January	1910)
(February	850)
(March	1193)
(April	1203)
(May	918)
(June	770)
Doctor for Perdreau [?]	110 francs
Medicines	562 francs
Vaseline	214 francs
Pinoflor	335 francs
Dry cleaning of clothes	120 francs
Packages of vegetables for Lyon	1 200 francs
Suitcase	350 francs
Shoe mending (115, 108, 152, 115)	490 francs
Personal costs (six months @ 4350)	26 100 francs
Bicycle tyres	1 700 francs
Bicycle for Jag	4 500 francs
Total..	<u>253 020</u> francs

It was all a long way from the five-star hotels and vintage champagne of later, fictional secret agents. That said, Tony and PIMENTO were operating on a shoestring in comparison with many of the other F Section circuits. The PHYSICIAN and SCIENTIST networks each managed to eat up budgets of a million francs a month while PIMENTO got by on an average of a mere 100,000, making it the circuit with the lowest expenditure at this time.[12] Moreover, another SOE file suggests that PIMENTO received even less than this figure. It shows that Tony received a total sum in 1943 of 199,970 francs making PIMENTO the third least well funded of the thirty-eight F Section networks; the highest, SCIENTIST and WHEELWRIGHT, absorbed 5,465,000 and 3,041,170 francs respectively during the same period.[13] Significantly, Claude de Baissac, the leader of SCIENTIST, reported to London that he 'always kept a good balance in hand' in the bank accounts he maintained in France. 'If he wanted to withdraw Frs. 5,000,000, he would make five separate withdrawals of Frs. 1,000,000 in order not to arouse suspicion.' De Baissac claimed he always kept 50,000 francs 'in his pocket' and a further 6-8,000 francs in his bag. Such largesse was in very stark contrast to the humble lifestyle of the young man working unobtrusively in Lyon and Toulouse.[14]

While assiduous in keeping his accounts, Tony did not neglect his first priority – PIMENTO's operational activities and the training of its personnel. In May his men attacked fodder wagons with incendiaries in the Lyon La Part Dieu railway marshalling yards and started a fairly substantial fire, although he had to admit that his other attempts to employ STS 17's 'passive methods' of sabotage 'all proved unsuccessful'. Better fortune was found in the south-west. Accompanied by Michel Comte, Tony carried out a reconnaissance of the Verlaghuet electricity/railway switching station with a view to mounting a sabotage attack against it. Meanwhile the PIMENTO training programme continued in all areas. Practical demonstrations were regularly being carried out to build confidence and raise the spirits of PIMENTO recruits and in June the Toulouse–Capdenac railway line was cut and two steam engines were attacked in the Montauban round house 'to lift the morale of the local team.'[15]

In July PIMENTO received a new recruit who soon became one of its stalwarts. This was Louis Pédémas, yet another member of the SRFD and, at least nominally, Bizot's boss. Known to the circuit as 'Perrier' or, less securely, as 'Ped', he and Tony had first met when he shared the flat above the customs office with Bizot. Pédémas, a man in his mid-forties, possessed a distinguished career in the First World War (being wounded and gassed) but had also fought as a captain in the Second. Captured during the German invasion, he escaped and rejoined the army in time to be demobilised in August 1940. He became a constant and loyal member of the team, not least because he sustained the essential customs service cover after some of Tony's original recruits became casualties of the clandestine war.[16] Pédémas's duties included ensuring that PIMENTO funds were kept securely in a safe at the SRFD headquarters. The envelopes containing the cash bore an impressive array of official labels to convince any prying eyes that they constituted part of an ongoing customs investigation rather than being the war chest of a secret, British-sponsored, resistance network.

Tony was by now totally immersed in Lyon life and clear proof of the strength of his 'Antoine Brévin' identity came at the end of July 1943.

When getting off a moving tram, an act forbidden by transport by-laws but an everyday misdemeanour committed by countless Lyonnais commuters, he was challenged by a gendarme. There being no way of denying his culpability, Tony was ordered to report to a local schoolhouse along with other malefactors. Here, he was told that the punishment for his 'crime' was a stint as a *Garde Voie* – a press-ganged auxiliary guard whose duty was to prevent sabotage to the railway line. The contrite secret agent humbly accepted the penalty and agreed to report for duty at a nearby station. As it transpired, the stationmaster responsible for overseeing Tony's duties was a member of PIMENTO, whose immediate response was an offer to relieve him of them. On the contrary, Tony wanted to undergo his 'punishment' to the full as it provided him with the opportunity of carrying out inspections of the railway lines and, armed with his *laissez-passer*, to wander freely around the city during the night curfew.

Far more important to Tony than a minor breach of a by-law were two crises that now hit PIMENTO in quick succession. The first was personal. Bizot's common-law wife, Germaine, fell gravely ill and he took her to Switzerland for treatment then, having arranged her medical care, returned to Lyon to resume his duties with the SRFD and PIMENTO. Understandably, Bizot was distracted, fretting over his partner's health and concerned about the care of their young son, Charles. Under the circumstances, Tony decided to transfer greater responsibility for PIMENTO's SRFD contacts to Jean Dorval, but then a new incident occurred that threatened to destroy the entire circuit.

Germain Laganne, the owner of a hardware store in Toulouse, was a schoolfriend of Bizot's. Tony tried to recruit him in late September 1942 as he possessed useful contacts with the local police. While sympathetic to the cause of resistance, Laganne 'considered it too dangerous a job to be undertaken for the time being'. That said, he was willing to supply Tony with synthetic grease ('against cash payment') for the special pumps with which saboteurs applied abrasives to railway car gearboxes.[17] He later had a change of mind and took a more active role in PIMENTO that included his recruitment of Pierre Charles Biou, a former army officer, who wanted to play a part in the Resistance. Laganne discreetly submitted Biou's name to Tony and, as it happened, there was at the time a pressing need for couriers to convey sabotage materials dropped to the PIMENTO grounds around Lyon to the less accessible south-west area. Following an interview with Tony, it was decided that Biou, bearing the codename 'Marcel', would undertake this task. His first commission was something of a dummy run, carrying a small amount of Cordtex instantaneous fuse for a group of railwaymen, friends of Laganne, who were seeking to establish a sabotage cell.[18]

His trial mission successfully completed, Biou's next task was the collection in Lyon of a consignment of explosives and its transportation to Toulouse. Coincidentally, he travelled on the same overnight train from the south-west as Tony who was returning to Lyon after a four-day spell in Montauban. The two members of PIMENTO were (quite rightly) unaware of the presence of the other and Tony had a host of more pressing commitments than linking up with a courier. Tony met Donoff soon after arriving in the city on 7 August and the two men spent the morning moving stocks of explosives.[19] Some came from Olga Vittet's, the rest were the contents of the railwaymen's caches at Les Brotteaux station and the accumulation was destined for storage at Combe's residence in the rue Montesquieu. Tony only learnt of Biou's arrival when he met Dorval for lunch and was told that the handover of the consignment for Toulouse would take place at seven o'clock that evening. After passing Tony some messages from London that had arrived via Alexandre Fourre, the three men met that afternoon to talk in particular 'about security on the mail route to Switzerland'.[20] Donoff turned up at Dorval's apartment around 5.30 that evening 'with a large suitcase full of 808 [plastic explosive] which was to be given to Marcel [Biou] to take to Toulouse'. Tony had laid down ground rules for transfers of such supplies and stipulated that contact should only take place in neutral locations or through cut-outs. The routine for passing over the explosive should therefore have seen a suitcase containing the consignment deposited in a railway station left-luggage office with the ticket passed to the courier either at a café or by a brush contact in the street. This is what *should* have happened when Biou met Dorval but, instead of the innocuous handover of a ticket, Dorval unaccountably took Biou back to his apartment in the rue Professeur Grignard. Here, he offered the suitcase containing the plastic explosive (with its characteristically distinctive smell of almonds) but Biou refused to take the whole consignment and merely left with three, twin-rail charges.[21] He also announced that he had changed his travel plans and would be taking the eight o'clock train instead of the eleven o'clock as derailments on the line had been reported. Later that evening at the Café des Variétés Dorval gave Tony an update on the arrangements but neither of them considered the alterations to the programme of any great moment. It was not until Tony had moved on to Bizot's that he decided that the surplus explosive refused by Biou should be removed from Dorval's apartment. It would be a tight squeeze to complete the job before curfew and Dorval was not at his flat. But with Donoff's help the explosives were shifted to Combe's by the 10.30 deadline.

A standard feature of the tradecraft used in conveying suspect packages on public transport was for the courier to disassociate himself from compromising material. At its most basic, this could be achieved by leaving the suitcase in one compartment while the courier took a seat elsewhere in the train. But Biou was a novice and on the journey to Toulouse, he simply put the explosives in the luggage rack above his seat. Consequently, when the German *Feldgendarmerie* made a snap search at Vienne of passengers and their luggage, Biou was caught red-handed.[22] Reports state that his hands were manacled behind his back and he was thrown onto the platform. He received a severe beating and was driven back to Lyon where the Germans embarked upon an investigation into the source of the explosives.[23] It did not take them long. There seems little doubt that Biou gave away Dorval (although apparently not Laganne) for, at 10.45 that same night (only half an hour after Tony and Donoff had left with the remaining explosives), the apartment in the rue Professeur Grignard was raided by the Gestapo.[24] Dorval and his mistress were arrested and taken away for interrogation while a search of the premises revealed no other stocks of explosives thanks to Tony's earlier intervention.[25] However foolhardy his behaviour in taking Biou to his apartment, Dorval now faced the consequences with exemplary bravery and he endured dreadful torture at the Saint-Paul and Montluc prisons.[26] In a subsequent report Bertholet wrote, 'He [Dorval] did not say anything bad' but in a later message to Tony added, 'Regarding Plouc [Dorval] I am beginning to learn that he has spoken about you under the name of Alphonse.'[27] After the war Tony gave the following summary: 'Poulet [Dorval] stated that he himself had received by parachute from LONDON the plastic which was found in MARCEL's [Biou's] suitcase and, when greatly pressed to give information on the whereabouts of ALPHONSE (also denounced by

MARCEL) POULET said that ALPHONSE was really himself, and that he had been dropped in from LONDON.'[28]

Dorval's courage could not detract from the immense potential damage to PIMENTO that his arrest represented. Unlike Pertschuk and Bloom who had been kept at a distance, Dorval occupied a place at the epicentre of the circuit's activities. He knew letter boxes, safe houses, courier lines to Switzerland and most of the leading personalities, not least Tony. By now the German security forces possessed several reports of a resistance leader 'Alphonse' with strong connections to London. It seems that they had neither the inclination nor the resources to collate the separate strands of information accrued in Toulouse and Lyon. However, with the benefit of hindsight, Biou could have provided that link. One can only conjecture that Tony's fate would have been very different had investigators with the malevolent ability of a Moog or Barbie involved themselves in his affairs.

Tony learnt of Dorval's arrest the following afternoon when he called at Bizot's apartment and found a note from Pédémas informing him of the tragedy and warning that the Customs Office had been searched by the Germans but nothing compromising had been found. Nevertheless, Tony ordered Bedat to destroy any PIMENTO records that were concealed in the SRFD offices. The danger to PIMENTO was not just the discovery of paperwork for there was no time to waste in securing the safety of vulnerable colleagues following the arrests. Rapid exchanges of messages between Tony and Bertholet led to the conclusion that Bizot must leave Lyon as soon as possible. The latter's intimate connection with Dorval was widely known and the enquiries that had been made in Paris in 1940 invited the assumption that Bizot was already regarded by the Germans with suspicion. His sudden absence at the time of Dorval's arrest was likely be interpreted as more than a coincidence but Bizot possessed a valid excuse in his need to see Germaine in Switzerland. Meanwhile the rest of the network had to be protected and Tony closed down all the circuit's letter boxes in Lyon and broke contact with Gauthier except via the link with Bottemer (who by this time had moved from Toulouse to Chambéry). Pédémas, who as both a close personal friend and a professional associate of Dorval's was at no little risk, went 'on holiday'.

The arrest of Dorval was a calamity for PIMENTO but Tony drew reassurance from the security preparations he had put in place for such an eventuality. Deeply dismayed by the arrests and, understandably fearful of both the short- and long-term consequences, Tony also felt Bizot's departure from the scene most acutely, describing it as the hardest to bear of all the losses sustained by PIMENTO during the war. Of course, any arrest of a comrade left its own irrevocable mark but Bizot's exile deprived him of his closest friend and mentor. It had been Bizot's wise counsels that had helped form Tony's first plans, guided his recruitment of helpers and established the strict security protocols that resulted in his remaining at liberty while so many other F Section agents had succumbed to the depredations of the Nazi forces. Bizot's sagacity and friendship had consistently sustained Tony whenever those inevitable, dark moments of doubt and uncertainty descended upon the young and isolated Englishman.

Amidst the uncertainties engendered by the crisis, Tony remained confident that no one knew of his bolt-hole at the Chemin du Panorama. Having issued security instructions to the network, he then kept well away from the customs office in Lyon, going to ground at his secret, safe house where he informed his landlady that he was suffering from a heavy cold. As he lay closeted in his room he had plenty of time to review his options. He could quit Lyon for the south-west where, unbeknownst to him, the earlier dangers of the PRUNUS *Funkspiel* had lessened after the Germans' abandonment of their operation in the middle of June. In the event, he decided to stay in Lyon and ride out the storm. He was reassured by his ability, if necessary, to drop the 'Antoine Brévin' alias in an instant. As part of his almost obsessive belief in security, Tony had devised a series of personal emergency caches. He buried large glass jars in discreet locations in Lyon and the south-west, each of which contained a full set of identity documents, money, bandages, scissors, a razor (to cut his hair or remove a moustache) and a small bottle of marc to sterilise a wound or raise the flagging spirits of the fugitive. Amongst the false sets of identities were those of 'Louis Dalibert', 'André Bonal' and 'Antoine Vialars'. For four or five days after the arrest of Dorval, Tony became 'Bonal' whenever he needed to leave his lair at the Chemin du Panorama. It was not a question of thinking just one move ahead of his adversaries but several. He was blessed with a remarkable group of followers, all of whom would have done their best to aid him, but Tony's own refined sense of security ensured that he would remain independent of any help.

As it transpired, the fallout from Dorval and Biou's arrests miraculously proved quite minimal. The only known casualty was the customs official, Alexandre Fourre, whose primary role was in passing PIMENTO messages across the border into Switzerland via Thonon-les-Bains and Saint-Gingolph. Perhaps Dorval felt the need to provide his interrogators with at least one name and it seems that he gave them Fourre's in the mistaken belief that no harm would befall his colleague.[29] Fourre was incarcerated along with Dorval in Montluc prison and here the two men were able briefly to meet and concoct consistent stories. Dorval instructed Fourre to admit to the Germans that he had passed on mail but should offer the explanation that he had assumed he was simply handling legitimate SRFD business. At the investigating tribunal, Dorval corroborated this version, Fourre was eventually released and was helped by Cusin to go into hiding.[30] 'There's no doubt,' Tony later reflected, 'if Dorval had not been a stubborn Breton, he would have talked under torture and then I think PIMENTO might have gone for a burton.' The range of knowledge possessed by Dorval and the little he gave away reflected a supreme dedication to his comrades in the circuit. He knew Olga Vittet's letter box at the Café Martel, all the connections with the SRFD, Laganne's identity and even the contacts with Zaksas in Toulouse. In a report recommending Dorval for a British decoration Tony wrote, 'By his unending gallantry he saved my life and also the lives of many other members of the circuit with whom he was in contact.'[31]

In spite of PIMENTO's wide range of contacts in the French civil administration, to all intents and purposes Dorval and Biou vanished from sight into the sinister twilight of German prisons. In post-war accounts, some members of the Resistance in Lyon have described their escapes from captivity; André Devigny wrote of an inspired breakout from Montluc Prison, Serge Ravanel narrated his liberation by means of a clever ruse and Lucie and Raymond Aubrac told of a spectacular ambush of a prison van.[32] But these successes were exceptions. For PIMENTO, it proved impossible to 'spring' captured comrades, not solely because of the level of German security but also that other pressing duties had to take priority. Time and resources could not be spared in planning speculative rescue operations when the bread-and-butter work of supply drops and sabotage was becoming ever more important. However, accounts written by Tony and Bottemer after the war, suggest that PIMENTO might have attempted to rescue its comrades. They affirm that on 21 October 1943 André Moch led twenty men in the hold-up of a lorry transporting prisoners from the Lyon Gestapo headquarters to Montluc prison. Some details are intriguingly specific including the assertion that twenty-one prisoners were freed and five Germans killed at a cost of two of Moch's men slightly injured. The inspiration for the attack was that Moch 'had information which led him to believe that DORVAL was on the lorry'.[33]

The arrest of Dorval and the subsequent German investigations offer insights into the efficiency of the Nazi security forces. Sturmbannführer Hans Kieffer, the deputy head of the Paris *Sicherheitsdienst*, in a post-war deposition emphasised the importance of security operations against SOE, 'Berlin attached extraordinary importance to the French Section ... All other matters were pushed into the background, and Berlin showed interest again and again only for French Section matters and we were always obliged to neglect other matters because Berlin considered the French Section particularly dangerous.'[34] Yet, in contrast to the intricate and highly successful Abwehr operation against PRUNUS in Toulouse and the Gestapo's arrests in Lyon, the probe into Dorval and his contacts seems slipshod. No significant attempt appears to have been made to investigate Dorval's SRFD connections. The enquiries made by a solitary German detective at the customs investigation office consisted of little more than a few cursory and rudimentary questions and a request for a copy of Dorval's personal file. The Lyon branch of the *Sicherheitsdienst*, with Klaus Barbie as head of its Section IV (Gestapo), had shown its malevolent efficiency on all too many occasions yet the opportunity to destroy PIMENTO was neglected. Explanations of the poor performance of the German authorities are at best speculative. Were they resting on their laurels after the affair at Caluire? Were they preoccupied with following up the leads revealed by this coup? Had Dorval's brave reticence shut the door on any further exploitation?

While the impact of Dorval's arrest was still being handled by his PIMENTO comrades, F Section in London informed Tony that he was to be withdrawn to England for consultation and a rest.[35] The decision was not inspired by the recent damage sustained by the network but, rather, it was simply recognition that more than a year undercover in Occupied France had taken a grievous toll of Tony's health. The agent's immediate response was to assert that his responsibilities made it an inopportune time to relinquish his duties but, equally, he could not deny his profound fatigue and ill-health. He still had not shrugged off the whooping cough contracted from Comte's daughter. The racking convulsions of coughing did nothing to improve his exhausted and weakened state and a trip to a doctor at Montauban resulted in nothing better than a black-market prescription for cough mixture and aspirin and the regretful comment that a *baptême de l'air* (a brief aircraft flight) as had been taken by patients in pre-war days would be the best treatment.[36] To make matters worse, Tony's psoriasis was particularly bad. For once, Buckmaster's usually unreliable memoirs possess more than a grain of truth –

> The tension in which Alphonse lived was mounting. His wise counsellors hinted to us that he should be temporarily withdrawn from France to rest and recuperate. The tone of some of his radio messages became querulous and testy. Alphonse was under great strain and he was tired.[37]

Some intimation of Tony's state of health had even penetrated the anodyne correspondence SOE permitted to reach his fiancée.* Hope Munday had received occasional notes and cryptic telegrams sent by Bertholet on Tony's behalf ever since his arrival in France. She had somehow managed to divine that all was not well and expressed her concerns to Baker Street about Tony's well being. On 17 July 1943, Flight Lieutenant André Simon of F Section wrote to reassure her (employing a certain economy with the truth):

> I can quite understand your anxiety about Lt. Brooks. Although he has not been well on one or two occasions, there is nothing seriously wrong and he is able to rest when he doesn't feel well. Quite recently we had news that he was better and that, in fact, he considers himself perfectly fit. I do not think, therefore, that you have any cause to worry.[38]

With Bizot in exile in Switzerland and Dorval in jail, the obvious candidate to act as Tony's stand-in during his absence in London was André Moch; he had

---

* The precise date of the engagement is unclear – it must have occurred before Tony's departure or it could have been part of their secret correspondence (that has not survived) – but Hope was described as Tony's fiancée in a letter of 6 February 1943.

the brains, stamina and dedication to fill the breach and, moreover, enjoyed a sound relationship with Bertholet. Moch came up to Lyon from Grenoble, met Tony (keeping a safe distance for fear of catching his leader's whooping cough) and readily assumed responsibility for PIMENTO in his leader's absence. He was just the man for a crisis; intelligent and strong with deep experience of clandestine life reinforced by a military aptitude for organisation and training. Already conscious of Olga Vittet's letter box in Lyon, he was now introduced to Gauthier and briefed on the reception committees in the Bourg-en-Bresse area. Moch then accompanied Tony on a trip to Toulouse and Montauban where they met with Zaksas and Comte, the leaders of the south-west outposts of PIMENTO.[39] Everything now seemed in order and Tony was confident that the arrangements would meet every eventuality during his absence that he assumed would be no more than a month.[40]

F Section sent final instructions for Tony's departure in a message that arrived via Switzerland.

> You should report on Tuesday 10 August at midday to barman of the Café de la Lorraine [*sic*?], Place des Ternes, Paris, and ask to see Monsieur or Madame Henri. On meeting Monsieur or Madame Henri, you should give following password: "Vous êtes Monsieur Henri?" Answer: "Non, mais je le connais fort bien." Similar contact can be made every Tuesday and Friday at midday. You will then be given necessary instructions for Lysander pick-up operation in August moon.[41]

Tony needed a cover story to explain his absence to Mme Dupeuple and informed her that he was going to Switzerland to marry his fiancée, 'Doreen Longchamp'.* Although he assumed that he would be away for just a few weeks, he took the precaution of paying his rent up to the end of the year. He felt he could not risk losing the accommodation should his absence prove more extended than anticipated. In addition to the pre-paid rent, he gave Mme Dupeuple a bar of luxury soap as a parting gift. The combination of cash and the expensive present brought about such a softening of the landlady/

---

* Although he showed Hope Munday's photograph to his landlady, Tony, with typical caution, had a real person living in Switzerland as his notional fiancée there. This was Doreen Wilkinson, the daughter of Bill Barton's second wife.

tenant relationship that Madame took the unprecedented step of wishing him *bon voyage*, and kissed him on both cheeks. Comte and Moch were the only PIMENTO comrades who knew he was leaving for England and he simply implied to others that he was going to Switzerland for a while. On 16 August 1943, having concluded some final details with Bottemer, he left Chambéry for Paris, taking (as was his custom) a return ticket. Typically, he prepared a justification for his trip: a visit to a dermatologist at the Salpétrière Hospital in Paris. The journey proved relatively trouble free, Tony's hacking cough ensuring that he was left alone by any would-be conversationalist and (involuntary splutters apart) he slept the whole way to Paris's Gare de Lyon.

Tony did not know Paris well, having only visited a few times on business trips with his uncle. Nevertheless, he could not fail to observe that the noisy, traffic-filled hubbub of pre-occupation days was no more. Uncertain of the regulations for buying metro or bus tickets, Tony decided to walk to his rendezvous at the Café Lorraine near the Étoile. The trek would have been pretty daunting for a Parisian commuter but for a man used to cycling fifty kilometres in a day it was no great trial. He had his camera with him and one of his surviving photographs records a near-deserted Place de la Concorde. Still finding himself with time to kill before the meeting, he located his rendezvous, carried out a surveillance of the neighbourhood and decided to check into a small hotel in the rue de Courcelles. Tony knocked at the sliding door of a reception cubicle and was greeted by a brassy, heavily made-up concierge wearing a black satin blouse. He enquired about the availability of a room for one or two nights and was surprised to receive a guffaw followed by the observation, '*C'est bien de votre âge.*' Only then did he realise that the premises were rather more than had at first appeared and it was a *hôtel de passe* where lovers engaged on secret trysts would rent a room for a couple of hours, rendering Tony's prediction of a two-day occupation worthy of approbatory comment. However, the choice of lodging proved fortunate. The concierge's good-natured admiration of the young man's stamina (or optimism) left unstated the fact that such establishments did not observe the registration of guests that were maintained by conventional hotels. Tony had unwittingly secured himself one of the safest bolt-holes in Paris.

At midday Tony arrived at the Café Lorraine and asked for 'Monsieur Henri'. The question was somewhat redundant as only one other customer was in attendance. Sure enough, the dark-haired man in his early thirties proved to be his contact. They introduced each other by their code names – his contact then switching from 'Henri' to 'Gilbert' – had a beer and together left the café in order to speak more freely. As they strolled along the avenue de Wagram, 'Gilbert' proposed and Tony agreed that they meet again the following evening at another café on the same street where the former would introduce a colleague, 'Marc'. 'Gilbert' suggested that Tony accompany him to a safe house but, self-sufficient as ever, Tony declined the offer. Any possible embarrassment at this refusal of hospitality was dispelled by 'Gilbert's' evident assumption that Tony was staying with a girlfriend. These arrangements having been concluded, the two men continued their stroll and 'Gilbert' offered the encouraging news that, if all went well, the operation ('*l'affaire*') would take place in two days' time. While Tony was pleased at the schedule, his customary reticence and innate sense of security left him disconcerted by the questioning to which 'Gilbert' subjected him. The Frenchman mentioned that F Section had informed him that Tony was an important organiser in Lyon who was returning to London for a briefing. Typically, Tony demurred and simply stated that he had been recalled for medical treatment and, as if his coughing was not sufficient corroboration, displayed patches of his psoriasis. With a shrug, 'Gilbert' told Tony he would see him again the next day and they parted company.

Tony was left mildly unsettled by the meeting and felt that something was not quite right about 'Gilbert'. He found it difficult precisely to identify the cause for his concern other than that his contact had seemed rather too keen to uncover more than was necessary about his activities. As it transpired, this was not a unique occurrence and other F Section agents in contact with 'Gilbert' shared similar misgivings. The wireless operator, Henri Despaigne, recalled, 'We agreed to meet … the next day on the Champs Elysées, where he ['Gilbert'] tried to find out what was my mission and where was I going and when I was going – to which I gave him no answer whatsoever. I mean you're not supposed to be interrogated by people who are only supposed to receive you. So I just wouldn't talk.'[42]

Subsequent events were to reveal that the concerns of these F Section agents were well founded. 'Gilbert's' real name was Henri Déricourt and he drew upon wide experience as a pre-war civil-aviation pilot for his new, clandestine role as F Section's Air Movements Officer. He had spent the 1930s flying with a barnstorming troupe and then on airmail runs for the French airline Air Bleu before being called up on the outbreak of war. His flying duties included service with an air transport squadron and, later, as a test pilot. Déricourt continued flying after the fall of France by securing a position with the Vichy government's Service Civil des Liaisons Aériennes de la Métropole. Eventually, he decided to leave France (his precise motives remain obscure) and, making contact with a British-run escape line, was brought out by sea and conveyed to Gibraltar. On reaching England, he was processed through the Security Executive's London Reception Centre where his talents were identified as being of potential use to SOE. He formally joined the organisation on 1 December 1942 and with the bare minimum of training was parachuted to France later that month. Déricourt quickly became a pivotal figure in F Section's clandestine air communication links (pick-ups rather than parachute operations) between England and France. As the new year began, F Section stepped up the development of existing circuits and created new ones as the Allies' plans for an invasion of France began to gather momentum. A sophisticated organisation was required to secure landing grounds and coordinate the flow of agents into and out of enemy territory; Déricourt and his team delivered this and became a vital part of Buckmaster's plans – the only trouble was that the agent was not all he seemed.

At first Déricourt seemed to justify all the faith F Section invested in him. He formed the FARRIER circuit and, with a team of helpers, located suitable reception grounds for pick-up operations. In April he was recalled to London for briefing, by that time having handled four aircraft receptions and received ten agents. He was not in England for long and returned to France by parachute on 5 May 1943 to resume his work. But soon after Déricourt's arrival, disaster befell F Section's major circuit, PROSPER. At the end of June, a succession of agents were captured by the Germans, including 'Prosper' himself, Major Francis Suttill, and his wireless operator, Major Gilbert Norman. Others soon joined them in captivity and the Germans embarked upon a wireless 'game' to deceive F Section of the recent calamitous events.[43] But word of the catastrophe eventually reached London, perhaps with a verbal contribution from Déricourt himself who made another, very brief, trip to England on 20/21 July. More important, on 22/3 July 1943 Nicolas

Bodington (who it will be recalled had earlier been sent to France to interview Jouhaux), a senior member of Buckmaster's staff and a man with extensive experience 'in the field', arrived in France on a mission of investigation and damage assessment. Together with his wireless operator, Flight Lieutenant Jack Agazarian, Bodington was received by Déricourt, who had just got back from England. Shortly after the agents' arrival, Agazarian was enticed to a compromised rendezvous in Paris and arrested by the Germans. Meanwhile, Bodington managed to stay at liberty until his return to England on the night of 16/17 August 1943, the day Tony arrived in Paris.

Buckmaster and his staff were desperate to limit the damage to their networks and discover the cause of the disasters. It is uncertain precisely when the first suspicions alighted on the Air Movements Officer but one disturbing report from Suttill (passed in June via Agazarian's wireless) mentioned that he 'thought Déricourt's security faulty'.[44] More sinister allegations followed in July with unsubstantiated but uncompromising reports claiming 'Gilbert is a traitor.' Yet again, for Tony, ignorance was bliss as he unwittingly found himself on the brink of another F Section disaster. He had been placed in the hands of a man who London was beginning to suspect was a double agent.

Utterly unaware of these sinister undercurrents, Tony arrived at the café the next day and found Déricourt accompanied by a tall, slim man, Rémy Clément, the aforementioned assistant, 'Marc'. Clément asked Tony whether he had been trained on pick-up operations and, going against the grain of disclosing anything about himself, he answered that he had. The meeting concluded with Déricourt instructing Tony to take a train to Angers the following day from the Gare Montparnasse. He was told not to give any indication at the station that he recognised his fellow passengers and was warned that he would be kept under friendly surveillance until all the parties met up at their final destination.

After a night rendered sleepless by the sound of amorous exertions in the neighbouring bedrooms, Tony checked out of the 'hotel' and walked to the station. At Montparnasse, he bought a third-class return ticket, having already mentally amended his cover story such that he was now in search of a dermatologist who had left Paris. He spotted Clément on the platform and, as instructed, took a seat in a different compartment. The journey passed without incident and, on arrival at Angers, he was pleased to discover that there were no security checks at the station. His optimism however took a knock when he saw that Clément was now the proud possessor of a tandem bicycle. This was Tony's first experience of riding such a machine and, in spite of being an accomplished cyclist, it proved a challenging journey as he found himself trying to 'correct' their line every time Clément leant into a corner. Eventually, they reached the Café de la Mairie at Briollay, ten kilometres north of Angers, where they met Déricourt.[45]

The trio waited in a private room at the back of the establishment until, in the early evening, Déricourt and Clément excused themselves to listen to the BBC's *messages personnels* for notification if the operation was 'on'. Before long, the Frenchmen returned with the encouraging news that *l'affaire* was going ahead. Clément retrieved two large rucksacks hidden in the well outside the café. These contained a selection of torches that he proceeded diligently to test. The agents then remounted their bicycles (with Tony now a little more in harmony with Clément) and headed off for the landing ground at Soucelles, some ten kilometres to the east. There, they left their bicycles by a hedge and crossed several fields until finally stopping at a large pasture. Clément fixed one torch to a stake, stuck it in the ground and then repeated the process some distance away. Handing Tony a torch, he instructed him that, on receipt of the recognition signal shone from the aircraft, he was to illuminate it while he and Déricourt would do the same. The final injunction was that Tony was to keep his torch pointed at the aircraft at all times. After about a quarter of an hour standing in the field, Tony began to hear strange, snorting noises coming from the darkness around him. The sounds emanated from neither Déricourt nor Clément and, straining his eyes to look into the gloom, he realised that the landing field was now occupied by a herd of cattle. Just at that moment, he caught the sound of an aeroplane. Clément had evidently heard its approach too and began flashing his torch that was soon followed by the illumination of those of his colleagues. At last spotting the aircraft, Tony was surprised that, instead of a Westland Lysander, it was a twin-engine aeroplane. His immediate concern was that it might be a hostile, German intruder but it made no aggressive movements and, completing a circuit of the landing ground, the aircraft started its final approach to land. Then, as if on cue, the cattle stampeded. Tony estimated that there were only about thirty of them but 'they sounded like a battalion' and galloped noisily past the three men who remained concentrated upon guiding in the approaching aeroplane. Miraculously, the aircraft landed without hitting the animals, turned at the end of the field, taxied towards the reception committee and switched on its landing lights. It was 01.35 on the morning of 20 August 1943.[46]

The pick-up operation, codenamed 'Dyer', had been entrusted to Wing Commander Lewis 'Bob' Hodges. He was immensely experienced and, moreover, had a personal commitment to clandestine operations having been assisted by the French Resistance in achieving a 'home run' after being shot down over France in September 1940. He joined No.161 Squadron in November 1942 and assumed command of the unit in May of the following year. For Operation 'Dyer' he was flying a Lockheed Hudson Mk III. Like the Lysander, the aircraft had not been specifically designed for clandestine work but its sturdiness and good handling made it an ideal choice for long-range pick-up operations and, especially, those requiring the transportation of relatively large groups of passengers. Hodges had already completed a successful Hudson operation (his first using this type of aircraft) on the same Soucelles ground where he delivered Bodington and Agazarian for their investigation of the PROSPER debacle. It was just as well that Hodges had some prior experience of the landing field for, on this occasion, a ground mist partially obscured the flare-path lights held by Tony, Déricourt and Clément and perhaps a lesser pilot might have aborted the operation.

If the size of the aircraft was a surprise, there was another shock in store for Tony. From out of the darkness there appeared a seemingly endless succession of people. With the aircraft's engines roaring and its propellers spinning, it was a dramatic and vibrant scene. The side door of the Hudson opened and a single figure, 'Dyer', emerged, his place soon being taken by no less than ten outgoing passengers.[47] They constituted a very distinguished collection of F Section agents:

Robert Boiteux, 'Nicolas' – Leader of the SPRUCE circuit based in Lyon.

Joseph Marchand, 'Ange' – Locally recruited member of Boiteux's circuit in Lyon.[48]

Jean Louis de Ganay – Locally recruited member of the PHYSICIAN network on the run following the PROSPER debacle. [49]

Marie-Thérèse Le Chêne, 'Adèle' – Courier for the SPRUCE circuit.[50]

Victor Gerson, 'Vic' – A veteran SOE agent who ran the VIC escape line for D/F Section.[51]

Robert Benoist, 'Lionel' – Locally recruited member of the CHESTNUT circuit who had made a dramatic escape from captivity and had kept one step ahead of the Gestapo for the last fortnight.[52]

Octave Simon, 'Badois' – Locally recruited, he worked with several F Section circuits but at the time of the pick-up was ill and on the run from the Gestapo.[53]

François Basin, 'Olive' – One of the very first agents sent into France, he had established the OLIVE circuit in the Unoccupied Zone. Arrested by the Vichy authorities in August 1942, he had been released in November and resumed his work.

Raymonde Mennessier – Basin's assistant.[54]

And Tony Brooks, 'Alphonse'.

Among the last of the group to embark was the middle-aged lady, Mme Le Chêne, whose tight skirt inhibited her stepping into the aircraft. No matter how high she hitched up her dress, it still prevented her raising her leg sufficiently to make the ascent. It was now up to Tony. Placing his shoulder underneath her backside, he hoisted her up and propelled her into the fuselage, the momentum forcing the unfortunate woman into an unintentional and less than elegant forward roll. His duty done, Tony climbed aboard, Clément slammed the door and Hodges took off. The aircraft had been on the ground for a mere thirteen minutes. Subsequent conversation amongst the passengers was, understandably, limited save for the occasional '*Bonsoir monsieur, bonsoir madame*'.

Apart from a single, speculative anti-aircraft shell that detonated some distance away from the aircraft, the two-hour flight was without incident and touchdown was made at RAF Tangmere in Sussex at 3.50 a.m. Hodges had scarcely landed when Buckmaster appeared on the tarmac. He greeted in turn each member of this large assembly of his returning agents but it was Tony who travelled back to London with him in his staff car. Presumably Buckmaster recognised that it was not the right moment for a debriefing and their conversation consisted of a few pleasantries such as the state of the exhausted agent's health. Only at that moment did it dawn on Tony that he had stopped coughing. The *baptême de l'air* had worked its wonders just as the doctor in Montauban had predicted. The SOE limousine had scarcely embarked upon its journey before Tony fell fast asleep. The next thing he knew was being woken outside the Norfolk Hotel in Surrey Street, off the Strand. Bidding the sleepy agent farewell, Buckmaster instructed him to report to Orchard Court later that morning.[55]

Tony was relieved to be back in England, but he would have been a great deal more thankful at his safe homecoming had he realised the true extent of Henri Déricourt's treachery. The accusations against the Frenchman were well founded: the man who had arranged Tony's flight was a double agent in the pay of the Paris branch of the Nazi *Sicherheitsdienst*.

Over the years, Déricourt has emerged as one of SOE's most controversial figures, finding supporters and detractors in almost equal measure amongst his colleagues within F Section and the Resistance. In the months following Tony's return to England, searching questions were asked about the Frenchman's probity. Accusations that he associated with German intelligence officers steadily increased and, as a result, on 4/5 February 1944, SOE mounted Operation 'Knacker'. Déricourt presumed that he was merely arranging the French end of a Hudson pick-up operation but, when the aircraft landed, in addition to six incoming agents there was an extra passenger aboard. This was Major Gerry Morel, Buckmaster's staff officer, who had orders to bring Déricourt back to England, using force if necessary. Déricourt expressed surprise at this turn of events, challenged the unexpected alteration to his plans and was unmoved by Morel's explanation that SOE wished to bring him to England to confer a British decoration. The Frenchman argued that he had important affairs to conclude in France (not least the disposal of the bicycles he had had brought to the field for the agents) before he could contemplate even a brief trip to London. But he promised Morel that, once appropriate arrangements had been made, he would willingly return to England on a future Lysander pick-up. Given the gravity of the charges being levelled at Déricourt, Morel's decision to accede to the agent's wishes is surprising. Perhaps the best explanation is that he feared that extended argument on the landing strip would put the safety of the aircraft and the nine returning passengers at risk.[56] As it transpired, Déricourt proved to be as good as his word and a few days later he was brought out, accompanied by his wife Jeanne.[57]

Squadron Leader Hugh Verity, one of the most accomplished of No.161 Squadron's pick-up pilots, had by this time taken up the post of Air Liaison-Operations (ALO) with SOE. He possessed knowledge of Déricourt in the extreme tension of a pick-up in a French field, as a sociable companion on the Frenchman's trips to London and now in his capacity as a member of the Baker Street headquarters staff. Verity later confessed to being 'shocked and incredulous' at the allegations levelled against Déricourt as he was 'a good friend of mine and his "Farrier" mission one of the most consistently successful at laying on good fields for pick-ups and efficient receptions.'[58] He joined Buckmaster at Déricourt's debriefing in Orchard Court following the Frenchman's arrival in London from Tangmere,

> Once we were all sitting comfortably in huge armchairs, Maurice [Buckmaster] told Déricourt that he had been accused of co-operating with the Germans in Paris. Déricourt's face showed absolutely no trace of emotion of any sort and, at first, he made no reply. He later explained that he had a number of German friends from his pre-war days as an international airline pilot. He kept up with them in Paris during the war and supplied them with black-market oranges as part of his cover. It was only by this method that he could ensure his safety to continue the good work he was secretly doing for us. So he said.[59]

The last three words say it all, but Verity 'still felt that he was a friend and a great partner in our operations'. Déricourt also appears to have possessed other, even more powerful, supporters in Buckmaster, Morel and Harry Sporborg, the Vice-Chief of SOE. But F Section's natural tendency to think the best of an apparently loyal and personable agent was offset by a more dispassionate, critical appraisal by MI5, which considered the accusations were of sufficient gravity that Déricourt should not be allowed to return to France. The principal argument offered in Déricourt's defence was that most of the agents he handled had either been safely brought back to London (like Tony) or remained operational in France. Moreover, others felt there was insufficient, concrete evidence that any of the arrests of F Section personnel could specifically be ascribed to Déricourt's actions. Nevertheless, SOE's Security Section argued, 'the fact that casualties do not appear to have occurred does not necessarily disprove his treachery.' They speculated that the Germans might throughout have been playing a long game, waiting for the right moment to exploit the entrées made by the double agent. The investigation proved inconclusive; Déricourt was forbidden to return to France but was by no means treated as a pariah in London. He was allowed to resign from SOE and join the Free French forces in the United Kingdom but scarcely had he done so than he was seriously injured in an air crash.[60]

After the war Déricourt returned to civil flying and, in April 1946, was convicted of smuggling gold, platinum and currency out of Croydon Airport. He managed to deploy an array of top legal counsel and (perhaps as a result) received a surprisingly small fine. His wartime endeavours resulted in the award of the Légion d'Honneur but the British criminal conviction ruined any hopes of his receiving the DSO for which he had been put forward. However, Déricourt's travails were far from over and, while the President of France was conferring one of the nation's premier awards on him, the Direction de la Surveillance du Territoire (DST) continued to investigate the accusations that he had collaborated with the Germans. On 22 November 1946 Déricourt was arrested in Paris and eventually went on trial in May 1948. The case against him appeared overwhelming but crucial German witnesses proved unavailable while, most tellingly, Bodington appeared for the defence. To all intents and purposes, the former SOE officer provided an exoneration and vindication of Déricourt's dubious actions.[61]

The interrogations of Déricourt and the post-war statements made by former German intelligence personnel reveal the naivety of some members of F Section in their assessments of the true allegiance of their colleague. The Frenchman eventually confessed to having worked for the Germans since the late spring of 1943, allowing them to put his landing grounds under surveillance and, when circumstances permitted, follow the incoming SOE agents to their ultimate destinations. In addition, Déricourt passed to the Germans the secret mail that had been entrusted to him for onward transmission to England. Apart from the acquisition of operational data, this information was skilfully exploited by Nazi interrogators in their questioning of captured agents. The nerves of the captives were shattered by the Germans' possession of such detailed, inside knowledge of SOE affairs. The enemy's insights into British secret operations appeared so comprehensive that several of the prisoners surmised that a German agent had infiltrated Baker Street. The captives' resolve was eroded by the dreadful assumption that withholding information was pointless as their adversary was omniscient.

Déricourt excused his actions by claiming that by appearing to cooperate with the Germans he would be able to protect his wife and assistants from harm. Moreover, he protested that his superiors in Baker Street were aware of his German connections and their failure to issue proper instructions or take protective measures exonerated him from any blame. There is also the possibility that Déricourt believed it was possible to serve two masters; after all, the careers of other double agents have shown throughout history that this is not a unique phenomenon. Espionage rarely falls neatly into absolutes of black and white and the conflicting demands of dual loyalties are far from rare. But there is no getting away from the conclusion that, even if the explanation Déricourt offered to explain his duplicity was truthful, he was hopelessly wrong in believing that he could serve the Germans without compromising the safety of the SOE agents he was handling. Whatever the complexities of the individual cases pursued by the Germans as they followed up the leads with which Déricourt furnished them, the blood of the British agents was on his hands – and there is no question that some of that blood might very well have been Tony's.

Chapter Ten
'Antoine Brévin' Will Die

On the morning of his return to London, Tony reported as instructed to the F Section apartment in Orchard Court. Mr Park, the janitor and general factotum, welcomed him with a warmth and kindness that did not fail to move the homecoming agent. Now, for the first time since he landed in England, Tony experienced a feeling of relaxation born of leaving the hazards of Occupied France behind him and he welcomed the prospect of being enveloped into the calm and comfort of F Section's Baker Street routines. That said, Tony was ardent in his desire to deliver a report on the current state of PIMENTO, brief his superiors on his own endeavours and discuss his future plans.[1]

Park's kindness touched Tony but the welcome he received from other F Section staff came as a complete surprise. He neither expected nor desired any fuss to mark his return but felt he was treated with a mild interest that bordered on indifference. Other returning agents have described their elation at the warm welcome given by London-based colleagues but, in contrast, Tony felt a tangible absence of empathy from the Baker Street staff – many of whom were new to the Section since he had departed for France more than a year earlier. No one seemed particularly keen to debrief him or to learn of the evolution of PIMENTO, never mind discuss its future. He dictated a report on 21 August but a copy has not survived and, presumably, was of such little moment that the interview failed to register in the agent's memory.[2]

Buckmaster's memoirs possess a grain of truth: 'We brought him back to England and refused, for three weeks, to discuss business with him.'[3]

The compassionate decision to provide Tony with a period of 'convalescence' was admirable but professionally questionable. He was amazed that the arrests of Dorval and Biou were not considered by his superiors of pressing importance. F Section's demeanour, however, was probably not indifference but, rather, a manifestation of flaws in the organisation's structure. Agents were not accorded an individual 'case officer' and London's oversight of the circuits in France was maintained largely on an *ad hoc* basis. F Section staff shared a variety of duties that resulted in no specific officer possessing an intimate knowledge of the personalities, activities and problems of each circuit.[4] Nevertheless, the 'neglect' of Tony is particularly surprising, for, on his return in August 1943, no other F Section circuit had enjoyed such an unbroken run of activity as PIMENTO. His superiors' desire to address the question of his ill-health and facilitate a well-deserved rest was commendable but it is remarkable that his up-to-date knowledge of France and specifically his own network were unexploited. Eventually, on 27 August he was interviewed again. His interrogator was Penelope Torr (F/RECS) whose write-up, 'Notes on Alphonse Circuit', was addressed to Buckmaster 'and for circulation'. While better than nothing, its two pages seem, if only on a question of scale, a profoundly inadequate survey of the work of the veteran organiser. It comprised a brief breakdown of PIMENTO's structure, an outline of the inter-relations between its members and some homilies from Tony on security measures. It also contained several factual errors that suggest deficiencies in Miss Torr's note taking.[5] The two F Section interviews (one account lost and one peripheral) having been completed, Tony was informed that he was being sent on leave and would be contacted 'in due course'.

In the absence of anything useful to do in Baker Street, Tony headed for his grandparents' home in Essex and a repeat of the 'wanderer's return' that had marked his arrival from Spain two years earlier. Strangely, it proved an easier reunion for a secret agent on leave than it had been for a refugee. His family's fortunes appeared to have changed little and, although Goldsmiths was not entirely untouched by wartime restrictions, it still offered a comfortable retreat for the Brookses' exhausted grandson. Day by day he built up his strength while his grandparents, suspecting that Tony was engaged on special government work, refrained from asking him questions. They did however possess some understanding that his military activities were unconventional from fragments of information they had received from Hope Munday. As early as 28 December 1942 Tony's grandmother had commented in a letter to Hope, 'Thank you so much for your letter & the good news it contained & we are glad to hear Tony is well, we had heard nothing since the letter you sent us. I wonder where he is & how he heard of his Uncle & Aunt we had been anxious about them & had heard nothing since the Germans took over.'[6]

Following the reunion with his grandparents, Tony wasted little time in seeing Hope. Their relationship, like countless others, had been handicapped by the exigencies of war. Tony's SOE training and departure for France had substantially restricted their courtship and the messages that Bertholet forwarded to Hope on his behalf related little more than that he was 'well' and thinking of her. Unsurprisingly, the young man with so many cares and responsibilities formed a strong emotional attachment to the girl 'back home'. Hope seems to have harboured similar romantic feelings for a boyfriend involved in 'secret' operations that contrasted with her own, more prosaic, war service as a WAAF stationed in the none too hostile environs of Cornwall. Moreover, their emotions were further cemented by Tony being warmly embraced into the Munday household on his visits to Leverington. For a 'loner' whose own family exhibited a tendency for emotional austerity, it is little wonder that he responded strongly to the kindnesses shown to him.[7]

While romance blossomed anew, some purpose returned to Tony's secret duties with orders to attend STS 17, SOE's sabotage training centre at Brickendonbury near Hertford. He harboured happy memories of the establishment from his initial course and hoped that this visit would offer opportunities for him to brief the training staff on his sabotage experiences 'in the field'. He already possessed a good relationship with one of the instructors, Captain Bill Hazeldine, and they discussed at length the lessons that Tony had learnt in France. He also explained to Hazeldine his theories on the amount of railway track that needed to be removed in order to achieve optimum derailment. Experience had shown Tony that if too little track was displaced, the locomotive merely jumped the gap and continued on its way. He therefore advocated taking out a section of railway line that was the combined length of the engine and the wheelbase,

There were many methods of doing this [railway sabotage] which were used according to the duration of the blockage intended. A cut of 6' could be made in the rail and initiated by a time delay which would cause a delay of a few hours before it could be repaired sufficiently to allow slow running and 6 hours before complete repair. A similar cut could be made but initiated by the engine itself. This caused greater damage but very rarely a derailment. To block a line for 12 hours or more, it was necessary to cause a derailment of an engine of several trucks. In order to do this a cut of 15' was needed. An alternative method of derailing an engine and train was the removal by unbolting of one length of rail. This method took a great deal of time and caused a lot of noise. In order to block a line for several days a derailment had to be made in a cutting or tunnel as the Germans cleared a derailment on an embankment by tipping the wreckage down the bank. In a cutting or tunnel the wreckage had to be removed by crane or by cutting up into small pieces. If a crane was used, it ran a great risk of being derailed itself as 50-ton breakdown cranes were very scarce.[8]

During his stay at STS 17 he took part in a heated debate regarding the merits and shortcomings of SOE sabotage equipment such as readymade railway charges, time pencils and fog-signal igniters. Time pencils, although intended for general use, were, in Tony's opinion, too sophisticated for novice saboteurs in the Resistance. He considered that robust handling of the device rendered it useless or, even worse, made it a danger to the saboteur himself. Tony explained it had become necessary for him to construct bespoke explosive charges fitted with an additional 10-second length of slow-burning fuse so that if the time pencil was accidentally initiated, the sabotage team had enough time to put sufficient distance between itself and the imminent explosion. PIMENTO had also encountered difficulties with fog signals: Tony had observed a tendency amongst his men to place the charge and the snout of the fuse on the inside of the rail 'for concealment'. The desire to hide the charge was admirable but it had an unfortunate consequence – the configuration resulted in the locomotive's wheel cutting the fuse that linked the igniter with the explosive and thereby curtailing any hope of detonation.[9]

To his great relief, Tony obtained news of PIMENTO when occasional reports from Bertholet arrived at Baker Street.[10] Few have survived but one, sent on 29 September 1943, reveals that, behind Bertholet's cool demeanour, the fallout from the arrest of Dorval was far from over. Written with the assumption that Tony's return to France was imminent, the message began with the disturbing news that Bertholet had lost contact with André Moch as a result of Fourre's arrest. The second part of the message was also uncompromising, 'For security obliged to change whole of your set up.' More optimistically, Bertholet suggested that the ever-reliable Bizot (who was now operating from Switzerland) had matters well in hand with arrangements for a new route to be taken by the cross-border couriers who could exploit his contacts with Swiss customs officials. A report that the Gestapo had searched the Lyon SRFD offices as a belated follow-up to Dorval's arrest was unsettling. PIMENTO was still not out of the woods and Bertholet advised that Pédémas should only be contacted with caution, that communications had been cut with Bottemer and that Bizot's Lyon apartment was 'probably brûlé'. Finally, he inaugurated a list of new codenames to be used in communications

- 'Alphonse' [Tony] to become 'Fleur'
- 'Geranium' [Bertholet] to become 'Tonton'
- 'Georges' [Moch] to become 'Jim'
- London to become 'Elizabeth/Elisabeth'
- 'Gaby' [Cordier] to become 'Juliette'
- 'Claude' [Bottemer] to become 'Julien'
- Pédémas to become 'Perrier'[11]

From the outset, Tony had hoped that his visit to London would be brief and he anticipated returning to France by the October 'moon period' at the latest. However, by the end of that month F Section showed no signs of sending him back. A rare and somewhat garbled wireless message on 18 October from Bertholet in Switzerland contained the hopeful statement 'Foresee Alphonse's return November'. But Tony did not share his friend's optimism and, feeling increasingly frustrated by aimlessly hanging around, he met Bourne-Paterson, the F Section staff officer who had overseen his departure in July 1942, to discuss the dilemma. The two men lunched at the White Tower Restaurant in Soho, then, as they walked back to Baker Street, Tony (fortified by Dutch courage) opened up his heart. 'Antoine Brévin' would 'die' if he did not get back to France soon. His rent at the Chemin du Panorama had been paid until 31 December but if he did not return by that date Mme Dupeuple's venality was likely to get the better of her and the room would be let to a new tenant. The loss of Tony's bolt-hole would be disastrous. Not only was it ideal for its location, configuration and security, it was a cornerstone of his 'Brévin' identity and the prospect of trying to find an alternative was deeply disquieting. Moreover, his official registrations for food, tram and railway passes would expire unless he renewed them by the end of the year. If these bureaucratic deadlines were not met, Tony would have to go through the tiresome and potentially dangerous business of re-registering (with appropriate explanations) when he finally went back to Lyon. A worst-case prediction was that he would need to create a whole, new, false identity. Part of the problem was that, unlike most other F Section agents, Tony operated as an 'illegal'; a term later used to describe Soviet Intelligence's Cold War placement of deep-cover agents living a perfectly normal, yet fictitious life in a foreign country.[12] Tony had made 'Antoine Brévin' into a 'real' Frenchman. In contrast, many of his F Section peers adopted the well-worn 'commercial traveller' type of cover or simply became human parcels passed from the care of one local guardian to another. Some agents made little or no attempt to develop full and convincing aliases and possessed barely enough documentation to pass a simple identity check. Lieutenant John Hamilton was arrested the morning after his clandestine arrival in France in December 1942. At a 'safe' house, he fell victim to a case of mistaken identity but, as his false documents and cover story did not hold up to close scrutiny, he was detained for further investigation. His ultimate fate was to disappear into the horrors of Gross Rosen concentration camp, never to return.[13] In complete contrast, Tony had from the outset built up a depth of 'legitimate' cover that was intended to frustrate any hostile attempt to penetrate his false identity.

Having convinced Bourne-Paterson of his operational requirements, Tony soon had another problem to resolve: F Section now suggested that he form a new circuit near Le Mans. The proposal came as a great surprise, not least because it had no justification. Tony had not been 'blown' in France and, notwithstanding the Dorval and Biou arrests, there were no attendant security risks in his being sent back to PIMENTO. Moreover, he did not consider himself a maquis leader and argued that sending him to a group of partisans hiding in the woods around Le Mans would be a waste of his talents and experience. For more than a year he had developed a formidable relationship with small cells of railwaymen and trade unionists assigned to specific objectives. He assumed that, if and when the need for paramilitary activity arose, either London would need to send someone else to lead PIMENTO in this new, operational phase or he would learn how to do it himself. But, for the present, he saw no sense in leaving his circuit when the work was half completed. The proposed transfer to another network was even more questionable given the glowing reports of Tony's work that F Section submitted to SOE headquarters. A plausible (but unconfirmed) explanation for Tony's redeployment was that he was needed to resolve a pressing problem in the Le Mans region. As this had been an important area for the now, virtually defunct network, PROSPER, was it intended that he revive the circuit? Whatever the motivation behind the proposal, Tony's assertiveness won the day and the Le Mans option was dropped.

Bourne-Paterson became a welcome ally in the fight to keep 'Antoine Brévin' 'alive' to lead PIMENTO. He accepted that Tony was resolute on this matter and strongly advocated within the Section that the agent be sent back to his original network. But the debate had absorbed a great deal of time and the onset of winter reduced flying opportunities to France. Tony therefore missed the November moon and had to wait his turn for a new slot in the special duties squadrons' heavily oversubscribed December schedules. [14]

Tony's time now began to fill with briefings preparing him for a return to France. One seemed to indicate the very real prospect of an imminent second front: during a broad strategic discussion with F Section staff officers, Tony was instructed to prepare sabotage plans to isolate Toulouse by severing its road and rail connections. Slipping into the role of an armchair strategist, he (inaccurately) predicted that the Allied invasion would be launched against south-west France with amphibious landings in the Bay of Biscay, possibly with a supplementary assault against the Mediterranean coast. [15] A much truer indication that the 'great day' was approaching was the issuing of PIMENTO's 'A' and 'B' coded messages that would be broadcast by the BBC as forewarnings of the invasion. SOE instructions laid down that on receipt of the 'A' phrases, F Section networks were to go on standby while the subsequent broadcast of the 'B' messages would signal that the assault was commencing and the Resistance groups were to begin their pre-arranged sabotage programmes. Tony was given microphotographs bearing the messages – an unusual departure for a man whose memory had already served him well with far more complex data of map references and *messages personnels*. They were concealed in a fountain pen that had been in among the 'equipment' SOE had given him on his previous departure. Although SOE's Camouflage Section had developed an extensive range of sophisticated, purpose-built concealing devices, the photos were simply placed inside the barrel of the pen, wrapped around the ink bladder.

For security reasons, unnecessary contact between agents in London was strictly avoided. But the hothouse atmosphere of Baker Street and the comings and goings at Orchard Court and F Section's 'conventional' offices meant that unintended lapses occurred. One face, that of a young courier, Anne-Marie Walters, registered with Tony (perhaps because of her looks) and this brief encounter was to have repercussions when the two agents later met in France. Another Orchard Court meeting was far from accidental and gave Tony the chance to meet his new wireless operator. Tony, the inveterate sceptic about wireless links, had now accepted London's decision: PIMENTO and the war had changed radically since the imposition of Bloom the previous year and reliance solely on the courier routes to Switzerland was foolish. His new colleague could not have been more different from Bloom. He was Roger Mark Caza, a French-Canadian, born on 29 November 1917 at Stanicet, Quebec Province. After graduating from the University of Ottawa in 1937 he remained in the city, becoming a reporter with its *Le Droit* newspaper. He enlisted in the Royal Canadian Corps of Signals in August 1939 and arrived in England later that year. When SOE recruited him in August 1943 he was still a signalman with the Canadian Army. Caza completed the usual agent training programme (with great distinction) between August and November, being rewarded with a commission as a lieutenant. Shortly afterwards, he was selected to join PIMENTO, but this process is not recorded in surviving SOE documents. The choice must have owed more to Caza's excellent wireless skills rather than his knowledge of France, for he had never visited the country and, although he spoke the language fluently, it was with a distinctive French-Canadian accent.[16]

Four and a half years in age separated the agents but the gulf in experience was immense. Unfortunately, there was little time in London for the two men to get to know each other and it was decided that Caza would be parachuted to PIMENTO after Tony had re-established himself in France. The latter would organise his wireless operator's reception committee and arrange safe houses for this new and vitally important member of his circuit. Concluding the meeting, Bourne-Paterson and Morel offered a few simple and timely words of advice to Caza (perhaps mindful of the shortcomings of his fellow Canadian, Duchalard) telling him that if he followed 'Alphonse's' orders he would be all right. On 7 December Tony wrote to Morel recording his impressions of PIMENTO's latest recruit, 'I am very pleased with him and he seems to be O.K. His French is not as bad as I was expecting, and I am sure he can pass as a peasant.'[17]

Caza was not the only F Section officer Tony met during his stay in London who was destined to play a future role in his work: Major Ernest van Maurik who was possessed of wide experience having performed SOE staff conducting and training duties in the United Kingdom. Like many of his 'backroom' contemporaries, van Maurik keenly sought a more active role and had been posted to Berne as Deputy Head of SOE's operations in Switzerland. Gubbins and Buckmaster explained to him that the local SOE head, 'Jock' McCaffery, was suffering from nervous exhaustion as a result of the immense burden of work. McCaffery was now in a Swiss sanatorium and, if he recovered, it was intended that he concentrate on Italian affairs while van Maurik would assume responsibility for F Section's interests. But the problem was how to get the SOE reinforcement into Switzerland. The country was isolated in the middle of Nazi-occupied Europe, without civilian or military air links to the United Kingdom and there was no hope of orchestrating a legal entry into the country, even with diplomatic accreditation. The Swiss would not be well-disposed to accept a parachuted 'diplomat', so it was decided to drop van Maurik into France and have him cross 'illegally' into Switzerland where he would declare himself a fugitive RAF airman. Nominally, he would be interned for the duration of the war, but it was anticipated that the Swiss authorities would leave him at liberty to carry out his SOE tasks. The plan was to drop van Maurik to a PIMENTO reception committee in the Ain near the Swiss frontier, and this was the primary purpose of the meeting. Tony agreed that on his return to France he would make the necessary arrangements and send final details of the operation to London via his courier link. Recalling his own rough landing in France, Tony offered to vet the ground himself but provisionally proposed 'Asticot' as the most suitable. Another, equally important reason for making the introduction was to allow Tony to brief van Maurik on his relations with Bertholet, a man who loomed large in the latter's prospective duties in Switzerland.[18]

In spite of Tony's impatience with some of F Section's staff, his outstanding achievements in France had not been overlooked and his superiors recommended the award of the Military Cross. In addition, he was promoted to the paid, acting rank of captain. The additional salary was welcome but it made little difference to him, for his bank account was brimming over with the accrued year's wages that had built up while he had been in France.

Away from these professional preoccupations, there were momentous developments in Tony's personal life. His courtship of Hope Munday had continued with regular visits to Leverington Hall where he found a welcome sanctuary from the frustrations of Baker Street, and on 9 November 1943 they married at Leverington Parish Church. Teddy Bisset, the first choice as best man, fell foul of pressing SOE duties and was replaced at the last minute by Tony's brother, Peter, on leave from the Fleet Air Arm. Wartime honeymoon opportunities were limited and the newlyweds spent their first days of married life at the Rembrandt Hotel in Kensington.[19]

Marriage did little to curtail Tony's champing at the bit to return to France. His impatience was not inspired by a burning sense of duty nor a heroic desire to return to the fray but from his preoccupation with the prosaic, practical need to be back in Lyon to re-establish the tenancy at his digs and register for the swathe of official documents required by the Vichy authorities. So much of Tony's cover in France had been underpinned by his 'Antoine Brévin' alias that worry over its being compromised engendered such anxiety that he suffered an acute attack of psoriasis. He slipped into a deep state of frustration while his deteriorating medical condition exacerbated the feeling of despair at his failure to get back to France. A visit to an SOE doctor offered no consolation, for the medical diagnosis suggested that it was now a borderline decision whether Tony was too unwell to be sent back to PIMENTO even if a flight could be arranged.

Tony's preoccupations with his return to France were understandable but in the winter of 1943 SOE had more to worry about than one grumpy and fretful agent. The number of circuits in France had greatly increased while the work of the long-established networks continued apace. The list of casualties grew too, illustrated by the casualty toll of F Section agents, more than two dozen of whom were killed or captured during Tony's brief period of sanctuary in England.[20] The scale of these tragic losses was probably a factor in F Section's belated decision to send Tony back to PIMENTO to carry on where he had left off. But if there was now a will, for the moment, there was not a way, for it was a difficult time of the year for parachute operations. Bad weather and aircraft shortages even led F Section to consider sending Tony back to France by sea. This was decidedly not to his liking; he was a poor sailor, an inadequate swimmer and the Germans had imposed a tight security zone on the coastal areas. In the best traditions of 'better the Devil you know', Tony refused the seaborne option and stipulated his preference for a parachute drop.

Buckmaster wrote in his memoirs that Tony was recalled to F Section's London office on Christmas Eve to be informed that he would be returning to France that very evening, thereby ruining 'his plans for celebrating Christmas with his *fiancée*'.[21] The account is hopelessly inaccurate; Hope was Tony's *wife* of six weeks and their separation predated the Christmas holiday. A telegram of 17 December from Tony to his bride, now at a WAAF billet in Farnborough, reveals that the couple had already succumbed to the calls of wartime duty and the honeymoon was long over. His final, muted message to her a few days later reveals how the demands of war dominated the lives of the young couple, 'Am going away as arranged. Bless you and all my love. Tony.'

SOE records concerning the circumstances of Tony's return to France have not survived. Neither operational instructions nor other briefing documents exist to provide insights into the decisions and planning that lay behind his resumption of the leadership of PIMENTO. Presumably these administrative processes kept Tony kicking his heels in London until, at last, on 20 December 1943, he was delivered to the SOE holding station at Gaynes Hall, close to Tempsford. No longer the novice of eighteen months earlier, he was now the seasoned campaigner. On this visit the ritual of the valedictory meal and the drive to Tempsford failed to leave a vivid impression on the agent. Even the repeat of his refusal to accept a pistol and an 'L' tablet did not cause anything like the same fuss as had been occasioned on his first departure.

Tony's feelings were dominated by an immense sense of relief that, at last, he was going back to France. In keeping with his original plans, F Section had confirmed that he would be dropped to a DZ on a curve of the River Tarn about 25 to 30 kilometres outside Montauban. In preparation for his return, a bicycle had been hidden in a local vineyard hut. Michel Comte was notified of the BBC warning message – 'Michou aime racler les plats' – that would herald his arrival but Tony had issued strict instructions that no one was to be at the DZ to receive him.[22] Instead of having a reception committee, he planned simply to hide his parachute in the hut and then cycle to Montauban.

When he reached Tempsford, Tony was surprised to discover that another agent was to share the aircraft, but he was informed they would be dropping to different DZs. For security reasons the agent's name and identity were not revealed to him and, as they boarded the aircraft, contact between them was restricted to nothing more than the greeting '*Bonsoir*' and a handshake.[23]

In contrast to the detailed record of Tony's first flight, his return is quite obscure. There were six operations to France from Tempsford on the night of 20/21 December 1943. Three were undertaken by No.161 Squadron, while No.138 flew the others, and analysis of each of the flights' details leaves only one as Tony's: Operation TRAINER 61/STOCKBROKER 1 & 3 flown by Flight Lieutenant John Perrins, which took off from Tempsford at 11.48 p.m. The pilot's report has not been located and the Squadron Operations Record Book merely states 'Operation STOCKBROKER 1 & 3 completed'.[24]

In later life Tony recalled that the only memorable feature of the flight was the RAF dispatcher informing him en route that the DZ near Montauban was impossible due to bad weather. He was then offered the option of being taken back to England or of dropping with his fellow passenger near Montbéliard, close to the Swiss border. Exhibiting a not untypical RAF sense of humour, the dispatcher quipped, 'Well, at least we got the first four letters right.' Tony had visited Montbéliard a few times before the war while making deliveries for the Grozon factory, and was consoled that he would not be arriving in uncharted territory. As far as he was concerned, the RAF could drop him wherever they liked as long as he stood a chance of getting back to Lyon before the New Year in time to breathe life into 'Antoine Brévin'.

But the sparse entry in No. 138 Squadron's record book, 'STOCKBROKER 1 & 3 completed', raises the disturbing question of whether Tony's return to France might, from the very outset, have been a STOCKBROKER circuit operation and that, contrary to F Section (and RAF) assurances, he had always been destined for Montbéliard. Tony's fellow passenger was Lieutenant Paul Sarrette of F Section, whose task was to develop some STOCKBROKER contacts into forming the GONDOLIER circuit in the Nièvre region.[25] This connection with the other F Section network explains the absence of a PIMENTO designation on the flight's documentation. There is no sensible explanation why the RAF would have sanctioned an aircraft undertaking two DZs at opposite ends of France. A Halifax would have been at the very limit of its operational range to complete a circuit that encompassed Montauban in the south-west and the STOCKBROKER task in the east. No specific evidence has been found to support an assumption that Tony was the victim of a deception in his SOE briefing but it is a theory that merits consideration. The most compelling justification for such a conclusion is that the young agent's insistence that he be returned to France had worn down F Section's staff officers to such an extent that they simply decided, after weeks of delays, to put him on the first available aircraft to France. If this was the case, it was reprehensible and regrettable; not least because, had he been consulted, Tony would have agreed to be dropped to a location in the Jura that was moderately well known to him.[26]

Such speculation was far from Tony's thoughts as he followed Sarrette out of the Halifax over eastern France. This parachute drop was markedly different from his 'blind' first operation for, as he descended, he could clearly hear the sounds of a reception committee rising up to him. On his landing, Frenchmen casually greeted him and did not seem in the least perplexed or intrigued by the arrival of a second, unexpected agent. Tony's parachute was whisked away but he made sure that he kept his striptease suit on until he could better comprehend the competence of the reception committee. If the arrival of the agents was not excitement enough, there was suddenly an explosion in the distance followed by a red glow seen on the horizon. The Frenchmen let out a cheer and when the celebrations ceased, one of the reception committee told Tony that members of their group had attacked a transformer.[27] Out of nowhere bicycles were produced and one resister told Tony that he would escort him to a safe house not far from the DZ. Tony took off his striptease and the two men cycled through woodland paths, onto a country lane and after a couple of kilometres finally reached a farm. Their host, a scruffy man in his sixties, had waited up for them. Having made the introductions, the guide said that he would return the next day having checked on German activity in the town following the drop, and then the farmer escorted Tony to a bedroom. Settling down for the night, Tony took off his shoes but not his clothes and, having checked that the roof of a chicken run underneath his window afforded a ready escape route, he lay down and went to sleep. The next morning the farmer gave him a simple breakfast before ushering him into a cellar underneath the farmhouse. Tony's first thoughts were that his host intended to show him a private arsenal of weapons and was surprised when the farmer approached a half-barrel full of liquid surmounted by a crust of mould that was topped off by a dead rat floating on the surface. Employing a length of cane, the farmer rolled back the mould until he noticed Tony's questioning look at the rodent. With a shrug he explained all by stating '*Il est mort heureux*' ('He died happy'). He then took two glasses, dunked them into the vat and proffered one to Tony who, feeling obliged to take a sip, found the concoction tasted a little akin to kirsch. The farmer drained his glass while Tony, having drunk sufficient to be polite, told his host that he considered the vintage excellent but that he was not used to drinking so early in the day. The farmer was pleased to help him out and poured the remaining contents of Tony's glass into his own and gulped it down.

The guide from the reception committee failed to return that day and Tony was obliged to stay another night. The next morning he was preparing to make his own travel arrangements when the contact appeared. He reported that there were no unusual German security measures since the drop and offered to escort Tony the few kilometres into Montbéliard. Leaving the farmer to his bucolic devices, the two men departed. They said their farewells before they reached the station for, typically, Tony did not want his companion to know where he was bound. Fortunately, the next Paris train soon arrived, and he slept most of the way, which perhaps accounts for his receiving no demands to present his papers during the entire journey.

It was only a few days before Christmas and Paris was displaying few signs of the festive season yet Tony allowed himself some celebratory thoughts at his return to work. He had no preconceived plans about which part of PIMENTO to visit first but decided on taking a train to Toulouse rather than Lyon. Although the latter was the place where he would revive 'Antoine Brévin', he considered that Michel Comte's garage offered the most secure haven from which to re-acclimatise himself and resurrect the career of 'Alphonse'.

On arriving at Montauban Tony took a long, precautionary walk around Michel Comte's garage before he gauged it safe to enter. There was no sign of tension from Michel Driffaud, the mechanic, who greeted him with a casual *'Bonjour, Monsieur Toni'*, as if he had never been away. The welcome from the Comtes was effusive, reflecting their heartfelt sentiment that the man who had returned to them was now a member of the family. When the embraces, eating and drinking had finally subsided, Tony received a detailed briefing from Michel Comte that revealed PIMENTO was still intact. No further security breaches had occurred since Dorval's arrest, the circuit's affairs in the Toulouse/Montauban area were sound and, as far as he knew, so were those in Lyon. But Comte kept one secret from his friend. It had nothing specifically to do with PIMENTO but it might have had a major impact upon their affairs. While Tony was absent in England, Comte had given refuge to Captain Henri Despaigne, an F Section wireless operator. He neglected to mention this to his leader – a decision that seems particularly strange given the close relationship between the two men. Moreover, Despaigne continued to operate in Montauban until 27 January 1944, more than a month after Tony's return to France, but without the latter knowing of his presence. In London, Tony had advised F Section that Comte could provide a 'safe house' for those '*de passage*' and it can be assumed that notice of the facility had been conveyed at some point to Despaigne. Notifying Tony of the arrangement with the wireless operator would have been more than an act of politeness for, by the beginning of 1944, Despaigne constituted a significant security risk; dual threats were posed by German direction-finding aircraft in the vicinity of Montauban and a reward of 15,000 francs had been put on his head.[28] Unaware of these links to Despaigne, Tony felt greatly reassured by Comte's favourable report on PIMENTO's state of health and, as a result, indulged himself with a few extra days in Montauban before departing to resurrect 'Antoine Brévin'.

On his arrival in Lyon, Tony wasted no time in going straight to his digs at the Chemin du Panorama where Mme Dupeuple's polite welcome became substantially warmer once he had presented her with gifts from his extended 'holiday in Switzerland'. He was relieved to find his room just as he had left it but derived his greatest consolation by being in ample time to register for his official documentation and achieve his overarching aim: 'Antoine Brévin' did not 'die'.

If Tony's domestic circumstances in Lyon were unaffected by his absence, there was no doubt that France had changed substantially in the four months that he had been away. The improvement in the Allies' military fortunes had not failed to register; the fall of Mussolini resulted on 8 September 1943 in the German occupation of those areas of France formerly held by Italian forces. Similarly, the Allied landings on the Italian mainland later that month provided further, incontrovertible evidence of the erosion of Axis power. Resistance in France was fuelled by these body blows to the Nazis' image of indestructible domination. A manifestation of this new self-assertion was the 'liberation' of the Savoyard town of Oyonnax by three hundred maquisards under the command of Henri Romans-Petit.[29] This was just a symbolic gesture recreating the pre-war national commemoration of the 11 November Armistice Day that marked the defeat of Germany in 1918. Security amongst the resisters was tight, the Germans were unaware of their intentions and, when control of the town was taken, there was no opposition (the local gendarmes sensibly refrained from taking any action). After the Resistance fighters held a parade, conducted a ceremony at the war memorial and sang 'La Marseillaise', Romans-Petit and his men disappeared into their rural hideouts or back to the anonymity of their everyday life in the town. The event raised morale amongst resisters in the region but undoubtedly the greatest impact was its contribution to Allied propaganda. The BBC and consequently the world learnt of this act of 'liberation' within Occupied France, and photographs of the wreath-laying ceremony were smuggled out of the country to appear in the free world's newspapers. But such an act could not escape Nazi retribution; a series of arrests and deportations followed the Germans' investigation into the demonstration.

Resistance activity was not solely concerned with propaganda opportunities and symbolic acts. In Grenoble, one of PIMENTO's operational areas but in which it functioned discretely and in isolation from other networks, a deadly series of tit-for-tat acts of violence unfolded between resistance groups and the occupiers. Following another 11 November demonstration, the Germans arrested hundreds of townspeople and deported 450 of them. In retaliation, a resistance group blew up a German ammunition dump. This act, in turn, incited the Gestapo to execute a number of hostages. The stakes were then raised even higher on 2 December 1943 when the Resistance attacked the German barracks in the Grenoble district of Bonne, killing fifty soldiers and destroying tons of explosives in a massive conflagration.[30] The escalation of violence was not confined to Grenoble and political opponents of the Vichy regime throughout France now faced punishments more deadly than simple imprisonment. The assassination in December 1943 of Maurice Sarraut, a Toulousain newspaper editor and politician, exemplified the new situation – his murderers were not the Gestapo but French fascists. Meanwhile the Vichy government's response to the upsurge of resistance was the appointment of Joseph Darnand as Secrétaire d'Etat au Maintien de l'Ordre (Secretary of State for the Maintenance of Order), supplementing his existing command of the Milice, the right-wing militia that served to enforce Vichy's anti-resistance policies.

Tony's re-acclimatisation continued with his renewal of contact with Auguste Bottemer at Chambéry where he was informed that PIMENTO was doing just as well in the east as the south-west. But this heartening news was offset by news of the executions of Dorval and Biou. They had been detained in prison in Lyon until their trial by a German military tribunal on 31 December 1943 resulted in sentences of death by firing squad. Little is known of their last days other than a proud, valedictory letter written by Dorval on the day of his execution, in which he declared that his last thoughts were for his friends and family and, typically, affirmed that '*j'affronterai la mort avec calme la tête haute et fière*'. As the prosecutors at his trial had sought to demean the motivation for his actions, he was keen to assure his parents that he was not 'a criminal or a bandit'. Dorval and Biou were executed at the military rifle range at La Doua in Lyon at four-thirty on the afternoon of 11 January 1944 with the Lyon press recording their demise in the following day's newspapers.[31]

In spite of his deep, emotional loss at Dorval's death, Tony could not allow himself to be distracted from his primary aims: the reassertion of his leadership of PIMENTO and handling of many concomitant tasks that included Caza's arrival. On the latter project, he decided he would utilise Donoff's extensive contacts to receive the Canadian in the Bourg area whence he would establish his wireless set at Gannat, fifteen kilometres west of Vichy. One of Donoff's cronies, Fernand Woreczyk, was deputed to act as Caza's 'minder' and assume responsibility (and the risk) of conveying the wireless transceiver to the transmission points (thereby reducing the threat to the operator). Codenamed 'Felix', Woreczyk was an Alsatian Jew of Polish extraction and, like Gauthier, possessed a nominal employment as a school assistant. Fearless and resourceful, he was an ideal choice for this important role. His sister Yvette also worked for the network as a courier, conveying documents between Lyon, Culoz and Chambéry. The Woreczyks were fully immersed in a clandestine life, operating under false identities not just because of their work for PIMENTO but also from the dire threat resulting from Vichy's anti-Jewish legislation. They were by no means the only members of Tony's team who were in this situation and by early 1944, PIMENTO included a significant number of Jews among its ranks. Tony gauged that their motivation was varied and derived as much from their individual, ideological convictions as socialists, anti-Nazis and French patriots as it was their response to racial persecution as Jews.

As Tony awaited the Caza reinforcement from England, the German inroads into PIMENTO seemed to be escalating. A tragedy befell the circuit soon after his return when André Malamard, alias 'Dédé', one of his earliest recruits at Pont de Veyle, was arrested by the Gestapo on 17 January 1944. Details of his capture are unclear and perhaps Tony was even unaware of it at the time. But Malamard later wrote of his misfortunes, recording a litany of the suffering that he had endured including having both arms broken, ribs cracked, teeth pulled out, being burned by cigarettes and subjection to the *baignoire* (a partial drowning torture process). His wife was beaten by the Germans, his properties were ransacked and his mother died from the shock and grief engendered by the arrest of her son. Condemned to death, Malamard escaped this fate 'by a miracle' but was deported to the Mauthausen and Auschwitz concentration camps from which he returned at the end of the war weighing 42 kilos.[32]

On 5 February 1944 the BBC *message personnel*, '*Adolphe a coupé la mèche*', announced the arrival that night of the wireless operator, Roger Caza. The

Canadian dropped onto one of Henri Morandat's grounds, 'Asticot', near Ceyzériat, a few kilometres south-east of Bourg, along with eight supply containers and two packages. Tony decided not to take an active part in the reception committee, deeming it prudent not to risk having both organiser and wireless operator together on the same ground, and instead observed the drop from a discreet distance,. His decision proved unfortunate for, as it transpired, it took some time before effective contact between the two SOE agents was to take place. Caza wrote that following his arrival he 'stayed a few nights in Bourg, but a state of siege threatened and [I] moved down to Lyon, then to Montauban, then back up to Naves near Gannat.' The whole trip took a week but the newcomer, unlike Tony who had largely fended for himself, was always accompanied by Woreczyk or other 'minders'. Caza's SOE documents stated he was Roger Marcel Pilon, a travelling salesman born at Louviers in the Eure who was currently resident in Bordeaux. However, Tony and the wireless operator's PIMENTO guardians were to consider this an unconvincing cover and alternative papers were forged describing him as a Yugoslav. This manifest slur on the agent's French accent did not sit well with the Canadian but he adopted a professional attitude and, perhaps recalling Morel's advice to follow Tony's instructions, accepted the amendment to his 'nationality'.[33]

The activation of Caza's wireless link proved troublesome. The need to move him around the now very extensive PIMENTO circuit resulted in his being separated from his equipment and, consequently, it took a month for the transceiver and crystals finally to reach him. As a result, radio contact with London was not established until the end of March, almost two months after Caza's arrival. Tony reported to London by courier on 8 March 1944:

Emmanuel [Caza] arrived safely and is now installed in the area agreed upon. He hopes to be able to work soon. Unfortunately we have had great difficulty in getting his equipment out of the departement [*sic*] where he arrived owing to the present police measures. But things are O.K. He has a permanent escort and a regular liaison with me.[34]

Caza's closest companion at this time seems to have been Jacques Pertuisot whom the wireless operator described as 'Always ready to look for and obtain anything I needed in the way of equipment, food, etc.' Pertuisot was the son-in-law of Monsieur Coulon, the Adjoint au Maire [Deputy Mayor] of Naves, who provided Caza with accommodation for a month and, doubtless, was instrumental in ensuring that the Mairie supplied ration cards and other useful documentation. Even at this early stage, Caza's aptitude for the clandestine life was in marked contrast to that of his predecessor Bloom, but, sadly, his contribution to PIMENTO's work proved similarly tardy. For many weeks after the wireless operator's arrival in France, Tony remained reliant upon the courier links to Bertholet, Bizot and Van Maurik in Switzerland for contact with London. Events would soon prove that these contacts were more critical than ever.[35]

Chapter Eleven
'Marguerite'

As Tony resettled into a 'routine' of daily life in France, he appreciated with some relish that the Vichy radio broadcasts and film newsreels were unable to conceal the changing fortunes of the war. No longer able to bask in a succession of unbroken German victories, the Nazi propaganda machine now placed great emphasis on the Wehrmacht's sacrifice and stoicism on the Eastern Front against an implacable and 'barbarous' foe. The constant pummelling of Germany and occupied Europe by the RAF's Bomber Command and the United States' Eighth Air Force was manifest and the best that the Vichy media could muster were lame castigations of 'indiscriminate' Allied 'malevolence'. But Vichy newspapers, radio and newsreels were not the only sources of information available to Tony and he kept up with the Allied version of the war's progress by listening to the BBC at his digs on his domestic wireless set. Reception was rarely good and sometimes the Vichy authorities' jamming meant that it was impossible to hear anything at all. But, when the British broadcasts did come through, they imparted a sense of optimism that sustained Tony's morale through his moments of worry and doubt.

If the violent struggles on the war's battlefronts did not visibly impinge on the daily life of the citizens of Lyon, Toulouse, Montauban, there was no escaping the major changes that had taken place in French society. As the war began to ebb away from the Germans and their collaborators, the forces of repression stepped up their efforts and PIMENTO did not remain untouched. An informant denounced 'Dodo' Donoff's brother to the authorities for handling false papers (probably furnished by his brother). On 2 February 1944 Robert Donoff and his wife were sent to the Drancy transit camp in Paris and then deported to Germany; neither returned.[1]

Politicians of the far right now dominated the French government while the German security forces and their collaborationist cohorts increased their brutal struggle against the Resistance. The explanation was simple; by the beginning of 1944, opposition to occupation had broadened greatly. In addition to the *réseaux* built up by the main resistance organisations sponsored by external forces such as the Free French, SIS and SOE, there was now a greater indigenous groundswell against German rule, reinforced by the ever-growing numbers of *réfractaires* – men on the run from the forced labour drafts being sent to work in Germany. Some young Frenchmen went 'underground' by adopting a passive, hidden life well away from their own homes. Secret refuge with family or friends offered one form of sanctuary but the fugitives' age made them immediately suspect to the authorities if they ventured into public places (unless they held documentation showing dispensation from forced labour). Another alternative was to seek a rural hiding place well away from the questioning eyes of the gendarmes, and for thousands of young men this led to their joining maquis groups hiding in the more remote areas of France. Sensibly, most of these youths lay low as their lack of martial experience and a shortage of weapons rendered it inadvisable to provoke confrontation with the enemy. These types of 'resisters' were not, in the main, suitable for PIMENTO. Tony wanted organised, controlled activity that could respond effectively to strategic or tactical requirements issued from London. An example of the tragic consequences of premature, local resistance activity occurred in the spring of 1944 when the maquis of the Glières Plateau clashed for a second time with Vichy and German security forces. Only a year earlier, a substantial force of Milice and Groupes Mobiles de Réserve (GMR) had fought a bloody campaign against resistance groups in the mountains. Now, the self-confident behaviour of the maquis provoked another enemy reaction. The maquisards were led by a charismatic Chasseur Alpin junior officer, Théodose Morel, and, although supplied with some arms by SOE, they numbered fewer than five hundred men. In contrast, the forces arrayed against them were daunting: GMR, Milice and Garde personnel supplemented by crack German military units. The brave but doomed resistance of Morel and his men highlighted the fragility of poorly armed resistance forces when confronted by seasoned, well-equipped and well-led opponents. It was a telling reminder that the French resistance was not going to expel the invader on its own; for the foreseeable future, its most efficacious role was to be found in the type of activities in which Tony and PIMENTO were engaged.

While prosecuting the network's continued sabotage operations, Tony's aim was also to step up PIMENTO's capacity for receiving supply drops, stockpiling more explosives, creating and training extra rail-cutting crews and forging an organisation that would be sufficiently robust and mature to meet the operational demands of D-Day – whenever it came. PIMENTO's leader travelled relentlessly, clocking up thousands of miles by train and an additional, Herculean stint by bicycle. Although he delegated as much work as possible, he remained the circuit's linkman; checking DZs, vetting recruits, instructing in sabotage techniques, taking part in operations and overseeing the complex links to London. A consequence of the inexorable increase of Tony's tasks was the need to reassess his personal security. By March 1944, the 'Antoine Brévin' cover as an itinerant collector of automotive spare parts for Michel Comte was pretty threadbare. Three and a half years into the occupation, the carcasses of vehicles abandoned in 1940 had been well and truly picked clean. Continuing to represent this activity as genuine employment was more likely to invite suspicion than deflect it. Gaston Cusin, the most senior civil servant on PIMENTO's books, therefore proposed that Tony assume bogus employment with the Vichy authorities. Always ready to listen to the advice of his colleagues – especially one as intelligent and experienced as Cusin – Tony appreciated the merits of the suggestion. He agreed to assume the amorphous post of 'agent technique' with the Ministère de la Production Industrielle et des Communications. But it was not enough simply to have business cards printed bearing his name and title. The 'legend' needed substance and, to establish the profile of a real civil servant, Cusin undertook to 'pay' a 'salary' on a regular basis by depositing the requisite funds (provided by Tony) into 'Antoine Brévin's' post office account. 'The payments were made in Vichy and the French Compte-Chèque Postaux system is such that the receiving Post Office only has a record of the point of despatch, but not how or by whom paid in.'[2] Thus, any check of 'Brévin's' finances in Lyon or Toulouse would lead an investigator to believe that Tony was a bona fide, salaried, Vichy employee.

The power and influence of Vichy officials were brought home to Tony when he struck up a brief relationship with an employee of the censor's department. Arriving for lunch at the Café des Jacobins in Lyon, Tony found the restaurant very busy and the waiter offered him a spare seat at a table already occupied by a middle-aged man who sported a francisque badge

Minor but important details from a clandestine agent's life and work. From top: business cards used by Tony under his 'Antoine Brévin' alias, using his cover employment as a Vichy civil servant; deliberately torn 10-franc notes used to identify a PIMENTO contact – matching the two halves established the bona fides of each person; train tickets purchased by Tony for journeys to Paris and then Angers for his flight back to England, August 1943.

in his buttonhole. The insignia marked the man out as a supporter of the Vichy regime, so Tony was immediately wary. Nevertheless, the two men struck up a conversation and the diner was not slow to reveal that he was a retired army officer now engaged on postal censorship. In the hope of picking up information, Tony affected an interest in the man's work and, suitably encouraged, the censor warmed to his subject, delved into his briefcase and produced bunches of letters exchanged between French prisoners-of-war and their wives. It was clear that the intimacies contained in the correspondence provided the official with a strong, salacious thrill. Tony was revolted but disguised his sentiments, consumed his meal and departed as quickly as possible. His reluctant forbearance stood him in good stead when he later returned to dine at the café and the censor pressed him to share his table. Tony felt it would be unwise to decline the pervert's invitation and it was soon evident that he had made the right decision. As they were eating their meal, the café was raided by the Milice and diners were subjected to interrogation and examination of their identity papers. All, that is, apart from Tony and the censor. The latter merely presented his official pass and ordered that he and his luncheon partner should not be bothered.

About this time Tony experienced a moment that threatened to derail the well-constructed myth of 'Antoine Brévin'. At the Gare Matabiau in Toulouse he was shocked to find himself addressed in English as 'Mr Bright' (his SOE cover name) by an attractive young woman. He instantly recognised her as the F Section agent that he had briefly encountered at Orchard Court the previous year. He feigned a total lack of comprehension, informed her (in French) that she must be mistaken, excused himself and rapidly boarded the nearest train. As it pulled out of the station (in the opposite direction to the one that he had originally intended taking), he reflected on the rebuttal he had just administered but, after much soul-searching, he was sure he had acted appropriately in protecting his security. The woman in question was the twenty-one-year-old Anne-Marie Walters and Tony's prudence in not getting involved with her seems justified. Sent to France in January 1944 to act as a courier for George Starr, the leader of the WHEELWRIGHT circuit, Walters eventually fell out with her superior and, on 31 July 1944, he sent a message to London accusing her of being 'undisciplined, most indiscreet ... also disobedient in personal matters. She constitutes a danger to security.'[3] Starr therefore ordered her to return to London via the Pyrenees and Spain. As Tony was in the Lyon area during Walters's summer departure, their meeting must have taken place earlier in the year before her break with Starr.[4]

Realising that preparations for the Resistance's support of D-Day were increasingly important, Tony worked tirelessly to maintain the flow of supplies from England. An excerpt from one of his scores of messages to Bertholet offers an indication of the volume and complexity of the work.

Results of February operations. Arcade, Euzèbe and Felix [DZs] successful. As Arcade message was retransmitted the following night I presume that the aircraft of Gauthier [DZ] dropped its load on Arcade. On Damien [DZ] the Milice arrived and the operation had to be abandonned [*sic*]. This ground must be cancelled. The warning message for ANANAS [DZ] was badly transmitted, it came over as BANANES. The actual message on the night was not complete and so the [DZ] crew were not certain that it was for them. They went to the ground all the same but left at 1.30 as all seemed to be quiet. On Brioche [DZ] nobody came as the operational message came over as something about oracles instead of 'Ne contez pas sur les miracles'. I'm sorry about that but I hope that you will repeat these rather important operations for me. Brioche will serve as general unloading ground. Transmit its message when you do another operation in the 5th Group. You can also use Brioche as general landing ground for the 3rd Group. On Salade [DZ] my best lieutenant, Jag [Gauthier], who has all operations to his credit was himself on the ground and the lights were worked off a car accumulator. No aircraft was seen or even heard … I hope you will repeat this operation. Please supply with every operation some torch batteries. In the material dropped on Arcade there are some queer things that seem to be anti-tank mines. Is this so? On all operations in the 4th and 5th Groups there will be fires as well as the usual lights. All operations can receive 24 containers.[5]

The dangers of working with PIMENTO seemed on the increase too, with Tony adding, 'We have been suffering very heavy casualties recently. 183 in the Martinet area [Bourg], 33 in the Gilbert area [Toulouse] and 33 in the Michel area [Montauban].' A consequence of these difficulties was his grudging recognition that he now needed a special courier to help share the burden. Breaking with his habit of using local recruits, he would ask London to send an F Section agent to assume some of the exhausting duties of conveying his orders throughout the vast PIMENTO operational area. The arrival of Caza and the prospect of a second wireless operator being sent to join him convinced Tony that he needed an SOE-trained courier capable in particular of handling the dissemination of radio messages. In the same message Tony requested, 'Owing to the difficulty for men to travel I should like you to send me a woman courier to replace me. As I do most of the main liaisons for security reasons. I should therefore like to have someone first class. Not young if possible.'[6] In particular, he wanted a mature woman, preferably plain in appearance, who might fit seamlessly into the blue-collar ambiance of his circuit. In the spring of 1944, young, male travellers in France readily aroused the suspicions of the security forces while, in contrast, the social mores of the time ensured that women were unlikely to be subjected to intrusive physical searches at spot checks. Tony hoped that F Section would send someone who had been trained at Beaulieu, could handle written or verbal messages, possessed prior operational experience and would hold no allegiance other than to himself. This request for an SOE agent was not a reflection of mistrust of his French comrades but rather owed an early realisation that the Resistance would soon be subjected to divergent political agendas.

He did not have long to wait for a response from London. Bertholet's note of 25 March 1944 informed him (in French) 'We are sending you at the beginning of April a very well-informed friend (Marguerite). A Lysander will bring her. Give us an address as soon as possible where she can contact you. On the day of her departure you will hear "The other side of the moon is full of green elephants".'[7]

On 5 April Tony wrote a note (partially in French) to London:

I will expect Marguerite as soon as I hear the message. The address she must go to is JULIEN'S [Bottemer's] (Tonton [Bertholet] will give you the precise address) and the pass words are the following. 1st. She must ask for Julien under his real name. (Tonton will add the real name of our friend) When in front of him she will say. 2nd. Do you have any soap?

Reply from Julien, None, Madame, 3rd. Not even Cadum for a child? She will then know that she is with friends. She will stay with Julien until my arrival. [8]

A message from Bertholet three days later contradicted Tony's proposal. He did not have Bottemer's current address and therefore proposed (in French) that 'Marguerite' be sent to Michel Comte's. 'As far as Marguerite is concerned, in order not to lose time, and as we do not have the address where she can join you, we are sending her to Michel's (I think that you are in agreement). I hope to receive this address today but the courier is doubtless a little late. The personal effects of Marguerite will arrive on 'Dinde' [DZ] 48 hours after Marguerite's departure.'[9] Another message from Tony appeared to have crossed with that of Bertholet, for he wrote from Bottemer's asking that, as part of her pre-departure briefing, 'Marguerite' be given the address and a description of her contact. The PIMENTO leader confirmed that he wanted

```
To Elisabeth from Fleur. 13.4.44.

Herewith the list of operations for May. Repeat any operations in the 1st, 2nd
and 3rd Groups of the April list. Cancel Octave,Cacahuette, and Dinde. Cancel
the whole of the 4th Group of April.
Results.. Dinde- Aircraft not even heard. Cacahuette- Aircraft replied to our
signals with his lights but dropped nothing. Canada- Aircraft failed to see
our lights. A petrol flare was lit. Other results not yet known. I hope that
soon you will send us some material. As deliveries have not yet been too
brilliant. "If you don't succeed the first time try and try again          "
For the Medecin operation. A nurse of the Red cross who has been looking after
RAF and USAAF men as well as patriots wishes to start a hospital in the Pau
area where any of our organisation could go to belooked after as well as any
airmen. If you are in agreement please include appropriate medical supplies.
Marguerite arrived safely at Michel's. Please note that I never confirmed his
address. I sent you Julien's. Also you gave an incomplete version of the pass
words. They should have been,"Je vous apporte des nouvelles des BUTEES T/126..
etc." and not les butes iex 126. Thanks for the 250.000. I am glad to hear
that you get my telegrams O.K. I do not intend to use Emmanuel until I have no
other method of communicating. I am awaiting with impatience the Eclipse oper-
ation.
As soon as you wish me to put Verlaguhet out of action for two months please
transmit the following message."Les trois diamands brillent toujours". We will
then cause a short circuit 48 hours later. Repeat the message to make sure that
it is heard. As soon as we get sufficient material we will attack the rail
sub-stations.
We have had to cancel Dinde and Cacahuette because there are some SS on the
ground or near-by. All farms in the region around Montauban and Toulouse are
billiting SS. Das Reich, Deutchland, Der Feurher, regiments. Their tanks are
mainly dispersed in the forest of Montech. They are going to be re-formed here
and trained. They are going to stay about two months. We have succeeded in
grease-gunning all their tank carrying wagons in the Montauban yards, about
82 in all.
For Marguerite I intend putting her in liaison with each of my area lieutenants
so that she can do the liaisons between them and me.
All well. Fleur.
```

Report from Tony ('Fleur') to SOE in London ('Elisabeth') that was smuggled across the frontier into Switzerland. He reports parachute drops, the arrival of his courier Lise de Baissac ('Marguerite'), plans for sabotage attacks and the appearance of Waffen-SS units in the south-west region of PIMENTO.

her to act as courier between Bottemer, Zaksas, Comte and himself because the burden of travelling and facing constant security checks was becoming too much. He even concluded by candidly admitting, for once, that the strain of his duties was beginning to tell upon him.

London decided to send someone who met several of Tony's criteria but who fell crucially short in others. The agent was Lise de Baissac. Born on 11 May 1905 in Mauritius, a British colony of French-speakers in the southern Indian Ocean, she had been brought up in France as a *jeune fille bien élevée*. Following the debacle of 1940, she made her way to Gibraltar where she met up with her brother, Claude. On arrival in England, he joined SOE and, in turn, brought his sister into the fold. Lise was a member of F Section's second training course for women and, after an abortive first attempt to parachute to France, made a successful landing the following night, 24/5 September 1942.[10] She and her companion were the first women agents of F Section to parachute into Occupied France. De Baissac's task was 'to form a new circuit and to provide a centre where agents could go with complete security for material help and information on local details'. It was later noted, 'Miss de Baissac accomplished both these missions, and organised a number of parachute operations.'[11] Her network, ARTIST, was successful but it took a heavy toll of her morale. De Baissac had adopted the cover 'Madame Irene Brisse', 'a widow from Paris who had regretfully decided that life in the capital was now too difficult for her; so she had come to live in Poitiers, attracted by the civilised ambience of the university town and by the fine old churches and buildings in the surrounding countryside, which she planned to visit.'[12] It was sensible to live a false identity that largely replicated her own but she suffered greatly from the pressures of the secret agent's life. 'I was very lonely. Very, very lonely. You grew to know very well what loneliness was. Because you are alone; you have false papers; you never have a telephone call; you never get a letter.'[13] Eventually there was more to worry about than loneliness and de Baissac was withdrawn from France by a Lysander pick-up on 16/17 August 1943 'having been seriously compromised by the Gestapo penetration of her Circuit in Poitiers.'[14] Her brother Claude and the ubiquitous Bodington were exfiltrated on the same aircraft. After a well-earned rest, she was brought back to Baker Street and given staff and training duties. A report recorded she was, 'One of our most successful girls. A good organiser and administrator. Was popular with her contacts and much loved in the region. She perhaps suffered from the family faults (excess of personal ambition and touchiness), but she is always ready to see reason and invariably put her work first. Is "difficult" but devoted and has made a very large contribution to the success of F Section.'[15] Such candour and prescience were frequent features of F Section assessments of its personnel but these observations about Lise de Baissac possessed a disturbing significance regarding her suitability for the new mission, to act as Tony's courier, 'Marguerite'.[16]

De Baissac's return to operational duties was delayed by her sustaining a broken leg in a practice parachute jump while acting as conducting officer for a group of student agents. The medical clearance for her PIMENTO mission bore the caveat that the injury required that she be delivered by Lysander. Consequently, de Baissac returned to France on Operation CHAUFFEUR on 9/10 April 1944 in an aircraft flown by Flight Lieutenant 'Willie' Taylor to a reception committee organised by 'Hector', Maurice Southgate, the head of the STATIONER circuit. After a day's wait for a train, she headed to Montauban, arriving at Michel Comte's on the morning of the 11th.[17] In the security-conscious PIMENTO set up, the appearance of any stranger was a source of immediate suspicion. The tension was exacerbated when the newcomer turned up at the Garage des Pyrénées looking as if she had just stepped off a Paris fashion house catwalk. Worse was to follow: de Baissac compounded matters by forgetting the password. Tony later conceded that this might have been a result of the unusual phrases that concerned a request for automotive spare parts, *Des butées T trente-six*.'[18] In spite of this inauspicious start, the courier was not rebuffed but asked to return later that afternoon by which time it was anticipated that Tony would have arrived. PIMENTO's leader had no idea that de Baissac was due that day so the meeting in Montauban was a fluke. The first he knew of the courier's arrival was when he called at Comte's and was informed that 'Marguerite' was waiting for him. The circumstances surrounding her appearance were explained and Comte reassured Tony that there was little risk of the woman being a Gestapo 'plant' for 'not even the Germans could have thought of sending someone like that to us'.[19] They agreed that a working-class girl with similar flaws in her tradecraft would have been far more suspicious. For her part, de Baissac realised from the outset that all was not well: 'He [Tony] appeared very surprised to see me and made me understand straight away that I wasn't at all the person that he wanted. I was disappointed by this welcome (I have to say that from the personal point of view, ALPHONSE had been very polite and would have been delighted if it had come off); but in spite of this we decided to begin work as soon as possible.'[20]

That evening, de Baissac joined Tony and the Comte family for a meal. It was not a relaxed repast with Michel Comte's working-class table manners evidently not to de Baissac's liking. Presumably trying to make polite conversation, she asked her host if it were possible to book a sleeping car from Montauban to Lyon and he replied that Tony was the expert on train travel. Trying to improve the atmosphere, the latter commented that she could travel by sleeper but it was unwise to do it too often. Records were kept of the registration number of a traveller's identity card and these details were then written on the back of the ticket. When checking in with the *wagons lits* attendant, the traveller's identity card had to be handed over and the number checked against that inscribed on the ticket. De Baissac appeared mystified by this complex procedure but accepted that the authorities imposed it to curtail the black-market trade in sleeper tickets. Later that evening, after quiet reflection, Tony concluded that, as with Bloom, London had let him down. His new courier seemed pretty well everything that he had not wanted notably regarding her demeanour and physical appearance. This assessment would prove well-founded and he soon discovered that she was temperamentally and politically unsuited for work with PIMENTO.

In spite of these misgivings, Tony took de Baissac to Toulouse to meet Zaksas and his associates. The trip proved far from successful and she reported that she had encountered similar *'visages formés et hostiles'* (fixed and hostile faces) to those she had received in Montauban. Her assessment was no exaggeration and Tony stated, 'Gilbert [Zaksas] who only saw her for five minutes found her completely unsympathetic.' The leader of PIMENTO added his own impressions: 'She was accustomed to military work and did not understand the political and socialist ideals that inspire us. She wanted to give brusque and military orders to pals … But, my friend, it won't do.'[21]

The next destination for the two, increasingly incompatible agents was Chambéry and a meeting with 'Claude' Bottemer. De Baissac showed a commendable keenness to learn more about her prospective duties, 'I asked questions and about work and understood I would have to collect and deliver written or spoken messages not knowing why or what.' It seems surprising that such an experienced agent should fail to appreciate that she had no need to know the content of messages she was carrying. But as someone with aspirations to run her own circuit (or at least part of one) she was unhappy with her prospective duties writing (in French), 'I was, in short, "a postman" and that was it, and that did not please me one bit.' Such apparently mundane (if dangerous) tasks as carrying secret messages were clearly unwelcome, the situation perhaps being exacerbated by the fact that her leader was seventeen years her junior. The frustration seems in keeping with the inherent personality traits of an agent whose SOE assessors identified as possessing 'an excess of personal ambition and touchiness'.[22] During discussions with Tony, de Baissac commented that F Section had led her to believe that she would be taking over the Lyon branch of his circuit rather than simply acting as a courier. He found this an astonishing revelation but further discussion had to be put on hold as the agents were called to lunch with the Bottemer family, which, for once, resulted in a 'friendly general conversation'.

De Baissac's report states that Tony told her at this meeting that he did not need her for the next week and gave her permission to try to contact her brother Claude who had returned to France on his third mission on 10 February 1944.[23] Presumably she had some idea of his whereabouts (he was, in fact, in Normandy) and she wasted little time in taking the opportunity to leave Chambéry.[24]

Lise de Baissac's departure allowed Tony time to take stock of the situation and report to Bertholet. He did not disguise his disappointment and confided his misgivings. Illustrating the ideological gulf that existed between PIMENTO and its new recruit, Tony related one of his courier's questions: 'Do you think it is a good idea to arm the socialist party?' He observed to his friend, *Je pari que tu ris.'* ['I bet you're laughing.'] Dispassionately, he forecast that de Baissac would find her future operational tasks physically taxing, in particular the strain and discomfort of frequent travelling under difficult, wartime conditions. In spite of these misgivings, Tony concluded the message by expressing his hope that the newcomer might yet settle down to her duties.[25]

But it was soon apparent that opposition to de Baissac was all but complete within PIMENTO's ranks. In addition to the adverse comments passed by colleagues at Montauban and Toulouse, Bottemer at Chambéry expressed profound antipathy towards the new arrival and refused to allow her across his threshold again. The situation was clearly untenable and only a few days after de Baissac's arrival, on 14 April Tony sent messages to Bertholet and London. To the latter he reported, 'I feel that Marguerite is not exactly the kind of person we need … She thinks that the job that I have for her, the liaison between my different groups, is not a sufficiently important one for her and that she would like to have a responsibility and be able to do something worthwhile. Also my job for her will require a lot of travelling.'[26] Understandably, Tony's message (in French) to his friend Bertholet was more detailed and came from the heart:

> I am counting on you to explain [to London] what I am about to tell you. Marguerite does not suit me. She is not at all the kind of woman we need for our affairs. She adopts a professional attitude to her work like a soldier but without idealism. If you ask her to make an extra effort she can't do it. I am not telling tales – you know me better than that – but she will never be a comrade. She turns up her nose at the prospect of eating with a worker or sleeping on the floor in a sleeping bag. There is another thing that is more serious which is that she is too curious. She wants to know and do everything but undertake the courier work which is precisely the task for which I asked for her, considering it a foolish thing without importance. For she finds it facile and without purpose and also pretty tiring. While the journey that I asked her to undertake is less hard than that of Juliette [Gaby Cordier]. I have asked Julien [Bottemer] to send you a few words on the subject. So put what I have said into a letter to Elisabeth [London]. But take care for her brother can pull strings and has the DSO. She remarked upon it first thing … I believe we will have more trouble than it is worth with her. So I suggest that she leaves for Parisian society and finds her brother in order to work for him. For she will do better there than with us.[27]

These statements engendered a torrent of messages between London, Switzerland and France. The time overlap between the receipt of information and instructions makes it difficult to plot the true course of events; a note from Bertholet dated 15 April stating de Baissac should have arrived on the 10th was sent the day *after* one from Tony in which he affirmed the courier did not meet his expectations. What is clear is that Bertholet and van Maurik in Switzerland accepted Tony's reservations about de Baissac and informed London of their opinions. Meanwhile, Bertholet sensitively sent a series of reassuring notes to Tony.[28] Supporting his protégé, he added an endorsement from van Maurik and dismissed concerns that Lise's brother, Claude, might have an influence upon the imbroglio. In the event, the matter was resolved as two separate sets of messages passed in transit. Tony laid out his reservations again and, with commendable open-handedness, forwarded a note to Switzerland from Lise de Baissac in which she expressed her own sentiments. PIMENTO's leader reiterated his case to London:

> With regard to Marguerite I am not in the least satisfied. Herewith a letter from her. I do not wish to make any comment on it. Tonton [Bertholet] will know its value. He knows Julien [Bottemer] and knows the value of his judgement. The question quoted by Marguerite is not the reason for the disagreement. But let that be. Marguerite finds the work a little strenuous and not in the least interesting owing to my security measures. I never confide the running of the whole organisation to anyone. Each groupe [*sic*] leader knows what he needs to know and only that. Secondly a courier, especially a woman need know only the minimum necessary. And that minimum will be learnt as time goes on. Marguerite was disappointed because she believed that she was going to have the chance to run an organisation and give orders to my groupe leaders, who are very experienced men and who naturally resent the intrusion of Marguerite.[29]

Of course, de Baissac's note to London offered a different perspective: 'I asked when I start he [Tony] answered Julien [Bottemer] did not want me because I asked such question as how many do you live here [*sic*] when I saw six new faces appearing simultaneously.' She expressed herself 'very surprised and angry' at Bottemer's criticism of her inquisitiveness and offered an alternative explanation, 'The truth is I am so different from his [Bottemer's] usual surrounding. He finds me strange and unsafe in that way I agree. My best security is to be myself. If I have to act the part of a "*fanatique militante politique*" I shall always be a "*fausse note*". Julien [Bottemer] feels it like myself but I would rather have discussed it openly and not [be] sent away and hit in the back. These ways are learnt by years of underground conspiracy. I have no such training my only answer is my sincerity and earnestness.' Written with annoyance, exasperation and with the pain of rejection still stinging, de Baissac's letter should not just be interpreted as a vindication of Tony and Bottemer's assessments and raises questions of London's judgement regarding her suitability. Anyone with the most basic understanding of PIMENTO should have realised that there was no place in the circuit for the bourgeois niceties that had sustained de Baissac as 'Madame Brisse' in Poitiers. Moreover, the disdain of the practicalities of clandestine life expressed in the courier's message to London seems naïve or foolish or both. The note concluded with the plaintive 'Please let me work with people I understand' and an appeal for instructions 'as wandering in hotels is not safe'. It was clear where de Baissac ultimately wished to go: 'Denis [her brother, Claude] can always find me Paris if I wait there with friends.'[30.]

Although concerned at the risk of incurring the wrath of F Section by his rejection of de Baissac and uncertain of the malign influence of her brother, Tony knew that he had made the right decision. Nevertheless, he assured Bertholet that if London instructed that he work with the courier, he would abide by their orders. In spite of the backing from Switzerland, the controversy over de Baissac rolled on through April and into May to the dissatisfaction of all concerned, especially the agents risking their lives in enemy territory. Lise de Baissac made a second, ill-fated attempt to contact her brother but the inconveniences of wartime travel did not improve her mood and provided further evidence of her unsuitability for the thankless tasks of a courier. She wrote, 'On the agreed day I arrived at Toulouse after a journey of 24 hours in the corridor of a packed train, 3 sabotage attempts, 1 change of train after having walked 500 metres along the track, in the middle of the countryside without having eaten or slept.'[31]

Tony was not at Toulouse and she carried on to Montauban where at Comte's garage she found him waiting for her. Bearing in mind de Baissac's troublesome journey, it was hardly the ideal moment to tell the tired and dispirited woman that the decision had been taken to dispense with her services. Consequently, de Baissac went into a *colère noire* in which she translated Bottemer's criticisms concerning her curiosity into an accusation that she was a double agent. But in spite of annoyance at the apparent slights to her character, she was delighted at her imminent release from a circuit whose aims and objectives she manifestly did not share. Tony had little more to say until he received formal approval from London and arranged to meet de Baissac in Lyon the following week.

But the impasse was still not completely resolved by the time of their rendezvous and de Baissac remained a 'member' of PIMENTO for a further week before official sanction was given for her to join her brother. With commendable honesty, she reported (in French) that during her period in limbo 'We, ALPHONSE and I, had several very amicable conversations' but with a sting in the tail 'that only confirmed my opinion.' Her opinion was:

> This circuit (which I don't deny has acted effectively against the enemy) was composed of militant socialists whose principal aim was political. I was not able to do the job because it was necessary to move in an environment which was totally alien to me and I would have always stood out and as a result of that perhaps compromised the security of the circuit. Someone said to ALPHONSE 'What do you expect old chap, she's not one of us.' Also, 'Again, if she was twenty, but a mature woman with her own ideas and an opinion …' What's to be done?[32]

Lise de Baissac had also concluded that PIMENTO's communication links with London possessed a sinister rationale. She did not accept that written messages sent across the frontier could convey more detail than wireless transmissions from Occupied France and speculated that '*le chef politique* [presumably Bertholet] *était en Suisse*' and he was exploiting Tony's reports in order to retain a Machiavellian control of the network's affairs.

Then, at last, they all got the green light. On 5 May Caza received a signal (No. 7) from London stating 'Marguerite's brother has sent us message saying he is awaiting her at personal address in Paris stop Please give her necessary instructions stop.'[33] Lise de Baissac wasted little time in departing for her brother's SCIENTIST network with which she served (with distinction) until the liberation. She received an MBE for her efforts, the citation recording that 'She proved of immense assistance to him [Claude], handling delicate contacts, of which there were many, in an extremely capable and diplomatic manner.'[34]

But such tributes were far in the future. In the spring of 1944 F Section agents in the field frequently criticised London for failing adequately to comprehend conditions in France. Lise de Baissac complained that, had she known the real make-up of PIMENTO before her departure, she would have immediately understood that she was unsuitable. Questions remain whether de Baissac was too inflexible, whether London had misunderstood the job description specified by Tony, whether he was uncooperative or whether, after almost two years, F Section still had not grasped the real essence of PIMENTO. The answer is surely a combination of all four. Tony's lack of confidence in his F Section superiors and his increasing sense of isolation was evident in a message to London on 17 May 1944, 'But if I get caught each area commander can take charge of his area and the work can go on. I haven't anyone capable of replacing me. And I do not wish you to send me one seeing the result with Marguerite!!!'

The de Baissac affair was not Tony's only preoccupation. Around this time he was terribly anxious about the health of Germaine, Bizot's partner, who remained gravely ill in Switzerland with tubercular meningitis. On 23 March 1944 Bizot wrote to Tony informing him that there was no hope of recovery and asked that photographs and keepsakes might be retrieved from his flat in Lyon. Tony willingly undertook the task and replied assuring Bizot that his mother was being looked after financially by PIMENTO. Then, on 8 April, Bertholet reported that Germaine had died. Touchingly, he wrote that Tony had never been far from the family's thoughts during the crisis – yet another clear manifestation of the close and enduring bonds between the members of the network whether in occupied France or neutral Switzerland.[36]

But soon another tragedy hit PIMENTO. Even while the wrangling over Lise de Baissac was at its height, Tony received garbled reports that his most trusted commander, André Moch, had been killed in a shoot-out with enemy security forces. Some seventy years later, the details of the incident remain sketchy. Tony's first intimation of the disaster arose when he travelled to Chambéry for a rendezvous with Moch at Bottemer's apartment. Arriving well before the appointed time, he spent a pleasant evening in the company of the Bottemers listening to Lizst's Préludes on the radio. But the musical idyll remained unbroken. Moch failed to appear and, at the end of the broadcast, Bottemer advised Tony to leave before the curfew prevented his reaching the station in safety. On the face of it, Moch's non-appearance held no sinister implications; nevertheless, Tony took the precaution of catching the next train back to Lyon. In the light of subsequent revelations, Les Préludes acquired a deep and lasting emotional significance for Tony.

In a post-war journal, Bottemer wrote an account of Moch's death. It offers a touching paean of praise to his fallen comrade but its grand, valedictory style is no substitute for an accurate description of the circumstances surrounding the death. Bottemer stated that Moch had been planning the rescue of a resistance comrade, 'François', who was being held captive by the Milice and SS.[37] He had met Moch on 10 April for the last time when they contemplated the terrible treatment 'François' would be enduring at the hands of the SS. The rescue attempt should have taken place on the 13th and Bottemer described how for hours he waited anxiously for Moch to return, 'He always came punctually to a rendezvous. This time he didn't come. And no one would admit to the others what we all suddenly knew.'[38] Unfortunately, the rest of Bottemer's account offers a poetic, not to say epic, representation of Moch's death rather than a factual narrative; 'No one knew how it happened. On the 12th April, in his deserted house in a park near Tronche where he held out, hidden with his relations ... He was alone with his Colt and his Sten. Some affirm ten, others twelve, were struck down by him before he himself fell.' Bottemer continued, 'He defended three young lives with which he had been closely tied. They disappeared into the great unconcealed chasm. No one saw these last heroic deeds.' Further information about the event is sparse. An inscription on a monument erected in 1947 outside the house where Moch was killed does not shed a great deal more light. It describes Moch as meeting his end, 'one against twenty' and choosing to die with a gun in his hand rather than be taken alive.[39] Other information on the affair is similarly anecdotal. One of Moch's neighbours related her version of events to Tony shortly after the war. She stated that Moch had been cornered in the house by German and Vichy security forces and, having held them off for as long as possible, killed himself.

Whatever the specific circumstances of Moch's death, his loss left Tony more isolated than ever; Bertholet could no longer cross into France, Bizot was in exile in Switzerland, Dorval was dead, and now, so too, was Moch. Meanwhile, support from F Section had been found sorely wanting; Lise de Baissac's appearance on the scene had hardly constituted 'reinforcement' while Caza's contribution had yet to have any real effect.

While Tony wrestled with the internal problems confronting PIMENTO, there was evidence that the German grip on France was not to be readily relinquished. Nazi and Vichy propaganda trumpeted the strength of Hitler's 'Festung Europa' with overblown images of powerful guns and huge concrete bunkers on the French coast that proclaimed Germany's power and resolution to repel an Allied invasion. But the photographs of an omnipotent Nazi war machine holding the frontline on the Channel held little relevance to members of PIMENTO in the relative backwater of the south-west. Then, in April 1944, a sudden and menacing German military presence descended on Montauban. This was the notorious 2nd SS Panzer Division, 'Das Reich', reinforcing the Wehrmacht's Army Group G that was entrusted with the defence of central and south-west France. The unit had participated in the invasion of France in 1940 and, by the conclusion of hostilities, had advanced deep into the south-west reaching Angoulême and Biarritz. The division enjoyed even more resounding victories during the assault on the Soviet Union in the summer of 1941 but it subsequently experienced the relentless decline of Hitler's fortunes on the Eastern Front. In the spring of 1944 the battered unit was finally withdrawn to France to supplement the German occupation forces and to refit, re-equip and regain its strength, 'They left behind their few remaining tanks, vehicles and guns, together with the memory of countless thousands of their dead in frozen graves from the Pripet marshes to the Cherkassy pocket. With infinite gratitude for their deliverance, they began to roll away through East Prussia, on the long journey from the eastern to the western extremity of Hitler's empire.'[40]

There was no question that the 'Das Reich' badly needed the respite. Its core unit, the Battle Group Lammerding, was to be the foundation of the virtual rebuilding of the division with an anticipated arrival of 9,000 new draftees needing accommodation in some fifty barracks and lagers in the Montauban area. PIMENTO reported some of these events, 'All farms in the region around Montauban and Toulouse are billeting SS, Das Reich, Deutchland [*sic*] Der Feurher [*sic*], regiments. Their tanks are mainly dispersed in the forest of Montech. They are going to be re-inforced here and trained. They are going to stay about two months. We have succeeded in grease-gunning all their tank carrying wagons in the Montauban yards, about 82 in all.'[41] *SS-Brigadeführer und Generalmajor der Waffen-SS* Heinz Lammerding had taken command of the division on 25 January 1944 and was to oversee its reformation and re-equipment in France with new Panzer IV and V tanks. In addition, he commenced extensive training exercises around Montauban to remould his unit into an effective fighting machine. While many Frenchmen and women were cowed by the presence of this elite force, others were not. Although the posting to France must have seemed like a holiday compared to the horrors of the Eastern Front, the division still found it necessary to mount guards on their supply dumps and installations. The local resistance had become confident and militant; violent incidents increased in severity from the theft of munitions and the odd pot shot at a sentry to more coordinated ambushes. In the early hours of 2 May a patrol from an SS tank battalion training near Montpezat-de-Quercy came under small-arms fire and, in reprisal, the Germans put several houses to the torch, property was looted and some civilians were assaulted before the unit returned to its barracks at Caussade.[42] This was to prove by no means the last or the worst such incident involving the 'Das Reich'.

It was about this time that Tony, Michel Comte and David Donoff called upon Pierre-Marie Théas, the Bishop of Montauban, to seek his help. It is hard to conceive of three supplicants with less impressive Catholic credentials: the sometime British Quaker, the French atheist and the émigré Jew. As he confessed to Tony, Comte's anti-clericalism had seen him throw eggs at church processions in his youth, but this had not prevented him respecting the man who had used his pulpit to denounce Vichy's anti-semitic and repressive policies and who took action to protect Jews from persecution. The reason for the trio's audience was, to say the least, unusual. The shortage of batteries for the reception committees' torches had become acute and, with none available for purchase on the black market, even the unlikeliest of sources had to be followed up. If the Bishop did not hold supplies, it was hoped that episcopal intervention might provide the solution. A housekeeper showed the members of PIMENTO into Théas's office and, as soon as she had withdrawn, the cleric opened a drawer and offered his guests a glass of wine. Toasting '*Vive les fidèles*' and reflecting on Hitler's achievement in bringing such a disparate group together, the Bishop listened to their request and within a week had produced some twenty much-needed batteries.[43]

By May 1944 Tony and PIMENTO were busier than ever. Supply drops were increasing while, at the same time, the training and organising of the sabotage groups continued apace. At the beginning of the month, Tony prepared special area headquarters with internal couriers and secret letter boxes to create a degree of autonomy for each of his groups. He briefed all the local leaders regarding their D-Day tasks and, with this infrastructure in place, was confident that even if the sub-groups found themselves isolated by unforeseen circumstances, there was a reasonable hope that they might meet their objectives. An impression of the size of the organisation and its development into a guerrilla force is revealed in Tony's message to London of 26 April in which he reported on the military strength of PIMENTO with 4,700 men armed in the south-west and 2,100 less well-supplied men north of Lyon.[44]

While the build-up of a combat force continued, PIMENTO's sabotage programme was unrelenting. In May, electricity pylons running parallel to the Montauban–Cahors railway line were attacked and other operations were carried out against power lines from the Pyrenees to Portet Saint-Simon, Verlaghuet–Colynac (Agen), Verlaghuet–Le Viviez and Le Viviez–La Mole. These actions deprived the railways of electricity to such an extent that the SNCF (French Railways) was compelled to return to steam traction for more than a week on the Montauban–Brive line. Naturally, there were some disappointments too and an attack on the Verlaghuet 220KV transformer was abortive due to faulty detonators that meant the charges failed to explode.

By now, Tony's workload and the range of his PIMENTO responsibilities ensured that he rarely participated in reception committees for supply drops, but he did attend the 'Eclipse' ground near Montauban on 30 April/1 May 1944. This was but one of seven separate parachute operations to PIMENTO that night as the circuit prepared for D-Day. The 'Eclipse' operation had been accorded a high two-star level of priority by the RAF and was undertaken by a Halifax aircraft of No 138 Squadron bearing nine containers and two packages. The crew commented 'lights bright but did not follow the a/c [aircraft] on circuit' and the illuminations went out after the first run. The correct Morse letter was given by the reception committee and they were confident that the pinpoint for the drop had been located. PIMENTO's own report confirmed the delivery but revealed some problems, 'Aircraft load dropped accurately from low altitude but 10th container dropped on German outpost. Half area surrounded but committee escaped. Only managed to take small portion of arms with them.'[45] Tony confirmed that one of the containers drifted away from the DZ and onto a farm occupied by elements of the 'Das Reich' Division. The hornet's nest had been well and truly aroused and the reception committee faced a real threat of capture. They therefore concealed the containers as quickly and effectively as possible then scattered. Two men escaped by swimming across a river, Michel Comte succeeded in walking through the back lanes to safety, four others were arrested, and Tony spent the next twenty-four hours hiding up a tree. From his vantage point, he was able to observe German patrols scouring the area for his colleagues and the containers. Thankfully, the search proved fruitless, Tony made a safe return to Montauban and three of the containers were eventually retrieved from concealment.

In spite of the increased tension in the region, the 'Das Reich' sometimes needed the assistance of the local community and, on occasion, Michel Comte was called upon to come to the aid of broken-down military vehicles with his heavy-goods tow truck. It made good sense for a resister to keep on the right side of the occupying forces but when a suitable opportunity presented itself he failed to respond with the diligence and rapidity that the Germans desired. One night a military motorcycle combination turned up at the garage and the soldiers asked Comte to attend a road accident in which several of their comrades were trapped under the wreckage of a lorry. He promised faithfully to get there as soon as possible, then returned to finish his meal, listened to the BBC on the radio and eventually made a very belated appearance at the crash site. The needs of the 'Das Reich' also nudged Comte and Tony a little closer to what might even have been considered 'collaboration' when Major Stückler, the division's senior staff officer, called at the garage asking for help with the manufacture of threaded bolts to draw tank-track links into their housings. There was a wonderful irony in the SS officer seeking the assistance of the young French mechanic who was really a British secret agent and who had for the last two years been engaged in frustrating German efforts at every turn.

Meanwhile, in the eastern area of PIMENTO, supply drops and sabotage activity were just as hectic. Teams carried out a succession of attacks against supply trains on the Macon–Lyon, Macon–Bourg and Bourg–Ambérieu lines. In addition, isolated electricity power lines were now particularly vulnerable to sabotage, and pylons were cut from Saint-Fons to Oullins. Railway turntables continued to be important but relatively easy targets for PIMENTO saboteurs in the SNCF work force. Access to the sabotage target and knowledge of the machinery's weak points were part of everyday life and, as a result, equipment at La Mouche in Lyon was attacked and partially damaged. The tried and trusted abrasive grease continued to be used and Tony reported to London that forty trucks, manufactured by the French company Berliet and destined for Germany were given hostile treatment. Meanwhile an unusual request was received from Bertholet in Switzerland for a consignment of German uniforms to be sent across the border. PIMENTO refrained from speculating on the clothing's use and ultimate destination, and Rudy Molter in Lyon merely set about fulfilling the order. The work was increasingly demanding but Tony and his men sensed that their endeavours were reaching a climax. They were not wrong.

Chapter Twelve
The Day Has Come

While Tony had been making his individual preparations for D-Day, so too, had F Section and the rest of SOE. Throughout 1944 more and more specialist organisers, wireless operators and sabotage instructors had been sent to France to reinforce existing circuits and establish new ones. In May, SOE's Headquarters estimated that there were 100,000 armed men in France ready to act on London's orders and, by the beginning of June, almost one hundred F Section circuits were in place from the Pas de Calais to the Pyrenees, from Besançon to Brittany. The masterplan was to carry out wholesale, systematic attacks on German communications throughout the country in coordination with the Allied invasion. Road, rail, telephone, telegraph and wireless links were to be severed and, once made, the cuts would be maintained. Even the most trusted and experienced of F Section circuit leaders such as Tony were neither informed of the date nor the specific location of the invasion, but they were fully aware that their groups' actions would be vital to the success or failure of the great venture.

The build-up of men, weapons and stores for the French Resistance was as nothing compared to the logistical feats taking place on the other side of the Channel, where years of preparation for the Second Front were finally about to come to fruition. The Allied planners had decided that Operation 'Overlord' would comprise a long-range assault on Normandy rather than the more direct, cross-Channel attack on the Pas-de-Calais. As with all plans, there were pros and cons to consider. The shorter route in the north would facilitate more comprehensive air coverage and a quicker sea voyage. On the other hand, the Pas-de-Calais's powerful defences made the less daunting Normandy coastline the better bet. A mighty armada of 7,000 naval vessels gathered in harbours all around the United Kingdom with millions of Allied soldiers poised to take part in the assault on Hitler's 'Festung Europa'. This was to be led by a spearhead of eight divisions carrying out the first phases of the airborne and amphibious attacks on the coast of Normandy. In order to confuse the Germans, Allied intelligence services surrounded the plans with a 'bodyguard of lies' and devoted immense resources and ingenuity to misleading the enemy (and the leader of PIMENTO) as to their intentions.

Tony had been briefed that PIMENTO's countdown to the invasion would begin with the 'A' or 'Apple' wireless messages. These would signal them to *stand by*, followed by the *action* 'B' or 'Beer' messages instructing the sabotage groups to commence their attacks. He and his teams knew the 'A' messages and listened for them on the BBC on the 1st, 2nd, 15th and 16th of each month. The 'A' and 'B' messages for PIMENTO were:

Ain, Saône-et-Loire and Lyon

A. CHRISTIAN [SIC] LAISSES TES CHEVEUX TRANQUILLES

B. NOUS N'AVONS PLUS D'ALLUMETTES

Grenoble, Savoie and Rhône Valley

A. SAMY EST UN CHIEN DE RACE

B. J'AIME LES FEMMES EN BLEU

Toulouse

A. NOUS GAVERONS LES CANARDS

B. BIENTOT TU VOLERAS

Guerrilla activity

A. L'ESPOIR BRULE TOUJOURS

B. LA GRAISSE DEVIENT RARE

Tony was staying at Michel Comte's home above the Garage des Pyrénées during the first week of June 1944. It was fitting that, as their work was reaching its culmination, he should be back at Montauban where his first, humble contribution to the war had been made with his decision to help Albert

Manser. His tasks were now very different as he devoted his time to visiting the PIMENTO groups in the south-west and instructing new members in sabotage techniques. He listened to the BBC as a matter of course for the *messages personnels* that warned him of the nightly supply drops, and 1 June was no different as Tony and the Comte family tuned into the radio in the flat above the garage. The eldest daughter sat, as usual absentmindedly fiddling with her hair when, amid the host of *messages personnels*, came the phrase '*Christiane laisses tes cheveux tranquilles*' ('Christiane, leave your hair alone'). The young girl was astonished to hear the voice on the radio admonishing her, but Tony and her father were listening intently to the PIMENTO warning messages that followed.

The broadcast was momentous, but Tony managed to keep his feelings in check. The previous month he had confessed to Bertholet that he did not feel optimistic; some of his supporters had shown a lack of fibre and he questioned his ability to find others willing to help with the work.[1] This war-weary frame of mind was surely an explanation for the absence of celebrations with the Comtes and, with years of false dawns behind them, he accepted that the messages constituted only the preliminary warning. Tony was also conscious of the need to prevent overreaction at the prospect of invasion and the next day he contacted his PIMENTO sub-groups to ensure they refrained from premature action and did nothing until the transmission of the 'B' messages. The same day, 2 June, he sent a note to Caza instructing him to inform London, 'Have heard Apple messages for all areas'. In spite of his outward restraint, the rest of Tony's message to F Section revealed a heightened sense of anticipation. He asked for more weapons to be dropped and confirmed, in accordance with London's instructions, that he would block the Route Nationale 20, the main road that ran north from Toulouse, through Montauban to Limoges. As the prospect of the great day loomed, Tony's thoughts turned to a more conventional, martial role. He requested London send him fifty uniforms, together with his own battledress 'so that I can put it on when I go underground in our maquis'. Tony's internal courier lines had kept him in touch with events in the eastern sector of PIMENTO and, in the same message, he reported on a recent air raid on Lyon during which thirty-two 'pals' had been killed in the district of Vaise and five at La Guillotière 'where very few bombs fell on the station, most in the road'. Such indiscriminate menace led Tony to consider his own safety and he requested a warning be sent via the BBC of bombing raids on Montauban 'as Michel is next to the station and I live there'. The days of PIMENTO eschewing the need for wireless communications were long gone and Tony confessed to 'awaiting with impatience the arrival of the new W/T'.[2] The network was now so large that it had outgrown many of his earlier administrative arrangements and the difficulties of keeping it functioning were manifest. But there was no question of Tony moving from Montauban at this time. He discussed with Michel Comte the momentous days ahead and, when the latter asked him about his plans, Tony simply commented, 'We started the war together and we'll finish it together'.

As the tension heightened, Tony regretted his failure to develop a close relationship with Roger Caza. The size and complex structure of PIMENTO meant that they were rarely in close physical proximity so, perhaps because of the absence of a personal rapport, Tony felt a need to meet his obligations as the Canadian's 'superior' officer by sending notes of advice and encouragement.

Note from Roger Caza to Tony sent shortly before D-Day. It comprises wireless messages from London concerning DZs, sabotage plans and the possible arrival of Jedburgh teams.

But the long years of waiting had rather blunted Tony's optimism and he confessed to being sanguine about the significance of the 'A' warning messages, 'I don't think there is any need to get excited yet, but nevertheless it is a good sign.' He instructed Caza to move back to the Bourg area as soon as the latest message had been sent to London and to take his crystals with him, leaving his radio sets behind as others were awaiting him in his new location.[3] The rest of the missive was, as Tony admitted, 'full of does and don'ts. I am sorry but they are very important' with the veteran twenty-two year old laying down a step-by-step series of orders. The primary instruction was 'in your new surroundings you must tighten up your security'. Caza was not to let Woreczyk and Gauthier know the content of wireless messages and he was forbidden to transmit anything that had not been cleared by Tony. He was also reminded of his position vis-à-vis other members of PIMENTO:

> Remember that you are a Lieut and therefore the senior officer present in your new hide out. That the others must obey you. Naturally, there are lots of things that they will know better than you, but for everything concerning your work or military affairs, you are in charge. If you use your authority well they will obey you and respect you. As every day conditions are changing and we are becoming more and more military. Insist for the very best conditions for your work and protection ... Be firm and severe. Be discreet with Felix [Woreczyk]. He is perfectly sure, but I do not like him to know all our goings on.

To soften the sternness of the message, Tony closed with a return to the vexed question of Caza's wardrobe. He had forwarded shirts and socks salvaged from Bizot's flat to tide his wireless operator over but now explained that a consignment of clothing sent from England had failed to be retrieved from a PIMENTO ground, 'So some one else, probably the Germans got your stuff again. My poor chap you haven't any luck with your clothes!!!'[4] At first glance, Tony's comments might have appeared severe or officious but the relationship between the two men was sufficiently sound for the wireless operator not to take offence. Caza, with his customary level-headedness, replied, 'Received instructions – I don't mind the do's and don'ts – you know them better than I do.'[5]

Caza's arrival had been vital to PIMENTO's development in the approach to D-Day and his performance played a significant part in removing Tony's prejudice about wireless links to London. His contribution had convinced Tony that as the network's affairs reached its culmination, he needed a second operator. But, ironically, after years of avoiding the imposition of a wireless link, his requests for reinforcement were denied. On 3 June London transmitted, 'Regret will be unable to send second W/T operator this moon stop will despatch him earliest July moon stop'[6] Although this was a disappointment, Tony consoled himself with the knowledge that the vital warning signals for the invasion would be conveyed by the BBC's *messages personnels* rather than having to depend upon clandestine wireless links. Each night at 9.15 p.m. Tony and Michel Comte listened for the 'B' phrases, straining their ears to pick out the messages through the atmospherics and German/Vichy attempts to jam the broadcasts. Such were the difficulties in receiving the British transmissions that not all of the phrases could be heard. This was the case on the night of 5 June when, having failed to pick up the BBC broadcast, the PIMENTO contingent at Comte's home resigned themselves to waiting for the following night's announcements. Thus, after years of hard work, danger and sacrifice, Tony and Comte were denied the opportunity of hearing the historic messages that revealed the invasion had been launched and PIMENTO was to go into action. Thankfully, PIMENTO members elsewhere had better fortune and throughout the south of France the 'B' messages, *'Nous n'avons plus d'allumettes'*, *'J'aime les femmes en bleu'* and *'Bientôt tu voleras'* were joyfully received by Tony's sabotage groups.

As Tony and Comte slumbered in Montauban, the first Allied airplanes began to disgorge over twenty thousand British and American airborne troops onto the fields of Normandy. The long-awaited invasion of France had begun. The paratroopers and glider-borne units were to seize and hold the flanks of the bridgehead; in the east, the British 6th Airborne Division landed south of Ouistreham while in the west, the US 82nd and 101st Airborne Divisions were dropped at the foot of the Cotentin Peninsula. After dawn, British, Canadian and American assault troops began to pour ashore on five separate bridgeheads on the Normandy coast. Although German resistance steadily increased, Allied mastery of both the air and the sea was all but total and, by the end of the day, some 156,000 men of the invasion force were on French soil.

Forged Ordre de Mission that provided 'official' cover for Tony to travel through Occupied France on PIMENTO business, 27 May 1944

On the night of 5/6 June SOE circuits all over France swung into action with attacks on rail, road and telecommunications links. One source makes an impressive claim for the effectiveness of F Section's sabotage teams, recording that '950 out of 1,050 planned interruptions of the railways were made.'[7] While PIMENTO's leader slept on in the apartment above the Garage des Pyrénées without any knowledge of these events, the weapon that he had created was unleashed to immense effect. On isolated stretches of rail track throughout southern France Tony's saboteurs placed their charges, telegraph wires were brought down and maquis groups set up hundreds of roadblocks.

Early on the morning of 6 June, Tony left the Garage des Pyrénées and took the train from Montauban to Toulouse to visit Zaksas, quite unaware that the invasion had commenced. Perhaps if he had heard the 'B' messages, his journey to the city might have given him cause for concern but the attempts to paralyse rail communications had not yet taken full effect. At Montauban there was no sign of tension for news of the landings seems not to have reached the south-west. Tony left the train at a stop in the suburbs of Toulouse, maintaining his usual policy that it was safer to take a tram into the city centre rather than run the risk of security checks at the main Matabiau station. He walked through a tranquil area of small, one-storey houses and market gardens where workers were thinning out rows of vegetables. Then, as he strolled past a house its shutters were flung open and a girl, of about eight years old, stark naked, shouted, 'They've landed!'

His thoughts full of the implications of the momentous news, Tony boarded his tram and, as it made its way into Toulouse, it became clear that word of the invasion had now spread. Inspired by the elation of his passengers, the tram conductor decided to make his own contribution to celebrating the liberation of his country by refusing to accept fares. However, the buoyant mood was quickly dispelled when the tram reached the Matabiau terminus where German soldiers and armoured cars were on full alert. This brief journey gave Tony an important understanding of the swings of elation and uncertainty engendered by the invasion. The shattered optimism of the passengers on the tram would be replicated time and time again in the succeeding weeks when Frenchmen and women found that the German occupation of their country was not to be readily relinquished. Throughout most of France in the days to come the Wehrmacht did not cave in, the Allies did not arrive, and the Resistance did not possess sufficient resources to take control.

At Zaksas's office, Tony was given a report of the night's activities. This was, of course, incomplete due to the fluid and uncertain state of affairs, but he was able to deduce that PIMENTO had taken major steps in fulfilling its obligations. As fragments of information came in of the landings in Normandy, Tony was still reluctant to discount his own theory (based upon the briefings he had received in London) that an invasion would also take place on the Atlantic coast south of Bordeaux. Like many generals in the German High Command, he suspected that the assault in Normandy was a feint and that the main landings would take place elsewhere. Amidst all the speculation there remained at least one constant – the presence of the powerful 2nd SS Panzer Division 'Das Reich' stationed around Montauban. The unit at first remained inactive in spite of the Allied invasion. When orders came for its deployment, it was not instructed to rush to the Normandy front but, instead, to implement a proposal from its commanding officer, Lammerding, that the division undertake counter-resistance activity 'in the Tulle-Limoges area, where substantial formations of gangs appear to be gathered.'[8] Thus on

8 June the tanks trucks, and paraphernalia of the division began to move northwards out of the Montauban area. Some of the 45-ton Panther Panzer Vs were loaded onto flat cars to be conveyed by rail but Tony's carborundum grease had done its work and, after a period of time, the axle boxes seized, forcing the tanks to take to the road. By this time the shortage of railcars was acute. Major Stückler, the senior staff officer of the divisional commander, had a request for extra rail space denied without explanation by 58th Panzer Corps headquarters.[9] Protests by Stückler failed and the 'Das Reich' tanks were obliged to eschew rail transportation and take the road to Figeac and Tulle. Incessant pinprick attacks by maquis groups beset the SS columns almost from the outset and, consequently, when opportunities to exact reprisals presented themselves, the division acted with great savagery. The beleaguered German garrisons in Brive and Tulle were relieved by the 'Das Reich' and, in the latter town, on 9 June, ninety-nine citizens were hanged from lamp posts. The next day, elements of the 'Das Reich' perpetrated what was arguably the most heinous war crime carried out by German forces in France. The 3rd Company of the 1st Battalion of the SS Panzer-Grenadier Regiment 'Der Führer' swept into the small, Limousin town of Oradour-sur-Glane and inflicted a monstrous massacre. The specific motives behind the atrocity have long been debated and deliberately obscured by the perpetrators. It seems that frustration, vindictiveness and sheer blood lust led the unit to massacre the entire population of the town; the men were shot, and the women and children herded into the church that was then set on fire. In all, 642 French civilians were murdered. If ever Tony and his PIMENTO comrades needed justification for their toils Oradour provided it.[10]

On 9 June the 'Das Reich' was ordered to curtail its local preoccupations and deploy to the Normandy battlefront, its tanks and half-tracks being instructed to entrain at Périgeux and Limoges. This was easier said than done as unrelenting sabotage operations had taken their toll. On the 10 the German High Command was advised 'in view of the transport situation' that departure would be a further two days at the earliest.[11] The Germans' difficulties were clearly a result of the desperate flatcar shortages and the sabotage cuts on the railway lines – PIMENTO's abrasive-grease teams had more than achieved their objectives. In the event, it was not until the 15th that the first of the trains bearing the 'Das Reich' moved northwards but, even then, the journey proved immensely difficult and the SS units were frequently forced onto the roads where they were vulnerable to the hit-and-run attacks of the Resistance and the predatory attentions of the Allied air forces. During the slow advance northwards from Montauban, the 'Das Reich' did not sustain heavy casualties at the hands of the Resistance and the balance of thirty-five SS fatalities set against hundreds of Frenchmen and women killed, most of whom were non-combatants, constituted a ghastly ratio. Nevertheless, with the German High Command desperate to staunch the Allied breakout from the Normandy bridgehead, the denial to them of an elite unit for over two weeks can only be considered as a truly significant resistance achievement in support of the 'Overlord' campaign.[12]

Although important, the 'Das Reich' constituted only one of PIMENTO's concerns. Tony's duties were to ensure that the whole circuit carried out its full range of tasks, cutting German road, rail and telecommunications, continuing to receive supply drops and, where appropriate, forming additional maquis groups. An appraisal written six months after the D-Day sabotage offensive recorded that no less than seventy-eight steam railway engines and twenty-nine electric types were destroyed by PIMENTO at this time in addition to a countless number of rail cuts.

It was a period of mixed emotions for Tony. Two years' work was reaching its culmination, but he struggled to keep control of the disparate activities of his sabotage teams and maquis groups. He remained initially in the Toulouse/Montauban/Lavaur area, encouraging the efforts of his men and trying to reconcile the sometimes conflicting demands of London and his own, local objectives. Few reliable documents have survived to gauge the full extent of SOE-sponsored resistance activity in the weeks immediately following D-Day. German situation reports would be invaluable, for the British and French accounts of the fighting have a tendency to overestimate maquis action. And it was not unknown for the same sabotage successes to be claimed by different groups. In a post-war report, SOE attempted to analyse resistance activity in an area west of Lyon where PIMENTO had a major presence:

ST. RAMBERT lies on the line CULOZ–AMBERIEUX, a line which was denied to the Germans almost without a break ever since D-Day. We were told that the ST. RAMBERT groups had carried out upwards of 30 cuts in a fortnight. This will illustrate the difficulty of properly assessing results. ST. RAMBERT is in the Ain, and cuts on this line were reported to us by MARKSMAN. They were probably also reported to us by PIMENTO, whose railwaymen were strong in this area, and now they were being reported by JEAN-PAUL's outlying group of the DITCHER organisation.[13]

Fortunately, some contemporary accounts by resistance leaders have survived amongst Tony's private papers. PIMENTO's Gauthier compiled a record of the rail attacks carried out under his auspices around the time of D-Day in the Bourg area. Even allowing for the possibility of exaggeration, the list is impressive. He reported that on 8 June a cut on the track was made near Servas on the line Lyon–Bourg, between 1 June and 8 July constant resistance attacks rendered the route between Bourg and Macon unusable and on 5 June a derailment at Turgon between La Vavrette and Pont d'Ain on the Bourg–Ambérieu–Lyon link proved highly successful. In addition, Gauthier stated that a wrecked supply train blocked the line for more than a month, with two other cuts helping further to increase the Germans' frustration.

It is understandable that members of the Resistance should seek to place great emphasis on their contribution to the fighting in France in the weeks following D-Day. The Australian war correspondent Alan Moorehead provides a dispassionate but laudatory estimation of the value of the Resistance.

Within a few weeks the maquis were holding areas of France three or four times the size of our bridgehead in Normandy. France was in a state of open rebellion. Very little of this was known to the outside world at the time, partly because the facts were largely secret, and partly because attention was focused on the more definite and understandable front in Normandy. It was not until the Allies broke out and began to run through France that it was realised how much the way had been prepared for us by the French themselves. From the moment of our landing the Germans were forced to fight a secondary battle against the maquis in their rearward lines, and that fight increased and continued right up to and after the fall of Paris.[14]

Chapter Thirteen
No Let-Up

Less than a fortnight after D-Day, the Allies were well established in Normandy but, far from slackening its efforts, PIMENTO was going full tilt. On 17 June 1944 Tony sent a message to London listing eleven dropping grounds 'standing by permanently for personnel and material' and giving details of numerous other DZs ready to receive drops of as many as seventy-two containers. It was now a time when the PIMENTO reception committees were happy to take whatever London could send and Tony requested the resources to maintain a private army, 'all possible material, anti tank guns, mines, machine guns, grenades, etc. Also plenty of plastic.' In addition, his need for another wireless operator remained as acute as ever. In an attempt to facilitate the arrival, he offered no less than nine different grounds to receive whoever F Section was able to send him.

Two days later, Tony sent Bertholet another message by courier for transmission to London. It reflected the hectic times through which he was living but conveyed a feeling of optimism for future PIMENTO activity. He asked his friend (in French) to help persuade London to increase the supply drops, claiming that he was confident that in Comte's and Zaksas's areas great things were possible and, with sufficient material, 'we will control the region, which will be good for the worker's movement'. It was also a time for Tony to allow himself a moment's brief consideration of how far PIMENTO had come during the last two years. He drew Bertholet's attention to the latest

ABOVE Matabiau Station, Toulouse, where Tony arrived to commence his clandestine career in July 1942.

BELOW Michel Comte's Garage des Pyrénées – Tony's Montauban base in the southern branch of PIMENTO.

ABOVE David Donoff 'Dodo' –
PIMENTO's 'fixer' until shot and
killed in Lyon, June 1944.

RIGHT André Moch 'Georges' –
Tony's second-in-command until
his death in a shootout with the
Germans in April 1944.

BELOW A memorial plaque for
Jean Dorval, one of PIMENTO's
earliest casualties.

À LA MÉMOIRE DE:
JEAN DORVAL
VÉRIFICATEUR PRINCIPAL DES DOUANES,
CHEVALIER DE LA LÉGION D'HONNEUR,
CROIX DE GUERRE 1939-1940,
MÉDAILLE DE LA RÉSISTANCE,
FUSILLÉ PAR LES ALLEMANDS LE 11 JANVIER 1944,
SES CAMARADES DE PARIS EN TÉMOIGNAGE
DE LEUR PROFONDE AMITIÉ ET DE LEUR FIDÈLE SOUVENIR

ABOVE Derailed railway wagons.

RIGHT The type of French railcar axle box that
PIMENTO saboteurs attacked with abrasives.

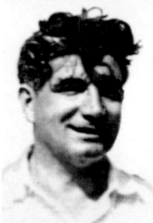

ABOVE The Kriegsmarine buildings on the Place de la Concorde, Paris, taken by Tony during his brief stay in the city, August 1943.

LEFT Henri Déricourt 'Gilbert' – the F Section agent who organised Tony's flight back to England but who was a double-agent in the pay of the Nazis.

BELOW Lockheed Hudson aircraft of the type that collected Tony from France in August 1943.

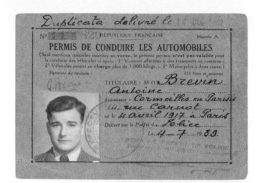

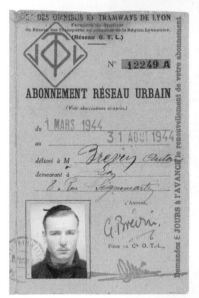

THIS PAGE The many faces of 'Antoine Brévin'. A false driving licence made by SOE in 1942 and fake travel documents acquired in France. 'Antoine Vialars' was one of several other aliases he adopted when he felt 'Antoine Brévin' was compromised.

ABOVE Roger Caza 'Emmanuel'
– Tony's wireless operator
from February 1944 until the
Liberation of France.

RIGHT Lise de Baissac
'Marguerite' – the SOE agent
sent to be Tony's courier in
France but who found it
impossible to work with her
PIMENTO colleagues.

ABOVE The Pont Pasteur in Lyon that was demolished by the Germans in spite of Tony's best efforts to save it in September 1944.

RIGHT A PIMENTO reception committee on the 'Bégonia' DZ near Bourg. The supply containers are laid out on the verge.

ABOVE A group of French Resistance fighters, summer 1944. Their impressive array of Sten sub-machine guns and the suitcase wireless set reveal the efficacy of SOE's supply operations by the time of the Liberation.

From a boy to a man; Tony Brooks's transformation during his wartime years as a secret
agent to Major Anthony Brooks, DSO MC, shortly after the war – an impressive, heroic
figure, but still only twenty-three years old.

request for drops of seventy-two containers 'what progress on 1942 when we took 3'. He reported that he had sent orders to Caza to work with Comte and that, when the second wireless operator eventually arrived, he/she would be entrusted to Zaksas and thereby Tony's main groups in the south-west could be in contact with London twenty-four hours a day. As ever, the existing courier links to Switzerland were operational and would continue to sustain a back-up channel for PIMENTO's communications with London.

The plans for Caza were decidedly optimistic for he had left the Naves area on 10 June and was escorted to Lyon en route for the Ain to work with Gauthier. The wireless operator explained the reason for the move to Tony in a note, 'J and I are sunk here – somebody talked too much – we are holing out but still working – can stay in this hiding place only a week or so – what with that and new D.F. [Direction Finding] station near Vichy, this spot is somewhat unhealthy – can you find us another spot? J can't stay here and is ready to keep on working with me wherever I go or do some other kind of work. Very sorry about this but it can't be helped.'[1] However, the maquis insurrection in the Bourg area prevented Caza from leaving Lyon and making contact with Gauthier. To make matters worse, the Canadian became separated from his wireless set and, in response to London's later enquiry as to why he had gone off the air, he testily informed them, 'You may rest assured that when I do not call it is because I cannot. Stop. Was stuck in Lyon with no set and could not receive much less send.'[2] The break in communication was extensive, with Caza estimating that he had gone off the air for three weeks during this crucial period.[3] Tony later recalled that his operator's problem was caused in large part by the blowing-up of river barrages on the Saône and Rhône that resulted in the wirelesses being stranded on the wrong side of the rivers. Given that this break in wireless contact occurred during the period immediately following D-Day, it was especially fortunate that PIMENTO's courier networks to Bertholet and Switzerland were still in place and working efficiently.

At a time when the achievement of all his hopes seemed but a short step away, on 27 June 1944 Tony was devastated by news of another tragedy. This time the casualty was the exuberant David 'Dodo' Donoff, the master 'fixer' and procurer of false documents. Tony was away from Lyon at the time of the disaster and therefore had to rely upon second- and third-hand accounts of what had happened. It seems that Donoff had taken a briefcase full of forged papers to a *mairie* in Lyon to have them endorsed with official authorisation stamps. This may have been one of his jobs for 'Amitié Chrétienne' rather than PIMENTO, although, in a later report, Tony affirmed that Donoff had been 'trying to get rations [cards] for my LYON circuit'.[4] A near-contemporary account by Tony suggested that Donoff 'was probably denounced by an employee in the town hall of the 5eme arrondissement in LYONS, who was arrested for trafficking in false ration cards.' Whatever the initial cause of the problem, it seems that Donoff, fearing that he was about to fall into a security spot check, made a dash to get away. It long remained a mystery to Tony why Donoff did not try and talk his way out of the situation, for his panicky reaction was decidedly out of character. It was sheer bad luck that German soldiers stationed in the street spotted the fugitive and fired at him. As Donoff lay mortally wounded in the gutter, the Germans showed little interest in their victim and it was left to French passers-by to call for an ambulance to take him to the Grange Blanche hospital. There, by yet another of those quirks of good fortune that sometimes blessed PIMENTO, the wounded man was spotted by Henri Combe, who was both Donoff's landlord and a member of the circuit. The resourceful Combe noticed his comrade's briefcase and a quick examination revealed that it was stuffed full of identity papers. In order to protect the anonymity of Donoff's clients, Combe threw the briefcase into the hospital incinerator and, once the former finally succumbed to his wounds, sent warnings to PIMENTO contacts explaining what had happened. Tony received accounts of the tragedy while in the south-west, enabling him to write to Bizot in Switzerland on 6 July that no damage to the circuit was foreseen. He related that when the authorities eventually searched Donoff's body, only a ration card was found and a subsequent investigation of the address featured on the document revealed nothing incriminating. For weeks Donoff's family, with the exception of his sister Herminette, believed him to be alive and detained at Montluc prison. When the news of his death finally reached them it invoked a second tragedy: one of Donoff's grief-stricken sisters committed suicide.[5] Tony's professionalism sometimes failed to mask his emotions and on 9 July 1944 he sent an impassioned message to Caza for transmission to London, 'Send funds urgently stop DODO shot in street 27 June in Lyon stop Breakage ceased stop Was my paper expert and responsible for Emmanuel [Caza] stop Worked with me from start stop Saved my life August forty three stop Please give rank and decoration stop am giving financial help to family who have lost other son too stop.'[6]

This message was accompanied by a personal note to Caza. It filled in the background to Donoff's death as far as Tony knew it and expressed his deep respect and affection for the forger. He also explained the reasons why London should recognise Donoff's contribution to PIMENTO's success:

The death of Dodo will no doubt cause you some sadness. You remember him? He was the chap who accompanied you with Felix from Michel's to Ganat. He was shot in the street by the Gestapo and the Milice. He had two bullets in the stomach, but he still managed to escape to the next street where by bad luck he was caught by three bullets in the back, which made him collapse. After leaving him there for nearly an hour they sent him to the hospital where he managed to warn us, he then went to sleep, believing that he would awaken but it proved to be his last sleep. He died mainly from an internal haemorrhage caused by a bullet in the liver. He did not suffer, thank God. With him goes one of my very best friends and the best man in our unit. But God wished it so and so we must not complain but must redouble our efforts to carry on to a victorious conclusion of this war now well on the way to success. Unfortunately he leaves a family of seven, father, mother and five sisters. His elder brother was deported about six months ago. Some people have all the bad luck. I hope for the family's sake that HQ give him a rank and the decoration that he deserves. It is so little for them and yet would give an outward sign to the family of the great service he has given to our common cause.[7]

After the war, Tony submitted an application for a decoration for Donoff but no record has been found of it having been accepted.

Meanwhile, Caza's travels had at last taken him to the Montauban area where he based himself in the countryside around the town of Lavaur. Here, he was protected and supported by a loyal group of men from Zaksas's network. In accordance with best operational practice, he frequently switched his place of transmission; his first location being the home of Ernest Fabries, a wine *négociant*, situated in the route de Belcastel where he used a bedroom on the first floor of the house for his work, passing a 15-foot length of aerial into the garden.[8] Caza, in a post-liberation report, stated that he stayed with Fabries for a week, and one of the local members of PIMENTO, Maurice Rouch, recorded that during that period the wireless operator restricted his transmission times to thirty to forty minutes.[9] The Canadian also had to travel a minimum of ten kilometres by bicycle each time he switched sites with the wireless strapped to either his or a companion's machine. The messages he received from London were passed to Zaksas in Toulouse both for the latter's edification and/or for onward courier to Tony. The bicycle was virtually the only means of carrying the messages with any rapidity over fairly long distances that by now were at best dangerous and at worse a battlefield. Rouch recalled that when called upon to carry out this task he hid the messages inside his bicycle pump. However, it was not Rouch but another member of the Lavaur group, Robert Marty, who was given the main responsibility for transporting Caza's wireless messages. Rouch testified (in French) to his comrade's diligence and bravery 'He travelled as the bearer of good news and of bad, of spoken messages and documents cycling around to bind us all together, weaving the threads of this cobweb which developed day after day.'[10]

With Caza now in the south-west area of PIMENTO, Tony decided to switch his own operational base to Lyon. The maquis was now predominant in the region around Toulouse, he felt he had little to contribute there and estimated that PIMENTO in the north had the greatest need of him. His intention was nothing less than to assume active command of his network's drop zones and resistance groups around Lyon. This decision was largely motivated by the need to exercise greater control over the activities of his representative, Gauthier. The surviving messages between the two men do not make comfortable reading, especially when compared to the warmth and mutual respect shown in Tony's correspondence with other PIMENTO leaders. In messages sent on 10 and 12 July, he castigated Gauthier for reports of the PIMENTO groups under his command that Tony judged too brief and inaccurate. Moreover, critically addressing his subordinate's requests for money, Tony enumerated Zaksas's and Comte's negligible financial demands on him. A further source of Tony's displeasure was the news that Gauthier had approached another resistance leader, Romans-Petit, for money. This act went counter to the fundamental PIMENTO precept of avoiding contact with other networks and Tony was unhappy that one of his chief lieutenants was now beholden to another group. Such was his ire that he informed Gauthier that he was considering ridding himself of the problem by transferring his troublesome comrade-in-arms to Romans-Petit's command. But Tony stated he had been dissuaded from this course of action by an unnamed confidant who was 'le représentant du General Koenig'.[11] It seems likely that the threat was simply a bluff to remind Gauthier that he was not indispensable and should toe the line.

A message from Caza mentioned that Tony left the south-west in 'the last week in July' and a note to Zaksas of 1 August confirmed his arrival with a request that a courier be sent to Olga Vittet's bearing news of developments in the south-west. In spite of the depredations of the Resistance and the efforts of the Allied air forces, Tony's rail journey to Lyon went without a hitch. On arriving there, though, he soon appreciated that major changes had taken place: a palpable air of tension and menace existed amongst and between the Germans and the French. Outside the city, the maquis had become ever more assertive and resistance activity within the conurbation was increasing. It was clear that the German commanders, with their thoughts preoccupied by the main battlefronts, were caught in a dilemma. The deployment of forces to crush resistance uprisings constituted a major distraction of their limited resources while a delayed response to the internal threat risked allowing insurrection to escalate into an even greater problem.

A major resistance uprising in the Ain, in which Gauthier had become involved, promised much but was soon subjected to a powerful German counter-offensive, Operation 'Treffenfeld'. On 9 July, German units including mountain troops and SS formations moved quickly and aggressively to reoccupy the region. Meanwhile a similar, if even more ruthless, assault was launched against the Resistance's precipitate 'liberation' of the Vercors plateau where the barbarous behaviour of the counter-attacking German troops ranked alongside that of the 'Das Reich'.

In Lyon the situation was different. The German and Vichy security forces were still operating 'at home' and although the city possessed a warren of side streets and alleyways, there was no urban insurrection to match that of the surrounding countryside. But violence was never far away and on the night of 26 July 1944 an attempt was made to sabotage the Café du Moulin à Vent, a hostelry popular with the Germans, on the Place Bellecour. A source states that a bomb was thrown and that several Germans were injured, but none killed. Another claims that a device (three packages of explosive) had been planted on the first floor of the restaurant amongst some telephone directories but had not detonated until after the restaurant had closed.[12] The failure to kill German soldiers did not stop the Gestapo exacting retribution. They removed five resistance inmates from Montluc prison the next day and summarily executed them at the scene of the previous night's incident. One of the prisoners did not die straight away but the Germans refused him medical treatment and the French police were ordered to let the corpses remain *in situ* on the pavement for the next three hours as a warning of the consequences of resistance. In spite of the very public unfolding of the incident, there was still a Nazi attempt at spin. Local newspapers printed stories claiming that the murdered Frenchmen had been responsible for planting the bomb and that they had simply been executed at the scene of their 'crime'. Such an excuse did not convince the local prelate, Cardinal Pierre-Marie Gerlier, who bravely visited Gestapo headquarters to remonstrate against the atrocity.

Tony became a victim of this heightened tension. One day, while innocently waiting for a tram in the centre of Lyon, he suddenly heard shouting and general commotion at a nearby German roadblock. The cause of the uproar was a cyclist who ignored the soldiers' orders to stop and whose intention was soon made clear when he threw a hand grenade that failed to detonate. As he sped away, one of the soldiers flung, a little optimistically, a retaliatory grenade back at him. By the time it exploded, the fugitive was long gone, leaving only the members of the tram queue as victims of the incident. Casualties were few, thanks to the grenade's design that created blast rather than shrapnel. Tony was the most seriously injured, receiving a fragment of metal in his knee. Reluctant to draw attention to himself in case of accusations that he was associated with the cyclist, he swiftly boarded the next tram. As it moved away from the scene, he could not help noticing that he was bleeding profusely and the other passengers were looking at him. Fortunately, a young housewife spotted his plight and discreetly placed her shopping bag in front of him to shield his bloodstained trousers from further inspection.

Eventually, Tony reached his stop and, thanking the woman for her concern, headed to the Chemin du Panorama. Finding an isolated spot, he surveyed the wound and fashioned a makeshift bandage out of his handkerchief. There was nothing he could do about his trousers but he realised that his bloodstained shoe would make a dreadful mess of Mme Dupeuple's floor. In the absence of a convenient source of water, his only option was to urinate on his shoe to remove the blood. At the house, he avoided other members of the household and reached his room without having to explain his appearance. Sterilising a pair of tweezers as best he could, he probed the wound and extracted a piece of hand grenade casing about the size of a ten-pence piece. He kept a small bottle of *marc* in the room for just such an eventuality and employed the alcohol to disinfect the wound, bandaged his knee and treated himself to a healthy belt of the liquor to fortify his resolve. Apart from the injuries sustained in his first parachute drop it was Tony's first war wound but, as the violence in Lyon increased, there was every chance that it would not be his last.

Chapter Fourteen
The Final Lap

Tony's main preoccupation had become the need to support the battle raging in Northern France. Every delayed troop movement, every German soldier kept on garrison duty in the south and every destroyed munitions train contributed to the erosion of the Nazis' hold on French soil. At first, the Allied progress in Normandy was slow, with the Germans putting up resolute resistance that restricted the breakout from the bridgehead. General Montgomery's British and Canadian forces became locked into a battle of attrition around Caen, then the Americans overran the Cotentin peninsula and built up their reserves for a renewed offensive. On 25 July 1944, Operation Cobra was unleashed and quickly developed into an unexpectedly successful Allied advance. Lieutenant-General George Patton's armoured formations pushed into Brittany and, by mid-August, swung round to reach the River Loire. The Germans in France were manifestly on the point of collapse and the Allied strategy demanded that, having broken out from Normandy, their armies would wheel eastwards, liberate Paris and push on towards the Reich itself.

Tony's leg wound did not incapacitate him and, far from holing up at the Chemin du Panorama, he remained in control of the disparate activities of PIMENTO. He felt the need to stay with his associates in the centre of Lyon as much as possible rather than base himself at his digs in the suburbs. The unwelcome consequence of this initiative was his arrest at a security check in the Place Bellecour while en route from Olga Vittet's to the Customs Office.

German troops and French police had blocked off the road ahead and, with other soldiers lingering behind him, he could not retrace his steps. Asked to show his identity card, he was then told to wait with a group of other young men. He was not comforted to note that his fellow detainees were all about his own age and colouring, leading him to speculate whether he might be the Germans' target. Then, together with his fellow prisoners, Tony was escorted to the Gestapo's new headquarters at 33 Place Bellecour.[1] After years of his trying to avoid this very predicament, it seemed that Tony's luck had finally run out. It was no consolation that his plight had not been brought about by his own failings – he simply put it down to the massive weight of the odds stacked against his survival. He was taken into a cellar that had once been a stockroom but was now an improvised dungeon and told to strip to his underwear – his other clothes and possessions (that included a large bundle of cash) were taken from him. The slamming of the door and sound of the key turning in the padlock brought back a flood of memories from his incarceration in Spain. He reflected that he had survived the last time he had been imprisoned and drew confidence and hope from past tribulations; he was a very different person from the callow youth who had crossed the Pyrenees in 1941. Years of clandestine operations, underpinned by his SOE training, had, he felt, equipped him with the skill and confidence to meet challenges such as this – which included being administered an emetic in case he had swallowed a compromising object. After a couple of hours, the door to his cell was unlocked and he was escorted into an office where the occupant, a German officer, instructed him to sit down. As he did so, Tony instinctively reached behind him to make sure that the chair was there. The lessons learned from Peter Follis's interrogation in the garage at Beaulieu gave him a surge of self-belief; he had been trained for this moment and felt that clear thinking and the strength of his cover story would see him through the crisis. The primary focus of questioning concerned the money found in his possession and, in response, his Beaulieu training kicked in: he answered slowly and indirectly, neither in an insolent manner nor one indicating deliberate obstructionism. He related a prepared story: he was hoping to buy a bicycle – not a clapped-out boneshaker but something with real rubber tyres. He presumed that his interrogator would understand that such an item would not come cheap as the exodus of German personnel from Lyon placed bicycles at a high premium. When asked for the source of his money, Tony explained that he had withdrawn it from his post office savings account and ventured that this could be corroborated by examination of the records. The German officer seemed mildly impressed by his confident statement and Tony was returned to his cell while the checks were carried out. Some hours later, the padlock and chain were once more removed. Tony's clothes were returned and he was led upstairs to the interview room. The demeanour of the German officer, although never hostile, was now affable. Ushering Tony to take a chair, he confirmed that his prisoner's explanations had all checked out. He expressed the hope that Tony, as a Vichy government official, would understand the need to hunt down black marketeers and, even worse, the agents of the 'Anglo-American-Judaeo-Bolshevik' conspiracy against whom the Third Reich was fighting a life-and-death struggle. Tony expressed his earnest agreement; the German officer apologised for any inconvenience, returned the money, shook the agent's hand and offered the salute and valediction '*Heil Hitler!*' Not to be outdone, Tony responded in like fashion, '*Heil Hitler!*' and left, a free, if more than slightly shaken, man.[2]

Meanwhile, resistance activity in the region continued to grow in intensity. Maquis groups proliferated and, in some areas, turned large parts of the countryside into virtual no-go areas for German military units. The need to provide weapons and ammunition for the fighting was all the greater. The face of resistance had radically changed; from the dark days of 1942 when Tony arrived and struggled to find loyal and willing helpers, France in the summer of 1944 was awash with recent latecomers to the cause. The maquis was full to overflowing, some towns that had never heard a shot fired in anger were 'liberating' themselves and skirmishes with the retreating Germans and remnants of the Vichy regime became fully fledged 'battles'. Many resistance units soon acquired the trappings of conventional forces such as headquarters staffs, 'official' paperwork and military protocol. Meanwhile, officers from the regular army of 1940 were taking their uniforms out of hiding (and mothballs – hence their nickname '*naphtalines*') and seeking a belated adherence to the Allied cause. Frequently ill-informed and just as frequently inclined to believe that they were the only people doing anything, these late arrivals engendered rancour and annoyance amongst veterans of the Resistance. The latter, including many strong-willed figures who had fought long and hard for this moment, were reluctant to share it with these newcomers. It was also a time when SOE and de Gaulle sought to impose their authority. These external claims for control were, in part, acknowledged by *résistants*, but others could not readily shed years of self-sufficiency and individual authority. Egos clashed with alarming regularity and reputations proved sensitive to the touch. This malaise was manifested in the Ain and Tony's lieutenant, Henri Gauthier, found himself in the firing line. His area had long witnessed significant maquis activity and, following D-Day, major engagements took place against the Germans. The FFI leader in the Ain was the aforementioned Lieutenant-Colonel Henri Petit, also known as 'Romans-Petit' or 'Romans', who had mounted the demonstration at Oyonnax and subsequently lent Gauthier money. Richard Heslop, an F Section officer who worked closely with Romans-Petit, testified, 'He had fought in the First World War, when he won the Légion d'Honneur and was mentioned in dispatches. Between the wars, he organised publicity for various fashion houses in Paris, but he left the elegant salons, the comfortable life, and a high income, to join the Resistance after Pétain surrendered to the Germans. In December 1942, nine months before I met him he formed the Maquis de l'Ain.'[4] F Section had recognised the importance of Romans-Petit's activities and, in September 1943 (while Tony was back in England) sent an inter-Allied mission to him comprising Heslop and a Free French officer, Lieutenant Jean Rosenthal. This team became the basis of the MARKSMAN circuit, an effective maquis network that was markedly different from PIMENTO in its make-up and its objectives.

Following his arrival in Lyon, Tony moved to exercise control over Gauthier and his network's activity in the Ain; a note of 2 August 1944 to his subordinate was measured and uncompromising. A sixteen-point set of instructions (in French) was reinforced by Tony's warning to Gauthier that he would hold him accountable if his orders were not followed to the letter. It constituted a clear move to rein in PIMENTO's local commander and ensure that he fell into line with Tony's strategy and – by extension – that of London. New BBC messages were issued instructing specific actions against railways and telephone communications. Stocks of explosives were to be hoarded for the commission of these tasks and orders issued that stores were not to be consigned to other groups or dissipated on small scale, local operations. Tony's instruction No. 13 gave Gauthier no opportunity for misinterpreting his orders, 'These instructions must be considered as cancelling every preceding instruction. They must be carried out to the letter and in the most efficient manner.' No. 14 was even more uncompromising: 'If you acknowledge this and confirm to me your intention of carrying out the task that I have asked of you, you shall have the funds and your position will be confirmed. But if you do not make an effort, you will have to make do on your own and submit to the judgement of a council of war once the Ain has been liberated, for I shall not be able to do anything to excuse the grave errors committed in the Ain and which have cost so many French lives.' The relationship certainly appears brittle for, in spite of the intimate '*tu*', Tony concluded, 'You now have your instructions, carry them out and all will be well. I still have confidence in you, perhaps wrongly, I don't know.'[4]

Tony was aware of Gauthier's problematic relationship with Romans-Petit, which had been exacerbated by the Colonel's avowed intention to control the *département* of the Ain, all the resistance activity within it and, just as importantly, the war materiel dropped there by the Allies. The previous year Gauthier had reported to Tony that Romans-Petit had engineered the appropriation of the contents of a supply drop at Chavannes. He claimed that Romans-Petit had lied to him so as to explain away the disappearance of the material and, when questioned further, had blamed the leader of the team ordered to carry out the expropriation of the supplies. The man had been arrested and Gauthier reported that, had the 'felon' not escaped he might have been executed as a scapegoat. Romans-Petit's teams did not confine their pillaging to this 'theft' and their depredations embraced the whole region, with the result that Gauthier was obliged to shift the location of PIMENTO's stores depots in order to prevent their being seized.[5] As the leader of PIMENTO, Tony felt that he had to exercise his authority and resolve the dispute with Romans-Petit rather than leave it to Gauthier. On 3 August, having promoted himself to 'Colonel' to possess an equal rank to his correspondent, the leader of PIMENTO wrote to Romans-Petit notifying him that Gauthier had been issued with a formal delegation of power.[6] While respectful to its addressee, Tony's letter categorically asserted PIMENTO's right to independent action. The sugary conclusion (in French), 'In the hope that our brotherly relationship will have the best of results and hasten a conclusive Allied victory, I beg you to receive my best regards', did not mask the fact that the document was an affirmation of Tony's intention to prosecute his own war without seeking Romans-Petit's sanction and gave notice that he would oppose any interference.

Tony's contemporary thoughts on the matter are revealed in a letter of 5 August 1944 to Colonel 'Alain', a relatively new addition to PIMENTO's cast of characters. 'Alain' was a friend of Rudi Molter, one of Tony's SRFD associates in Lyon.[7] Tony alluded to Gauthier's report on events in the Ain and speculated that Romans-Petit's strategic errors in adopting tactics to hold ground and liberate towns rather than maintain guerrilla operations, had provided sabotage opportunities for PIMENTO. If Gauthier were to develop this work, he would need money and, as Tony was short of cash, he asked 'Alain' to lend it to him. Never a spendthrift and reluctant to be indebted to others, Tony's financial difficulties were acute. An F Section summary of the monies sent to France records that PIMENTO did not receive any cash in June and July 1944 and that the circuit remained amongst the least well-funded of the networks.[8] The shortage of cash was critical for, as PIMENTO's work developed, its members increasingly curtailed their regular occupations in order to become 'full time' resisters. To prevent family hardship, the men required financial help and, in the absence of money from SOE, Tony's financial arrangements with 'Alain' became vital. There was also a non-financial element: in addition to 'Alain's' loan of 100,000 francs, Tony asked for his assistance in confirming PIMENTO's status with local Free French authorities.

On 7 August 1944 Gauthier sent Tony a 'Rapport de l'activité dans l'Ain, des FFI, sous le commandement du commandant Romans'. Handwritten and limited by Gauthier's preoccupation with other priorities, it recorded a rather muddled picture of the maquis's performance. While it conceded Romans-Petit's qualities – '*Bon officier, très courageux et dynamique*' – it also described him as having been influenced by questionable counsel and of taking on too many tasks. Gauthier described Romans-Petit's disputes with his subordinates (Heslop being an exception with whom he worked in perfect accord) over strategy. The picture was made even clearer on 9 August in a note from Tony to 'Alain'. In spite of stepping up the number of supply drops, the material now being delivered to the Ain was frequently of the wrong type, comprising small-arms ammunition instead of much-needed stocks of plastic explosive for PIMENTO's saboteurs.[9] Nevertheless, Tony reported (in French) that Gauthier was coping although still in a tricky position vis-à-vis Romans-Petit: 'Every day Roman's men come offering their services, for they no longer want to work with Roman because the latter talks of holding ground. Jag's [Gauthier's] position is very delicate. If he accepts the services of Roman's men the latter will accuse him of having played a mean trick on him. The situation is very difficult. I have ordered Jag to accept the services of anyone but only in the field of sabotaging communications. That will leave Roman the direction of real military operations.'[10] At a time when connections and 'pull' were becoming ever more important, Tony attempted a little bit of 'networking' himself and had met with 'Marie', the FFI departmental chief for the Rhône, Raymond Basset.

Then, on 11 August 1944, Gauthier received a formal note from Romans-Petit asking for a report on '*Le Colonel* THEODORE' as neither l'Etat Major Régional nor Heslop had heard of him. Moreover, Romans-Petit affirmed that Colonel 'Bayard' – in reality Colonel Marcel Descour, the Chief of the FFI's Alpine Zone – did not know of 'Theodore' either. There is little doubt that this demand for information was a retort to Tony's earlier message affirming Gauthier's freedom of action.[11] Meanwhile Heslop had sought F Section's assistance in checking out the bona fides of 'Theodore'. On 13 August Caza received a message from London, 'we have received following telegram from Ain circuit quote Lt Col Theodore alias Alphonse alias Fleur styling himself Chef saboteur zone sud has sent us commandant Jag [Gauthier] with orders take over all sabotage groups unquote stop there must be misunderstanding stop this circuit is under disciplined command Lt Col with whom you are free to cooperate at your discretion and under his authority.' It was but one more manifestation of the extremely complex state of F Section's circuits in France. London was scarcely in a position to arbitrate in the dispute and Tony resolved to make personal contact with Romans-Petit and Heslop to try to iron out the difficulties.

The rivalries, sensibilities and claims to precedence of the disparate elements of the Resistance absorbed a disproportionate amount of the organisers' attention but the real war was still raging on other battlefronts. On the night of 14/15 August 1944, Operation 'Dragoon', the Allied

LAISSEZ-PASSER

Je soussigné, Lieutenant-Colonel THEODORE, du Service du Sabotage
des Communications, des FORCES FRANCAISES DE L'INTERIEUR, demande
aux autorités interessées d'accorder libre passage à:

BREVIN, Antoine, né le 4 Avril 1917

Fait à LYON, le 28 Aout 1944

Theodore.

Lieutenant-Colonel THEODORE

Laissez-passer issued by Tony as 'Lieutenant-Colonel Theodore'
to himself as 'Antoine Brévin', 28 August 1944.

invasion of southern France, commenced. Although the high command
in the Mediterranean was concerned that the undertaking would denude
the Italian front of badly needed troops, the assault had been endorsed by
Churchill, Roosevelt and Stalin at the Tehran Conference. In contrast to the
Normandy invasion, French military units were in the majority (four Free
French divisions to three American) and the amphibious landings between
Toulon and Cannes soon achieved great success against the very indifferent
performance of the German 19th Army's defenders. As the French troops
advanced westwards towards Toulon and Marseille, Lieutenant-General
Alexander Patch's American 7th Army pushed north to Grenoble and up
the Rhône valley. The original Allied plan anticipated that Lyon would
be liberated within three months but matters proved substantially more
promising: 'So thoroughly had the termites of resistance eaten away by now
the pillars that German authority rested on in southern France that the whole
structure crumbled to powder in days.'[12]

Tony's secret correspondence reveals the immense problems confronting
him and his circuit at this time. The constant shortage of money and the complex
arrangements for the supply drops were conducted against a background of
persistent political strife amongst resisters. In a note to Bertholet of 20 August
Tony gave an update on the current state of affairs.[13] He was at the time unable

to move out of Lyon and estimated that the scale of the fighting in the area prevented any chance of his returning to the south-west region of the circuit. Lack of funds continued to worry him. While acknowledging that a little cash had arrived, he bemoaned the fact that the money due to be sent to the 'Paris' DZ had not materialised and pleaded that consignments be included in the next drops. He described (in French) how the political dimension of the resistance was coming to the fore now that victory was in sight, 'Unfortunately we are meeting a great deal of opposition from former army staff officers. The reasons for this opposition are both political and personal. The bulk of FFI officers are reactionary and distrustful.' But the news was not all bad and Tony reported that he had also encountered some decent FFI types and hoped to work alongside them. He urged that with Caza still in the south-west, London send a wireless operator to Gauthier. Tony also related that Louis Pédémas was in hospital. The SRFD man had cracked his head in a bicycle accident and, although the injury was serious, it was hoped that he would make a full recovery. Tony asked Bertholet to formally record that the mishap had befallen Pédémas while on official resistance duty and that, in due course, the FFI should meet the costs of his medical care and convalescence. A post-war account stated 'At the end of August PEDEMAS was found wounded on the edge of a road near LYONS on his way back from a parachute reception, suffering the loss of one eye and a severe shock to his mental faculties. It has never been possible to discover who the aggressor was.' While the injuries were at first assumed to have been meted out by either the Germans, the Milice or even a rival resistance group, there was nevertheless some suspicion amongst members of PIMENTO that perhaps the 'aggressor' was, in truth, a bottle (or bottles) of wine consumed by Pédémas during his travels to outlying detachments of the circuit.

Meanwhile, the situation in the south-west was improving all the time. On 17 August the German High Command conceded that its parlous position was now hopeless, and ordered the evacuation of those Wehrmacht units still stationed in the region. Their intention was to withdraw northwards to form a defence line in conjunction with other formations recoiling from the Allied push out of Normandy. Some garrisons moved precipitously while that of Toulouse only began to pull out at two o'clock in the morning of Saturday the 19th. It did not take long for the local resistance to recognise what was happening and go into action. That same day, units received instructions to seize the towns, maintain order and neutralise German formations. PIMENTO's group in Lavaur was particularly quick to react and took control of the town, arresting officials and collaborators with a minimum of trouble. With scarcely a moment to draw breath, the Lavaur fighters were on their way to Toulouse, responding to Zaksas's request that they assist in the liberation of the city.[14] It was a time of great elation. Serge Ravanel, the commander of the FFI's Region 4 that encompassed the Toulouse area, wrote that the liberation of the city had been achieved at the astoundingly low cost of thirty-five French casualties. In the light of a post-war imperative to assign as much credit as possible to the resistance's contribution to the liberation of France, such a relatively bloodless victory was almost an embarrassment. Most of Toulouse's population had merely stood back, observed the departure of the occupying forces then witnessed the Resistance stepping into the vacuum. But this pragmatic, prosaic succession of events lacked any hint of martial glory so:

> Four days *after* the liberation of the city, the local MLN [Mouvement de Libération Nationale] paper called on the population to build barricades: 'as in 1793 our people must conquer their liberty'. The justification for this 'posthumous' insurrection was that the Germans still were not far away, but symbolic considerations were probably more important: the German evacuation had cheated the population of its insurrection.[15]

Meanwhile, in Lyon the Nazi occupation continued, the atmosphere becoming increasingly threatening as the Franco-German enmities that had built up over four years rose to the surface. It was therefore all the more important to secure good intelligence on counter-resistance operations and Tony managed to acquire a first-rate source. This was Jean-Lucien Feuz, 'Petit Jean', 'a funny little effeminate chap … During the war he played a very useful double role with the Germans, Drives a car like a maniac.'[16] Feuz worked for one of PIMENTO's contacts, Monsieur Ailloud, a Lyon garage owner, and his extra-mural duties included being a driver for the Gestapo when they mounted their frequent raids in the city. Perhaps a pawn or perhaps a pragmatist, Feuz provided intelligence to PIMENTO on his German employers. Tony's men were thereby furnished with the make and registration number of the Gestapo's cars and the radio-direction-finding vehicles that scoured the streets seeking to locate clandestine wireless transmissions. As soon as a raid's destination was announced to the Gestapo team and its French drivers, Feuz would make the excuse that he was out of cigarettes and call in at the tobacconist's opposite the garage. It was no coincidence that the woman serving behind the counter was a member of PIMENTO, and Feuz's intelligence would provide warnings for those in danger. The tip-offs were a great boon to the network's security at a time when the German and Milice forces were becoming ever more jumpy and violent. It was increasingly dangerous to be out on the street for the resistance's violent actions ensured that similarly brutal responses were meted out by the Germans.[17] Reprisals became almost an everyday event. On 19 July 52 prisoners from Montluc were 'executed', on 20 August 120 more were killed and between 17 and 21 August 115 others were massacred at the Bron airfield.[18]

While Tony was still getting over the shock of his arrest and ploughing his way through the complexities of resistance politics in Lyon, another muddle orchestrated by London was taking place in the south-west region of PIMENTO. On the night of 16/17 August 1944 a trio of special forces soldiers was parachuted into France 'to work with PIMENTO (ALPHONSE) in TARN ET GARONNE; to assist in the organisation of F.F.I. and Resistance elements under his control, and to report on the potentialities of his groups.'[19] The three men, Captain David Stern, Aspirant 'J. Le Rocher' (Maurice de Galbert) and Sergeant Donald Gibbs, constituted the 'Jedburgh' team, JOHN. They formed part of a major SOE plan to reinforce F Section circuits around D-Day with teams of specially trained British, French and American soldiers who could provide tactical leadership for the maquis, convey the need to work in concert with Allied strategy and, perhaps most important of all, offer a direct wireless link to the United Kingdom. Overall, the 'Jedburgh' teams made a significant contribution to post-D-Day resistance activity, linking effectively with maquis groups and providing important 'on the ground' assessments of where the Allies' supply resources should best be deployed. But through no fault of its own, JOHN failed to make an impression on the secret war. Not the least of their difficulties was the simple fact that Tony had not received any clear notification of the decision to send them.[20] The astute post-operational report written by Captain Stern offers a clue that the team was sent in haste, 'Briefing was ably handled and no trouble was spared in the effort to do the best possible in the short time available.' However, Stern had little difficulty in identifying the fundamental flaw in the JOHN plan: 'It turned out that whereas the brief stated that we had been asked for by ALPHONSE, ALPHONSE, had in fact asked for instructors to work in civilian clothes in June 1943.' He concluded, 'From this it would seem that it would have been better to have had ALPHONSE's agreement before our departure, or failing this, to have sent us elsewhere.'[21] A consequence of this bizarre decision not to involve the circuit leader in the planning of the 'Jedburgh' team's activity was the selection of its dropping zone. 'Pinocchio' was not a PIMENTO ground and seems a peculiar choice given the abundance of the circuit's DZs in the south-west. The crassness of this error was not lost on Stern: 'Had it [JOHN] arrived at a suitable ground on August 16th, it might have been able to achieve a limited amount of good work.' He implied that he was uncertain where the blame lay, writing that 'Pinocchio' was chosen 'in the brief "by ALPHONSE" and according to ALPHONSE "by London"'. Stern was however sufficiently well informed to comment 'ALPHONSE had suitable and better grounds in this area.'

If the planning for JOHN was bad, the implementation was lamentable. With many arrangements still to be settled ('There was as yet no safe house or letter box available'), Stern and his men valiantly declined the offer to remain in Algiers and opted to press on. En route to their DZ, the American pilot of their aircraft gave them the opportunity of aborting the mission as there was adverse weather ahead but, once again, JOHN elected to proceed. Their pluck was commendable but further difficulties awaited them. Although the bonfires of a DZ were identified, no recognition signal was offered but the pilot then announced that he had spotted the correct letter being flashed from the ground. The team jumped and landed safely although a pannier containing their personal kit dropped without a parachute 'and caused solid objects within, including our carbines, to change shape rather drastically'. The reception committee was pretty incompetent but this setback was nothing to the discovery that the aircraft had delivered them no less than 150 kilometres from their intended location. Undaunted, team JOHN thereafter diligently endeavoured to make contact with Tony or, as time passed, began to settle for locating someone who had even heard of him. The appearance of this small Anglo-French military presence did something to boost the morale of the maquis groups with whom they came in contact. 'At this stage came a short period of embracings, hand shakings and laying of numerous wreathes. The reception which we received as representatives of the British and F.F.I. was unforgettable.' After a week's journey, JOHN arrived in the PIMENTO heartland but 'Searches for ALPHONSE in MONTAUBAN and TOULOUSE were of no avail.' Perhaps some consolation was found when Stern and his men made contact with the SOE agent George Starr and other 'Jedburgh' teams in Toulouse on 25 August. After a week or so trying to make themselves useful in the area by helping to engage the retreating Germans, they returned to Toulouse and on 1 September met Caza. A meeting was arranged with Zaksas but Stern conceded, 'The interview showed that there was nothing left for us to do.' The JOHN report offers a clear indication of rivalries within the Resistance that were later to degenerate into a virtual civil war known as the *Épuration*. Stern wrote that Zaksas 'was trying to form a Batallion [*sic*] as he wished to keep the members of his political group Libérer et Fédérer together. He was very frightened of the F.T.P. [the communist Franc-Tireurs et Partisans] so much so in fact, that when we suggested visiting his Maquis he said that he would not like us to go in our uniform, as certain people might say that his party were mercenaries employed by a foreign power.'

Team JOHN remained in France until October 1944. They had clearly sought to make themselves useful but the abiding retrospective impression is one of futility brought about by bad luck and bad planning. Stern could legitimately claim that some 'of our work though not in accordance with our mission, had certain value and the simple fact of our appearance especially in the first days of the liberation was of definite morale value.' However, JOHN was a failure. Not only had the preparation been inept and their insertion incompetent but Stern felt that the timing was wrong, 'Had we been sent in a month or more earlier we should have been of more value and wasted less of our training.' Long after the war, when Tony heard of the team's story he was incredulous. He could not fathom London's failure to inform him adequately of the decision to drop a 'Jedburgh' and, secondly, asked why they were not sent to one of his own dropping grounds. But the last word must be with the blameless leader of JOHN, 'It is quite evident that team JOHN did none of the things it was intended to do.'[22]

Meanwhile, in the north, after weeks of secret correspondence, Tony, accompanied by Gauthier, finally met Romans-Petit and Heslop.[23] On arrival at the maquis's farmhouse headquarters, Tony was surprised by the degree of military formality present, noting an abundance of clerks, orderlies and staff officers. The arrival of the singularly unassuming young British officer in civilian dress engendered a mixture of mistrust and hostility. Tony found Heslop cordial and professional while Romans-Petit seemed aloof and possessed an elevated view of his own importance. Nevertheless, both sides expressed the desire to resolve their differences. Tony reiterated the statements made in his correspondence, especially emphasising that he did not seek to interfere with Romans-Petit's activities in the Ain. Moreover, he was happy to allot to him all the parachuted stores for which PIMENTO had no pressing need. But, in return, Tony wanted a commitment that there would be no tampering with PIMENTO supplies and, in particular, he needed Romans-Petit to recognise that the explosives and sabotage material required by the 'original addressee' were to be deemed sacrosanct. To Tony's great relief a deal was struck and he emerged with one less headache.

The fighting between the Germans and the Resistance was no longer restricted to the countryside. In Lyon on 24 August 1944 the communist 'Carmagnole' group decided to liberate two prisons near the central railway station. It was not a success; most of the inmates had already been released and German troops fired upon the attackers. The 'Carmagnole' actions nevertheless fanned the embers of revolt in the working-class, communist-dominated district of Villeurbanne and soon crowds were gathering and barricades being constructed in the streets, 'The Carmagnole group found itself at the head of an insurrection that it had not planned. Setting itself up in the town hall, it appealed for help from the Resistance outside the city. No help arrived because the regional FFI leaders felt that the insurrection was premature.'[24] If the FFI representatives outside the city were unwilling or unable to help then Tony, inside the city, with close connections to the working-class resistance groups and no political agenda of his own, was keen to render whatever assistance he could.

Tony's first step was a meeting with leaders of an unspecified communist group who, it can now be assumed, were from the 'Carmagnole'. There was no little risk attached to the contact and he decided that he needed 'back up', choosing for his companion Pierre Moucot, a member of PIMENTO, who was also a police inspector and Villeurbanne resident. This was undoubtedly a wise move as his colleague's attributes proved vital in what was a tense encounter.[25] Nerves jangled on all sides, not least those of the British officer whose later reflection, 'I was a bit apprehensive', belied his conviction that one wrong word could see him taken out and shot as a capitalist intriguer. At the headquarters of the resistance group, an indoor swimming pool in Villeurbanne, Tony outlined his credentials as 'Alphonse', a British officer, and asked how he might help. He soon concluded that the communists viewed him with suspicion both as a foreigner and a resister who was not a member of the Party. Nothing could be done to overcome the communists' reservations about accepting material aid from such a 'tainted' source. The conversation over, the two PIMENTO men emerged from the meeting unscathed, disappointed and rather shaken by the experience. In hindsight, Tony's offer to provide weapons for the Villeurbanne fighters might have proved crucial, for their lack of arms and ammunition (not to say leadership) ensured that, on 26 August, the Germans regained control of the district. Similar setbacks prevailed in the outlying suburbs – Oullins was 'liberated' by the Resistance on the 25th and retaken by the enemy on the 30th.

But the German occupation of the city was drawing to a close. Lyon (like Toulouse) was not to be fought over street by street, and the German commanders finally gave orders for their troops to pull out. While the military exodus continued, the bridges across the Rhône and Saône were left intact but, as the Allied forces approached, the Germans prepared the river crossings for demolition. Wehrmacht engineers mined the bridges one by one and then waited in readiness for the order to destroy them. Fully aware of the irony of such a role reversal, Tony now made attempts to frustrate his enemy's sabotage programme by removing explosive charges from the Pont Pasteur, the last bridge before the confluence of the Rhône and Saône. 'Jean', a junior member of PIMENTO, volunteered to assist Tony and the two young men crawled under the bridge by means of a water pipe and removed connections linking the Germans' explosive charges.[26] Their work completed, Tony and his comrade now had to decide whether to escape by working their way back along the pipe to the riverbank or drop into the water. A combination of fatigue and the slipperiness of the pipe made up their minds for them and, after struggling valiantly to hold on, they had to let go. 'Jean', seemingly a good swimmer, turned in the air and dived into the river. Simultaneously, Tony, who lacked any confidence in water, hung on to the pipe for as long as possible and then, clumsily, dropped feet first. He was delighted to find that the river was sufficiently deep to break his fall but its shallowness did not put his swimming skills to the test and he was able to scramble to the riverbank. Tragically, Tony's good fortune was 'Jean's' undoing; the Frenchman must have struck his head following his dive and he failed to join Tony in the safety of the reeds that grew along the riverbank. 'Jean's' body was found weeks later, miles downstream from the bridge. Sadly, his sacrifice proved purposeless. As Tony watched from his riverside hiding place, he observed German lorries parked on the centres of the bridges and, all too soon, realised that the explosives he had removed were not the only means of demolishing the structure. Suddenly, the vehicles exploded, the central spans of the bridge collapsed and Tony found himself threatened by a shower of masonry. Disconsolately he walked back to the sanctuary of the Customs Offices where he stayed the night. Meanwhile the rest of the Rhône bridges followed the fate of the Pont Pasteur, and that evening those across the Saône were also destroyed.

Tony's encounters with the enemy were not confined to the city. In forays out of Lyon, he used a Citroën car that Rudi Molter had acquired by some dubious means from the German *Sicherheitsdienst*. It still retained its German markings but, when occasion demanded, Tony fixed a Union flag to the bonnet.[27] In an official report he wrote, 'At the end of August I equipped it with two Bren guns, one firing forward through the wind-screen which had been removed with all the other windows and the other firing through the rear window. In this set-up it proved very successful.' Accompanied by Molter, Tony took part in a skirmish with a German armoured car near Les Echets to the north of the city. Although he and his comrade survived the encounter, their vehicle was not so lucky, and Tony admitted, 'Unfortunately this car had to be destroyed by incendiaries after being heavily damaged by one of our own grenades.' This 'friendly fire' mishap came about when Molter threw a 'Gammon' grenade at the enemy vehicle but it bounced off the armour plating and detonated against the Citroën. Further evidence that the liberation would not always prove 'heroic' occurred when Tony encountered a patrol of US armoured cars during another of his ventures out of Lyon. He had earlier spotted a German Panzer IV tank being dug into a defensive position and surmised that it would remain vulnerable to attack until it had been properly sited. Having fortuitously come upon the American combat unit down the road he offered to lead them to a suitable vantage point from which they could direct fire upon the enemy. The briefest reconnaissance was all that the American commander needed to satisfy himself that the target was not sufficiently 'vulnerable' for his unit to attack it and he ordered his vehicles to depart the scene.

More effective liaisons with the main American force converging on Lyon now became a major priority for Tony. He was kept well informed of tactical developments by his numerous contacts both inside and outside the city and consequently predicted that a show of strength by US units would both intimidate the Germans and inspire the Resistance. To this end he made contact on 2 September with an armoured car patrol of the 142nd Regiment under Lieutenant James Crocker that had found its way into the suburb of Villeurbanne but then showed little desire to advance further towards the river and the heart of the city.[28] Ever the optimist, Tony procured a bottle of brandy and set about encouraging the American unit to toast the Allies' success with their new French comrades-in-arms. After a while, the drink took effect and the British agent felt empowered to appeal to the Americans' alcohol-inspired bellicosity and suggest they make a foray towards the Rhône. His exhortation proved successful and the armoured cars advanced to the riverside *quai*, turned right and headed northwards, 'I led this patrol in the morning of 2 September, not at nightfall, along the Cours Emile Zola, Cours Vitton, and the Cours Morand down to the east bank of the Rhône, and then south along the Quai du Général Sarrail and the Quai Victor Augagneur.' Their presence failed to intimidate the Germans and Milice who still held the opposite bank and the appearance of the American vehicles encouraged bursts of ineffective sub-machine gun fire from the other side of the river. This fusillade was mere bravado and the bullets fell harmlessly into the water. But once the crews of the armoured cars recognised that they were being subjected to hostile fire, they responded with their 37mm gun and heavy-calibre machine-guns. Perceiving that the enemy fire had come from the imposing bulk of the ancient municipal building the Hôtel-Dieu (or perhaps this just constituted the best and largest target), the Americans blazed away at the unseen foe across the river. The building soon caught fire and one of Lyon's most treasured civic buildings was all but destroyed.[29]

At dawn on 3 September 1944, units of the Free French army reached the Lyon suburbs of La Pierre-Levée and Oullins and the 1st Battalion of the Foreign Legion took up positions to the north. At the same time, American elements advancing from Grenoble reached Vénissieux and Bron. By ten o'clock the French forces had penetrated to the heart of the city and General Diego Brosset, the commander of the 1st Division, soon took control of the Hôtel de Ville. The victory was marked at noon by a ringing of the city's bells.[30]

Safe-conduct pass issued to Tony by 4 Special Force Unit that was attached to the US 7th Army during operations in and around Lyon at the time of the Liberation.

It must have been a momentous moment for Tony. More than four years after the German army motorcyclists had swept past him as his family fled to Montauban and nearly two years after he had witnessed the Nazi occupation of Lyon, he now saw the Wehrmacht in full retreat. The arrival of the American and Free French forces also marked to some extent the end of his wartime clandestine life. Within days of Lyon's liberation, he reported to Special Forces Unit No. 4, the SOE/OSS liaison team attached to the US 7th Army. His contact was Lieutenant-Colonel Edward Head, the British deputy to Lieutenant-Colonel William Bartlett, the American commander of No 4 SFU.[31] Tony supplied an update on PIMENTO's recent local activities but also furnished the unit with the name and address of Robert Dick as a useful contact when the Allied advance eventually reached the Jura. By a splendid irony, Dick arranged for No. 4 SFU to be billeted at the château of Tony's uncle, thereby at last facilitating the opportunity for Norman Brooks to make an unwitting, belated and minor contribution to the Allied cause.[32]

It might be assumed that the final achievement of Tony's wartime aims would have seen the young man indulge in a well-deserved round of celebrations with his comrades but any such thoughts were rudely halted when he suddenly fell ill. While en route to one of PIMENTO's teams outside Lyon, he was struck down by violent stomach pains. These became so acute that he was incapable of driving and had to take the drastic course of giving Molter – a non-driver – the wheel. Thankfully, they managed to locate a US Army field hospital without mishap. Explaining his predicament to the doctors, Tony was swiftly examined and diagnosed as suffering from duodenal ulcers. There is little doubt that the illness was as much an injury of war, caused by the stresses and strains of the last two years, as the shrapnel from the German grenade that had entered his knee. A painkiller was administered and Tony was transferred to an American hospital in Lyon, from which he emerged after a few days, if not cured, at least able to resume his remaining, somewhat uncertain, obligations to PIMENTO.[33]

Chapter Fifteen
An End and a Beginning

The elation engendered by liberation from the Nazi yoke was for many members of the French Resistance short-lived and quickly replaced by recrimination and persecution. Conflicting political ideologies and personal animosities resulted in fierce disagreements that sometimes degenerated into violent clashes between groups of resistance fighters. Perhaps inevitably, some SOE agents found themselves caught up in this post-liberation backlash. At the very hour of victory, a few of the most senior F Section organisers were rudely dismissed from the country and their local comrades-in-arms left to look to their own fates as seismic internal divisions within newly liberated France overwhelmed the common bonds of resistance to German occupation. In Toulouse, George Starr, whose power and influence as leader of the WHEELWRIGHT circuit had reached substantial proportions, was not prepared to pander to de Gaulle's brittle sensitivities when the Free French leader visited the city in September 1944. At a time when congratulation and mutual respect seemed most appropriate, a heated exchange took place between the two men that led to the British officer concluding his interview with de Gaulle with the less than polite *je vous emmerde* [screw you]'. The Free French leader responded by threatening to have Starr arrested before he accepted assurances that the SOE agent would leave France immediately. A similar fate befell Roger Landes of the ACTOR circuit in Bordeaux, in spite of the conciliatory intervention of Tony's friend and PIMENTO colleague, Gaston Cusin, the recently appointed Commissaire de la République. Meanwhile, Richard Heslop of MARKSMAN, as a result of his close relationship with Romans-Petit, found himself embroiled in factional strife. The latter was arrested by the recently appointed Free French authorities while Heslop 'narrowly escaped imprisonment at the hands of the new men who did not understand who he was.'[1]. In contrast to the travails of these contemporaries, Tony, a man not possessed by a desire either to confront or rub shoulders with the high and mighty, managed to remain in the background.

While other F Section circuits became engaged in argument and recriminations, Tony gradually recovered from his illness and made contact with SOE's rear elements as its staff officers began to arrive in Lyon. Amongst them was Commander Brooks Richards, a naval officer with a distinguished career in clandestine operations. He had participated in secret cross-Channel naval missions, taken part in the Allied invasion of North Africa in November 1942 and from October 1943 commanded an F Section North African offshoot, AMF. After a couple of days in Lyon, Richards received orders to report to Paris and, as Tony also had business there, the two young officers embarked on a journey that took them through dangerous territory where scattered groups of German soldiers were still at liberty and undisciplined bands of resistance fighters engaged in brigandage. Tony's choice of transport, his latest expropriated vehicle, another Citroën saloon car with German number plates and a Union flag arranged over its bonnet, was not the most inconspicuous form of transport. But the two SOE men were armed to the teeth and, although fired upon on one occasion, they completed the otherwise uneventful trip in good time. For Tony the most memorable moment came when Richards asked him where they were. Consulting a map, the driver rather ambiguously indicated somewhere in the middle of France. Richards did not seem in the least disturbed by such uncertainty for he clearly had received the information he was after; they were now sufficiently far north for him to adjudge he was within 'Home Waters' and he set about removing the white cover from his naval cap.[2]

In Paris, Tony called on the new British Ambassador, Duff Cooper. The diplomat had performed the same function with the Free French authorities in North Africa and, with the liberation of metropolitan France, on 13 September 1944 he took up his duties in Paris. Tony's knowledge of the country and, in particular, trade union and socialist circles impressed Cooper and a request was soon made by the Ministry of Labour for his services with a view to a permanent appointment as a labour attaché at the Paris Embassy. At the conclusion of his meeting with the Ambassador, Tony mentioned that he was en route to London and Cooper responded that he should call on Clement Attlee, the Deputy Prime Minister, and Ernest Bevin, the Minister of Labour. This somewhat intimidating proposal proved more than idle chit-chat and Tony duly received letters of introduction to both politicians.

At last, on 25 September 1944, Tony returned to the United Kingdom and to Hope, the wife with whom, due to his SOE and her WAAF commitments, he had spent less than eight weeks of married life. For the previous nine months, Tony's only means of communicating with her had been the few letters and cryptic telegrams forwarded by Bertholet from Switzerland. She had known little of his activities and the all-consuming effort to push PIMENTO towards victory, not to say the personal crises her husband had faced – such as his arrest by the Germans and his recent illness. The rekindling of their relationship was not the only challenge. Once back in England, Tony had to get used to speaking his mother tongue on a daily basis, to wearing army uniform and living in a country that was almost as alien to him as it would have been to a foreigner. His sense of dislocation was further increased when he discovered that F Section was winding down. Its focus was now the transfer of some staff to France where the primary obligation was to liquidate the networks, assist personnel who had suffered hardship as a result of their war service and commence the melancholy task of investigating the fate of captured agents. In the midst of all this disconcerting change and uncertainty, there was at least one source of reassurance: Tony was the recipient of a substantial amount of back pay accumulated during his service in France. Whatever the returned secret agent's problems might be, for the foreseeable future, money was not to be one of them.

Amidst sundry SOE meetings and debriefings in London, Tony submitted Duff Cooper's letters of introduction that resulted in appointments with Attlee and Bevin. While the interview with Attlee was brief and formal, it brought about a treasured opportunity to meet Winston Churchill who called into the Deputy Prime Minister's office to discuss another matter and, consequently, was introduced to Tony. While his acquaintanceship with the nation's foremost leaders was fleeting, the encounter with Bevin was lengthy and convivial being sustained by copious amounts of tea consumed by both parties. Tony emerged from the encounter with a full bladder and the strong impression that the Labour politician and trade unionist was genuinely engaged by the agent's tales of the workers' role in resistance and his assessment of the current state of French politics.[3]

Within a month of his arrival in England, Tony received orders to return to France as part of the JUDEX mission. This was F Section's grand tour of inspection of its former circuits; a not always comfortable mix of investigation, congratulation, commiseration, liquidation and gastronomic indulgence. Buckmaster conceded:

As we proceeded on our course through France, civic receptions multiplied and banquets became more frequent and, despite food shortages, more luxurious. We became hardened to *extempore* public speaking. Indeed, the audiences were far from being critical and welcomed our little convoy with extravagant enthusiasm. Demands for our visit came from all districts and we were very pressed for time on our itinerary. Watch in hand, we made our adieux to one group in order to drive at speed to the *mairie* of the next town, where we knew a large crowd would be awaiting us.[4]

Tony arrived in France on 17 October but it took a while for him to catch up with the mission and, in the PIMENTO leader's absence, 'Rudi' Molter received JUDEX in Lyon on the 24th. Three days later Tony joined the British team to give a report of his wartime activities that included an explanation of the difficulties he had experienced with his subordinate, Gauthier. The JUDEX mission report (perhaps resulting from a disinclination for anything but celebratory matters) records that Tony was 'counselled to go and see CARRE concerning his problems'. Bearing in mind London's failure to grasp the workings of PIMENTO during the war, Tony was not particularly surprised that F Section was found wanting even at this late stage.[5] There were several JUDEX missions to France and, overall, their reports reflect a commendable desire by London head office staff to express their gratitude to the men and women who had made such a vital contribution 'in the field' to F Section's endeavours. However, the accounts of these missions are also suffused with indications that they were, at least for some participants, little more than an engaging excursion for Baker Street office staff. Perhaps as a consequence, Tony felt uncomfortable participating in the forays and restricted his JUDEX contribution to the bare minimum. He did not stay in France with the junket any longer than was necessary and returned to the United Kingdom on 2 November.

Once back in London Tony prepared citations for awards to his comrades-in-arms. In spite of his abhorrence of paperwork, he produced on 10 November 1944 a list of twenty-one recommendations for the award of the Médaille de la Résistance.[6] This exercise constituted the opening shots in a bureaucratic war that Tony ultimately lost: his defeat proving a source of deep and enduring disappointment. He eventually came to the reluctant conclusion that he was more successful in helping to achieve French official recognition of his helpers' deeds than convincing SOE that his comrades' service in PIMENTO merited British decorations. Throughout the war Tony had sent messages to London requesting formal acknowledgement of his followers' bravery and dedication. In spite of these recommendations and his post-facto representations, the members of PIMENTO received a disappointingly meagre number of decorations. A note of 9 August 1946, from an officer handling the residue of SOE's affairs informed Tony that only three of the PIMENTO comrades whose names he had submitted for British recognition were still up for awards. The feeble explanation offered was 'I am afraid that your recommendations must have been shot down by the old Personnel Board'.[7] The three, highly deserving recipients were Auguste Bottemer, Henri Morandat and his brother Roger; Bottemer was to receive a King's Commendation and the Morandats were awarded the King's Medal for Courage in the Cause of Freedom. But even the latter achievement proved something of a hollow victory as the Morandats' medals were attributed to an RF Section proposal that, not unnaturally (given their brother's prominence in Free French circles) but inaccurately, described them as members of SOE's Gaullist section. At least Roger Morandat's citation included a reference to his working 'on the instructions of a British officer'.[8]

Meanwhile the residual F Section bureaucratic processes in London continued and Tony was interviewed by a very experienced F Section staff officer, Major Robert Angelo, about PIMENTO's activities. The result of their deliberations, dated 16 November 1944, was a six-page overview of a network that had operated in enemy territory for more than two years. The apparent inadequacy of this document was not necessarily Angelo's fault; Tony's dislike for paperwork perhaps owed something to its brevity and occasional inaccuracies.[9]

Meanwhile, in France the JUDEX bandwagon was still rolling along and on 23 November 1944 Tony was instructed to proceed by military aircraft for temporary duty with the mission commanded by Colonel 'Benson' (Buckmaster's pretty superfluous *nom de guerre*).[10] He reached Paris by 5 December 1944 and drove to Toulouse via Bourg, Lyon and Chambéry, arriving at his destination on the 11th. It was yet another JUDEX *grande bouffe* with various SOE staff officers and agents including Buckmaster, George Starr (persona grata again) and George Hiller attending with local French dignitaries. Once again, Tony appears to have constituted a somewhat peripheral figure, for analysis of his endeavours and those of his circuit seems to have been of secondary importance to the prevailing social and culinary niceties. At least he did not have to kick his heels for long; an order of 18 December 1944 instructed him to proceed to London 'on or soonest' to 23 December 1944 and he flew back on the 24th from Paris with two other F Section headquarters staff luminaries, Captain Nancy Fraser-Campbell and Mr Ivor Lloyd, on Christmas Eve.

While he was handling the remnants of his F Section responsibilities, Tony was still being considered for the Foreign Office post; his wartime successes, personable character and intimate knowledge of France and the French making him a strong candidate for employment with the Paris Embassy. The bureaucratic process to convert the secret agent into a diplomat/civil servant proved a challenge but a note of 16 December suggests that Tony's audiences with Attlee and Bevin had made some impact. 'BROOKS has been instructed by the Paris Embassy to apply personally to Mr ATTLEE and Mr BEVIN in case of difficulty and it would appear desirable that we should if possible in some way facilitate the desired arrangement.'[11] Duff Cooper seems to have continued to agitate for Tony's appointment to a post in Paris. This was very much in keeping with the Ambassador's unconventional recruitment policy, 'Duff felt happier with non-professional diplomats, finding many of the regular Foreign Office men "dull dogs".'[12] But an impediment to Tony's appointment loomed with the perennial reluctance of government departments to meet staff costs when they hoped that the financial obligation might be vested elsewhere. On 3 January 1945 Lord Selborne, the Minister for Economic Warfare and the politician responsible for SOE, attempted to cut through what he incisively described as 'red tape nonsense'. He minuted to CD, Major-General Sir Colin Gubbins, 'I certainly think it is an S.O.E. job to maintain contacts founded on S.O.E. work in France at the request of the Deputy Prime Minister, the Minister of Labour, & the Foreign Secretary. I want Brooks posted to Paris Embassy at once & retained on S.O.E. books. Please see me personally if there is any further difficulty.'[13] But the barriers of official process triumphed over the wishes of even as influential a figure as Selborne and within twenty-four hours the job had 'fallen through'.[14] An intimation of the talent that the embassy had lost is to be found in reports written by Tony at this time including an assessment of the current state of affairs in France and two political analyses submitted to SOE on 8 February 1945.[15]

Given his outstanding success as the leader of PIMENTO, it might have been expected that Tony would have been considered for further operational duties. Several members of F Section, especially wireless operators such as PIMENTO's Roger Caza, and some veterans of 'Jedburgh' operations in France undertook important work for SOE in South East Asia. But Tony was neither a signaller nor a paramilitary commander of guerrilla units and, in the absence of any recorded explanation of what might have lain behind the decision not to deploy him, these seem the most likely reasons why SOE refrained from using him in the final campaigns against Japan.

Tony was far from idle, however. Once the celebratory preoccupations of the JUDEX missions had retreated, he undertook a practical task that was closer to his talents and interests. He was assigned to a wide-ranging, forensic assessment of SOE's sabotage activities in France and in February 1945 was transferred from the agents' pool to the Evaluation Staff of the Directorate of Research, Development and Supplies (AD/Z). Nevertheless, there still remained some residual PIMENTO obligations and on 1 March 1945, together with Buckmaster, he lunched with Jules Moch, the father of his late comrade-in-arms, André. It was a difficult meeting, for although Moch *père* had come to terms with his son's death, his wife still suffered dreadfully from her loss. However, she had sufficiently recovered her equilibrium a week later to write to Tony thanking him for his glowing testimonies of her son's wartime achievements. Such had been the depth of feeling occasioned by their conversation that Mme Moch was moved to ask if he would *'puisque vous n'avez plus vos parents de nous considérer comme un peu de votre famille, vous qui avez été le frère de combat de notre grand garçon.'*[16] This deeply moving encounter and the painful memories it evoked in Tony made a return to duty something of a relief. On 11 April 1945 Lieutenant-Colonel William Dennis sent him a memo instructing him to proceed to France 'as the representative of the Evaluation staff'. He was to be responsible for 'obtaining as much information as possible from ex agents, representatives of French Government Services and Industrial concerns' to inform the Evaluation Committee. This would entail visiting 'certain factories, and installations to ascertain as far as possible the effect on the enemy's war effort of action taken by agents and the French resistance movement.'[17] He travelled to France the next day, where, together with the distinguished Free French saboteur, Capitaine Pierre Henneguier, he embarked upon a detailed and lengthy investigation of the efficacy of the myriad acts of industrial sabotage carried out in France under SOE's auspices during the occupation.[18] They travelled the length and breadth of the country for the next eight months, their reports offering an analytical commentary on the methods and success of individual attacks, the immense range of the Resistance's operations, the damage inflicted upon industry and communications and the potency of modern sabotage equipment and techniques.[19] For Tony it was a most fulfilling commission, bringing together his first-hand experience of sabotage and his keen interest in the more technical aspects of engineering and explosives. There was a downside; his work with the D/EV Section permitted only sporadic returns to the United Kingdom to see his wife who had been invalided out of the WAAF in March 1945.[20]

While Tony was working in France on the evaluation project, he was obliged to handle a constant stream of correspondence concerning the fortunes of his wartime colleagues. Enquiries ranged from the mundane such as the fate of PIMENTO vehicles to the more pressing, never-ending questions of the bestowal of awards, decorations and pensions. One important case concerned funds to support Paulette Morandat whose husband, Roger, was still missing and believed to be a captive in Germany. There was also the continued need to provide financial assistance to the parents of Dorval and Donoff.[21] Thankfully, a cadre of F Section staff, based at the Hotel Cecil in Paris, were able to assist in these matters. Tony worked with them and, as the occasion demanded, pronounced upon the validity of individual cases – not least because some key PIMENTO figures (especially those from the south-west) were absent on active service with the reconstituted French Army. Regrettably, Tony's SOE duties did not always permit attendance at PIMENTO events either to celebrate or to grieve. On 11 June 1945 he wrote to 'Yvon' Morandat expressing his regrets that he would be unable to participate in gatherings to mark the return of his brother Roger from captivity while Tony's work also prevented him from attending a service in Lyon on 17 June to commemorate the anniversary of Donoff's death.[22]

When the Second World War finally ended in August 1945, almost a year had passed since Tony's endeavours with PIMENTO had come to their triumphant end. Now his wartime feats were to achieve formal recognition and, on 12 September, Vera Atkins, one of the few remaining F Section staff, notified him of the award of the Distinguished Service Order (DSO).[23] Maurice Buckmaster wrote on the 17th, 'I am delighted to hear your long-awaited D.S.O. has come through. All my heartiest congratulations. You have a record which has rarely been beaten in either war for distinction & youth combined.'[24] Tony's French decorations took a little longer to be conferred. A decree of 16 January 1946 signed by de Gaulle (shortly before his resignation from office) announced that Tony had been awarded the Légion d'Honneur and Croix de Guerre.[25]

At the beginning of September 1945 Tony was back in France and on the 19th he attended an 'unofficial' interview at the Embassy as a 'prospective candidate' for an unspecified job. He evidently made a good impression for a note of the meeting stated 'Very conscious of his youth, and of unassuming manner and appearance, this officer nevertheless creates a feeling of confidence, trust and ability, and I think, should the opportunity occur, would be well worth interviewing in London after checking with River.'[26] He spent at least part of the rest of the month in the south-west on his sabotage evaluation survey but was in Lyon on the 30th to attend the ceremonies marking the formal exhumation from a communal grave of the remains of 78 resisters executed by the Germans at the rifle range at La Doua. He

*Cartoon drawn by a friend or colleague of Tony depicting
the award of his DSO by HM King George VI.*

was therefore able personally to honour one of the victims; his friend and comrade-in-arms, Jean Dorval. The civic ceremony took place in the city's main square, the Place Bellecour, in which the coffins were arranged in the form of a Cross of Lorraine. After the religious services and speeches Tony accompanied members of the SRFD and other PIMENTO comrades to the customs office for their own, more intimate ceremony, during which Cusin presented Dorval's younger brother, Yves, with his sibling's posthumous Médaille de la Résistance.[27]

While Tony was pondering joining the Foreign Office, he was also being sounded out for a job in the United States. Peter Masefield was the Civil Air Attaché in Washington and on 13 October 1945 wrote, 'there seems every hope that, if you are interested, I should be able to offer you an appointment here on my Staff as my Diplomatic and Political Assistant dealing expressly with the United States Department of State, the U.S. Civil Aeronautics Administration, Congress, the Senate, and in fact the whole Governmental and Political aspect of the Civil Aviation picture out here.'[28] Rather than being intimidated, Tony found the job description very appealing and promptly replied expressing interest. However, he warned Masefield that he foresaw potential difficulties in that he was not due to sit his examination for the Senior Branch of the Foreign Office until the summer of 1946 and was unlikely to be demobilised until a year later. He had obviously had his fingers burned (not to say his trust damaged) by earlier experiences, and disappointment over the Labour Attaché post at the Paris Embassy still lingered. Moreover, exhibiting a confidence belying his years but not his depth of experience, he was keen that Masefield understood that he was not prepared to be paid a pittance. Clearly tempted by the offer, he needed more details before making his final decision while another factor was that Tony's brother, Peter, had also been offered a position by Masefield. By 7 November his options remained open, writing to Buckmaster that he hoped to continue the residual SOE work 'for some time' but his future employment remained unresolved, 'The moment will naturally arrive when I shall have to pick between this job [Washington] if it comes off, and that of remaining at H.Q., but it is so unlikely that two jobs will turn up that I am not seriously concerned.'[30] Typically, he did not confine himself to these options but was also in touch with the Associated Equipment Company and several other transport firms in the revival of his somewhat bizarre 1943 scheme to establish an agency in France for heavy-goods vehicles.[30] Masefield remained keen to secure Tony's services and on 21 November 1945 wrote clarifying the terms and conditions of the job (a total sum of about £1000 a year made up of salary and allowances) and stated that the Embassy had already begun to process the appointment with the Foreign Office. Tony replied (perhaps inspired by a concern that his formal education had been curtailed by the war) that while the remuneration appeared acceptable, he was less certain than Masefield that he would pass the necessary exams.[31] On 10 December he wrote to his brother, 'I have another offer of a good and interesting job. I am awaiting the final details of each before making up my mind'.[32] In January 1946 he sat the Foreign Office Examination, mentioning in a letter to a school friend that he was still awaiting the result.[33]

During this period of uncertainty about his future career, Tony continued to be beset by requests for help from his wartime colleagues that arrived on an almost daily basis. The favours ranged from the booking of hotels in London to the securing of passports, visas and official accreditation. Eighteen months after the end of the war, never mind the two years since the liberation of France and the conclusion of PIMENTO's activities, Tony's wartime responsibilities still weighed him down. Some old comrades asked for help in securing travel visas for the United Kingdom while others requested his intervention with the French authorities to secure financial assistance or letters of attestation for themselves or the families of fallen comrades. The correspondence was mostly affable in tone, notably with the supplicants showing great solicitude regarding Hope's uncertain health and their entreaties for Tony to return to France on a visit. But a few members of PIMENTO found it difficult to comprehend that their erstwhile leader had a different job (not to say a sick wife) and was therefore unable to replicate his wartime, daily engagement in their lives. Tony conceded that perhaps he was not an assiduous letter writer and therefore failed to meet the necessary output to satisfy his friends, but his surviving papers reveal that his epistolary activity was substantial. He pressed the French authorities for official recognition of his comrades' work and responded to a range of questions from individuals who affirmed they had worked for him.[34] The wartime colleague who seems to have generated the most problems was Woreczyk. Tony received complaints about him from both the French and British authorities, while 'Felix' bombarded him with page after page of scrawled, handwritten letters bemoaning this, that and the other perceived slight regarding his wartime endeavours.

On 6 November Tony wrote to Pédémas mentioning that he was planning to write an account of their wartime exploits – not for publication but as a souvenir for the *'vrais copains'* ('real mates'). He also informed Molter of the project, mentioning that he hoped to obtain photographs of PIMENTO locations including 57, rue Racine, the office in the rue Jarente, Olga's bistro, 38 rue Montesquieu, and damaged bridges and derailments.[35] His life was evidently still very dislocated and on 7 November 1945 he wrote to a Chillon schoolfriend, 'I am at present in London working at my headquarters, but I don't know for how long. The beginning of next year

I hope that Hope will be well enough to come and live with me either in London or somewhere in the suburbs, which will be pleasanter for both of us as living in digs is pretty boring.'[36]

After the war Tony clearly felt an attachment to his two alma maters; Chillon and Felsted. Correspondence with Chillon schoolmates debated the impact that the 'DBs' [Day Boys] had exerted on the pre-war life of the school and he expressed the hope that the school would eventually return to its former 'glory'. He also advocated that Felsted commemorate the wartime sacrifice of his schoolmates, and on 7 November 1945 wrote to the school supporting a memorial for pupils who had lost their lives in the war.[37]

Meanwhile, the list of Tony's career options showed no signs of decreasing. In November 1945 he was invited to become a member of a British youth delegation being sent to the Soviet Union under the auspices of the Anglo-Soviet Youth Friendship Alliance. In a letter to his brother, Tony explained that the 'War Office' had asked him to go on a visit scheduled to last four or five weeks. It is perhaps a little ironic that the well-meaning secretary of the Alliance in her letter to Tony requested 'a full biography of yourself, including education, military service and so forth? This would be for publicity purposes both here and in Russia.' The wisdom of sending a wartime secret agent to represent the British Army in the Soviet Union seems questionable unless there was an official, hidden agenda that has left no trace in Tony's private papers.[38] With an understanding of secrecy that seems rather more advanced than his superiors' (not for the first time), on 22 November 1945 Tony wrote, 'I have come to the conclusion that my personal security would be blown if I went on this mission to Russia to represent the Army in the British Youth Delegation.' He foresaw that the delegates would find themselves in the full glare of publicity (both from the Soviet Union and the United Kingdom) and his proposed cover as a member of the Parachute Regiment or the Devonshire Regiment (with whom he had been billeted in Gibraltar in 1941 and for which he evidently retained affection) was decidedly flimsy. Nevertheless, he stated his willingness to make the trip if wiser heads could come up with a better cover but, if this was not possible, he recommended that an alternative member of SOE be substituted. Officialdom endorsed his proposals and the following day he notified the Anglo-Soviet Youth Friendship Alliance that he would not be participating.[39]

Tony's voluminous personal correspondence throws little light on the process by which Masefield's job in Washington disappeared, neither is the result of Tony's Foreign Office examination evident. But to a certain extent these were now academic. SIS's absorption of SOE saw it welcoming many of the members of this supposedly 'rival' organisation into its ranks and Tony was to be one of them. There is a wonderful irony that, as SOE was closed down and SIS began to take an interest in recruiting members of its 'rival' for post-war work, the same Commander Kenneth Cohen who had spurned Tony after his escape from France in 1941 should have asked SOE for his details. Vera Atkins, one of the few residual F Section staff officers, responded on 12 October 1945 with a paean of praise: 'an exceptionally capable person … excellent security … exceptionally good organiser, a very shrewd judge of character and capable of assuming great responsibility … he is absolutely reliable … he is in fact one of the rare people whom one could recommend for any job as he holds not only a good record in the field but also an excellent record for the office work he has done in the past twelve months.'[40] In the light of such a recommendation and his outstanding wartime achievements, it is little wonder that Tony became one of the SOE personnel to whom SIS offered post-war employment. An official note simply states 'posted to M.I.6. for Special Duties w.e.f. 15.1.1946'.[42] That he was now 'in the fold' is clear from a memo addressed to CSS (Chief of SIS) through DTD (Director Training Department) dated 21 February 1946 referring to a form for conditions of service that Tony had signed. These, sparse documents clearly indicate that he had embarked on a career in the post-war Secret Intelligence Service.[42]

Finally, after so many invitations and regretful declinations, on 9 September 1946, Tony and Hope embarked upon a pilgrimage to the scenes of his wartime triumphs. His wife's account of their motor trip to France offers vivid impressions of PIMENTO personalities and insights into their post-war lives. At the very beginning of their journey, Tony revealed his finely-honed, persuasive skills to good effect. Having declared everything to French customs (apart from 100 contraband cigarettes), he was asked 'Any presents for friends over here?' Hope recorded the ensuing exchange:

> To [Tony] then shot a beautiful line saying 'Yes, I've got coffee and tea for
> the chaps in my maquis.' While this was sinking in he offered the chap

a cigarette. Nothing more was said, and he never opened the door of the car, but retired with the Churchman No.1 [cigarette] wreathed in smiles.[43]

It was soon evident that 'Antoine Brévin' still lurked beneath the surface, 'In a few hours To seems to have changed from a perfectly respectable English Gent into an excited little Frog. The way he eats is quite different from the way he eats at home.' Young, impressionable and unaware of the complexities of Tony's resistance past, Hope's observations are both naïve and clear-sighted. Their tour was to be a long, long way from the elaborate celebrations that had characterised the JUDEX missions. Through Hope's eyes emerges a vivid impression of the bond between Tony and his French comrades. As the couple drove through the French countryside and visited the towns and cities in which Tony had fought his war, members of PIMENTO welcomed them with overwhelming friendliness and generosity. Tables groaned with food and drink and Hope was subjected to a crash course in French gastronomic and epicurean excess. In Lyon she witnessed the emotional impact of Tony's return upon the Combe family noting, 'They were a dear old couple, who had tears in their eyes at the sight of To again.'

The Brookses encountered more than affectionate tributes and Hope reflected on the war's harsh legacy:

> It was on this road that after two years you could still see the devastation of war. In some places there were burnt out German vehicles every few yards on either side of the road, and even in the fields where they had gone to find shelter from the bombing. The Germans must have gone through hell on that road.[44]

But in spite of their hosts' efforts, Hope manifestly felt a degree of isolation. The unity enjoyed by those who had worked together in the clandestine war was something that even the most welcome of outsiders could never fully share. It had nothing to do with age, sex or sharing a common language. To her credit, Hope was not insensitive to the intimacy of her husband's bond with the Frenchmen and women with whom he had experienced so much. This was perhaps most evident in Tony's return to the Citerne farm, the scene of his arrival in France by parachute in July 1942:

We had not warned them of the day of our arrival, though To had written from England to say that we hoped to be in France this Summer. Madame was at home and seemed really excited to see us … Madame went into the yard to call her husband. She has a most wonderful call, which must carry for miles. It was not long before the tall straight figure of Monsieur appeared in the doorway of the kitchen. It was touching to see his expression as he shook hands with To. I have never wanted to have a command of the language so much as I did at that moment. I should so like to have thanked him really properly for all he did for To that night, at the greatest risk to himself and his whole family. The Farmer and To and I went out at once to the field to look at the very spot where To had landed. There was the very tree he had fallen into, and there was the hedge where he had crawled to hide. At luch [sic] the whole scene was clearly put before me. They remember every detail. The old woman sat away from us at the end of the table gazing with wrapt adoration at Tony. She kept speaking to me in a faint quavery old voice of the night when To arrived. 'It was a miracle I say, down he came with all the village to see him, and my son he runs out and brings him here, and we give him rum and coffee. It was a mirical [sic] I say. It was the good God that sent him.' Over and over again she kept muttering this to herself. I really think that she thought To was a Messiah or something … for it was the Good God that sent him! When she talks of it being a mirical, I dont [sic] think she is far wrong. When I think that the whole of St Leonard flung open their windows and pointed to the sky as poor old To came tumbling down, and as I think that it was at just that second that Monsieur Citerne happened to be looking out of the window, and that he happened to be a patriot and a man of quick action, it was a mirical of its own kind. But I am afraid it was only the English that sent him down and not the good God.[45]

The visit was concluded with the suggestion of a photograph: '[The Citernes'] eyes lit up at the idea, and Monsieur at once wanted to shave and change his shirt. To assured him that this was quite uneccassary [sic], but he still insisted of [sic] ducking his head into the bucket of water standing by the well in the yard.'[46]

The demands of Tony's post-war secret duties inhibited the maintenance of close links to his wartime colleagues. His comrades never left his thoughts but opportunities to meet them were limited. But decades after the end of the war and now retired from government service, he returned to France on a few occasions to attend commemorations. These included the unveiling of an F Section Memorial at Valençay in May 1991, and PIMENTO reunions where he met his comrades-in-arms and finally received local honours bestowed by the Toulouse and Lavaur authorities. He also revisited his old haunts in Lyon and the Bourg where he discreetly renewed contact with some remaining PIMENTO veterans. On these occasions the years slipped away, revealing a bond that the passage of time had failed to erode. The Frenchmen and the Englishman, now far from their first flush of youth, did not need to speak of specifics – such as individual sabotage operations or details of reception committees – they were, once again, simply *copains*.*

---

* On several occasions the author was privileged to be present. The decades slipped away while amidst all the conversation and back slapping, much was left unspoken. The outsider could not fail to notice the PIMENTO veterans positively basking in the presence of their returned leader and comrade-in-arms.

Life After PIMENTO

Tony tried very hard after the war to keep a custodial eye over the members of his network, but this proved far from easy as his unconventional government service involved a variety of overseas postings. Later, he seemed reluctant to engage in the increasing formality (and frequency) of Resistance reunions and declined to participate but, in later life, in spite of his increasing physical infirmity, they took on substantial importance for him. The following pen portraits have been compiled from Tony's correspondence, verbal anecdotes and the author's personal knowledge.

'Jean-Marie Alain' – Tony corresponded with 'Alain' after the war, usually via Molter, but the relationship gradually soured. In 1954, an SRFD investigation of 'Alain' revealed that he had dropped his *nom de guerre* and was now Charles Kalis de Frontac. The report suggested that this aristocratic lineage was one of many falsehoods and he was really just Charles Kalis, the son of a post office worker. His misdemeanours may have extended beyond a 'Walter Mitty' dream of a noble ancestry and there were suspicions of his being an embezzler and confidence trickster.[1]

Théo Bernheim – After the war he became a youth worker but no further trace of him is evident in Tony's papers in spite of contact with his relative, Auguste Bottemer.[2]

René Bertholet – He visited Britain in autumn 1944, assisted in mounting operations into the Reich and then participated in a post-war SOE mission to Germany to identify reliable German contacts. As a citizen of a neutral state, the bestowal of a British award or decoration for his war service was problematic but SOE put him up for a Certificate of Commendation.[3] The citation concluded, 'During all this time he gave unstinted support to our work, at great risk to himself and out of purely idealistic motives, namely the social, political and moral well-being of his fellow men, without ever seeking to gain any advantages therefrom for himself.'[4] Bertholet then disappeared from sight but eventually sent Tony a New Year card in December 1949. He became the leader of a socialist commune in Brazil and it was there that he died in 1969.

Raymond Bizot – By April 1946 Bizot's official career had been fully re-established. He was 'Inspecteur Principal' of the Service National de Répression des Fraudes Douanières' at the Ministry of Finance.[5] He subsequently took employment in the petrochemical industry but old habits died hard and, in post-war years, he pursued unofficial, personal investigations into the activities of alleged collaborators including the infamous Joseph Joinovici.[6] Bizot died in 1978 aged eighty. In addition to his numerous French honours, Great Britain awarded him the King's Medal for Courage in the Cause of Freedom in 1948.[7]

Auguste Bottemer – He wrote a frosty letter to Tony in October 1945 berating him for not staying in touch and returned a gift of cigarettes. Tony related this to Bizot, expressing his sadness at the schism and his failure to understand it.[8] Bottemer sent Tony a New Year card in December and their correspondence was renewed until Bottemer died in the 1960s after a '*terrible maladie*'.[9]

Roger Caza – Following his work in France, Caza volunteered to serve with SOE in the Far East. After jungle training he was parachuted into Malaya on 5 August 1945 as part of Operation 'Tideway Green'. It proved a far from pleasant venture: 'It was a nightmarish 85 miles trek in swamps and jungles. We had three days rain. Our boots deteriorated into nothingness. We had blistered feet and Lt. R. M. Caza arrived at destination by sheer courage – his ankles twice their normal size.'[10] With the operation achieving little, less than a fortnight after their arrival the war was over. Caza received an MBE and a Croix de Guerre avec palme from the French for his service with PIMENTO. He corresponded with Tony from Ceylon asking for news and hoped they would meet up on his return to the United Kingdom.[11] Caza later became a press attaché in France of the Canadian Department of External Affairs. He died on 2 May 1971. A selection of his wartime documents, his uniform, medals and wireless set are held by the Canadian War Museum. His widow, Chantal, attended PIMENTO reunions with Tony and Lena Brooks in and around Toulouse in 1990.

Jean Citerne – He continued to farm. After his death in 1975 (aged eighty-six) Tony remained in contact with his family.

Michel Comte – Awarded the King's Medal for Courage in 1948, he continued to run the Garage des Pyrénées where Tony visited him after the war.[12] Comte wrote to Tony in December 1961 concerning his wife's battles with cancer, asking if he could help find treatment; Tony did what he could, but Mme Comte died in 1962. The garage was sold two years later and Comte retired to a seaside home. He died in 1983.

Gabrielle 'Gaby' Cordier – She worked for the Socialist politician Guy Mollet after the war then for the SFIO in Paris. Tony and Lena Brooks met her in Paris in 1954. Cordier corresponded with Tony in December 1983 over an historian's research into Bertholet's life. She died as Mme Gabrielle Boehme-Cordier on 14 December 1986.

Gaston Cusin – Appointed Commissaire de la République at Bordeaux following the liberation, Cusin went on to hold senior government posts in economic and colonial roles. Tony remained in regular contact with him including a visit to his home at Saint-Gingolph in September 1991; Cusin died two years later aged ninety-one.

Lise de Baissac – In 1950 de Baissac married Gustave Villameur and resided in the South of France until her death in March 2004 aged ninety-eight.

Marcel Guerret – He was punished for his role in Pétain's assumption of power but later wrote a treatise that explained and justified his actions. He died on 22 January 1958; a school and a road in Montauban have since been named in his honour.

Odette Laroque – She returned to France at the end of hostilities after incarceration in Ravensbrück concentration camp. Reporting to F Section's team in Paris at the Hotel Cecil on 24 May 1945, she was debriefed and Tony was on hand to assist in her formal accreditation.

Albert Manser – Released from German captivity at the end of hostilities, Manser returned to his trade as a bricklayer. He lived the rest of his life in Kent, dying at Rolveden in 1998 aged seventy-nine. Tony (and the author) attended his funeral.

Jacques Megglé – He returned to France from captivity in Germany on 17 May 1945 but doubts about his conduct resulted in his imprisonment in Toulouse. A military tribunal in 1946 found him innocent by a majority verdict but he nevertheless remained under a cloud of suspicion.

Jean Monier – After the liberation he was appointed to the important position as 'liquidator' of the PIMENTO *réseau*, winding up its affairs (repayments, benevolent obligations, etc.). He resumed his work as 'Régisseur' at the Théâtre du Capitole, Toulouse and maintained a very active role in Resistance old comrades' affairs until his death in 2003 aged ninety-two.

Henri Morandat – He continued to work the family farm and Tony met him on several occasions including in Paris in 1987 for the inauguration of a '*place*' in honour of his brother 'Yvon'.

Roger Morandat – Post-war he worked with his brother in L'Agence Européenne de Presse. Highly decorated by the French, he was initially recommended for an MBE but was eventually awarded the King's Medal for Courage in the Cause of Freeedom as was his brother Henri.[13] He died in 1998.

Léon 'Yvon' Morandat – He pursued a high-profile career in French post-war politics during which he made major contributions to the coal industry and social affairs. He died in 1972 and the 'Place Yvon Morandat' was inaugurated in Paris on 21 February 1987.

Gilbert Zaksas – He served as a Socialist deputy for Haute Garonne from October 1945 to June 1946 and subsequently took up a government post in the French colonies. Zaksas appears to have severed all contact with his Libérer et Fédérer associates and died in Paris in December 1978.

And …

Tony Brooks – One of his first important duties for SIS was as head of station in Sofia, establishing an early British intelligence presence behind the Iron Curtain. On his return to the United Kingdom he brought his remarkable range of skills to benefit SIS's training department. He was divorced from Hope in September 1951, married Elizabeth 'Lena' Erskine in February 1952 and the same year resigned from SIS. He returned to France to join the family plaster works in the Jura but left in 1956 following management disputes. He therefore was available for re-recruitment by SIS in order to participate in the Suez campaign, after which his experience was deployed to great effect in Cyprus as an adviser on counter-terrorist operations. Tony subsequently held various SIS postings abroad and in Britain. He was seconded to MI5 in 1971 as part of a joint section seeking to recruit Soviet intelligence officers stationed in London. Following retirement from government service he pursued a career in various commercial projects. Tony died in London in April 2007. Amongst his many anecdotes was that he took great pride in having voted in post-war French elections as 'Antoine Brévin'.

Parachute Operations

Arranging parachute supply drops was, along with carrying out acts of sabotage, Tony Brooks's primary duty. His network, PIMENTO, would be toothless without the explosives, weapons and ammunition that SOE and the RAF would deliver. Moreover, the drops would include a wide range of other material to ease the life of a resister including money, food, cigarettes, first-aid supplies and even printer's ink.

While Tony's arrival on the night of 1/2 July 1942 was faultlessly achieved by his No. 138 Squadron crew, subsequent flights proved more problematic. It was not until the night of 23/24 November 1942 that Tony and PIMENTO received the first of what was to be more than one hundred supply drops over the next twenty months. Initially the drops were primarily made to the DZs (dropping zones) around Lyon but from the beginning of 1944 greater numbers were devoted to PIMENTO's groups in the south-west. At this time the loads increased too. Throughout 1943 they were usually confined to five or six containers on each operation but from February 1944 reception committees had to be prepared for drops of fifteen containers or more. In the build up to D-Day and during the French Resistance's subsequent open war with the German occupying forces, daylight drops were made and some DZs were designated as 'dump grounds' for aircraft that had failed to locate their designated sites.

Among the other changes occasioned by the evolution of clandestine supply, not all of the operations were conducted by the Special Duties Squadrons, Nos. 138 and 161. Other Bomber Command units based in the United Kingdom were diverted to parachute supply duties while PIMENTO was also serviced in some twenty-seven operations flown by RAF and American USAF aircraft from bases in North Africa.

PIMENTO's reception committees only received one agent – Roger Caza on 5/6 February 1944. Tony's arrival in July 1942 was a 'blind' drop and his return to France in December 1943 was to a STOCKBROKER DZ. Marcus Bloom, who was intended to serve as Tony's wireless operator, arrived by sea in November 1942, while Lise de Baissac, PIMENTO's short-lived courier, was brought to a Lysander landing ground run by another network in April 1944.

Tony's private papers contain many contemporary documents concerning PIMENTO's supply drops, ranging from very detailed listings of DZs through to messages sent to London via Switzerland in which he reported the success or failure of operations. He was justifiably proud of his achievements in coordinating this remarkably complex and demanding facet of his duties as leader of PIMENTO. In the 1990s he prepared a detailed listing of his parachute operations that included confirmation of the primacy of the DZs around Lyon (the Département of the Ain) with seventy-four operations compared to fifteen in the south-west. Hardly surprisingly, Tony did not feel the need to cross-reference his account with RAF records but in the research for *Saboteur* an attempt was made to do so. Regrettably this exercise revealed that the compilation of a definitive list of PIMENTO supply operations would all but impossible and its compilation would add little to an appreciation of Tony's astonishing achievements. By his own calculations, PIMENTO air operations delivered nearly a thousand containers with a total weight of 132,000 kilos of stores.

Tony Brooks's Citations

Citation of the Award of the Military Cross
A/Capt. Anthony Morris BROOKS
(231617) General List

Captain BROOKS went into the field in July 1942. Although the youngest organiser despatched by his section, being now only 20 years of age, his performance has been a model example of superlative efficiency.

On going to the field, he was given one contact only, but, by his quick-wittedness, resourcefulness, and discipline, he has built up an organisation which is the perfect clandestine circuit. His amazing power of command has inspired all with whom he has come in contact with confidence and a supreme faith in his ability as a leader.

He has implemented his orders on long term policy with speed and precision and in addition the group which he leads have the following actions to their credit:

1. 150 kw power plant out of action for three months.
2. 50 ton crane at LYONS out of action for one month.
3. 30 locomotives out of action for one month and five for three months.
4. Destroyed by fire:
    (a) 50,000 litres of ether
    (b) German cables store
    (c) Two tankers of naphthaline
    (d) Twelve tankers of petrol
    (e) Four trucks of resin
    (f) Eight hundred aircraft wings
    (g) One transformer

(h) Machine tools sabotaged in three factories

(i) On 21 Oct 43, 20 armed men held up a lorry conveying prisoners from Gestapo building to Fort Montluc. Twenty-one prisoners liberated, five Gestapo guards killed. Own casualties, two men slightly injured.

Thanks to his own skilful creation and administration of his circuit, Captain BROOKS has remained in action in the field for fourteen months. The average period in action without arrest or enforced withdrawal for an officer fulfilling a similar role is six months. This lengthy period of work under conditions of great strain and hardship and in constant danger of arrest by the Gestapo is all the more remarkable as Captain BROOKS does not enjoy good health. I most emphatically recommend that he be awarded the Military Cross.

Citation for the Award of the DSO
Major Anthony Morris BROOKS
(231617) General List

In December 1943, Major BROOKS was parachuted into FRANCE for resistance work in collaboration with members of the French Trades Unions and to prepare concerted action for D-day and post D-day activities. The nature of his circuit made his organisation the most widely scattered in FRANCE with groups working in many areas.

In order to control all these groups, Major BROOKS was continually travelling, thus risking the danger of arrest. His main connections were with the French railway workers. Among them he formed and trained grease-gun crews, railway cutting crews and stores distributing crews.

These crews were responsible for rail sabotage on a large scale. Many of the attacks were led by him personally and by great courage and technical ability he inflicted many severe blows on the enemy's rail communications.

Cranes were also destroyed and altogether 107 locomotives were put out of action. By his sabotage work, Major BROOKS forced the Germans to use the roads, and when German convoys moved along the highways he continued to attack them by laying ambushes. As the U.S. 7th Army approached LYON he intensified these attacks on German transport and at the same time, organised and carried out telephone cuts around LYON and BOURG. He led the first American tank patrol into LYON.

In the execution of his work he received 70 successful parachute operations. Although these operations were scattered over a large area, the committees trained by Major BROOKS were most reliable, and receptions were always well-organised. He never spared himself, and never hesitated to carry out a reception himself in order to experiment in the type of method most suitable. It was his personal contact which gave unity and cohesion to his groups and which made possible concerted action on D-day.

Notes

Chapter One: An Unusual Childhood

1. I am indebted to Christopher Dawkins of Felsted School for supplementing Tony's recollections with details from school records.

Chapter Two: 'This Country is at War'

1. *The Times*, obituary of Peter Brooks, 3 February 1996.

2. Lelette Mornand continued to work in Lons-le-Saunier until, after her marriage in January 1942, she moved to Dijon where, Tony wrote, he visited her and she agreed to help him with PIMENTO ('Narrative', p. 29). He later stated that she had been a member of an escape line assisting Allied servicemen to evade capture, with her uncle's hotel, Le Chapeau Rouge, being an important staging post for the fugitives.

3. Unfortunately, entries in Tony's pocket diary for 1940 only commence on 9 May and no record of his movements for the first months of the year is available.

4. Paxton, *Vichy France*, p. 13.

5. Ousby, *Occupation. The Ordeal of France*, p. 46.

6. This was a patented system by which motor vehicles were fuelled by gases generated by burning charcoal or coal, which were cheaper and more available than petrol or diesel.

7. Registration document is amongst AMB Papers.

8. Hirschfeld was later reinstated in his post but not for long. Four other officers of the Senate denounced him as a Jew ineligible to exercise public service as a result of anti-Semitic legislation.

9. Tony kept the postcard, and his diary for 3 July states, 'Uncle and Mr Guerret went in Citroën to Vichy and Clermont-Ferrand.' Guerret's apparent apostasy (and not a little post-war settling of old scores) was to earn him exclusion from the Socialist Party and led to his abandoning political office for the rest of his life. www.assemblee-nationale.

10. Adant, *René Bertholet*, offers the most reliable source on his career.

11. Letter from Manser to Tony, 11 May 1966. AMB Papers There is no contemporaneous mention in Tony's diary of their meeting. This can be interpreted as an early example of his security-mindedness or perhaps a reflection of his amorous preoccupation with Colette Hirschfeld that comprises most of the diary's cryptic entries. Intriguingly, much later, on 2 and 25 December he records receipt of letters 'from Albert'.

12. Manser reached Foix but was apprehended by French gendarmes as he tried to cross the frontier. He was interned near Marseille and Grenoble, then, on the German occupation of Vichy France, he was transferred to prisoner-of-war camps in Italy and Germany. At the end of hostilities, he returned to Kent and, in 1966, contacted Tony following the publication of Foot, *SOE in France*. The two men remained in touch until Manser's death in 1998. This account of Manser's experiences is based upon

tape recordings of his reminiscences, his correspondence with Tony and the latter's recollections.

13. Chilver's charge, William Simpson, described their journey in his memoir, *I Burned My Fingers*. Coincidentally Simpson later joined SOE's planning staff in Baker Street while Chilver became a member of its Training Section specialising in testing students' cover stories. HS9/307/3.

14. A photograph of Caskie, reproduced in this book, inscribed by Tony 'Photo taken at Marseille in May of the Padre' is amongst the latter's papers.

15. Caskie, *The Tartan Pimpernel*, p. 35. Albert Manser briefly encountered Caskie during his adventures after leaving Tony.

16. Foot, *MI9*, pp. 65–6.

17. Neave, *Saturday at M.I.9*, p. 78.

18. AMB Papers.

Chapter Three: A Walk in the Mountains

1. 'My trip from Proby to Goldsmiths', a typescript account of this period (May to October 1941) written by Tony in October 1941 was discovered in September 2010 amongst his papers and, along with interviews, forms the basis of this account.

2. Nouveau worked on the escape lines until arrested by the Germans in January 1943. He survived Buchenwald concentration camp and returned to Marseille. In *Saturday at M.I.9*, Airey Neave described Nouveau as 'witty and uncomplaining, a magnificent and a great Frenchman' (p. 122). After the war the British authorities awarded him the George Medal. Disappointingly, there is no mention of Tony in Nouveau's memoirs, *Des Capitaines par Milliers*, but it is a record of the servicemen he assisted rather than his escape-line colleagues.

3. Murphy, *Turncoat*, p. 73.

4. Ibid., p. 76.

5. Cole's MI5 file is in the National Archives at KV2/15, while *Turncoat*

offers the best published account of his life.

6. Cole's subsequent activities saw him plumb even deeper depths of treachery. His collaboration with the Germans led to the deaths of some fifty resisters and the incarceration in concentration camps of three times that number. He was finally killed in a shootout with French police in Paris in 1946.

7. 'My trip from Proby', p. 4.

8. Ibid, p. 3.

9. Ibid, p. 4.

10. Ibid., p. 4 The sixth member did not feature in Tony's recollections.

11. Ibid, p. 5. Tony's report states that the group simply divided into two on setting out but contact between the parties was soon lost. His later recollections have been cited here as there must be a suspicion that in his contemporary account he was in some way reluctant to concede that as the leader he had 'failed' to keep the group together.

12. Tony's near contemporary account of his arrest is prosaic and his record of the time he took to complete the journey into Spain is far from clear. He affirmed that the arrest took place at 10.30 on the evening of the 17th but failed to include the colourful details of the Spanish official's amorous preoccupations. The description here is one Tony gave in his later life.

13. 'My trip from Proby', p. 6.

14. Instone, *Freedom the Spur*, pp. 242–3.

15. 'My trip from Proby', p. 11.

16. Confirmation of Darke's identity can be found in www.conscript-heroes.com and Clutton-Brock, *RAF Evaders*, p. 68.

17. Instone, *Freedom the Spur*, p. 247.

18. 'My trip from Proby', p. 11.

19. Ibid.

20. 'My trip from Proby', p. 12. A fellow Miranda inmate, Bob Sheppard, offers an account (*Missions secrètes et Déportation 1939–1945*) at variance with Tony's recollections of events. In addition to claiming that he shared

a furlough from the camp to visit the village of Miranda with Tony, he states they were released at the same time, and describes a train journey to Madrid, followed by a breakfast at the Madrid Embassy. He also maintains that he was a member of the party that accompanied Tony to Gibraltar. This account is neither reflected in Tony's 1941 report nor his later recollections.

21. Billeting details from 'My trip from Proby', p. 16. Tony was clearly proud of this sojourn with the British Army and when completing an official form in later years even claimed that he had been 'seconded' to the regiment.

22. 'Subject A. M. BROOKS', 26 August 1941. Information supplied by the SOE Adviser. Another list of helpers compiled by Tony gives addresses in Lyon, Paris, Marseille, Perpignan, Arbois and Besançon. In January 1942 Bigay met Tony while he was making contacts for his network at Lons-le-Saunier. She offered to help him but when he asked if the factory's trucks might move explosives, she refused, explaining traces to her 'would be suicide'. He refrained from informing her that his former workmates, Bouillet and Jeunet, had been transporting sabotage material for several months. 'Narrative', p. 30.

23. Note, 14 September 1941. Information supplied by the SOE Adviser. During the war SIS only sent a few British citizens to France to serve undercover as Frenchmen; these agents were older than Tony and tended to fulfil specialist roles such as wireless operators. Details of Cohen's SIS career are to be found in Jeffery, MI6.

24. The convoy appears to have consisted of the light cruiser Edinburgh and the destroyers Cossack, Zulu, Piorun and Garland with the City of Durban as the other merchant ship. www.naval-history.net This reference states, however, that it left Gibraltar on 2 October.

25. Early in 1941, the warships slipped through the British blockade and made a foray into the Atlantic where they sank 22 merchantmen before finding sanctuary at Brest in March. Thereafter, there was acute British apprehension of the German raiders launching another breakout, but they remained in the French port until March 1942.

Chapter Four: 'We'll be in Touch'

1. Curry, The Security Service 1908–1945, p. 396

2. Note for Captain Guy Liddell, 18 October 1941. Information supplied by the SOE Adviser.

3. Langley, Fight Another Day, p. 129

4. Tony's November 1941 personal report reveals a reason for his criticisms of Garrow – the latter's dilatoriness over the scheme to rescue the RAF airmen from a Marseille hospital. Minute 'Anthony Morris BROOKS', 30 October 1941. Information supplied by the SOE Adviser.

5. AMB Papers. The RAF's interest in Tony may have been reinforced by his having taken photographs of aircraft that he entrusted to his former girlfriend Lelette Mornand in Lons-le-Saunier, in May 1941, employing on the package the false name, 'François Bertrand' that had been given him by Capitaine Faure.

6. Minute 'Anthony Morris BROOKS', 30 October 1941. Information supplied by the SOE Adviser.

7. 'My trip from Proby', 16 November 1941.

8. Information supplied by the SOE Adviser.

9. Tony's Identity Card was stamped 'attested' Euston Combined Recruiting Centre. AMB Papers. This recruitment was to generate a considerable amount of bureaucratic correspondence between the Air Ministry and SOE and it was not until 8 April 1942 that Tony's RAF 'service' was officially terminated.

10. Bob Sheppard, Tony's fellow inmate in Miranda de Ebro, does not appear to have encountered similar difficulties. In

his memoir he states he was finishing the second phase of training when he learnt of the attack on Pearl Harbor (7 December 1941). However, Yarnold, *Wanborough Manor*, p. 48 indicates that he had begun the first phase of his training on 3 December.

11. Buckmaster, *They Fought Alone*, pp. 56–7.

12. Foot, *SOE in France*, p. 179. Buckmaster's Personal File is at HS9/232/8. It records both praise and criticism of him as head of F Section and confirms Buckmaster's comment to the author that Gubbins was no great admirer.

13. Foot, *SOE in France* p. 522.

14. Mackenzie, *The Secret History of SOE*, p. 226. Such niceties were in marked contrast to the tragic and violent Anglo-French struggles in Vichy-held colonial territories, see Smith, *England's Last War Against France*.

15. Buckmaster, *Specially Employed*, p. 167. Unusually, Buckmaster's memoirs are accurate concerning Tony's RAF connections. He was enlisted on 26 November 1941 and placed on deferred service the following day. No note of a meeting between the two men at this time features in Buckmaster's diary.

16. Amongst the many casualties of the official destruction of SOE's records are its training files. Lists of the complements of each party have not survived and, short of scrutinising every Personal File (such a mammoth task would founder on the incompleteness of the files), the training group lists cannot be fully reconstituted. The prefix '27' was a carryover from SIS's numerical designation for France.

17. Coppin's Personal File, HS9/350/9. Coppin's membership of 27L was only confirmed after Tony's death.

18. Flower's Personal File HS9/522/5, and Tony's recollections.

19. A possible candidate amongst the dozens of Evanses who served in SOE is Jack Etienne Olivier Evans but a personal file for him has not survived. Another is Raymond Jack William Couraud who served in SOE under the cover name Raymond 'Lee' although he does not completely fit Tony's description of 'Evans'. Couraud's rejection due to youthfulness is thrown into question by his being eight years older than Tony. However, the former underwent SOE training for F Section at about the same time as 27L and later took part in the St Nazaire raid. By a remarkable coincidence he arrived in England on the same ship as Tony, the SS *Leinster*. Couraud's extraordinary wartime experiences are too complex to describe here but if he was 'Josephine' he is another addition to the remarkable gallery of colourful and dangerous characters that Tony encountered during the war years. HS9/1647.

20. HS9/865/7. Tony's recollection was that 'Maurice' was highly strung and talked in his sleep (in English) and this was considered enough to render him unsuitable for further training. This was clearly one of the rare occasions when Tony's memory let him down. Krumhorn was sent on a mission to France but only got as far as Gibraltar when it was aborted. Back in England he showed a lamentable sense of security, left SOE in February 1943 and was convicted of living off immoral earnings in June 1944.

21. Stonehouse Personal File, HS9/1419/8. Yarnold in *Wanborough Manor* erroneously states that one of the 27L students was Robert Boiteux. After training with an earlier party, 27G, he served with distinction on two missions to France.

22. Bisset's correspondence is held by the Imperial War Museum. I am grateful to Mrs Winifred Bisset Rigg for her recollections of this period.

23. 'Preliminary Report', 21 January 1942. Information supplied by the SOE Adviser.

24. Ibid.
25. The times are confused. Bisset wrote from Surrey on the 22nd but his next letter is postmarked 5 p.m. 23rd and dated 23rd, but, in the text, he stated that they had arrived at six o'clock that morning instead of at 9.50 'yesterday' i.e. 22nd, when he was still in Wanborough. To further confuse matters, Tony recalled that after Wanborough he had gone to Goldsmiths and spent time at the Norfolk Hotel in London before going to Scotland.
26. Coppin's SOE Personal File offers no amplification of Tony's recollections of the high-wire act and restricts itself to broadly complimentary comments on his character, 'Extremely keen on Demolitions and any form of training requiring physical effort'. TNA HS9/350/9.
27. 'Para-Military Report', 14 February 1942. Information supplied by the SOE Adviser.
28. List of training drops drawn up by Tony after the war. His source is not known but the details are very precise. AMB Papers.
29. HS9/350/9. Krumhorn is not mentioned perhaps because he only completed one parachute descent.
30. HS9/1419/8.
31. HS/16.
32. HS 7/51.
33. 'Finishing Report', 6 April 1942. Information supplied by the SOE Adviser. Woolrych had served with British Intelligence in the First World War; an account of these activities can be found in Morgan, *The Secrets of Rue St Roch*.

Chapter Five: 'For Christ's Sake Let's Get Going'

1. Dansey had a particular interest in Switzerland and acted as SIS's senior liaison officer with SOE. At this time he saw most of the latter's wireless traffic. See Foot, *SOE in the Low Countries*, p. 36.
2. Memo from AD/X to D/R 18 March 1942. Information supplied by the SOE Adviser.
3. McCaffery Papers, April 1942.
4. Ibid. Buckmaster's diary does not include any mention of meetings with Tony at this time. This does not mean that they did not take place but rather that they were perhaps deemed of insufficient importance to be noted.
5. Pimlott, *Hugh Dalton*, p. 318.
6. Robin Brook became a highly influential SOE staff officer handling European affairs. He affirmed to the author that he was a great admirer of Tony's wartime feats, and the two men remained in touch until Brook's death in 1998.
7. Foot, *SOE in France*, p. 178.
8. Bourne-Paterson had joined SOE in February 1941. An accountant and fluent French speaker, at the time of his appearance in Tony's story he was a civilian for he was not commissioned until December 1942.
9. Buckmaster, *Specially Employed*, p. 168. It will not be a surprise that Buckmaster's recollections do not correspond with Tony's who had never attended a university lecture. The other agent could not have been the celebrated Michael Trotobas, for he did not return to England from his first mission to France until the autumn.
10. Howe, *The Black Game*, p. 87.
11. It is likely that Tony received another briefing from SOE's political warfare expert, John Hackett.
12. 'Finishing Report', 19 May 1942. Information supplied by the SOE Adviser.
13. An account of its early days is provided in Kim Philby's, *My Silent War*, although the Soviet spy and most of the other original staff were long gone by the spring of 1942.
14. Foot, *SOE in France*, p. 57. Rheam's SOE Personal File is at HS9/1250/7. A civilian instructor, William Blackden, made a favourable impression on Tony. HS9/160/5.

15. 'Finishing Report', 19 May 1942. Information supplied by the SOE Adviser.

16. Buckmaster, *Specially Employed*, p. 167.

17. Jackson, *France: The Dark Years*, pp. 219–220.

18. AMB Papers. The argument was sound but his youthful appearance rendered a cover story that he was in his mid-twenties of doubtful veracity. Moreover, he possessed no experience of soldiering in the French Army. His forged demobilisation certificate is among his papers.

19. F Section circuits were eventually given the names of professions but its early networks, such as Tony's, enjoyed more eclectic inspiration. Buckmaster's diary simply records that he met with 'Theodore' on 31 May, while SOE records reveal that both this name and 'Alphonse' were employed throughout Tony's service.

20. Telegram from Berne, 12 May 1942. Information supplied by the SOE Adviser. Henry Hauck was an academic, socialist, trades unionist and Free French official based in London.

21. Telegram to Berne 19 June 1942. Information supplied by the SOE Adviser.

22. Sainsbury (ed.), *The F Section Memorial*, p. 10, and his Personal File HS9/350/9.

23. Foot, *SOE in France*, p. 196.

24. King, *'Jacqueline'*, p. 242. Perhaps as a consequence of this infighting and his undistinguished performance, Flower was brought back to England on 17/18 March 1943. He remained on SOE's staff for the rest of the war in its Training and RF sections. HS/9/522/5.

25. Sheppard, *Missions secrètes et Déportation*, pp. 234–40.

26. Interrogation Report in Bloch's Personal File, HS9/165/8. She suffered an even worse fate than Stonehouse and was killed at Ravensbrück concentration camp in 1945. Some of Stonehouse's astonishing adventures are recorded at HS9/1419/8 while he personally related some of his experiences to the author. A brief narrative of Stonehouse's SOE career is to be found in Sharf, *Brian Stonehouse*.

27. In Cambridge, Tony and Hope met Vivian Collum, an old Felsted schoolmate. After the war Tony wrote to him mentioning the chance encounter. AMB Papers.

Chapter Six: 'Je Veux Voir Monsieur Pierre'

1. This aircraft had been in service with the squadron for a little over six months and in December 1941 had been flown by Flight Lieutenant Ron Hockey to drop agents in Czechoslovakia who carried out one of SOE's most controversial operations, the assassination of Reinhard Heydrich. Walczak was killed in a flying accident in February 1945.

2. AIR 20/8458.

3. AIR 27/956.

4. Corby's unpublished 'Memoirs', p.109. A description of the A Type and an illustration of the configuration of the parachute on board the aircraft is at HS7/14.

5. The aircraft made a safe return to Tempsford at 5.10 a.m. on 2 July. AIR 20/956.

6. 'Narrative', p. 1.

7. 'Narrative', p. 2.

8. 'Narrative', p. 2 and Tony's oral testimony of the circumstances of his arrival.

9. 'Narrative' p. 3. While Tony later stated that he stayed only one night, his injuries and the freshness of his recollections in this near contemporaneous document suggest that he most likely stayed for a few days. In a formal SOE interview more than two years after the event the period had stretched to 'about six days'. HS6/567.

10. The technique of dropping agents 'blind' later became a method of handling networks suspected of being compromised. Of the ninety-one F Section agents commemorated on the

Valençay memorial, eighteen were captured on landing.

11. Tony later arranged for a postcard to be sent to the Citernes from Aix-les-Bains informing them that he was well and at liberty. Subsequently, he requested that the BBC transmit a message, in suitably guarded terms, informing Citerne that the agent had returned to the United Kingdom. In 1993 Tony and Lena Brooks visited René Citerne who still possessed some of Tony's equipment. Perquin, *Clandestine Parachute and Pick-Up Operations*, Volume 1.

12. De Vomécourt, *Who Lived to See the Day*, pp. 31–2.

13. 'Narrative', p. 3.

14. Tony did not mention de Vomécourt in his own post-war narrative either.

15. Subsequent events confirmed the wisdom of Tony's decision not to discuss his affairs with de Vomécourt. A report sent to London by another F Section agent, Lieutenant Ben Cowburn, of 9 July 1942 stated, 'Teodore [Tony] landed blind in a village near Gauthier's [de Vomécourt] residence. All the village turned out to watch and one person was heard by Teodore himself as he floated down to say: "Ca doit être encore un Juif que les Anglais nous envoient." In case you have not already been advised, Teodore was able to tear off his harness and hide motionless a few feet away while some of the village people purposely miss-directed the hurrying gendarmes. Teodore got in touch with Gauthier and went away on his travels and we believe he is ok.' This tittle-tattle continued, for in a report of 28 October 1942, Cowburn stated (erroneously) that Tony's aircraft had 'circled 13 times' before dropping him. HS9/1651. Yet another wireless operator, DIVIDEND, on 9 July 1942 reported Tony's arrival, HS7/244 p. 31.

16. Tony recalled it as one night but wrote soon after the war that it was two. 'Narrative', p. 3.

17. HS6/423 Interrogation of de Vomécourt in London, 8 March 1944, p. 5.

18. Narrative', p. 3 *The Great Waltz* is an American 1938 'biographical' film about the composer Johann Strauss II.

19. Although Tony's journey passed without incident, there were real perils attached to moving around the Unoccupied Zone. Six weeks later, another F Section agent, Richard Heslop, was arrested at Limoges station.

20. Cubero, *La Résistance à Toulouse et dans la Région 4*, p. 23.

21. Ibid.

22. HS6/1005.

23. Mackenzie, *The Secret History of SOE*, pp. 691–2. Bertholet was described by his SOE controller in Switzerland as 'the most hopeful person in our field whom I have come across'. HS6/1005.

24. SOE had to protect its agent from the envious approaches of the Americans. A telegram from London to Berne on 21 May 1942 stated 'United States SO organisation having seen reports from Robert thought he would be useful man. They telegraphed their Legation Bern suggesting he should be sent to America. We have telegraphed our people New York to tell them to lay off. Try convey similar request to their man at Bern.' Information supplied by the SOE Adviser.

25. It cannot be claimed with any certainty that all of Bertholet's numerous clandestine contacts have been traced. The US National Archives reveal his OSS connections, NARA RG226; E194; Box 93 Fold 404. I am indebted to Jacques Baynac for this reference. SOE records reveal Bertholet met Allen Dulles, the OSS representative in Switzerland, in November 1942. HS7/262. He was also involved in helping the Centre Américain de Secours to smuggle refugees into Switzerland, Sullivan, *Villa Air-Bel*, pp. 407–8.

26. HS6/1005.

27. Telegram from SOE for JQ, 12 November 1941. Information supplied by the SOE Adviser.
28. 'Narrative', p. 4.
29. Ibid. In a letter written in 1984 by Perret to Bertholet's biographer she stated she only saw him occasionally and briefly during the war and did not allude to the personal relationship claimed by Tony. AMB Papers.
30. AMB Papers. During extensive interviews for this book, Tony never commented upon the telegrams he sent to Hope. A more formal and anodyne notification of his safe arrival was sent to her on 5 August 1942 when F Section wrote, 'Lieutenant Brooks requested that news of him might be sent to you from time to time. I am very pleased to be able to inform you of his safe arrival at his destination and that he is in excellent health and spirits.' During his return to England in 1943 Tony informed Hope, 'Your first letters, i.e. up to 23.5.41 are in my room at Proby. So are some letters from Rhona, my nurse at Felsted. Your letters during 1942 and '43 are either in my room, in my suit-case at 3, Chemin du Panorama, Caluire, or at Montauban at Michel's.' For someone who throughout his professional career in secret service was considered to be obsessive about operational security, these revelations constitute noteworthy indications of human fallibility.
31. 'Narrative', p. 6.
32. Péan. *Vies et Morts de Jean Moulin*, p. 151.
33. A eulogy in 'Ceux de la Résistance' among the AMB Papers states Dorval had worked for the intelligence branch of the resistance movement 'Libération' in Paris from its formation until his forced departure for Lyon in June 1942. A letter from Tony to Bizot of 6 December 1946 gives Dorval's departure from Paris as 30 June 1942 with a mention of the *réseau* AJAX. AMB Papers. *Les Fusillés (1940–1944)* (Pennetier et al.) states he was a member

of the 'Johnny' and 'Adolphe' networks, but the entry is littered with errors.
34. Léon Morandat was a close associate of Bertholet's who, in addition to arranging for the transmission of the report to London, had lent the Frenchman 50,000 francs in the spring of 1942. Telegram Berne to London, 18 March 1942. Information supplied by the SOE Adviser. Morandat played no further part in Tony's war but continued to work in the Free French cause. He left France on the night of 17/18 November 1942 by a clandestine RAF pick-up and was brought back to England. On his return, SOE noted, 'Yvon has been in touch with ALPHONSE and has left his brother and others to continue working with him.' HS8/233. Morandat later became the youngest member of the Assemblée Consultative Provisoire d'Alger. In January 1944 he was parachuted back to France where he served as a deputy of Alexandre Parodi, the délégué general of the Provisional French Government.
35. This had been acquired through the auspices of Abbé Glasberg, a leading light of l'Amitié Chrétienne, a charitable organisation that was involved in securing safe refuges for victims of Vichy and German oppression.
36. 'Narrative', p. 6
37. Ibid.
38. Goubet and Debauges, *Histoire de la Résistance dans la Haute-Garonne*, p. 29, and Jackson, *France the Dark Years 1940–1944*, p. 439.
39. If Tony felt that Guerret was not the man for PIMENTO, the politician nevertheless seems to have engaged in some political aspects of resistance notably with the organisations 'Libération' and 'Combat'. See www.assemblee-nationale for details.
40. 'Narrative', p. 7.
41. F Section War Diary, HS7/244.
42. Cowburn's messages announcing Tony's arrival have already been mentioned in note 15.

43. 'Narrative', p. 7. An SOE report by Tony written on 16 November 1944 states that she was recruited in February 1943. Such inconsistencies render attempts at a definitive narrative decidedly problematic.

44. 'Narrative', p. 8.

45. An indication of the challenges inherent in creating an accurate chronology of a clandestine network is Tony's claim in a 'Draft Report' on PIMENTO of 11 January 1945 that he did not contact Comte until September 1942. AMB Papers.

46. Tony's 'Narrative', p. 25, an Imperial War Museum oral history recording, and a photograph he took on a visit to Lyon of the address.

47. The citation for his British decoration stated that he was an escaped prisoner-of-war. It is not without inaccuracies and states RF Section as the sponsor. HS8/394.

48. 'Narrative', p. 9.

49. Ibid., p. 10.

50. Ibid., p. 11.

51. Message 21 July 1942. HS7/244.

52. Enthusiasm seems to have outstripped numbers and one source affirms 'it only had nine members at the end of the 1942', 'Action and Ideology of "Libérer et Fédérer"', p.10. One of this handful was Jean Monier, a council employee, who after November 1942 became a pillar of PIMENTO in Toulouse during the war and oversaw its residual post-war affairs.

53. 'Narrative', p. 12. The group's lack of martial competence was exemplified by a request that Tony advise them what to do with a meagre store of explosives that had remained untouched for a year in a sepulchre in a Toulouse cemetery.

54. Figarol wrote a post-war account of his resistance activities (*Pour ne pas oublier*). The number of inaccuracies identified by Tony renders it an interesting evocation of the time rather than a reliable description of PIMENTO's work. For example, Figarol states that

he was introduced to Tony in April 1943 (p. 60) while an SOE report by Tony dated 12 January 1945 affirms Figarol 'Has worked with me since July 1942'. This latter document formed part of Tony's advocacy of a British decoration for Figarol – realised in 1948 with the award of a King's Medal for Courage in the Cause of Freedom. The Frenchman was evidently proud of this recognition and four pages of his book are devoted to reproductions of documents relating to it.

Chapter Seven: PIMENTO's First Steps

1. War Diary of F Section p. 9 HS7/244.

2. Foot, *SOE in France*, p. 210. If Tony faded out of the picture regarding Jouhaux, Bertholet did not. On 19 November 1942 Berne informed London 'that ROBERT had been asked to visit JOUHAUX who was at Cahors and had done so'. Bertholet advocated that the Frenchman should be brought out of France but SOE argued that the occupation of the Southern Zone had rendered this impracticable. The Swiss agent was dissatisfied by this response and still affirmed that Jouhaux should be exfiltrated or, failing this, an SOE wireless operator should be provided to facilitate a link with London. He urged that Free French connections should not be used, for Jouhaux's intimates considered the Gaullists to be heavily tainted by political right-wingers. Bertholet's entreaties proved fruitless; London maintained that it could not move Jouhaux and a wireless link (possibly Newman) was already available to him. HS7/245 p. 259.

3. 21 July 1942, F Section War Diary. HS7/244.

4. HS7/244 p. 81.

5. Ibid. The story is a little confused, for, presumably, the trip was the one Norman Brooks had made in 1940.

6. At this time of unsophisticated navigational aids, the RAF's special duties squadrons were heavily

7. 'Thibaud's' identity remains elusive.
8. 'Narrative', p. 16, and AMB Papers.
9. Ibid.
10. 'Narrative', p. 17 This seems a very robust stance taken by the inexperienced agent but is in keeping with Tony's abundant, youthful self-confidence. Forgues was a leading figure in the resistance movement 'Libération'.
11. His CV is in AMB Papers.
12. Ibid., pp. 17, 26.
13. Ibid., pp. 15–16.
14. Ibid., pp. 19–20.
15. Presumably the grease had come from Switzerland. An SOE report of January 1945 states (erroneously) that this link was maintained until June 1943. 'Le Docteur's' identity is not known but he could have been one of a couple of former French army doctors connected with Bertholet. Report from JQ100 (Sullivan) to JQ (McCaffery) of 16 March 1942. Information supplied by the SOE Adviser.
16. The date of the first contact with Cusin is taken from the 'Narrative' but other timings are found amongst Tony's papers and the commencement of his involvement in PIMENTO's affairs is uncertain. Some notes suggest he joined as late as June/July 1943. Details of Cusin's clandestine career can be found in Baynac, Les secrets de l'affaire Jean Moulin. The date of the first meeting with Cusin is not the only discrepancy. Tony's comments on SOE in France shortly after its publication, stated that Bertholet introduced him to Augustin [sic – Charles] Laurent, the Secretary of the Civil Service Trade Union, and even Léon Jouhaux, the man F Section had originally charged him to contact. AMB Papers. Tony's post-war 'Narrative' states that Dorval, acting on Tony's behalf, met Laurent.

17. HS7/244, p. 83.
18. A report from JQ100 (Sullivan) to JQ (McCaffery) of 16 March 1942 relates to Bertholet's Marseille connections and includes mention of a Lieutenant Weidenfeld of the Deuxième Bureau. Information supplied by the SOE Adviser.
19. 'Narrative', p. 20 At this time the abrasive grease was either sent secretly into France from Switzerland or was locally produced.
20. 'Narrative' p. 16. Littlejohn, The Patriotic Traitors pp. 236–7.
21. HS7/245.
22. Ibid., p. 252.
23. A surprising comment about PIMENTO's staffing needs appeared in a telegram in October 1942 asking 'Please telegraph whether you are (a) willing (b) able to supply complete French identity papers for Robert [Bertholet] and for D'ASTIER's sister who will ensure liaison between Alphonse and Urbain.' McCaffery Papers. This is the first and only time this proposal appears in the PIMENTO story and Tony never mentioned it. The d'Astier de la Vigerie family were stalwarts of the Resistance.
24. 'PIMENTO Supply Operations' notes written by Tony after the war. AMB Papers.
25. AIR20/8252. HS7/245, pp. 252 and 254. Even the ostensibly empirical fact of the supply drop has been open to debate. The account given in RAF's records have been assumed to be the most accurate. Interestingly, Tony failed to mention the abortive operation in his 'Narrative'.

Chapter Eight: There but for the Grace of God Go I

1. Richards, Secret Flotillas Volume II, p. 372. This official version is not without discrepancies and I am grateful to Rod Bailey for identifying Giacomino Sarfatti of SOE's Italian Section as another passenger on the

Seadog, HS9/1311. There is a further PIMENTO link to Sarfatti's story: maps intended for the agent's use were sent on one of Tony's drops, PIMENTO 12, 17 January 1943.

2. Bloom was born in 1907 making him some fifteen years older than Tony. Details of his early life can be found in his SOE Personal File HS9/166/7 and 'Lieutenant Marcus Bloom: a Jewish Hero of the SOE', Martin Sugarman, *Jewish Historical Studies*, volume 39, 2004, pp.183–96.

3. At his preliminary SOE interview it was noted that he had an accent 'but he says it will disappear'. Another F Section agent who met him in France stated 'he could not speak French properly'. Rabinovitch report, HS6/423.

4. A reference in Bloom's Personal File, regrettably, merits special note. The training record of this man who had volunteered for exceptionally dangerous duties includes anti-Semitic remarks made by the counter-signing officer. These remain distasteful even when allowances are made for the vocabulary and social attitudes of the period: 'Mental and physical effort seems to come hard to this pink yid. In conversation, at least with myself, he is dull-minded and by no means forthcoming; though not an oyster, maybe he keeps under the shell the usual racial nimbleness.' HS9/166/7.

5. An SOE report stated that, in August 1942, there were six wireless operators in the Unoccupied Zone of which only four were in contact with London. They were servicing twenty-five SOE-trained organisers and nineteen locally recruited personnel. HS7/121. A note on Bloom's personal file includes the exculpatory comment from F Section (or perhaps Buckmaster himself), 'the risk of sending to the field this officer with his imperfect French and his Anglo-Saxon-Jewish appearance was only justified by our extreme penury in W/T.O's.' HS9/166/7.

6. The document also includes details of an escape route to Spain, 'If you are escaping by your own means make for the Consulate General, 35 Passeo de Gracia, Barcelona.' HS6/422.

7. F Section War Diary, p. 252. HS7/245.

8. Tony's post-war testimonies affirmed that a meeting with Bloom had taken place a few days after the scheduled rendezvous. Moreover he stated that their relationship began and effectively ended at this time. There are now strong grounds to suggest that this was not the case and that Tony had telescoped the narrative. A measure of the complexity of the story is shown by a document found amongst Tony's papers stating that the meeting with his wireless operator took place as late as 12 February 1943 – some three months after Bloom's arrival in France. This is clearly incorrect for F Section's War Diary records that on 17 November Bertholet 'reported that URBAIN had safely arrived'. Tony's post-war narrative states that he met Bertholet in Lyon on 12 November and he might well have informed Bertholet of the wireless operator's arrival, facilitating the message sent to London. The SOE War Diary reveals that F Section considered Bloom to be in touch with Tony throughout the winter of 1942/3 in spite of the former's inability to send and receive wireless messages. The situation is further confused by an assertion in the same document that SOE in Berne advised London on 7 December 1942 'that as ROBERT [Bertholet] was away on military service until the beginning of January any December operations would have to be arranged by London direct with ALPHONSE [Tony] via URBAIN [Bloom].' HS7/245, p. 254. So, just where does the burden of evidence lie? How could Tony be so misplaced in his recollections of his meeting with Bloom, not least because this formed part of his testimony to the official historian

of SOE in France? Moreover, if he was wrong on this very important matter what else of his recorded memoirs was inaccurate? Thankfully, there is good reason to put trust in the veracity of the chronology of Tony's post-war narrative written when memories of these events were fresh and his account was seemingly supported by a journal that, sadly, no longer exists. The description given in this chapter of a brief meeting with Bloom in November 1942 followed, after a break of three months, by reconnection in February 1943, offers the most plausible version of the complex PIMENTO/PRUNUS story.

9. 'Narrative', p. 21. It was however via Bertholet in Berne that London was informed of Bloom's safe arrival. F Section War Diary HS7/245, p. 253.

10. Bloom's conduct was in marked contrast with his training report, 'The student is security-minded and most discreet both in his conversation and in his habits.' HS9/166/7.

11. There is some debate about the precise date and vessel involved. The official history, *Secret Flotillas*, states that it was 21/22 April 1942 on the *Seawolf* while a pro-forma on Pertschuk's Personal File gives the date as 13 April by submarine.

12. The official history of SOE in France asserts that he was originally a PWE agent but his Personal File offers no corroboration of this. Foot, *SOE in France*, p. 217 and HS9/1172/7.

13. HS6/469, 'The British Circuits in France', p. 91.

14. Foot, *SOE in France*, p. 217.

15. Tony later recalled that Bloom had explained that he had met Pertschuk in England and been given an address in case he ever needed a reliable contact in Toulouse. This account now seems highly unlikely and Bloom was probably furnished with the link after he had arrived in France. Tony also recounted that Bloom stated he had trained with Pertschuk, but the dates of their courses do not match nor is it likely that

Pertschuk could have had a Toulouse operational contact address while in England.

16. Marcel Petit, a member of the PRUNUS network, was arrested and interrogated by the Germans. He stated that his captors showed him a photograph of Pertschuk in British Army uniform. Petit subsequently broached the matter with Pertschuk when he encountered him in Buchenwald concentration camp but merely elicited the response that the Germans' possession of the photo could only be explained by a leak in London. 'Interview with M. Marcel PETIT, 1 June 1945'. Information supplied by the SOE Adviser.

17. Bloom's indiscretions contrast with Bertholet's preoccupations over the security of the Colis Suisse. When the latter suspected that its address was being indiscriminately distributed amongst London's agents, he threatened to hand unexpected visitors over to the Vichy authorities. F Section War Diary, HS7/244, p. 77. In the event, the establishment's legitimate existence did not have long to run following Bloom's arrival. On 20 December 1942 Berne informed London that the Toulouse Colis Suisse premises had been requisitioned by the Germans. HS7/245, p. 257.

18. Written statement by Tony, 14 May 1998, AMB Papers. It was not unknown for agents in the field to change London's arrangements unilaterally and then seek Baker Street's confirmation of the local emendation of plans. For example, Peter Churchill informed London that he needed to retain Odette Sansom rather than release her to fulfil her original tasks.

19. This feature of the narrative parts company both with the official history and some of Tony's statements in later life regarding his connections with Bloom and Pertschuk. Most of his descriptions of events are present but

their order has been reconfigured to take account of new sources.

20. 'Narrative', p. 21.

21. Ibid., p. 22.

22. Goubet and Debauges, *Histoire de la Résistance dans la Haute-Garonne*, p. 45

23. Pilot's report, AIR20/8452, and No. 138 Squadron Operations Record Book, 22–23 November 1942, AIR27/956 and 'Narrative', p. 24.

24. No. 161 Squadron Operations Record Book, 22–23 November 1943, AIR27/1068. On its return the aircraft encountered problems with its compass and was obliged to divert to Exeter. Tony's normally reliable post-war narrative fails at this point and his account has been amended to accommodate data from RAF records.

25. 'Narrative', p. 24.

26. Ibid.

27. Ibid., p. 25,

28. Ibid., p. 27.

29. Ibid.

30. Tony's 'Narrative' gave a slightly different version of this story from the one he offered the author but the import remains the same; pp. 25–6.

31. 'Narrative', p. 27.

32. Description of Molter in Hope Brooks's post-war narrative, p. 9.

33. Tony also stated, on a different occasion, that the date was October 1942.

34. 'Narrative', pp. 28–9 Details of Moch's wartime activities (including contributions by his family) appear in *Les Nouvelles de Corenc*, Avril 2014, No.175 pp. 6–7.

35. HS6/422. Throughout November and December London continued to send messages to Tony via Bertholet, complaining that they had heard nothing from Bloom and another wireless set would be sent for him. McCaffery Papers.

36. Loubet, 'Le réseau "Prunus"', pp. 53–5.

37. Foot, *SOE in France*, p. 208.

38. F Section War Diary HS7/245 p. 255. An irascible character by nature, the tensions of being a clandestine wireless operator did not improve Rabinovitch's temper and a message to London sent on 22 January 1943 reflects his mood, 'Spare my sending or you will be sorry – last warning.'

39. HS6/423 Interrogation of 'Catalpha' [Rabinovitch], 1 October 1943.

40. HS6/422, p. 10 and HS6/423, p. 8.

41. This chronology is reconstructed from Tony's 'Narrative'. The original does contain some errors such as this being the moment of Bloom's first appearance and that he had befriended Pertschuk during their training.

42. 'Narrative', p. 31.

43. Ibid., pp. 31–2.

44. Ibid p. 32.

45. Ibid, p. 33.

46. HS6/422 Berne had sent a message to London on 18 February 1943 advising of Bertholet's arrest and the need to inform Tony. Information supplied by the SOE Adviser.

47. Information from the SOE Adviser. Tony's post-war 'Narrative' states that Bertholet's last trip was 12 November 1942, the day after the German occupation of Vichy France, although in a message to London in April 1943 Bertholet stated, 'Just returned from good fortnight's stay in France'. McCaffery Papers.

48. 'Narrative', p. 33.

49. 'Jules' was Jean Arnault who acted as a courier between PRUNUS and other networks in Lyon and Marseille. 'Martin' – Fernand Hanon – later stated that Arnault had fallen out with Pertschuk and left the network around the time of the lunch. Hanon left Toulouse in May and, after a long and frustrating journey, finally reached England in October 1943. HS9/653/3. Jean Arnault is not to be confused with Claude Arnault of the WHEELWRIGHT circuit.

50. 'Narrative', p. 33.

51. The 15th is the date given in Morandat's death notice but the arrest is given as 16th (Ceux de la Résistance article on

Dorval) and 23rd in 'Narrative', p. 33.

52. 'Narrative', pp. 33–4 and note on Dorval in AMB Papers.

53. The passage of time obscured some of the wartime detail. During a conversation with Roger Morandat in 1980 following a ceremony to name a square in Paris in 'Yvon' Morandat's honour, Tony was upbraided by his wartime comrade for not having helped his wife during his incarceration. The archives, never mind Tony's recollections, show otherwise. A telegram from Bertholet to London on Tony's behalf states, 'For Yvon. Your brother who worked with me arrested by Gestapo in course of big Liberation [the resistance organisation 'Libération'] round-up. Arrest unconnected with my work. Are in contact with and looking after his wife.' HS6/653. One reference from June 1943, indicates a sadly unrealised effort to free Morandat, 'Tournesol [Bertholet] has direct line to him via prison guard who will arrange escape if he can accompany Morandat.' McCaffery Papers.

54. 'Narrative' p. 35.

55. Ibid. Bedat was yet another member of the SRFD to join PIMENTO.

56. Ibid., p.35 In a note presumably written following the publication of Foot's *SOE in France*, Tony described Megglé's visit to Lyon but placed it *after* the arrests in Toulouse and offered an account of Bizot 'arresting' Tony at the station to prevent him falling into a German security check. Corroboration of Tony's suspicions concerning Megglé is amongst the fragmented copies of telegrams sent to and from SOE's Swiss outpost. A message from London in May 1943 included, 'Theo [Tony] is therefore quite right to assume envoy is agent provocateur. Although this may not be so, he will probably be contagious therefore avoid contact.' McCaffery Papers. The F Section wireless operator Rabinovitch reported to SOE that

'LE BOITEUX was arrested and set free again.' [Interrogation 1 October 1943] Megglé, not surprisingly, makes no reference in his post-war reports to being released for any period but his deposition confirms that he visited Lyon on PRUNUS business. In spite (or because) of the accusations made against him, at the end of the war Megglé embarked upon an investigation into the collapse of PRUNUS. Tony later speculated that the man in Lyon may have been a Gestapo plant pretending to be Megglé. In his post-war deposition (in Pertschuk's Personal File) Megglé affirms his captivity in Toulouse until a transfer to Fresnes jail on 28 May 1943. Around 15 January 1944 he was moved to Compiègne and then sent to Buchenwald concentration camp on 29 March. A similar account of the Lyon affair appears in Tony's 'PIMENTO Notes', AMB Papers.

57. Hanon Personal File, HS9/655/3.

58. Megglé's own version of his resistance career appears in Pertschuk's personal file. File HS6/423 states that one of Pertschuk's men reported 'MAUDIT' [Megglé] had previously worked for 'NICOLAS' for two years in Bordeaux but had escaped when that circuit was 'blown'.

59. Interview with Marcel PETIT, 1 June 1945. Information supplied by the SOE Adviser.

60. 'Narrative' p. 35.

61. Telegram April 1943 in McCaffery Papers. The stress and fatigue of a clandestine life were evidently taking their toll and, as will be seen, Tony's condition worsened.

62. A message from SOE in Switzerland reported some impressive PIMENTO sabotage figures to London in April 1943, 'Theo's [Tony's] operations till end March were average of one thousand axles plus several engines per month.' McCaffery Papers.

63. Description of Laroque by Rabinovitch in HS6/423.

64. There was a tendency amongst some of the F Section agents to indulge a need to converse in their mother tongue. The PROSPER network was notorious for indiscreet meetings and, as has been noted, Tony's training colleague, Brian Stonehouse, spoke English while in France.

65. Tickell, *Odette* p. 199, Churchill, *Duel of Wits* p. 264. Sansom's SOE interrogation of 12 May 1945 records 'on the occasion of this visit to TOULOUSE source [Sansom] had met an agent from the UK who was tall and wore a moustache. He is known to RAOUL. Source points out that her memory is very indistinct about these matters, and the above is all that she can remember.' The mention of this unidentified agent serves to illustrate the complexity of tracing the movement of personalities and the fragility of memory.

66. 'Narrative', p. 36.

67. Tony later said that Megglé and Bloom were present, but neither is mentioned in the 'Narrative' as being there.

68. 'Narrative', p. 36.

69. HS6/323.

70. KV6/18.

71. Hitter's deposition of 1 June 1945 stated that he met Megglé on 8 April and introduced him to 'Bobby'. Information supplied by the SOE Adviser.

72. Deposition by Megglé 30 November 1945 in HS9/1172/7 and wireless message HS6/422.

73. Megglé states in his deposition that he had an appointment to visit Petit at 0900 on the Monday.

74. Megglé affirmed in his deposition that he was to collect the material from Petit on Monday 12 April but then stated that he called at Moog's at that time and does not mention Petit.

75. Miannay, *Dictionnaire des agents doubles dans la Résistance*, p. 204. Further details of Moog's nefarious activities are to be found in Baynac, *Présumé Jean Moulin*, pp. 635–8.

76. In his otherwise excellent history of SOE, William Mackenzie follows Bourne-Paterson in erroneously suggesting that the German agent responsible for the fall of PRUNUS was Roger Bardet (p. 569).

77. Megglé's own account of his arrest and (partial) understanding of the downfall of PRUNUS is to be found in his deposition. Hitter commented: 'Il semble que ces renseignements ont été donnés par Megglé. Celui-ci déclare qu'au cours des conversations qu'il a eu avec Boby entre le 8 et le 12 Avril, il a été mis suffisamment en confiance pour lui donner certains renseignements sur l'organisation dont il faisait partie à Toulouse.' Information supplied by the SOE Adviser.

78. 'Le réseau "Prunus"', p.71.

79. Ibid., p. 73. Marcel Petit was very critical of Megglé and believed 'that MEGGLE, after arrest, had given away everything he knew about the group, which was proved by the fact that the Germans only knew those things which MEGGLE knew.' 'Interview with M. Marcel PETIT, 1 June1945.' Information supplied by the SOE Adviser. Rabinovitch later commented in a debriefing, 'LE BOITEUX [Megglé] was arrested and set free again. At any rate, he was seen in TOULOUSE after EUGENE'S arrest.' HS9/1223/4.

80. Laroque claimed that Megglé was in the car that drove her to Gestapo headquarters. She was eventually sent to Ravensbrück concentration camp in Germany. Following her repatriation, she reported to F Section's office in the Hôtel Cecil in Paris on 24 May 1945 where Tony formally identified her. Memo from Captain Hazeldine to Flight Office Atkins, 25 May 1945. 'Paris' file, Vera Atkins Papers, 12636 Imperial War Museum,.

81. Statement of 17 July 1945 by M. Colle reporting Bloom's descriptions made to him in Fresnes prison. HS9/166/7.

82. Moog was present at the arrest. Megglé statement, HS9/1172/7. Hitter was brutally interrogated at the Gestapo Headquarters at the avenue Foch then held at Fresnes prison for six months before eventually arriving in Buchenwald concentration camp in January 1944.

83. This was by no means the last of Moog's operations against the Resistance. His services were loaned to the SD and he became a pivotal figure in the momentous destruction of the Conseil National de la Résistance. His ultimate fate is disputed. There are claims that he died in a road accident in 1944, was killed in an aircraft accident in 1945 in Germany, or vanished with two suitcases of resistance documents, 'although while doing good work for us, he did good work for the other side as well. After the Gestapo headquarters was bombed in May 1944, we discovered that "Pierre"[Moog] had disappeared with two suitcases filled with documents.' Bower, *Klaus Barbie* p. 63.

84. Accounts by members of PRUNUS testify that both Bloom and Pertschuk showed signs of having been beaten when held at the Gestapo headquarters in Toulouse and any possible complicity must have come at great personal cost.

85. Overton Fuller, *Déricourt: The Chequered Spy*, p. 304.

86. Report, 11 January 1945, AMB Papers. This is confirmed in a contemporary message from Tony to Bertholet on 18 May in which he stated he had 'closed down his two post-boxes and has cancelled passwords known to Eugene [Pertschuk]'. McCaffery Papers.

87. HS6/422.

88. BISHOP report, HS6/422, Churchill, *The Spirit in the Cage*, p. 10

89. KV6/18.

90. Ibid.

91. HS6/422.

92. Marks, *Between Silk and Cyanide*, p. 16.

93. KV6/18.

94. Written statement by Tony 14 May 1998, AMB Papers.

95. 'Narrative', p. 38.

96. Ibid.

97. HS6/422. A version sent to Bertholet using 'Theo' instead of 'Alphonse' is in the McCaffery Papers. While uncertainty remained over the fate of Pertschuk and Bloom, SOE in Switzerland offered London possible contacts to aid them including, 'Third possibility is by contacting Olga at Brasserie Martel (in the café en bas) Rue de la Republique (near Progress building) in Lyon. Password "Je viens voir Monsieur Alphonse" Olga replies "Quel Alphonse" Contacter "Alphonse tout court" Then give name.' McCaffery Papers.

98. HS6/422. Version to Bertholet in McCaffery Papers.

99. HS6/422.

100. Ibid.

101. Ibid.

102. Ibid. The version of the message in the McCaffery Papers includes 'We request this as there is possibility of German trap.'

103. Bernard was Bloom's brother who was serving in the British Army.

104. There is no reference to the case in the memoir written by Leo Marks, the head of the Codes Section. Given the importance of the affair and Marks's claims to have unmasked other German deceptions, perhaps this was not one of his investigative triumphs. It did not feature in the author's interviews with Marks either.

105. HS6/422.

106. Ibid.

107. HS6/422. BISHOP report, p. 8. With some justification MI5 considered this an ill-considered test.

108. HS6/422. BISHOP report, July report, p. 9. When the author gave a copy of this document to him for his comments, Tony wrote in the margin, 'Who was the idiot who thought this?'

109. HS6/422.

110. HS9/1223/4. A message to SOE from WHEELWRIGHT's George Starr in

July 1943 reported: 'Just learned that 18 arrested in connection with Eugene [Pertschuk] transferred to Fresnes prison.' Then in August he inaccurately stated: 'Am informed by Inspector of Surete that Urbain [Bloom] executed by Germans at Fresnes and probably Eugene [Pertschuk] at the same time. Inspector was not actual eye witness but affirms that above facts are true to best of his belief.' McCaffery Papers.

111. Fayman report, 24 June 1945. Christopher Burney, an F Section agent who befriended Pertschuk in captivity, stated, 'He was very savagely interrogated.' Information supplied by the SOE Adviser.

112. Foot, *SOE*, p. 136. This account echoes Goetz's other statement but it would be surprising if the German wireless expert had managed to arrive in Toulouse by the night of Bloom's arrest.

113. 1 October 1943, HS9/1223/4.

114. After the war, SOE honoured its obligations and reimbursed Mrs Bloom the money that she had borrowed in order to purchase expensive, black-market items for her husband.

115. Letter by Victor Pistora to Lieutenant Commander P. A. O'Leary, 4 December 1945 in Mauthausen File, Vera Atkins Papers, 12636, Imperial War Museum.

116. Seaman, *Bravest of the Brave*, p. 170.

117. After the war Hitter published them as *The Leaves of Buchenwald*. Several other figures involved with PRUNUS were present in the camp including Jacques Megglé and Marcel Petit.

118. Eugen Kogon, an inmate of Buchenwald, speculated that Pertschuk was mistaken for Wing Commander Forest 'Tommy' Yeo-Thomas, an SOE agent who, months earlier, had escaped from the camp. Were the SS prepared to execute a 'Perkins' because the name was faintly similar to Yeo-Thomas's alias 'Dodkin'? Another inmate, Alfred Balachowski, reported that Perkins's and Dodkin's names were called out on 10 April and 'Perkins was hanged on

this day.' Vera Atkins Papers, 12636, Imperial War Museum.

119. Pertschuk also had connections with George Starr but there was no fallout. Denise Bloch reported that she went with Starr to a private address at Agen in case of Pertschuk's escape or release – the house was not raided. She revealed to SOE that Starr was 'in a "terrible mess". He needs someone to help him as soon as possible because he is now the only one left to control five departments (he is taking on LYONS and TOULOUSE), and if he is arrested there is no one else.' HS9/165/8. It is further vindication of Tony's security that an agent as well-connected as Bloch seems not to have known of his existence and assumed that Starr was the only F Section organiser operating in southern France. After the war Tony corresponded with Pertschuk's brother and tried to help discover the circumstances surrounding the arrests in Toulouse.

120. BISHOP report, September version, p. 7, HS6/423. A message from SOE in Switzerland to London in June 1943 included 'Theo [Tony] says that some of Eugene's [Pertschuk] friends state that it was PILLS (who limps) who sold out, or possibly parents of girl known as Eugene's fiancée.' McCaffery Papers. By June 1943 SOE in Switzerland reported that SIS had confirmed Moog's responsibility for the arrests. McCaffery Papers.

121. Memo, 5 November 1944, HS9/1172/7. Marcel Petit stated that Megglé had confirmed their association during his interrogation in the Toulouse Gestapo headquarters. Other accusers included Christopher Burney who reiterated Pertschuk's claim that Megglé had identified him following his arrest. It also seems that the PRUNUS Buchenwald prisoners brooded over where the guilt lay and alighted on Megglé without giving any real consideration to Moog's role.

122. Unrelated to the other arrests, Gauthier, Roger Morandat's successor in PIMENTO, was brought in for questioning by the authorities in June 1943 but was released due to lack of evidence. Veyret, *Histoire de la Résistance armée dans l'Ain*, p. 44.

Chapter Nine: The Going Gets Tough

1. The controversy remains unresolved. Intriguingly, Tony commented shortly after the publication of *SOE in France*, 'Yvon [Leon Morandat] also introduced me to Jean MOULIN (Max).' This is the only reference to a meeting with de Gaulle's emissary and it failed to reappear in the extensive interviews conducted by the author with Tony. 'PIMENTO's Comments of SOE in France', AMB Papers.
2. Message of 27 June 1943 from Bertholet in AMB Papers.
3. 'Rebecca' was a homing beacon developed by SOE to direct RAF aircraft to the parachute dropping grounds arranged by the circuits and Baker Street.
4. Telegram from Switzerland to London reporting the approaches, McCaffery Papers.
5. MacLaren, *Canadians Behind Enemy Lines*, p. 37.
6. HS9/452/7. Duchalard Personal File.
7. 'Pimento Notes', p. 20, AMB Papers.
8. Message of 27 June 1943 from Bertholet in AMB Papers, and in McCaffery Papers.
9. *SOE in France* (2004 edition) p. 247.
10. June 1943 McCaffery. Presumably 33 and 53 were safe havens.
11. AMB Papers.
12. HS6/322.
13. HS7/121.
14. The astonishing disparity in funds between the circuits suggests that a detailed analysis of SOE finances is a worthwhile project for a future historian. The seemingly profligate financial arrangements claimed by de Baissac are in an interrogation report

made in August 1943 on his return to England, HS9/75.
15. 'Report', 11 January 1945. HS6/567.
16. In a message to Bizot in Switzerland on 25 May 1944 Tony wrote (in French) 'Perrier [Pédémas] treats me like a real pal. Every time I am passing by he invites me to a meal at his place and he helps me with many little things.' AMB Papers.
17. 'Narrative', p. 19.
18. Two sources (card index amongst Tony's papers and 'Narrative') give the date of Laganne's recruitment as September 1942 while another has it as late as April 1943. The 'Narrative' states that Tony recruited Biou on 4 May 1943, p. 40. Biou was always known to his comrades as 'Marcel' and, in a letter to Tony after the war, his father asked that his son be recognised for his deeds under his real name. AMB Papers.
19. 'Narrative', p. 44.
20. Ibid.
21. 'Narrative', p. 45 and letter to Biou's father of 16 July 1945 in AMB Papers.
22. 'Narrative', p. 45. *Les Fusillés* curiously states that he was arrested in Lyon 'au cours' of a trip on 3 August 1943.
23. Description of the arrest provided by Tony. The aforementioned letter to Biou's father of 16/7/1945 states that Biou was not tortured because Dorval convinced the Germans that his colleague was a minion and knew nothing. It cannot be discounted that Tony offered this benign version of events to spare the Biou family unnecessary emotional suffering.
24. Citation for Dorval. AMB Papers. Tony's card index gives Biou's arrest as '8th August 1943 in train "SP" south Lyon'. In a memo from Tony to Major Bill Hazeldine who was responsible for much of F Section's post-war liquidation process in France, the former wrote that Biou 'worked as courier between Toulouse and Lyon for three months, was arrested, and within four hours

gave the address of Poulet, my second in command'. AMB Papers. The 'Narrative' suggests that Biou was arrested on the evening of the 7th, p. 45.

25. The woman was later released. 'Ceux de la Resistance' states that no explosive was found but that the smell of the 808 explosive lingered. AMB Papers.

26. Tony stated that he had been informed that Dorval's teeth were knocked out with a chisel then ice cubes were placed in his mouth to accentuate the pain from the exposed nerves. When later spotted in prison he was virtually unrecognisable.

27. Note from Bertholet to Tony, 8 February 1944 AMB Papers.

28. HS6/567. The note of 12 January 1945 comprised recommendations for gallantry awards to Dorval and Moch.

29. In a 1945 report Tony stated erroneously that Fourre 'was arrested with him [Dorval]'. Gaston Cusin gave another version in a post-war speech about Dorval. His account (based upon Fourre's statement) suggested that Dorval had given the Germans Fourre's name in the *mistaken* belief that the latter was already under arrest and that by nominating a man in custody he would not be pressed to denounce resistance fighters still at large.

30. An entry for Fourre in a card index amongst Tony's papers states that the former was released on 3 February 1944. A message from Bertholet to Tony of 31 January 1944 states (in French) 'Alex is at liberty. But he is very ill and can be found at a hospital where Poulet [Dorval] lived.' AMB Papers.

31. 12 January 1945 AMB Papers.

32. They wrote accounts of these events in *Je fus ce condamné*, *L'esprit de résistance* and *Ils partiront dans l'ivresse*. The complete veracity of these accounts has been questioned by some readers.

33. AMB Papers and *Les Nouvelles de Corenc*. The accounts seem very similar to the celebrated operation to liberate Raymond Aubrac but Moch's name

does not appear amongst the substantial published literature. Perhaps members of PIMENTO had simply assumed that the famous escape attempt was mounted to free Dorval, not Aubrac.

34. 'Deposition of Hans Kieffer', 19 January 1947, Vera Atkins Papers, 12636, Imperial War Museum.

35. The surviving SOE files do not record the precise process by which Baker Street decided to order Tony's return. A telegram from London to Bertholet dated 4 June 1943 intimated that consideration was being given to his recall, 'Very sorry about ALPHONSE agree we [*sic*] should go 53 to recover strength or would try pick up July moon if so let us know immediately stop have sent pommade [*sic*] on several ops and also wired prescription stop sending more by other line.' HS6/653. It was clear that Tony's departure had been arranged by 21 July for it is mentioned in a telegram from Berne on that date. HS9 1045/5. However, an SOE document, 'Future Programme', submitted by Buckmaster on 29 July 1943 gives no hint of a recall, 'A CGT organiser with excellent railway contacts has done most valuable work, which is growing rapidly, principally near Lyon and Toulouse and to the north of Lyon.'HS7/121. Tony's 'Narrative' states that he had a meeting with Moch on 2 August to discuss future parachute operations so that he could take the information back to London 'as H.Q. had informed me that I was to be allowed to go on leave shortly', p. 44.

36. A telegram of early July 1943 from SOE in Switzerland to London stated, 'Unless said day [D-Day] intervenes Theo [Tony] would like to return now for leave between two moons. Plane trip might cure his whooping-cough and get him thoroughly fit for big things. Please instruct.' McCaffery Papers.

37. The 'wise counsellors' were probably Bertholet. Buckmaster, *Specially Employed*, p. 171.

38. Copy in AMB Papers. The letter was signed by Isabel Norris, one of F Section's unsung backroom staff.

39. Tony arranged funds to maintain PIMENTO during his absence and a message from Switzerland to London on 9 August 1943 acknowledged that Tony had received 100,000 francs from Bertholet. McCaffery Papers.

40. Tony's 'Narrative' does not dwell on the arrangements for his return to England. Rather than a planned departure, it suggests a 'crash' evacuation. However, the text is highly abbreviated, does not describe events in detail and reads as if the author has run out of time to complete the narrative properly.

41. Telegram 'for Theo' [Tony] July 1943 from London to Switzerland, McCaffery Papers.

42. IWM Sound Archive 9925. These sentiments also appear in Despaigne's unpublished memoirs, 'Les notes des mes missions militaires', 1983. AMB Papers.

43. For the definitive account of PROSPER see *Shadows in the Fog* by Suttill's son.

44. *SOE in France*, p. 299. This message was sent by Agazarian on his first operational tour. Concerns regarding Déricourt's probity began long before the summer of 1943; a Security Service file reveals that as early as 7 December 1942 the Free French had expressed their doubts about Déricourt's links to the Germans. KV2/1131.

45. Déricourt had accompanied another prospective passenger, Octave Simon, to Angers. It is not known whether they were on the same train as Tony. KV2/1131.

46. AIR20/1068.

47. 'Dyer' was Erwin Deman, a member of SOE's D/F Section that created escape lines for agents. He was a Viennese Jew who served in the French Army, was captured by the Germans in 1940, escaped, reached North Africa and joined the Foreign Legion. Not a man to languish in inactivity, he deserted,

made his way to the United Kingdom and was recruited by SOE. Deman was tasked to form a clandestine cross-Channel sea link but the first attempt to land him in April by sea was aborted and he had to wait until August for this flight. He went on to create the successful VAR escape line.

48. His SOE Personal File offers nothing about his arrival in the United Kingdom. HS9/987/4.

49. De Ganay later returned to France in May 1944 to work with the MINISTER/DIETICIAN network.

50. She had arrived in France on the same naval operation as Bloom.

51. His SOE Personal File does not make mention of this flight.

52. Benoist returned to France in October 1943 to form the CLERGYMAN network. Arrested in June 1944, he was killed at Buchenwald in September.

53. He returned to France in March 1944 but was arrested on landing. He perished at Dachau concentration camp in August 1944.

54. I am grateful to David Harrison for helping identify her.

55. Buckmaster's diary reveals that the excursion to the Sussex airfield did not impact upon his other F Section duties and he was back at Orchard Court at 6.55 a.m. for a meeting with Gerry Morel at 7.30. Buckmaster Diary and AMB Papers. See Saward, *The Grand Prix Saboteurs* for a detailed account, if regrettably without notes, of the 'Dyer' operation. Details of F Section's use of the hotel (5 guineas a week board) are to be found at HS8/535.

56. It was the first Hudson operation flown by the No 161 Squadron pilot, Squadron Leader Len Ratcliff. AIR27/1068. With his customary sangfroid, Ratcliff later related, 'I knew Déricourt and didn't personally believe these accusations. I was prepared to trust him and didn't have any fear about flying to the field.' *Memoirs*, p. 30 and the author's conversations with Ratcliff

in November 2015. With hindsight it seems questionable, given the suspicions about Déricourt, that incoming agents should have continued to be entrusted to him.

57. Flight Lieutenant Leslie Whitaker collected him by Lysander on 8–9 February.

58. Verity, *We Landed by Moonlight*, p. 164.

59. Ibid., p. 165.

60. The saga is fully discussed in Déricourt's substantial SOE Personal File, HS9/421–5.

61. Controversy surrounded Déricourt until (and after) his death in an air accident in Laos in November 1962.

Chapter Ten: 'Antoine Brévin Will Die'

1. Buckmaster's diary for 20 August 1943 states 'Lunch – Park Lane with incoming Joes'. Tony did not mention that he was part of the gathering. He evidently possessed a different status to some of the other agents on his flight, for several were obliged to pass through MI5's London Reception Centre for refugees arriving from Occupied Europe.

2. It is mentioned in Moch's Personal File, HS9/1045/5.

3. Buckmaster, *Specially Employed*, p. 171. This is, in part, corroborated by Buckmaster's diary for there are no references to his meeting Tony prior to the latter's return to France in December, never mind after 'three weeks'.

4. This assessment is based upon SOE records and interviews with several members of F Section including Maurice Buckmaster, Vera Atkins and, of course, Tony Brooks.

5. HS9/1045/5. Amongst the paper's imperfections is the description of Lelette Mornand, Tony's onetime girlfriend, as a truck driver. Torr had only been appointed to the post of F/RECS a month earlier, HS9/150/7.

6. Copy in AMB Papers. This seems a surprising lapse by the normally

security-obsessed Tony. He also had Bertholet (employing the alias 'Baumer') send birthday or seasonal greetings from Switzerland after the occupation of Vichy France. F Section also sent Hope anodyne updates by letter and telegram of Tony's well-being, and purchased birthday presents for her on Tony's behalf.

7. Amongst Tony's private papers there exist handwritten notes evidently intended for Hope (presumably in the event of his death) describing his closest PIMENTO associates. There is no indication that this was ever given to Hope and it is reasonable to assume that, in the event of his demise, it was to help her piece together his wartime activities.

8. Four-page report c. October 1945 in AMB Papers.

9. It was intended that Tony attend a training course at STS 40, Howbury Hall, Waterend, to be instructed on aircraft reception techniques but the booking was cancelled on 26 November. Information supplied by the SOE Adviser.

10. One of the happier exchanges concerned London's notifying SOE in Switzerland of Tony's safe arrival: 'Delighted to inform you Theo [Tony] arrived safely this country this morning' followed two days later by the reply, 'All here delighted. Give him good wishes from Charles [Bertholet] and us for pleasant leave.' McCaffery Papers.

11. Telegram from Berne to London, 29 September 1943. Information supplied by the SOE Adviser.

12. Manuscript drafts of a lecture on 'Illegals' delivered by Tony in the 1970s exist amongst his papers.

13. Le Chêne, *Watch for me by Moonlight*, p. 113, *The F Section Memorial*, p. 12. Neither Hamilton's Personal File nor the testimony of a colleague present at his arrest offer corroboration of the specifics of this account.

14. A telegram from Berne to London of 18

October 1943 included the comment 'foresee Alphonse's return November'.

15. Tony later speculated whether the briefing was bogus and he had been used as a pawn in the monumental Allied deception scheme 'Fortitude'. A stratagem involving the south-west of France *did* feature among the planners' wiles. The deception, Operation 'Ironside', was that an Allied expeditionary force, largely American, would embark at west-coast ports in the United Kingdom and proceed to capture Bordeaux, which would then be exploited by US forces sailing directly from America – 'The deception staffs did their best to implement this rather implausible story, but their hearts were not in it.' Howard, *British Intelligence in the Second World War* Volume 5, p.125. Tony's briefing in late 1943 seems far too early for 'Ironside', which was only put into effect on 23 May 1944, Hesketh, *Fortitude* p. 102.

16. Caza Personal File, HS9/283 One report commented, 'He is concerned about his ignorance of the country to which he is going and his inadequate knowledge of the language'. A member of PIMENTO reflected that Caza spoke *français mais avec un accent repérable à vingt mètres* ('French but with an accent identifiable at twenty metres'). Rouch, *La Résistance à Lavaur (Tarn) et dans sa région*, p. 79.

17. AMB Papers.

18. Tony did not have time to report on the DZ before van Maurik was dropped on 4 January 1944 to the MARKSMAN circuit. The latter claimed in his memoirs that Tony had cancelled the drop to PIMENTO 'since he was not satisfied with the security of his parachute ground near the Swiss border.' You Must Be Paterson!, p. 136. Ironically, the 'Asticot' ground that Tony had recommended was used but this was probably a result of members of PIMENTO and MARKSMAN reception committees working for both

circuits. Van Maurik crossed successfully into Switzerland and took up his duties for SOE. He met Bertholet in Geneva on a regular basis: 'My meetings with René were always a pleasure as he had a quick wit and we were able to indulge in mutual admiration of Tony. It was good to get first-hand news of this paragon and operational data was passed both ways – proposals for or acceptances of new parachute landing grounds, details of derailments and other operations and much else.' 'You Must Be Paterson!', p. 159.

19. Winifred Bisset and Hope became friends and remained in touch while their husbands were away on active service. Teddy Bisset was sent to France in July 1944 as part of the 'Tilleul' Inter-Allied Mission but, tragically, he was killed in a firearms accident on 24 September.

20. *The F Section Memorial*, passim.

21. Buckmaster, *Specially Employed*, p. 172. This is by no means the book's only flaw. One of the more absurd passages is a graphic description of Tony's ambush of a German motor column and capture of a general. No such action took place; not least because on the date cited (October 1943), Tony was in England.

22 'Narrative', p. 44. The original plan was that Comte and Petit Michel were to form the reception committee. In his notes for Hope, Tony wrote, 'On my departure moon the actual night will be shown by this message 'La Rivière coule vers la mer'. AMB Papers.

23. Tony never mentioned whether the agents had dined together at Gaynes Hall.

24. AIR 27/956 and AIR 20/8459.

25. Sarrette served with distinction in France until killed by a mortar misfire on 5 September 1944.

26. The account of the flight was related by Tony to the author.

27. An SOE document records among STOCKBROKER's achievements: 'Maillard works, Montbéliard.

Transformer attacked and out of action for 1 month. December 1943.' HS6/469 'The British Circuits in France', p. 65.

28. HS6/569, HS9/427/9 and Despaigne's unpublished memoir, 'Les notes de mes missions militaire', 1983.

29. His real name, Petit, was usually amalgamated with his *nom de guerre*, 'Romans', into Romans-Petit.

30. Peschanski et al., *Collaboration and Resistance*, pp. 204–5 and Giolitto, *Grenoble 40–44*, pp. 247–75

31. Note and ts from 'Ceux de la Resistance' and copy of the letter in AMB Papers. In May 1977 Gaston Cusin gave a speech at the opening of the Jean Dorval room at the Direction Nationale des Enquêtes Douanières.

32. Letters from Malamard to Tony 20 September 1945 and 23 November 1945. AMB Papers. Tony never mentioned this dreadful episode in his later verbal accounts of PIMENTO.

33. Caza's post-liberation report of 2 October 1944, HS6/567 and his papers held at the Canadian War Museum (ref. 19720178). The latter do not include documents about the Yugoslav identity but contain papers in the name of 'Roger Jadbois'. These feature entries in Tony's handwriting but, when questioned about them by the author, he denied any involvement with the forgeries.

34. Courier 'To Elizabeth from Fleur' 8.3.44, AMB Papers.

35. In a note to London of 7 April 1944 Tony specified how he intended exploiting Caza's wireless, 'But he is of no use to me to transmit [details of air] operations as these messages are far too long for him. So I will not let him work for the time being and keep him for D-Day.' In fact, Caza's set played a vital role in the arrangements for supply drops. AMB Papers.

Chapter Eleven: 'Marguerite'

1. Note on David Donoff in AMB Papers.

2. Tony's words in 'Recollections of a Secret Agent', Cambridge 1986, AMB Papers.

3. HS6/469 'The British Circuits in France', p. 97.

4. Tony's apparent heartlessness was not unique amongst F Section's best agents. A similar situation confronted Francis Cammaerts, the leader of the JOCKEY circuit, 'Only foolish agents would make rendezvous with others in the field before they left England; but only strong-minded ones would have the resolution to ignore a former training companion they ran into by chance. Yvonne Cormeau, George Starr's wireless operator, met Francis Cammaerts in a crowded train in Toulouse, a few days after she had reached France in August 1943; she tried to catch his eye, but he simply looked through her; she remembered to be discreet; and both of them lived to tell the tale.' Foot, *SOE in France*, pp. 111–12. Walters's memoirs, *Moondrop to Gascony* are perhaps the best written by a female F Section agent but the work fails to mention the meeting with Tony.

5. Note from Tony to Bertholet, 8 March 1944, AMB Papers.

6. Ibid.

7. Ibid. This was one of the more surreal messages of a code system noted for its eccentricity. It was later the title of a book by Dominique Decèze. Unfortunately no reference is made to the real origin of this code phrase and the book affirms that it was one of twenty-six *messages personnels* broadcast the day before D-Day.

8. 'To Elisabeth from Fleur', 5 April 1944. AMB Papers.

9. 'Note' 8 April 1944. AMB Papers. This suggests that in spite of the difficulties with delivering Caza's personal effects, similar complications loomed in getting de Baissac's material to her on the DZ 'Dinde'.

10. Lise de Baissac's training reports were favourable, 'Intelligent, extremely

conscientious, reliable and sound in every way. Is quite imperturbable and would remain cool and collected in every way.' HS9/77/1. It has been alleged that the abortive drop was due to incompetence on the part of the chief of the reception committee, Raymond Flower, Tony's friend from his training days. *'Jacqueline'*, pp. 234–5.

11. HS9/77/1. Perhaps significantly in the light of later disputes, she admitted a reluctance to become engaged in parachute drops, 'She had given it up towards the end of her stay as she felt that it was not suitable work for her.'

12. Jones, *A Quiet Courage*, p. 71.

13. Ibid., p. 75.

14. De Baissac's Personal File, HS9/77/1.

15. HS9/77/1.

16. SOE training assessments (both favourable and critical) revealed great insights into the character and capabilities of students – including Tony's.

17. HS6/567.

18. The most detailed account of Lise de Baissac's career, based upon interviews and briefings from the SOE archive, erroneously suggests 'After passing her first night in a Stationer refuge, Lise set off for Lyon where her new mission lay.' Jones, *A Quiet Courage*, p. 240. Tony's statement and de Baissac's own contemporary account confirm that she made for Montauban not Lyon.

19. Although Comte told Tony of de Baissac's failure to remember the password, in her own official report she claimed to have delivered the agreed exchange.

20. 'Rapport de Marguerite Avril–Mai 1944'. HS9/77/1.

21. 26 April 1944, AMB Papers.

22. HS9/77/1.

23. This is a little surprising given Tony's disinclination to have contact with other F Section networks. Perhaps he was looking to relieve himself of her services in the shortest possible time in a similar fashion to the arrangements concluded with Bloom and Pertschuk.

24. In the event, she failed to locate him and returned after a week's furlough.

25. Undated note from Tony to Bertholet, AMB Papers.

26. 'To Elisabeth from Fleur, 14.4.44', AMB Papers.

27. Ibid.

28. These included one on 22 April 1944 in which he stated he had decided upon a 'radical solution' by dispensing entirely with de Baissac's services. Bertholet gave a robust and uncompromising set of instructions to Tony including ordering de Baissac's dismissal and that Bottemer was to have nothing more to do with her. He felt that there was no point in trying to convert de Baissac to their ways and she should be removed from the PIMENTO scene forthwith. The solution of this problem did nothing to resolve Tony's pressing need for a special courier but Bertholet came up with a substitute – Gaby Cordier. Tony had considered using Colette Hirschfeld (known to Bertholet, the niece of Guerret and already one of PIMENTO's couriers) but he appreciated that Cordier was immensely experienced and probably the better bet. In fact, Bertholet had already taken the decision and informed Tony that he had written to Cordier, relieving her of her current obligations and affirming that he was confident she would accept her new duties.

29. 'To Elisabeth from Fleur 24.4.44', AMB Papers.

30. Original manuscript letter by de Baissac, 23 April 1944, AMB Papers.

31. 'Rapport de Marguerite, Avril–Mai 1944' 13 November 1944, HS9/77/1.

32. AMB Papers. Such allegations of gender and age discrimination have particular resonances in the twenty-first century, but Tony's contemporary and subsequent statements reveal that his criticisms of de Baissac did not turn on either of these factors.

33. Original note in AMB Papers.
34. HS6/469. 'The British Circuits in France', p. 20. Lise de Baissac did not forget the perceived slight she had received at Tony's hands and in a post-liberation SOE report criticised the political influences within PIMENTO that she felt had rendered her unsuitable. Tony was not as exercised as de Baissac over the affair but he neglected to make reference to her arrival and departure in the brief official summary he wrote after the war describing PIMENTO's activities. In 1991 the two agents met at a reunion at Valençay when de Baissac replied to Tony's fraternal greeting with a denial that they had ever met.
35. AMB Papers.
36. Ibid.
37. A message from Tony to Bertholet of 27 March 1944 included 'François has been arrested in Grenoble. Four of his pals have been killed in a skirmish with the Milice.' A letter from Bottemer to Tony of 10 May 1946 contained a copy of a missive of 27 March 1946 from Robert Warnant to Jules Moch. Warnant stated that he had served with André Moch and suggested that 'François' was François Schaeffer who died after deportation. This correspondence illustrates the difficulty in delineating the precise membership of each resistance group and the fact that many resisters worked for several networks. Tony recognised this state of affairs and sent a letter confirming Warnant's application for recognition of his service in PIMENTO. AMB Papers. *Les Nouvelles de Corenc*, avril 2014 pp. 6–7 No. 175 reaffirms the plan to rescue Schaeffer.
38. This seems likely to have been the failed rendezvous that Tony recalled but the dates do not tally. On the 13th the leader of PIMENTO was already in the south-west at the beginning of the 'Marguerite' crisis. The original article was written by Bottemer in German (published in *Le Républicain du Haut-Rhin*), translated into French and retranslated into English. It is little wonder that the text is stilted. AMB Papers.
39. Tony was invited to the unveiling of the memorial on 16 November 1947 by the organising committee, and Moch's parents wrote to ask if he would say a few words on the occasion. Unfortunately he was serving in Bulgaria at the time.
40. Hastings, *Das Reich*, p. 23.
41. 'To Elisabeth from Fleur', 13 April 1944, AMB Papers.
42. *Resistance R4*, No. 12, June 1980 p. 30.
43. Bishop Théas was eventually arrested by the Gestapo on 9 June 1944 and liberated by French forces in August. Tony related that Comte had been to school with the Bishop, but the former was not local although they might perhaps have both been educated together elsewhere.
44. 'To Elisabeth from Fleur 26.4.44' AMB Papers.
45. AMB Papers. PIMENTO's report claimed that the problem had been with the tenth container but the RAF record states that the load was only nine. That said, it also rather mystifyingly cites *two* packages were part of the load but comments that '5 packages returned to base'.

Chapter Twelve: The Day Has Come

1. Message to Bertholet included in a note to London 11 May 1944, AMB Papers.
2. A near identical letter written on the same day was sent to London via Switzerland. In a note to Tony on 22 April 1944 Bertholet had stated that London would shortly be sending another 'musicien' (wireless operator) to complete his 'orchestra'. AMB Papers.
3. Note '2.6.44 To Emmanuel from Fleur'. The arrival of his wireless operator failed to curtail Tony's acrimonious exchanges with London. Misconceptions were frequent and inevitable given the

difficulties and tensions of the time but in a written message of 11 May 1944 sent to London via Switzerland, Tony seemed particularly exercised by F Section's queries regarding Caza's whereabouts. He wrote, 'Re the question where Emmanuel [Caza] is working ... I repeat that he is working a few kilometres north of Gannat. But you already know that. It was decided when I was at H.Q. Both Captain N... [Noble] and Major M...[Morel] discussed with me his future working place. It was agreed that he could not work in the Martinet area as there were too many already but that the Allier would be alright. It was also agreed that there he could be easily in liaison with both the southern and northern end of our circuit. What difference does it make to you where I receive his equipment? Please note that the new W/T will work in the TOULOUSE area. So don't ask me in a month why he isn't in Grenoble.' The message offers an example of Tony's irascibility with what he considered to be London's fussiness that he felt masked inherent incompetence. Moreover it reveals an extraordinary level of assertiveness from a young man of barely twenty-two years towards his superiors. AMB Papers.

4. Caza's difficulties with his wardrobe continued. In a note to Zaksas on 30 July he reported that London had promised to send a suitcase containing his clothes on the DZ 'Fontainebleau'. The 100,000 francs in the consignment almost seemed of little consequence compared to the prospect of the wireless operator getting his smalls. He asked that the suitcase be brought to him as soon as possible as he had now been waiting for his clothes for three months.

5. Message 'To Emmanuel from Fleur', 2 June 1944 AMB Papers.

6. AMB Papers.

7. Foot, *SOE in France*, p. 342 (2004 edition).

8. Hastings, *Das Reich*, p. 97.

9. Ibid., p. 98.

10. The literature on the massacre includes Beck, *Oradour: Village of the Dead* and Farmer, *Martyred Village*.

11. *Das Reich*, p. 165.

12. The Resistance's actions against the 'Das Reich' has been seen as one of its most significant military successes, highlighting the joint contribution of maquisards and SOE to the liberation of France. The accounts have been burnished by time so that the actions of a couple of schoolgirls (the Comte daughters) have even been hailed as rendering the division immobile: 'The division did not get into action in Normandy till D+17. The two young sub-agents who had delayed its start were sisters: the elder was sixteen, the younger fourteen.' Foot, *SOE*, p. 227. In contrast, revisionist views have posited the Resistance's role was peripheral or inconsequential, 'It is certainly not true, as was once alleged, that the Maquis delayed the progress of the Das Reich Division from Toulouse to Normandy, prolonging a journey of three days to two weeks.' Jackson, *France: The Dark Years, 1940–1944*, p. 556. As ever, the truth lies somewhere between the two extremes. PIMENTO's doping of the railway cars with abrasive grease was not the only factor in impeding the division's movements while the German High Command's initial order for the division to undertake counter-terrorist operations in the south-west does not necessarily mean that the Resistance's actions were ineffective when it was eventually ordered to move to Normandy.

13. JUDEX report, 'The Cluny Maquis', AMB Papers.

14. Moorehead, *Eclipse*, p. 108.

Chapter Thirteen: No Let-Up

1. The identity of 'J' is not known despite Caza having left a detailed account listing his primary helpers. AMB Papers.

2. AMB Papers.

3. Caza's interrogation, HS6/567.
4. Report 11 January 1945, AMB Papers.
5. Message '6.7.44' AMB Papers. A later message from Tony to London reported that for security reasons he had been unable to attend a Mass said in Lyon for Donoff. The ceremony is unusual given Donoff's presumed religious beliefs. The family contacted Tony after the liberation asking him to attend the reburial of Donoff's body but his work commitments prevented his being present.
6. The claim that Donoff saved Tony's life perhaps relates to the fallout from the arrests of Biou and Dorval. On the other hand, Tony was never reluctant to boost the contribution made by his fallen comrades in order to secure London's recognition of their service.
7. AMB Papers.
8. Rouch, *La Résistance à Lavaur (Tarn) et dans sa région*, p. 79.
9. HS6/567 and *La Résistance à Lavaur*, p. 80 This was longer than recommended and the duration of Caza's transmissions was, perhaps, a reflection of the pressing demands of the time.
10. *La Résistance à Lavaur*, p. 56.
11. Message 10 July 1944 AMB Papers. Prior to the Allied invasion Koenig had been appointed head of the Forces Françaises de l'Intérieur – effectively supremo of all French resistance fighters.
12. Bower, *Klaus Barbie, Butcher of Lyons*, p.124; Linklater et al., *The Fourth Reich*, pp. 125–6.

Chapter Fourteen: The Final Lap

1. Its former premises in the avenue Berthelot had been damaged in May by an American air raid, necessitating the move. Doré-Rivé, *Une ville dans la guerre*, p.13.
2. Tony's obsession with possessing a full cover story, in particular over the large sum of money in his possession, had been his salvation. This was in stark contrast to the practice of Claude de Baissac, who always kept large amounts of cash on him – 'The reason for this is that if he is in danger, the money can always be used to buy help. If the police search you and find the money, they ask you to prove how you came by it and they will then return it to you. When you fail to prove how you got it, they keep it.' This stratagem was not one with which Tony concurred. HS9/77/1.

3. Heslop, *Xavier*, p. 151.
4. Note, 2 August 1944 AMB Papers.
5. There had evidently been other disputes between rival resistance groups. In a message to London on 28 May 1944 Tony wrote, 'In the Martinet [Lyon] area we have had a lot of trouble with the Communist Maquis who have raided, with an armed crew, two of our dumps. I managed to get an interview with the regional boss and I hope to be able to stop their thieving.' AMB Papers.
6. A wireless message sent by London to Caza in late June included 'Personal for Alphonse delighted inform you your promotion rank acting Major with effect from fifteenth June'. AMB Papers.
7. AMB Papers. The use of *noms de guerre* was endemic throughout the resistance. 'Alain' was later assumed to be Jean-Marie Alain. Tony thought he was an Alsatian (perhaps because he spoke excellent German) and a former seminarist. In spite of 'Alain's' successful career in the resistance (Légion d'Honneur, Croix de Guerre and Rosette de la Résistance), Tony later considered him suspect and believed him to have profiteered from helping refugees cross the demarcation line. After the war he was described by Tony's wife as 'a very wealthy young man who before the war was given six months to live. With money and influence and a large estate he started a very successful maquis. He came out of the war with a brilliant past, full of wounds and chest full of ribbons, but he still lives. He is a very charming young man, with perfect manners and an aristocratic bearing.' See 'Life After PIMENTO'.

8. HS7/121.

9. Tony attended one drop where a substantial amount of the material was of Italian origin and markedly inferior to the usual British-manufactured military equipment.

10. Note 'Yves' [Tony] to 'Alain', 9 August 1944. AMB Papers.

11. AMB Papers.

12. Foot, *SOE in France*, p. 412.

13. Letter '20.8.44', AMB Papers.

14. Rouch, *La Résistance à Lavaur*, pp. 85–6.

15. Jackson, *France: The Dark Years*, p. 560.

16. Hope Brooks, post-war narrative, p.20, AMB Papers.

17. The danger was such that, on 7 August, Tony asked Gauthier to send him a Colt pistol – a radical departure from his customary disinclination to carry a firearm. AMB Papers. Bertholet had already sent Tony a Swiss Army Luger but it seems likely that a more readily concealable weapon was needed. The weapon is in the Imperial War Museum.

18. Zeitoun and Foucher, *Lyon 1940/1944*, pp.54–6.

19. HS6/534. All the quotations that follow are from the JOHN post-operational report.

20. Caza's wireless messages only record hints of JOHN's arrival. On 3 August 1944 London offered, 'Can send team of 3 uniformed officers with own communications who could take over some of your groups in Tarn et Garonne.' Another message of 11 August indicated they (or some other team) would be arriving on the 'Canada' DZ, AMB Papers. There was a world of difference between such vague comments and the fait accompli of the team's arrival in France.

21. An SOE document of 3 August 1944 summarising Tony's activities stated: 'In view of the extent covered by these groups [the various components of the circuit] it has been decided that a Jedburgh team should be sent to take over certain of these groups, preferably in TARN et GARONNE, after consultation with ALPHONSE.' Information supplied by the SOE Adviser. It must be more than a coincidence that the wireless message to Caza advising that the team could be sent and the SOE report inferring that a clear-cut decision had been made to send JOHN should have occurred on the same day.

22. By happenstance, the author was able to discuss JOHN with David Stern at an SOE ceremony in 2015. In a draft report of PIMENTO's activities written by Tony dated 11 January 1945/ he wrote: 'Jedburgh team supposedly dropped to me was landed 150 Kilometres to the South West.' AMB Papers.

23. The date is uncertain. There is nothing in Tony's papers (official and unofficial) describing the visit but it is known that Heslop was in England between 7/8 July and 6/7 August. Romans-Petit was in the United Kingdom from 5/6 September to the 13th. The uncertainty of Tony's precise whereabouts suggests that must have been between 7 August and 5 September. Heslop had his first contact with the Americans on 27 August so, probably, the meeting took place in the period 7–26 August.

24. Jackson, *France: The Dark Years*, p. 559.

25. Tony was not averse to supplying communist groups when he felt it necessary. In a note of 13 April 1944, he wrote that he provided arms and money '*au parti*' under Camus in Agen but expressed his disappointment at the absence of comradeship and cooperation shown by the beneficiaries of his largesse. In a post-war letter to Tony, Rudi Molter stated that Moucot had provided an astonishing total of 5,000 false identity cards to the Resistance registered through the Commissariat de Police of Villeurbanne. AMB Papers.

26. As with many, if not most, of the members of PIMENTO, surnames were rarely used and *noms de guerre*

frequently adopted. 'Jean's' real name is unknown.

27. The flag had been acquired by Donoff's sister when she visited London for the Silver Jubilee of King George V in 1935. Tony also carried a *laissez-passer* issued to Antoine Brévin under the authority of Lieutenant-Colonel 'Théodore' whose signature looked suspiciously similar to his own handwriting. AMB Papers.

28. Letter from Tony to Brooks Richards, 1 July 1989 AMB Papers and Funk, *Hidden Ally*, p.248.

29. Letter to Brooks Richards, 1 July 1989, AMB Papers. The reconstruction of the Hôtel-Dieu was not completed until the 1980s.

30. *Revue de la France Libre*, No. 219, 1977.

31. Chalou, *The Secrets War*, p.179. Regrettably the OSS War Diary of No. 4 SFU offers little information on this contact. HS6/612.

32. Norman Brooks was no longer in residence. With his customary pragmatism, he fled to Switzerland once the German occupation of Vichy France threatened his being interned. Some details of the requisitioning of the château are to be found in the US National Archives and the OSS No. 4 SFU War Diary at HS6/612 that confirms occupancy by 9 September 1944.

33. No official record of Tony's medical condition has survived, and the account is based solely on his recollections. The only reference to him in the No. 4 SFU war diary states that he and Molter left for Toulouse on 6 September, but the trip may have been unrealised due to his illness.

Chapter Fifteen: An End and a Beginning

1. Foot, *SOE in France*, p. 423.

2. In his autobiography, *The Drums of Memory*, the SAS officer Stephen Hastings claimed that he drove Brooks Richards to Paris. Unless this was a different occasion, it reveals the fragility, never mind the drums, of memory.

3. On 23 October 1944 Selborne wrote to Atlee apologising 'for not having written to you before about Major Brooks and S.O.E. contacts with the Trade Union movement in Europe' and regretting that (due to his ill health) he had not had the opportunity of seeing Tony himself. HS8/234.

4. Buckmaster, *Specially Employed*, p. 196.

5. 'Carré' was the nom de guerre of Paul Leistenschneider, who had been the Free French Délégué Militaire Régional for the Region 'R3' that encompassed the south-west area of PIMENTO.

6. Information supplied by the SOE Adviser and drafts amongst Tony's papers.

7. Minute to 'Major A M Brookes [sic]' 9 August 1946. AMB Papers.

8. HS6/567, HS8/394. André Moch was one of the other PIMENTO figures put up for an award, the King's Commendation for Brave Conduct, HS9/1045/5. Raymond Bizot and René Figarol also received the King's Medal for Courage in the Cause of Freedom in 1948. A full list of the names Tony had submitted appears in a note of 2 August 1946 divided into 'Decorations' and 'Kings Medal'. On 6 August he asked, perhaps sentimentally, that Jean Citerne's name be added to the list. The problem did not end there. In a letter of 31 July 1947 Buckmaster wrote to Tony informing him that the War Office had lost the citations for PIMENTO personnel and they needed to be resubmitted. The former head of F Section asked that Tony 'send me from memory, & urgently, a list of at least the most meritorious, with names + addresses'. AMB Papers.

9. HS6/567.

10. Order in AMB Papers.

11. Memorandum 'Major A M Brooks MC', 16 December 1944, Information supplied by the SOE Adviser.

12. Charmley, *Duff Cooper*, p. 200. Cooper also recruited other SOE 'old boys' onto his staff including Brooks

Richards from SOE's AMF Section and Robin Hooper, one of the RAF's Special Duty pilots.

13. Memorandum 'Major A M Brooks MC', SO to AD/S.1, 3 January 1945. Information supplied by the SOE Adviser.

14. Information supplied by the SOE Adviser.

15. AMB Papers.

16. Letter 10 March 1945. AMB Papers.

17. Ibid.

18. Amongst Henneguier's many achievements had been the sabotage attack on the Bronzavia factory at Courbevoie on 3 March 1944. This operation ensured that a planned RAF raid – that would doubtless have resulted in civilian casualties – was not required. Albertelli, *Histoire du Sabotage*, p. 376.

19. The reports can be found at HS8/424-7

20. Letter from Tony to Vivian Collum, 1 December 1945, AMB Papers.

21. In a letter of 24 May 1944 to Bizot in Switzerland, Tony mentioned that he was sending Dorval's parents 1,500 francs a month along with other monies due to their son. Writing to Pédémas on 24 July 1945 Tony hoped that Dorval's brother had returned from Germany because the parents 'ont l'air bien âgé et bien paysan'. The same letter carried a comment on Biou's father's false suspicions of Dorval being responsible for his son's arrest. AMB Papers.

22. The appointments diary of Major-General Sir Colin Gubbins, the executive head of SOE, indicates Tony should have had an audience with him on 18 June but a record on Tony's PF claims he arrived in the UK from Paris on 21 June 1945, and, confusingly, an air ticket indicates he flew back on the 17th. AMB Papers.

23. The investiture eventually took place on 12 March 1946 at Buckingham Palace. Tony recalled that the King made the quite understandable observation, 'You were pretty young'. A cartoon depicting the occasion appears in this book.

24. Letter from Buckmaster to Tony, AMB Papers.

25. Note from Brooks Richards, February 1946, AMB Papers.

26. Memorandum, 19 September 1945, information supplied by the SOE Adviser. Neither the author nor the other figures mentioned – 'Tiny' and 'River' – have been identified.

27. Reports in *La Marseillaise* and *La Liberté* 1 October 1945. Letter from Tony to Lacoste, 6 October 1945. AMB Papers. A photograph of Tony with his PIMENTO colleagues is among his papers. They stayed in touch with each other regarding Dorval's reburial but no news was forthcoming from the family until, in March 1946, Bizot wrote that their friend had had been interred back in Brittany but no wartime colleagues had been invited to attend. AMB Papers.

28. AMB Papers. Disappointingly, Masefield's autobiography contains no references to Tony, only some to his brother, Peter Brooks.

29. Letter from Tony to Buckmaster, 7 November 1945, AMB Papers.

30. AMB Papers.

31. Ibid.

32. Ibid.

33. 11 January 1946 Letter to 'Mac', AMB Papers.

34. Among the more imaginative claims was that of André Chell who professed to have joined PIMENTO in November 1940, had been parachuted seven times and was arrested on 23 June 1942. Tony informed the French authorities that Chell's statements were impossible. Chell's claims to wartime service seem to have been an attempt to mitigate post-war charges for swindling. AMB Papers.

35. Letters from Tony to Molter and Rykebusche 6 November 1945. AMB Papers. Sadly, although Tony's records contain many photographs, there is no suggestion that these near contemporaneous images were taken.

36. Letter to George Schreiber (?), 7 November 1945 AMB Papers.

37. In his later life Tony did not express any emotional attachment to his schools but his post-war sentiments are evident in his correspondence. Letter 7 November 1945. AMB Papers.

38. Letter from Helen Guiterman to Tony, 17 November 1945. AMB Papers.

39. Memo from Tony to 'RW', 22 November 1945 and letter to Guiterman, 23 November 1945, AMB Papers. Tony also said that he was 'warned off' participating in the mission by John Willy Munn.

40. Letter from Atkins to Cohen, 12 October 1945. Information supplied by the SOE Adviser.

41. Information supplied by the SOE Adviser.

42. AMB Papers.

43. Hope Narrative, p. 2, AMB Papers.

44. Hope Narrative, p. 23, AMB Papers.

45. In September 1945 Tony had written to Citerne asking for the return of his parachute as Hope had asked for it as a souvenir of his wartime exploits. In a letter to Peter Brooks of 25 September 1945 he reported that he had picked it up. 'The canopy is intact and in very fine condition. A peasant kept it very carefully and was rather sorry to see me take it away but I feel it's a worthwhile souvenir.' AMB Papers.

46. Hope Narrative, p. 33, AMB Papers.

Life After PIMENTO

1. SRFD report, 1 April 1954, in AMB Papers.

2. According to a letter from Bottemer, 27 March 1945. AMB Papers.

3. The file states: 'In the event of this award being approved it is requested that in no circumstances should this citation be published and that the Swiss Government should not be informed.' For a period of time Bertholet employed the alias 2/Lt. 'Charles Arnold' and wore British Army uniform. Information supplied by the SOE Adviser.

4. Information supplied by the SOE Adviser. There is also a suggestion that he received a personal letter of thanks from Winston Churchill.

5. Memo from Tony to Bourne-Paterson, 26 April 1946. AMB Papers.

6. Correspondence with Tony in AMB Papers. See also entry on Joinovici in Miannay, *Dictionnaire des agents doubles dans la Résistance*.

7. Notification of his 'King's Medal' is in a letter from Tony to Buckmaster on 2 December 1949. AMB Papers, 1947–53.

8. AMB Papers.

9. Information from letter of 1967 by Gaby Cordier. AMB Papers.

10. HS1/118.

11. AMB Papers.

12. Citation in HS8/389.

13. HS8/394.

Bibliography

Abel, Sabine, 'René Bertholet in der Französischen Emigration und in der 'Französischen Resistance', thesis, Kassel, 1984

Adant, Philippe, *René Bertholet*, Paris, 1995

Albertelli, Sébastien, *Les services secrets du général de Gaulle*, Paris, 2009

Albertelli, Sébastien, *Histoire du Sabotage*, Paris, 2016

Aubrac, Lucie, *Ils partiront dans l'ivresse*, Paris, 1984

Baynac, Jacques, *Les secrets de l'affaire Jean Moulin*, Paris, 1998

Baynac, Jacques, *Présumé Jean Moulin*, Paris, 2006

Beck, Philip, *Oradour – Village of the Dead*, London, 1979

Bernier, Olivier, *Fireworks at Dusk*, Boston Mass., 1993

Bertaux, Pierre, *Libération de Toulouse et de sa région*, Paris, 1973

Bird, Michael J., *The Secret Battalion*, London, 1965

Bobenrieth, Charles, *39/45 à Lyon*, Lyon, 2002

Body, Robert, *Runways to Freedom*, privately printed, 2016

Bower, Tom, *Klaus Barbie, Butcher of Lyons*, London, 1985

Boyce, Frederic and Everett, Douglas, *SOE: The Scientific Secrets*, Stroud, 2003

Buckmaster, Maurice, *Specially Employed*, London, 1952

Buckmaster, Maurice, *They Fought Alone*, London, 1958

Burney, Christopher, *The Dungeon Democracy*, London, 1945

Burrin, Philippe, *Living with Defeat*, London, 1996

Caskie, Donald, *The Tartan Pimpernel*, London, 1958

Chalou, George C. (ed.), *The Secrets War*, Washington DC, 1992

Chappat, Marie Christine, 'Yvon Morandat, Une Figure du XXe Siècle', unpublished thesis, Université Jean Moulin, 1987–1988

Charmley, John, *Duff Cooper*, London, 1986

Churchill, Peter, *Duel of Wits*, London, 1953

Churchill, Peter, *The Spirit in the Cage*, London, 1954

Citrine, Lord, *Two Careers*, London, 1967

Clark, Freddie, *Agents by Moonlight*, Stroud, 1999

Clutton-Brock, Oliver, *RAF Evaders*, London, 2012

Cubero, José, *La Résistance à Toulouse et dans la Région 4*, Bordeaux, 2005

Curry, John, *The Security Service 1908-1945: The Official History*, PRO, Kew, 1999

Dank, Milton, *The French against the French*, London, 1978

Dear, I. C. B. (General Editor), *The Oxford Companion to the Second World War*, Oxford, 1995

Decèze, Dominique, *La lune est pleine d'éléphants verts*, Paris, 1979

Devigny, André, *Je fus ce condamné*, Paris, 1978

Doré-Rivé, Isabelle (ed.) *Une ville dans la guerre*, Lyon, 2012

Dreyfus, Michel, *Libérer et Fédérer 14 Juillet 1942-Avril-Mai 1944*, Paris, 1985

Estèbe, Jean, *Toulouse 1940-1944*, Paris, 1996

Farmer, Sarah, *Martyred Village*, Berkeley, 1999

Figarol, René, *Pour Ne Pas Oublier: 1941– 1944*, privately printed, n. d.

Foot, M. R. D., *SOE: The Special Operations Executive 1940-1946*, London, 1984

Foot, M. R. D., *SOE in France*, London, 1966, 1968, 2004

Foot, M. R. D., *SOE in the Low Countries*, London, 2001

Foot, M. R. D. and Langley, J. M., *MI9:Escape and Evasion, 1939–1945*, London, 1979

Funk, Arthur Layton, *Hidden Ally*, Westport Conn., 1992

Garnett, David, *The Secret History of PWE*, London, 2002

Gildea, Robert, *Marianne in Chains*, London, 2002

Giolitto, Pierre, *Grenoble 40-44*, Paris, 2001

Goubet, Michel and Debauges, Paul, *Histoire de la Résistance dans la Haute-Garonne*, Cahors, 1986

Griffiths, Frank, *Winged Hours*, London, 1981

Groussard, Georges, *Chemins secrets,* Tome 1, Paris, 1948

Guidoni, Pierre and Verdier, Robert (eds), *Les socialistes en Résistance (1940-1944)*, Paris, 1999

Guillin, François-Yves, *Le Général Delestraint*, Paris, 1995

Hardy, René, *Derniers Mots*, Paris, 1984

Hastings, Max, *Das Reich*, London, 1983

Hastings, Stephen, *The Drums of Memory*, London, 1994

Hesketh, Roger, *Fortitude: The D-Day Deception Campaign*, London, 1999

Heslop, Richard, *Xavier*, London, 1970

Hoare, Rt. Hon. Sir Samuel, *Ambassador on Special Mission*, London, 1946

Hochard, Cécile, *Les cheminots dans la Résistance*, Paris, 2011

Hoffman, Ruth and Helen, *We Married an Englishman*, London, 1939

Hoffman, Ruth and Helen, *Our Arabian Nights*, London, 1941

Howard, Michael, *British Intelligence in the Second World War*, Volume 5, London, 1990

Howe, Ellic, *The Black Game*, London, 1982

Instone, Gordon, *Freedom the Spur*, London, 1956

Jackson, Julian, *The Fall of France*, Oxford, 2003

Jackson, Julian, *France: The Dark Years, 1940-1944*, Oxford, 2003

Jackson, Robert, *The Secret Squadrons*, London, 1983

Jeavons, Stefan, 'Action and Ideology of "Libérer et Fédérer"', unpublished thesis, Anglia Higher Education College, 1991

Jeffery, Keith, *MI6: The History of the Secret Intelligence Service 1909–1949*, London, 2010

Jones, Liane, *A Quiet Courage*, London, 1990

Kedward, H. R., *Resistance in Vichy France*, Oxford, 1978

Kedward, H. R., *Occupied France: Collaboration and Resistance, 1940-1944*, Oxford, 1987

Kedward, H. R., *In Search of the Maquis*, Oxford, 1994

King, Stella, *'Jacqueline'*, London, 1989

Kogon, Eugen, *L'enfer organisé*, , Paris, 1947

Langley, J. M., *Fight Another Day*, London, 1980

Le Chêne, Evelyn, *Watch for me by Moonlight*, London, 1973

Linklater, Magnus, Hilton, Isabel and Ascherson, Neal, *The Fourth Reich: Klaus Barbie and the Neo-Fascist Connection*, London, 1984

Littlejohn, David, *The Patriotic Traitors*, London, 1972

Long, Helen, *Safe Houses are Dangerous*, London, 1985

Lormier, Dominique, *La Gestapo et les Français*, Paris, 2013

Loubet, Didier, 'Le Réseau "Prunus"', unpublished thesis, University of Toulouse, 1990

Mackenzie, William, *The Secret History of SOE*, London, 2000

MacLaren, Roy, *Canadians Behind Enemy Lines 1939-1945*, Vancouver, 1982

Marino, Andy, *American Pimpernel – The story of Varian Fry*, London, 1999

Marks, Leo, *Between Silk and Cyanide*, London, 1998

Marnham, Patrick, *The Death of Jean Moulin*, London, 2000

Merrick, K. A., *Flights of the Forgotten*, London, 1989

Miannay, Patrice, *Dictionnaire des agents doubles dans la Résistance*, Paris, 2005

Moorehead, Alan, *Eclipse*, London, 1968

Morgan, Janet, *The Secrets of Rue St Roch*, London, 2004

Morgan, Ted, *An Uncertain Hour*, London, 1990

Murphy, Brendan A., *Turncoat*, San Diego, 1987

Neave, Airey, *Saturday at M.I.9*, London, 1969

Noguères, Henri, Histoire de la Résistance en France, five volumes, Paris, 1967–81

Nossiter, Adam, *France and the Nazis*, London, 2003

Nouveau, L. H., *Des Capitaines par Milliers*, Paris, 1958

Ousby, Ian, *Occupation: The Ordeal of France 1940–1944*, London, 1999

Overton Fuller, Jean, *Déricourt: The Chequered Spy*, Salisbury, 1989

Paxton, Robert O., *Vichy France*, New York, 1982

Péan, Pierre, *Vies et morts de Jean Moulin*, Paris, 1998

Pennetier, Claude, et al., *Les Fusillés (1940–1944)*, Ivry-sur-Seine, 2015

Perquin, Jean-Louis, *Clandestine Parachute and Pick-Up Operations*, Paris, 2012

Peschanski, Denis et al., *Collaboration and Resistance, Images of Life in Vichy France 1940–1944*, New York, 2000

Philby, Kim, *My Silent War*, London, 1976

Pimlott, Ben, *Hugh Dalton*, London, 1986

Poirier, Jacques R. E., *La girafe a un long cou…*, Périgueux, 1992

Ratcliff, Leonard, *Memoirs*, privately printed, 2005

Ravanel, Serge, *L'esprit de résistance*, Paris, 1995

Richards, Brooks, *Secret Flotillas*, two volumes, London, 2004

Robbins, Christopher, *The Test of Courage*, London, 1999

'Robert, Pierre', *Spain Calling!*, London, 1937

Rouch, Maurice, *La Résistance à Lavaur (Tarn) et dans sa région*, privately printed, Aix-en-Provence, 1994

Sainsbury, J. D. (ed.), *The F Section Memorial*, Welwyn, 1992

Saward, Joe, *The Grand Prix Saboteurs*, London, 2006

Seaman, Mark, *Bravest of the Brave*, London, 1997

Seaman, Mark, 'Introduction', *Secret Agent's Handbook of Special Devices*, PRO, Kew, 2000

Sharf, Frederic A, *Brian Stonehouse: Artist, Soldier, War Hero, Fashion Illustrator*, Boston Mass., 2014

Sheppard, Bob, *Missions secrètes et Déportation 1939–1945*, Bayeux, 1998

Simpson, William, *I Burned My Fingers*, London, 1956

Smith, Colin, *England's Last War Against France*, London, 2010

Spencer, Geoff, *Beloved Alien, Walter Fleiss 1901–1985*, privately printed, 1985

Stafford, David, *Britain and European Resistance 1940–1945*, London, 1980

Sullivan, Rosemary, *Villa Air-Bel*, London, 2006

Suttill, Francis J., *Shadows in the Fog*, Sutton, 2014

Sweet-Escott, Bickham, *Baker Street Irregular*, London, 1965

Sweets, John F., *Choices in Vichy France*, New York, 1986

Tickell, Jerrard, *Odette: The Story of a British Agent*, London, 1949

Van Maurik, Ernest, 'You Must Be Paterson!', typescript memoir

Verity, Hugh, *We Landed by Moonlight*, London, 1978

Veyret, Patrick, *Histoire de la Résistance armée dans l'Ain*, Châtillon-sur-Chalaronne, 1999

Vomécourt, Philippe de, *Who Lived to See the Day*, London, 1961

Walters, Anne-Marie, *Moondrop to Gascony*, London, 1946

Yarnold, Patrick, *Wanborough Manor*, Guildford, 2009

Zeitoun, Sabine and Foucher, Dominique, *Lyon 1940/1944*, Rennes, 1994

Archival References

The two most important archives are the private papers of Tony Brooks described as 'AMB Papers' and those official records held at the National Archives, Kew. The latter can be identified in the footnotes by their 'department' designations such as HS (SOE), KV (MI5), AIR (Air Ministry) and WO (War Office). Unattributed statements by Tony Brooks are from recorded interviews with the author. I am grateful to Rod Bailey for helping to make the McCaffery Papers available to me.

Index

(The initials AB refer to Anthony 'Tony' Brooks)